THE
Contemporary Soviet City

Contributors

Richard B. Dobson, Analyst, Soviet and East European Affairs, United States Information Agency, Office of Research, Washington, D.C.

Mark G. Field, Professor of Sociology, Boston University, Boston, Massachusetts.

Zvi Gitelman, Professor of Political Science, University of Michigan, Ann Arbor, Michigan.

Sigurd Grava, Professor of Urban Planning, Columbia University, New York, New York, and Technical Director for Planning and Vice President, Parsons, Brinckerhoff, Quade & Douglas, Inc.

Peter H. Juviler, Professor of Political Science, Barnard College, New York, New York.

Henry W. Morton, Professor of Political Science, Queens College, City University of New York, Flushing, New York.

William Moskoff, Professor of Economics, Lake Forest College, Lake Forest, Illinois.

Henry J. Raimondo, Assistant Professor of Economics, Rutgers University, New Brunswick, New Jersey.

Gertrude E. Schroeder, Professor of Economics, University of Virginia, Charlottesville, Virginia.

Louise I. Shelley, Associate Professor, School of Justice, American University, Washington, D.C.

Robert C. Stuart, Professor of Economics, Rutgers University, New Brunswick, New Jersey.

THE
Contemporary Soviet City

Edited by

Henry W. Morton
and
Robert C. Stuart

M. E. SHARPE, INC.
Armonk, New York

*This book is dedicated to the students
of Queens College.*

Copyright © 1984 by M. E. Sharpe, Inc.
80 Business Park Drive, Armonk, New York 10504

Library of Congress Cataloging in Publication Data

The Contemporary Soviet City.

    Bibliography: p.
    1. Cities and towns—Soviet Union—Congresses.
I. Morton, Henry W., 1929–   . II. Stuart, Robert C., 1938–
HT145.S58C66   1984   307.7′64′0947   83-8543
ISBN 0-87332-248-7
ISBN 0-87332-254-1 (pbk.)

Printed in the United States of America

Contents

Contributors   ii

Preface   vii

Introduction   ix

PART I: AN OVERVIEW

1 The Contemporary Soviet City/*Henry W. Morton*   3

2 The Sources of Soviet Urban Growth/*Robert C. Stuart*   25

PART II: THE SOVIET URBAN SCENE

3 Financing Soviet Cities/*Henry J. Raimondo and Robert C. Stuart*   45

4 The Soviet Urban Labor Supply/*William Moskoff*   65

5 The Urban Family and the Soviet State:
   Emerging Contours of a Demographic Policy/*Peter H. Juviler*   84

6 Urbanization and Crime:
   The Soviet Experience/*Louise I. Shelley*   113

PART III: SOVIET URBAN SERVICES

7 Soviet Urban Health Services: Some Problems
   and Their Sources/*Mark G. Field*   129

8 Soviet Education: Problems and Policies
   in the Urban Context/*Richard B. Dobson*   156

9 Urban Transport in the Soviet Union/*Sigurd Grava*   180

10 Retail Trade and Personal Services in Soviet Cities/
    Gertrude E. Schroeder   202

11 Working the Soviet System: Citizens
    and Urban Bureaucracies/*Zvi Gitelman*   221

Conclusion   244

Bibliography   251

Index   257

Preface

This volume had its origin when the two editors met as members of a program committee, chaired by Henry Krish (University of Connecticut), to plan panels for the 1979 national convention of the American Association for the Advancement of Slavic Studies (AAASS). Our mutual interest in Soviet urban problems led us to plan a workshop on this theme, an idea suggested by Alvin Z. Rubinstein (University of Pennsylvania), who was chairman of the program committee for the 1980 national convention of the AAASS, which was held in Philadelphia in November 1980. Encouraged by the enthusiasm of our participants and the positive response from the audience, we proceeded to organize a full-day conference on this topic, with the support of Alexander Dallin, who was chairman of the program committee for the 1981 convention of the AAASS that met in Asilomar, California, in September 1981. All the papers that appear in this volume were first presented there.

At the conference we received valuable assistance from David T. Cattell (University of California at Los Angeles), Jeff Chinn (Minnesota University System), and Robert Osborn (Temple University) through their oral and written commentaries, which were invaluable in helping us revise our manuscripts. Donald Graves (State Department) also participated productively in the discussion. Although James H. Bater (University of Waterloo) was unable to attend our conference, he too contributed written suggestions.

Our sincerest thanks to all those mentioned above (and to our universities which supported our travel expenses and provided us with typing and copying services). Without such combined support this volume could not have been put together.

Last, but far from least, is our great appreciation to our contributors, who were faithful to our deadlines and willingly rewrote their chapters guided by the comments they received. We thank them sincerely for their splendid cooperation. It was a great pleasure working with them.

Henry W. Morton
Robert C. Stuart

Introduction

The urbanization of our world is a relatively recent event. Until a short time ago the vast majority of humanity lived in villages growing food and fiber, handcrafting tools, clothing, and other goods. Before 1850 no society could be considered to be predominantly urban, and by 1900 only Great Britain was. Today in the industrialized countries of Europe, North America, and Japan, cities are the primary centers of human activity, and the majority of people in those countries live in cities. Even in the economically less developed countries of Asia, Africa, and Latin America, where urbanization is less pervasive, urban centers are the locus of economic and cultural activity.

Although the process of urbanization actually began over 5,000 years ago when the first cities appeared, the transformation of the world into an urban society only took off with the advent of the industrial revolution. Improved technology and techniques in agriculture greatly reduced the need for farm labor, and the many who thus became unemployed and underemployed were drawn to industrial sites in cities to work in factories where the recently invented steam engine revolutionized the productive process. Products that had previously been made by hand were now manufactured by machines, sold at relatively low prices, and widely distributed.

Rapid industrialization was thus chiefly responsible for the mercurial growth of cities. However, a major obstacle to their development in the past had been an excessive mortality rate. It was slowly overcome in the West by the latter half of the nineteenth century, as epidemics of cholera and other diseases were prevented by sanitizing wells and rivers from which water for drinking was drawn and by controlling and treating waste products.

Rapid urbanization came later to the USSR than to the West. The Stalinist policy of rapid industrialization in conjunction with forced collectivization of the countryside, begun in 1929, drove millions of peasants from their farmlands to new industrial sites and converted small towns into large cities almost overnight. The urban population more than doubled between December 1926 and January 1939, from 26.3 to 56.1 million. By 1962 the majority of Soviet citizens resided in urban communities. Today the USSR is indisputably highly urbanized.

In the relatively short contemporary experience of rapid urban growth, few, if any, polities, the USSR included, have managed the urban process well. While each had to deliver similar urban services, not only systemic differences but also historical and cultural traditions and each society's pattern of economic development shaped its ranking of priorities, its methods of financing, and the way it chose, implemented, and monitored its policies and practices. Yet the rapidly increasing urban population, whether governed by the representative multiparty system in a mixed economy found in most Western societies or by the one-party system in a state-owned and directed economy found in the Soviet Union, still had to be provided housing, schools, water, electricity, sewerage, transportation, shopping facilities, medical care, police and fire protection, and recreational and cultural facilities. The difficulties of furnishing these services in quantity and quality while trying to cope with negative manifestations of city life like crime, pollution, and overcrowding have all been part of Soviet, as well as Western, urban policy concerns.

The purpose of this book is to provide information about and analytic insights into the contemporary Soviet urban experience—which in many ways is so different from ours. Cities play the central role in Soviet life. They are the industrial engines of the Soviet economy. Soviet industry, shops, hospitals, universities, and cultural institutions are located primarily in cities. And the majority of Soviet citizens live in cities and towns, in multifamily dwellings. In 1980 the USSR had twenty-two cities with a population of over one million, compared to six in the United States.

In contrast the majority of American urban residents live in suburbs, primarily in free-standing single-family homes. They drive to shopping centers and malls for their consumer purchases. Over fifty percent of those living in suburbia also work locally in commerce and industry.

The suburban life style as we know it hardly exists in the USSR. The city *is* the Soviet urban experience, and how well the city functions is of vital importance to the Soviet leadership. The productivity of the Soviet worker is affected by the quality and quantity of urban services provided, such as housing, shopping facilities, transportation, education, and cultural activities. A serious lack in one or several of these areas results in lower labor productivity and increases the turnover rate of workers leaving their jobs, already one of the highest in the world.

Such problems and complexities of rapid urban growth are analyzed in Part I of this book, an overview of the contemporary Soviet city.

For most Soviet citizens, as Morton shows in his essay, cities are the most, indeed the only desirable places to live; and the larger the city, the better—ideally Moscow or the capitals of republics. The millions who live in satellite communities or in middle-sized and smaller cities are frequently the urban poor of Soviet society because of the scarcity in their areas of food and other consumer products and the lack of restaurants, good medical facilities, repair services, and cultural activities. But permission to move into large urban centers is restricted and monitored. Thus the three major problems facing Soviet cities are an immobile labor force; a still serious housing shortage which prevents factories, offices, and stores from importing needed workers because there is no place for them to live; and a consumer goods crisis in which the lack of meat, poultry, butter, and milk has forced Soviet authorities to introduce food rationing. Moreover, comprehensive urban planning in response to these problems remains more myth than reality because factories belonging to industrial ministries are still a major funding source in most cities for such urban services as housing, schools, shopping facilities, transportation, and utilities. Consequently managers of these factories, and not local government officials, are the people who determine the siting of industrial and civil construction, often in violation of planning ordinances, and they also frequently administer those city services that they own and control.

Stuart analyzes the reasons for the rapid transformation of Soviet society from a rural into a predominantly urban one since 1929. The expansion of the Soviet urban population has been the result of three principal factors: first, the movement of population from rural to urban areas; second, the natural increase of population resulting from a larger number of births over deaths in urban areas; and as cities expanded, third, the administrative reclassification of rural areas into urban ones. Of these the migration from rural areas to urban ones has been the dominant portion of urban growth, although in recent years the natural growth of cities has become more important. Throughout the period of rapid industrial development and urbanization, both the birth and death rates have fallen. The net impact of these trends has been a substantial slowing in the rate of growth of the Soviet population. This means that Soviet society as a whole is aging, a trend that holds important consequences for the Soviet urban labor force.

In Part II the financing of Soviet cities, the reasons for the labor shortage, the crisis in the urban family, and the problems of crime in the USSR are described.

Our knowledge of how Soviet cities are financed is, according to Raimondo and Stuart, limited and incomplete because little information has been published on the subject by Soviet authorities. There are two principal sources of funds for urban services: those which a city government receives from a superior soviet on the district, province, or republic level, and those supplied by enterprises belonging to ministries to finance the construction of housing and other urban services. Cities, although they want to exercise control over urban civil construction, do not always succeed in convincing enterprises to finance such projects through the city budget process. A significant number of enterprises still prefer to finance and build them independently. Consequently, because the city budget is not all-inclusive, it is difficult to determine who pays for and administers what services in a city.

In his study Moskoff explains why the USSR faces a severe labor shortage which if not corrected will accelerate the slowdown in Soviet economic growth that Soviet leaders are now trying to reverse. The shortage is due to demographic developments and to inefficiencies in the allocation of labor. In the past factories and service industries attracted peasants to work in cities, but this pool of surplus labor has dried up. Moreover, because of the low birth rate characteristic of a maturing urban society, no natural increase in the labor force can be expected between 1986 and 2001. Inefficient labor allocation compounds the problem. Labor turnover is four to five times as high as in the West because of unsatisfactory work and living conditions. Additionally, plant managers hoard labor in order to be able to "storm the plan" in the last days of each month when supplies and equipment are finally in place. Factories are also required to send workers to state farms to assist with planting and harvesting. These demographic and labor utilization factors will significantly limit economic growth and thus consumption by Soviet society beyond this century.

As has happened in other industrialized countries, the Soviet family's economy, values, and motivations have changed dramatically with urbanization. Juviler's study shows how the three-generation extended family unit has broken up. Grandparents live separately, children have become consumers rather than helpers, and women have become a major component of the work force. The high rate of female employment has caused a sharp decline in the birth rate (except for Central Asia) and a steep increase in divorces as women have become more economically independent. The Soviet political and economic system requires full employment, but the decline in births and the rise in the mortality rate have aggravated the already serious labor shortage. To reverse this trend the government has launched a pronatalist policy that provides modest money incentives to encourage families to have more children. The success of this program may very well depend on the availability and quality of food and other consumer goods and services; otherwise families will not be persuaded to have more children.

The growth of urbanization in the USSR, according to Shelley, has also led to an increase in the crime rate, as it has in the West. But unlike in other urbanized societies, the incidence of crime has been highest in middle-sized and smaller, but rapidly growing, cities and not in the large urban centers. This is because Soviet authorities have to a large degree succeeded in exiling serious offenders. After completing their sentences, those convicted of major crimes are, as a rule, banished to spend the next five to ten years in remote regions of the USSR. At the end of that period their chances of receiving permission to resettle in Moscow, Leningrad, Kiev, or any other large city in the European part of the Soviet Union are slim.

The quality of urban services is discussed in Part III, which looks at the areas of health, education, transportation, and urban retail trade.

The principle of free and universally accessible medical services, in the view of Field, as pioneered by the USSR, has gained wide acceptance by the Soviet public. Soviet health services are administered primarily in cities and towns, where most hospitals and clinics are located. For the Soviet leadership a healthy worker and soldier are essential for a productive economy and a robust defense system. Health care is labor intensive in the Soviet Union. Medical salaries are low, compared to the West, and the Soviet government has not invested heavily in advanced diagnostic equipment and in the development of new drugs. The system is two-tiered—one level exists for the general population, which uses local clinics and hospitals; the other operates for the privileged groups of society that have access to a closed network of medical services that provide a higher quality of medical care. Medical care is financed by the state but paid for by citizens in the form of taxes. It is not entirely free because surgeons and nurses expect to receive covert payments for services rendered.

A primary purpose of Soviet education, as described by Dobson, is to prepare children for a vocation that will make a purposeful contribution to society. Soviet youngsters enter school at age seven and, if successful, graduate from secondary school ten years later. Beginning with the ninth year, their choice of curriculum, academic or vocational, shapes their career opportunities. But a child's family background also affects academic peformance and vocational choice. Children of the Soviet middle class, which is concentrated in urban areas, tend to earn higher grades in school and are more likely to apply to universities for admission. Institutions of higher education, which are also clustered in cities and hence are more accessible to urban residents, are free and provide a small stipend for student expenses.

Grava's study analyzes urban public transportation, a vital service used by practically everyone for getting to work, shopping, and leisure activities. Privately operated automobiles are still owned only by a small minority of the Soviet population. Consequently the urban transportation system is overcrowded, even during non-rush hour periods. In large cities the metro (subway) is the backbone of Soviet urban transportation, and it is fast, clean, and efficient. Subways are currently operating in eight cities, with many more under construction. (A city with a population with over one million is eligible to receive subway service.) Other modes of transportation are buses, trolley buses, and trolley cars. Buses are the workhorses of Soviet surface transportation and because of their age are frequently in poor repair and not properly heated or ventilated; but they are always jammed with passengers. Soviet urban transportation shows little evidence of long-range, purposeful planning. Decisions, except for subway construction, appear to be made on an ad hoc basis and to be governed by current resource restraints.

The availability and quality of consumer goods and services for Soviet urbanites, according to Schroeder's study, continue to compare unfavorably with countries in both Western and Eastern Europe that have similar GNPs per capita. Retail shopping facilities and services still are too few in number, poorly equipped, and inadequately serviced. A centrally targeted economy has proved unsuitable for managing production and distribution of goods and services for an increasingly affluent population. Prospects for improvement are dim, and the 1980s will almost certainly be a decade of stringency for the Soviet consumer unless productivity can be raised substantially. The problems of irregularity of supply and poor quality are rooted in the nature of the economic system. Hence solving them would require radical reform geared to satisfying consumer demand rather than meeting planned production targets, as well as prices that would reflect the cost of items produced and of services rendered.

Citizens' contacts with government officials in the USSR are much more frequent than in the West. They take place most often on the local level between citizens and the government employees who allocate housing, dispense pensions and other welfare payments, and provide a wide range of retail services. Since official agencies provide the basic necessities of life, contacts with them are vitally important to the Soviet people. Gittelman describes Soviet citizens' evaluation of Soviet urban services based on interviews with former Soviet citizens from various ethnic backgrounds and geographic regions. Their overall disposition toward local officials was generally negative, although not uniformly so. The housing sector received the worst marks, and the pension system the best, perhaps because obtaining satisfactory housing is the greatest struggle for people, while applying for a pension is a relatively routine procedure that entails the dispensing of money, not a very scarce resource. Among respondents there was wide agreement on the existence of ethnic discrimination; that communist party members were definitely favored in job assignments and other areas; and that the less well educated are more inclined to use bribery while the better educated utilize personal connections to convince bureaucrats to give them what they want.

The contributors to this volume, experts in their specialties, have based their analysis primarily on Soviet sources and have visited the USSR to interview people and make on-the-spot observations of urban conditions. Because of their disciplinary diversity (four economists, three political scientists, three sociologists, and one city planner) they have used a variety of approaches in analyzing Soviet urban problems.

After perusing this volume the reader can draw his or her own conclusions about the ways in which the contemporary Soviet city is similar to or different from its Western counterpart. As we wrestle with the problems of our urban centers, it is useful to compare the experience of urban developments in different settings.

PART

I

AN OVERVIEW

—————— Henry W. Morton ——————

1

—————— The Contemporary Soviet City ——————

The USSR in the 1980s is a land of city dwellers, with over 63 percent of the Soviet people living in areas designated as "urban." This is a recent development. Over the past fifty-six years Soviet society recorded one of the fastest urbanization rates in the world. In 1926, 26.3 million (or 17.9 percent) of the population lived in urban areas, and there were just two cities with populations over one million (Moscow and Leningrad) and thirty-five over 100,000. By 1980 the number of urban residents had increased more than sixfold, to 168.9 million, and there were twenty-one cities with a population of over one million and 271 with more than 100,000.[1] (See Tables 1 and 2.)

Table 1
Urban Growth, Russia–USSR, 1897–1980

	1897	1926	1939	1959	1970	1980
Cities with populations over 100,000	14	35	82	148	221	271
Their total population (in millions)	4.4	9.5	27.0	48.6	75.6	96.3
Average population (in thousands)	314	306	329	328	342	353

Source: Jirí Musil, *Urbanization in Socialist Countries* (Armonk, N.Y., 1980), 47; *Narodnoe khoziaistvo SSSR v 1980 g.* (Moscow, 1981), 18-23.

What are the social, economic, and political consequences of this rapid urban growth? What are the problems of Soviet cities, and do they differ from the current American experience?

The United States is now in a period of posturban development, particularly in the Northeast and the Middle West, characterized by inner-city decay and poverty, with affluent suburbs surrounding the central city. Mayors of cities have become mendicants seeking handouts at the national and state capitals. American cities need to attract commerce and industry and to hold on to their middle-class

Table 2
Large Soviet Cities, 1979
(population in thousands)

Population over 1 million		Population between 500,000 and 1 million	
Moscow	8,203	Alma Ata	975
Leningrad	4,676	Rostov on-the-	
Kiev	2,248	Don	957
Tashkent	1,858	Volgograd	948
Kharkov	1,485	Saratov	873
Gorky	1,367	Riga	840
Novosibirsk	1,343	Krasnodarsk	820
Minsk	1,333	Zaporozhe	812
Sverdlovsk	1,239	Voronezh	809
Kuibyshev	1,238	Lvov	688
Dnepropetrovsk	1,100	Krivoi Rog	663
Tbilisi	1,095	Yaroslavl	608
Odessa	1,072	Karaganda	583
Cheliabinsk	1,055	Krasnodar	581
Erevan	1,055	Izhevsk	574
Baku	1,046	Irkutsk	568
Omsk	1,044	Vladivostok	565
Donetsk	1,040	Frunze	552
Perm	1,016	Novokuznetsk	551
Kazan	1,011	Barnaul	549
Ufa	1,009	Khabarovsk	545
		Kishinev	539
		Togliatti	533
		Tula	521
		Zhdanov	511
		Dushanbe	510
		Vilnius	503

Note: There were 271 cities with populations over 100,000
Source: *Narodnoe khoziaistvo SSSR v 1980 g.* (Moscow, 1981), 18-23.

inhabitants. Desperately they search for means to keep their tax bases from shrinking in order to pay for essential city services, whose costs have escalated. Instead they attract lower-income groups and the poor. Those with means have flown to the periphery, seeking a better life-style.

A sharply contrasting situation exists in the USSR. In the eyes of most Soviet citizens, cities are the most, indeed the only, desirable places to live, and the larger the city, the better—ideally Moscow or the capitals of republics. The millions who live in satellite communities near large cities are frequently the urban have-nots of Soviet society. Not because of unemployment—a singular success of Soviet policy has been the providing of full employment, although at much lower pay than in the West—but because of poor consumer services: a dearth in the variety and quality of goods, a scarcity of food, particularly meat and dairy products, and the paucity of restaurants, movies, theaters, good medical facilities, and repair services. These are only to be found, if at all, in large cities.

Many commute to the center city for work, but not by choice. The regime, unsuccessful in controlling urban population growth, has closed off Moscow, Leningrad, Kiev, and other large centers to newcomers to prevent them and other cities from developing into shanty towns. Permission to move to them is rarely granted. Numerous illegals reside in them, but their numbers are difficult to estimate.

For the Soviet citizen, therefore, the question of living within the center city or in surrounding settlements is not a casual but a crucial one. Beyond the city line, with the last high-rise structures still in sight, a harsher life style prevails, greatly lacking in creature comforts and time-saving devices. Suburbs as Americans know them, which extend uninterruptedly from one adjoining community to the other beyond the city line, with shopping centers and malls, simply do not exist.

Because of a critical housing shortage, permission to move to major cities is granted only by exception. If a factory or institution wishes to hire an employee or worker who will be domiciled in Moscow, Leningrad, Kiev, and other large cities, proof must be submitted to the city soviet (council) demonstrating an urgent need for his services. Even then permission is rarely given. If it is, the worker and his family will most likely receive only a temporary permit with a stipulated time period, usually for three years or less. Such workers are called *limitchiki*. They may possess special technical skills, may be semiskilled, such as construction workers, or may even be unskilled, like *dvorniki*, the combination janitors and *concierges* who clean and maintain housing inside and outside the premises. Such people are principally recruited from the provinces because Muscovites rarely apply for such menial positions.

Despite strict regulations, those wishing to move to large cities may attempt to do so illegally by entering into a fictitious marriage with a person who has a *propiska* (residence permit) for that city or by bribing the authorities. The price for a *propiska* ranges from 500 rubles for a provincial center to 2,500 to 3,000 rubles for Moscow.[2]

Three Major Problems of the Contemporary Soviet City

In the eyes of Soviet leaders, the most serious problems of the contemporary Soviet city in the European part of the USSR are that its population is aging and immobilized, which has led to severe labor shortage; that it suffers from a severe housing shortage, which directly contributes to the immobility of the urban population and prevents cities from importing needed personnel; and that chronic food shortages have forced Soviet leaders to ration meat and butter.

Population immobility and the labor shortage. Soviet society is aging. More people are retiring than are entering the labor force. (The retirement age for women is 55; for men it is 60.) Currently between one-sixth and one-fifth of the population living in large cities in the European part of the USSR is of pensioner age. Pensioners do not consider leaving Moscow, Leningrad, Kiev, and other large urban centers to move to the Soviet "sun belt," the Caucasus and Central Asia, for several reasons. Entry into those cities is also restricted, and they are as overcrowded as those in the north. Moreover, in many instances they would have to lower their housing standards, and they would lose the network of contacts they have spent a lifetime developing to acquire scarce consumer goods and access to officials who can assist in side-stepping bureaucratic red tape.

But since the introduction of the first five-year plan in 1928, increased production has largely been achieved by attracting rural workers to industrial sites in cities. Every additional worker added incrementally to output. Now there are no places in the city to put rural émigrés, and moreover the reservoir of rural surplus labor has dried up—except in Central Asia and the Caucasus. Soviet officials estimate that 800,000 additional workers are needed annually between 1981 and 1990. Even if cities were not restricted and housing were abundant, the numbers needed are simply not available. And the situation will get worse before it gets better. The USSR's largest generation was born in the second half of the 1950s and reached working age in the latter half of the 1970s. A smaller generation born in the second half of the 1960s will reach working age between 1985 and 1990. At the same time, a large generation born during the late 1920s will reach retirement age. Therefore the demographic forecast is that the Soviet Union will realize virtually no increase in labor resources during the last fifteen years of the century.[3] Because of an uneven distribution in population growth, the European part of the USSR will face an actual reduction in the number of people reaching working age, whereas Central Asia and Azerbaidzhan will have a labor surplus.

Soviet authorities are understandably concerned that this situation will exacerbate the labor shortage and affect production. They will intensify their efforts to persuade those who are eligible to retire to continue working. In 1981 seven million pensioners, or 30 percent of all people of retirement age, worked.[4]

The USSR would not suffer from a serious labor shortage if it could rationalize its labor force and the work process by substituting mechanized work for manual labor (40 percent of Soviet laborers in industry still work manually); if employers would stop hoarding labor (because 50 to 80 percent of a plant's output takes place during the last days of the month, a large labor reserve is needed for "storming" the plan); if employers were not required to dispatch millions of production workers annually to the countryside to help bring in the harvest (about eight million production workers performed this task in 1979); if losses in workdays could be reduced (currently averaging 20 days a year) and in work time (15 to 20 percent), much of it due to alcoholism; and if the high labor turnover rate (about 21 percent of the work force or 15 million workers in industry and construction) resulting in millions of lost workdays, primarily caused by work dissatisfaction and poor living conditions, could be significantly lowered.[5]

A primary reason why the Soviet worker is unproductive is that he lacks incentive to work hard. This is well expressed by a Soviet saying: "I'll never get fired, I'll never get a raise, I'll never get promoted."

The Soviet regime has experimented, but only on a limited scale, with a program (the Shchekino experiment) that permits factory directors to dismiss ineffective workers and reward the most productive with higher pay. Pledged to a policy of full employment, Soviet authorities have so far been unwilling to introduce meaningful incentives that would rationalize productivity, perhaps because they are fearful that it might also lead to structural unemployment—a most serious problem currently troubling Western nations.

The housing shortage. The lack of housing and overcrowded housing conditions exacerbate the acute manpower problem. Factories, offices, and stores cannot hire people if there is no place for them to live.

After decades of neglect, the Soviet regime, shortly after Stalin's death, launched an ambitious residential construction program in the mid-1950s to eliminate the critical housing shortage that forced the majority of urban families to live communally, sharing their apartment, kitchen, bathroom, and toilet with strangers. The average living space per person was only five square meters (about 55 square feet) in 1950.[6]

Thirty years later a majority of urban families lived in separate dwellings, and the average space per person had increased to 8.7 square meters (a 10-foot-by-10-foot span).[7] Some cities provided much better housing accommodations in terms of space than others. Differences ranged from Moscow's 11.2 square meters to Dushanbe's 6.6 square meters per person. (See Table 3.)

However, the promise made in the 1962 Party Program that each family would have a separate apartment by 1980 has not been kept. Approximately 20 percent of the urban population still live communally, and an additional 5 percent are sheltered in workers' dormitories.[8] They are the housing poor of the USSR. The problem is that there are still many more households (families and singles) than housing units. The figures for both categories have so far not been published by the Soviet government. We do know, however, the annual number of housing units built and marriages performed for selected cities.

A glance at Table 4 shows that of twenty-eight Soviet cities in 1979, only Kiev managed to build more apartments than it registered marriages. In such a comparison Kiev, Sverdlovsk, Dnepropetrovsk, Minsk, Baku, and Kharkov fared the best, whereas Odessa, Frunze, Ashkhabad, Donetsk, and Novosibirsk did worst. (See the last three columns of Table 4.) Since it is very likely that each city still carried a huge backlog of unsatisfied housing needs, this meant that

Table 3
Per Capita Living Space in 28 Cities, 1979

Cities	Per capita living space in m²	Urban population in thousands	Density of population (1,000 inhabitants per km²)
USSR	8.6	166,200	
Moscow*	11.2	7,915	9.0
Baku*	10.9	1,030	4.7
Tallin*	10.7	436	2.5
Leningrad	10.7	4,119	6.6
Riga*	12.2	843	2.8
Kiev*	9.6	2,192	2.8
Donetsk	9.6	1,032	2.9
Kharkov	9.6	1,064	4.8
Dnepropetrovsk	9.3	1,083	2.7
Vilnius*	8.9	492	1.9
Cheliabinsk	8.8	1,042	2.1
Sverdlovsk	8.8	1,225	2.5
Minsk*	8.7	1,295	7.0
Tbilisi*	8.7	1,080	3.1
Novosibirsk	8.6	1,328	2.8
Gorky	8.5	1,358	4.1
Kishinev*	8.4	519	4.0
Omsk	8.3	1,028	2.3
Alma Ata*	8.2	928	5.6
Kuibyshev	8.2	1,226	2.6
Odessa	8.3	1,057	7.7
Perm	8.1	1,008	1.4
Kazan	7.8	1,002	3.6
Erevan*	7.1	1,003	4.7
Ashkhabad*	6.9	318	3.8
Frunze*	6.9	543	4.4
Tashkent*	6.8	1,816	7.1
Dushanbe*	6.6	501	4.0

Note: Living space includes bedrooms and living rooms, but not kitchens, bathrooms, hallways, and storage areas. For the Russian Republic the minimum standard was 9 square meters.
Source: *Vestnik statistiki*, 12 (1980), 66-68.
*Capitals of republics.

newlyweds were seldom able to move into an apartment of their own. They invariably had to live with in-laws. In the cities with more severe shortages, such situations can last for decades.

A modern housing unit that has electricity, gas, central heating, hot and cold running water, a bathroom and flush toilet is the most expensive consumer good in the USSR and in the West. Without government support, in the form of direct subsidies, tax relief, or loans, few dwellings would be built in either society.

In the West, where the majority of dwellings are privately owned, housing is primarily rationed by price. This means that the apartment or home one decides to rent or purchase depends on the price and what the buyer can afford. This quickly narrows the choice to the type of housing and location that are both desirable and affordable.

In the Soviet Union the rationing of urban housing is primarily by governmental allocation.[9] More than 70 percent of all urban units are owned by the state. The exceptions are cooperative apartments, which amount to slightly more than five percent of the total. The rest are privately owned and found primarily in smaller cities and towns. They accounted for 22.5 percent of all urban housing in 1980. Four republics, Georgia (38.9 percent), Kirghizia (36.7 percent), the Ukraine (35.6 percent), and Uzbekistan (34.8 percent), had the highest amount of urban housing privately held.[10] State and cooperative housing in cities consists of low-, medium-, and high-rise apartment buildings. Therefore owning a home of your own with a garden, which many urbanites in the West prefer, if they can afford it, is not a possibility for Soviet citizens living in medium-sized or large Soviet cities.

Rents and utilities in state-owned apartments are nominal, usually less than 5 percent of a family's income. Since rent is not a factor, the great majority living in Soviet cities could easily afford to reside in the most luxurious and spacious apartments, in the most desirable location—that is, in or near the center, which has the best shopping areas, is the locus of cultural activities, and requires the minimum use of chronically overcrowded public transportation.

But the fact is that every major city suffers from a serious deficit in housing units even in its least desirable area, the outer ring, which offers poor shopping facilities, an unpaved and frequently muddy walk to the bus, and a long trip to work. Circumstances are worse in new towns where housing construction particularly lags behind industrial development and in small towns, which, having been bypassed by the momentum of industrialization, except for electricity and television, still live under nineteenth-century conditions.

Those who wish to improve their housing situation try to get on the city's waiting list. Eligibility usually begins with five square meters, or less, per family member. Since government officials control the limited supply of housing, it is not surprising that housing bureaucrats are the focal point for bribes. For those on the waiting list, jumping the queue is a universal wish because it can reduce one's waiting time from ten years to zero. For this to take place, influence, a bribe, or both are needed.

Table 4

Surplus/Deficit: Marriages and Housing Units Built in Major Soviet Cities, 1979
(in rank order)

	Marriages	Housing units built	+ Surplus − deficit	Marriages per 1,000 population	Units built per 1,000 population	+ Surplus − deficit
Kiev	24,113	25,200	1,087	11.1	11.4	+0.3
Sverdlovsk	13,185	13,100	−85	10.8	10.7	−0.1
Dnepropetrovsk	13,039	12,700	−339	12.1	11.7	−0.4
Minsk	15,298	14,500	−85	10.8	10.7	−0.1
Baku	8,494	7,500	−994	8.3	7.2	−1.1
Kharkov	17,210	125,400	−1,810	11.8	10.5	−1.3
Moscow	90,430	76,900	−13,530	11.2	9.7	−1.5
Tallin	4,771	4,100	−671	11.0	9.4	−1.6
Gorky	14,377	11,400	−2,977	10.6	8.4	−2.2
Kazan	9,748	7,600	−2,148	9.8	7.6	−2.2
Perm	9,736	7,100	−2,636	9.7	7.0	−2.7
Tbilisi	10,969	8,000	−2,969	10.2	7.4	−2.8

Alma Ata	12,077	9,600	−2,477	13.2	10.3	−2.9
Leningrad	57,554	39,400	−18,154	12.5	9.6	−2.9
Tashkent	18,434	13,400	−5,034	10.3	7.4	−2.9
Dushanbe	4,849	3,400	−1,449	9.8	6.8	−3.0
Kishinev	6,411	5,000	−1,411	12.6	9.6	−3.0
Omsk	12,032	9,000	−3,032	11.8	8.8	−3.0
Erevan	10,364	7,200	−3,164	10.1	6.9	−3.2
Cheliabinsk	11,121	7,600	−3,521	10.7	7.3	−3.4
Riga	9,675	6,800	−2,875	11.5	8.1	−3.4
Kuibyshev	13,111	8,800	−4,311	10.7	7.2	−3.5
Vilnius	5,701	3,800	−1,901	11.7	7.7	−4.0
Novosibirsk	16,844	11,000	−5,844	12.8	8.3	−4.5
Donetsk	12,150	7,600	−4,550	11.8	7.0	−4.8
Ashkhabad	3,389	1,400	−1,989	10.8	5.9	−4.9
Frunze	6,268	3,300	−2,968	11.7	6.1	−5.6
Odessa	12,030	4,600	−7,430	11.4	4.4	−7.0

Source: *Vestnik statistiki*, 12 (1980), 66-68.

The Soviet Union is a "society of connections"; who you know may well determine how well you are housed, what food you eat, what kind of clothing you wear, and what kinds of deficient goods (from quality tape recorders to refrigerators) you can obtain. It is not simply a question of money, although that may be essential at some point to "buy" an official; more important are one's connections because there are many commodities and services that money alone cannot buy and that can only be obtained as favors, to be paid back immediately or at some future date. The society of connections is composed of interacting networks of friends and acquaintances who, by virtue of their positions, have access to scarce resources they trade for others. A good apartment is one of the scarcest commodities, and to get one quickly one must be well connected. "Too often the decisive factor is not the waiting list," *Pravda* explained on February 16, 1973, "but a sudden telephone call . . . [after which] they give the apartments to the families of football players and the whole queue is pushed back." It helps immensely if your father has influence, as was the case in Magnitogorsk, where the director of a large factory obtained a flat illegally for his son.[11]

The still acute housing situation is the government's responsibility because it was pledged to eliminate the shortage. It invests heavily in industry, attracting workers and managerial personnel to urban areas, yet *under*invests in housing construction and other consumer services needed to take care of them and their families. It restricts consumer choice to high-density apartment-style living in cities, thereby discouraging consumer initiative for private home building, and it limits cooperative housing construction, which is largely self-financed.

As long as the state remains the principal financer of urban housing construction and does not get even a partial return on its investment, the housing deficit in relation to households can only be reduced incrementally. However, if rents were raised to pay for a significant portion of the construction costs and for the upkeep of the housing stock, then the state could be in a much more favorable position to substantially increase its investment in housing. (But additional funds by themselves would not guarantee significant increases in housing construction because the required materials and equipment, due to poor economic management, would not be produced.)

Since such a change in policy is not feasible at the present time, because of the government's stated commitment to assign public housing free of charge, which the urban consumer finds very attractive and expects as a matter of course (not realizing that he is paying higher prices for clothing, durable goods, and other products to pay for the state's huge housing subsidy), the housing shortage will continue for many years to come.

The food shortage. Scarcities of meat, butter, milk and other dairy products, poultry, fish, and even potatoes have burst the bubble of expectation, floated by Soviet leaders since Khrushchev, that the supply and quality of food and consumer goods would slowly but steadily improve. In November 1981 Leonid Brezhnev acknowledged that "the food problem is, economically and politically, the central problem" for the next five years.[12] Moscow, Leningrad, and the capitals of the republics remain the best supplied, but even they have felt the pinch. Frequent trips from the provinces to large urban centers are necessary to buy whatever food is available. Even in large cities with a population of over one million, meat is seldom stocked in state stores. At the collective farm markets found in all cities and in most towns, where price is determined by demand and supply, meat may be available, but at three to five times the price that would be charged in state stores. Chronic shortages also exist for quality clothing, appliances, furniture, and other goods. In 1981 a Soviet reporter was sent to Krasnodar, a city with a population of over half a million, to check the availability of everyday items: a toothbrush, soap, shaving cream, socks, and underwear. In a day's shopping he could not find any of them for sale.[13]

After Stalin's death the Soviet public was led to expect a slow but steady increase in the flow of foods and other consumer products, which in fact did take place. Between 1950 and 1980, according to a U.S. government study, per capita consumption of all goods nearly tripled.[14] Of these, the food supply was the slowest category to grow; nevertheless the average Soviet citizen consumed over twice as much meat in 1975 as he did in 1950.[15] Despite such advances the Soviet diet still lags behind Western nutritional standards. Although the daily caloric intake is about the same, 3,300 for Soviets as against 3,520 for Americans, starchy foods (grains and potatoes) represented 44 percent of the average Soviet diet, compared to 26 percent of what the average American eats; meat and fish account for only 8 percent of the Soviet diet, compared to 21 percent for the American diet.[16] Because of a chronic shortage of fresh fruits and vegetables, the average Soviet citizen's "consumption of vitamins, particularly of vitamins E, A, B_1, B_2, and nicotinamide is insufficient, especially during winter and spring."[17]

With meat and butter very scarce, the government has initiated a rationing system, which has not been publicized in the national press. (This is in addition to the existence of elite food stores, long established in major cities, to which only the highly privileged have access.) In Moscow and some other cities, when meat and butter are available, customers are limited in the quantity they can buy (usually a kilo, or 2.2 pounds, per purchaser), or special times are set aside when residents in a housing development may shop at their local store for meat and butter.[18]

In the Siberian city Irkutsk (pop. 568,000), ration coupons, red for 2.2 pounds of meat and green for two-thirds of a pound of butter, are distributed monthly by the local housing administration.[19] Having a ration coupon does not automatically guarantee the shopper will be able to buy meat or butter because the item may not be available in stores.

Direct distribution of meat, butter, and other scarce food products at factories and other places of work is a third variant of rationing. Employees at such places are most favored because they can buy hard-to-get foods without searching for them in stores and then having to wait in long lines until served, as are those whose plant has a cafeteria that provides nourishing meals at subsidized prices. Both ways of supplying food are important factors in combatting labor turnover and helping factories hold on to their work force. The increased distribution of food at places of work has undoubtedly reduced food deliveries to state stores, thereby aggravating the food problem for the majority of shoppers.

The immediate cause for the decrease in food supply is the unprecedented failure of four consecutive grain harvests. Grain production reached a record high 237 million tons in 1978 but has not reached the 190 million-ton mark since. A poor grain yield means a severe cutback in feed stock for animals. To prevent serious declines in meat and dairy products consumption, the USSR, which had been a grain exporter, imported $12 billion worth of grain and other agricultural products in 1981, which was 40 percent of its hard currency purchases that year.[20] Even with grain imports, meat production declined slightly, from 15.4 million tons in 1979 to 15.2 million tons in 1981, and milk production fell for the third consecutive year to 88.5 million tons, the lowest level since 1974.[21]

Soviet agriculture has never recovered from Stalin's policy of forced collectivization of farms in 1929 and 1930, which removed Russia's best farmers from the soil. Today an aging and shrinking rural population longs to leave the village, although financially peasants are perhaps better off than many of their city cousins. With income earned primarily from their private farm plots, many could afford good clothing, color television, a motorcycle, and some even a car. But whatever they want to buy, and whatever needs to be repaired, can only be bought or serviced in cities and towns.

The Brezhnev solution was to pour money into agriculture: 315 billion rubles have been spent since 1965, with more in the pipeline, to pay state and collective farmers higher prices for their products, provide better pensions, equip farms with new machinery, construct new buildings and facilities, produce more fertilizers, and pave rural roads—most still have dirt surfaces that make them difficult to navigate after heavy rain.[22] The yearly expenditures for agriculture are higher than annual expenses for defense. The Brezhnev farm policy is currently being continued by his successor, Yu. V. Andropov.

Left largely untouched by the Soviet leadership is a counterproductive incentive structure. Most farm workers get paid for piece-rate work: the amount of land plowed, for example. Consequently the final product, the harvest, is not the major concern for them. Thus they might plow shallowly to make more money even though the field needs deep plowing. Contributing to the problem is the fact that farm machinery is in chronic disrepair, and spare parts are difficult to obtain. Moreover, up to one-third of the harvest is lost because of spoilage, inadequate storage facilities, during transportation, or due to pilferage.[23]

A major responsibility of cities is supplying their populations with food. Because of persistent shortages and the unreliability of food deliveries from other parts of the country, large and medium-sized cities are dependent on their immediately surrounding territory for food. In Irkutsk the deputy head of the provincial party organization explained that "local farms supply 60 percent of the meat we need and 80 percent of our milk, and we don't get enough from the outside."[24] This is why rationing was introduced.

Even factories and the armed forces now have to farm to provide food for workers and servicemen. The formation of factory "agrarian shops" was urged by a Central Committee of the CPSU and USSR Council of Ministers resolution in December 1979 and endorsed by L. I. Brezhnev in his May 1982 statement "that every industrial enterprise and every organization that is capable of managing [an agrarian shop] should have one. . . ."[25] The military also receives much of its food from military-run state farms. Commander of the Northern Fleet, Admiral A. Mikhailovskii, revealed in June 1982 that all the milk and eggs consumed by the navy are provided from its own resources.[26]

Officially a large part of the blame for the food shortage is placed on the rapid rise in the population's monetary income, the fact that "the food supply is increasing by an average of less than one percent a year, while the population's ability to pay for its requirements is growing almost seven times as fast." This has increased effective demand for food products, "and in conditions of unstable food supply, it has led to a tendency to hoard."[27]

This argument is not very persuasive. The output of meat and dairy products has declined, but the Soviet population is still increasing by two million persons a year. The question that has not been addressed by party leaders is why food prices in state stores are far below production costs (a fact of which most consumers are probably not aware). By holding meat (and butter) at the 1962 price, the state subsidy for meat in 1975 was 12 billion rubles, the equivalent of a 40 percent markdown in the retail price.[28] By 1982 the retail price for meat products covered only half of the cost,[29] and meat became even scarcer. Had the government raised the price of meat and other foods in relation to cost, the demand for these products would have decreased. Then a greater number of previously hard-to-get foods would have been displayed, permitting the consumer to make choices.

A primary reason why the Soviet leadership may be reluctant to raise food prices in accordance with supply and demand is the memory of 1962, when prices for meat and butter were increased by 25 percent. This triggered protest demonstrations in a number of cities, a repetition of which the regime wants to avoid.

Mission Impossible—
the Search for Comprehensive
Urban Planning

The reasons for Soviet urban problems are many. Historically the rate of industrial investment far exceeded the financing of urban services, and this vitiated the practice (but not the theory) of comprehensive urban planning, which was supposed to provide a balance between industrial growth and urban development.

Urban planning came late to the USSR. In the 1920s various groups heatedly debated what form the new "socialist" city should take. Numerous theories for new communal living and urban design were advocated by various groups, including a radical proposal by the "disurbanists" to abandon cities as a way of life. Because of lack of funds, though, none of these proposals was implemented, and little urban construction of any kind took place during this period.

The party abruptly ended the debate in 1931, declaring that the existing cities were already "socialist" by definition, and it opted for traditional, neoclassical themes for architecture and city planning. Ornate public buildings and ornamental subway stations were constructed, as were large squares and broad boulevards—useful for parades. These grandiose configurations were intended to be symbolic supports for the glorification of Stalin and the power of the Soviet state. Also approved at that time was the concept of green belts of forests and meadows, which were to encircle cities, providing recreational opportunities for urbanites.[30]

Moscow was the first city to adopt a long-range plan (known as the general plan) for urban development, but not until 1935. It served as a model for other cities, which, however, did not approve theirs until after the war, in the 1950s and 1960s. It was also in the postwar period that the office of the Chief Architect of the City functioned as a department of local government responsible for city planning.

Practically all problems of city growth stem from the model Stalin chose to rapidly industrialize the country in the late 1920s. The building of new factories, which spurred the rapid population growth of cities, was not matched by a corresponding investment in the urban infrastructure. Responsibility for both kinds of investment was placed in the hands of industrial ministries, and little thought was given to town planning:

> Ministries and plants literally tore cities to pieces. Each
> one attempting by all means fair and foul to build "its own"
> housing right next to the plant, create at any price "its
> own" private workers' community near the plant with "its
> own" water supply, sewerage, steam plant . . . in short
> to do everything for itself and give nothing to the city.[31]

The enterprises became fiefdoms of ministries. Controlled from Moscow and the capitals of the republics, today they remain, in many instances, the dominant force in urban decision-making.[32] They still predominantly control the purse strings for urban investments and frequently the productive capacities for building housing and other urban facilities.

City party committees and soviets have been trying to whittle away at the power of enterprises in this sphere but have achieved only limited success. Ministries in the mid-1970s still accounted for 70 percent of all appropriations for housing construction, 65 percent for building kindergartens and day-care centers, and 30 percent for constructing hospitals and clinics. (Ministries spend disproportionately for urban services. Those employed in plants belonging to heavy industrial ministries have an 18- to 20-times better chance of receiving new housing than those working in light industry. Those employed by municipalities are less favored since they are solely dependent on city housing resources.)[33]

The present arrangement was inherited from a previous era and will not change by itself. The post-Brezhnev leadership is unlikely to attempt radical surgery on the system. Khrushchev did in 1957 when he dismantled the central-ized economic ministries and created economic regions instead. This was one of several reasons for his ouster. Brezhnev and company, who succeeded him, did not tempt fate by repeating his political error.

In the past several decades a series of reforms, principally advocated by planners and city party and government officials, were adopted to limit the power of enterprises, but they met only partial success. *Gosstroi* (the State Committee for Construction) was formed in 1952, which helped many large cities, over a period of years, to develop their own construction capacities—a function the ministries had monopolized. Today practically every major city has its own construction agency.

Of great significance was a joint party and government resolution of July 1957 that called for city soviets to become single-developers (*edinye zakazchiki*) for all city construction projects funded by enterprises and municipalities. If this law were enforced, a city agency, the capital construction administration, would collect all money and would coordinate the scheduling of all civil construction, which until then had primarily been done independently by enterprises.

The resolution has still not been fully implemented to this day. Moscow, which once had as many as 500 developers, finally achieved single-developer status in 1967, as did the capitals of republics and many larger cities in the USSR a number of years later.[34] Because of the lag in application, the Central Commit-tee of the CPSU and the Presidium of the USSR Supreme Soviet issued separate resolutions in March 1971 requesting that the single-developer model be adopted in cities, and again in 1978, when a deadline was set—that came and went—of 1980. But in 1978, 65 percent of all capital investments for civil construction in Russian Republic cities and only 39 percent for the USSR were funneled through the capital construction administrations of city soviets.[35] A number of state agencies—the armed forces, the Committee for State Security (KGB), and certain USSR ministries—are simply too powerful to willingly transfer their planning and construction capacities to city governments.

The 1971 party and government resolutions also urged city governments to use powers they already possessed to take charge of coordinating city planning and improving municipal services. They were instructed to review plans of enterprises belonging to federal and republic ministries that wanted to expand their plants or build new ones, and to transfer those enterprises to city subordina-tion that primarily service the city population.

They were also directed to improve the maintenance and repair of urban housing owned by enterprises, which accounted for about two-thirds of the total, by setting deadlines for their gradual transfer to a city agency—a move that had been previously advocated by a 1967 decree.[36]

The 1971 resolution was slowly and indifferently implemented. Take the transfer of enterprise housing to municipalities. This is not a simple matter. City governments lack the equipment, money, materials, and the skilled manpower necessary for proper maintenance and repair. Consequently they will only accept buildings from enterprises if they are well maintained and are not in need of capital repairs, for which municipalities, understandably, are not willing to pay. This is a primary reason why deadlines for the transfer of housing stock were not established. Cities also see little advantage in accepting buildings that are already fully occupied. They need empty apartments to distribute to families that have been waiting for many years. Enterprises, for their part, hesitate to turn over buildings to local soviets because they want to hold on to their housing to attract workers to their plants.[37]

Ten years later (in 1981) a joint resolution on "Further Enhancing the Role of the Soviets in Economic Construction" was issued by three leading party and government bodies: the Central Committee of the CPSU, the Presidium of the Supreme Soviet, and the Council of Ministers of the USSR. More forceful in tone, and shifting the responsibility from soviets to enterprises, the resolution ordered factories belonging to the USSR and republic ministries, before they send drafts of five-year and annual plans to higher agencies, to *submit* them for examination to the appropriate bodies of jurisdiction, the councils of ministers of autonomous republics or to executive committees of territory, region, province, district, or city soviets, "where questions of land use, environmental protection, construction, utilization of labor resources, production of consumer goods, and also social, cultural, consumer, and other services to the public are concerned." The appropriate soviet body is to inform the enterprise and, when necessary, the higher level agency as well of the results of its examination and proposals for change. USSR and union republic ministries are to take these proposals for change into account in drawing up the final plans of enterprises under their jurisdiction.[38]

Will this resolution be more successfully implemented? Will it prevent the unauthorized siting of new plants and the expansion of existing ones? Only time will tell.

Who Governs

There is still the matter of who governs the city. Constitutionally it is the executive committee (*gorispolkom*) and the departments of the city council (soviet) that plan and administer services under the city's control. They are nominally responsible to the members of the city soviet, who are elected from a single slate, and who in turn "elect" the executive committee and the chairman. City soviets usually meet for a day, bimonthly or quarterly.

Organizationally every city government is responsible to a superior soviet depending on a city's subordination, either district, province, or republic. The higher the subordination, the more prestigious the soviet, and the fewer bureaucratic channels an executive committee or a city department has to clear. Moscow and Leningrad report directly to the Council of Ministers of the Russian Republic. The city of Zagorsk's superior is the Moscow Province Soviet because Zagorsk is a district center. Functionally certain city departments, such as finance and police, will be accountable to the superior soviet's departments of finance and police respectively and to the city soviet and its executive committee as well. Local service departments, such as the restaurant trust, report only to the city soviet.

But this still does not tell us where the locus of power in cities resides or how the decision-making process works. The power play of Soviet politics may be viewed within the context of bureaucratic politics. "The Soviet political system is a huge bureaucratic arena in which bureaus compete, bargain and negotiate to such a degree that although all are officially subordinated to one central leadership there is virtually no sphere of administration immune from bureaucratic politics." [39]

In the game of bureaucratic politics some bureaucracies are more powerful and successful than others. This also applies to the triangular struggle over who controls Soviet cities: the managers of enterprises, the first party secretary of the city, and the chairman of the executive committee of the city soviet are all party members. Most participate in an interlocking directorate, the city party bureau. But all are not equal. Because of the institutions they represent, they pursue different interests and carry different responsibilities. They are also backed by and responsible to higher authorities whose political and economic influences play an important role.

Although the chairman of the city soviet executive committee is nominally the mayor, the first secretary of the city party committee is invariably in charge. The party's mandate is broad: "to direct all soviet, economic, trade union, and youth organizations." [40] This means that the first secretary and the party bureau function as leaders and coordinators of the city's political, economic, ideological, and cultural activities.

The first secretary is boss unless in the unusual case he is outranked by the director of a large plant or the chairman of the city executive committee by virtue of either one's membership in a higher party body (the provincial party committee or, in rare instances, the central committee of the republic or the USSR). In this *troika* the mayor has huge responsibilities but little authority. He is most concerned about but least effective in reordering the balance between municipal and industrial needs.

In official sources and interviews the function of the city party leadership is frequently described as one that primarily guides policies and reviews important (*nomenklatura*) appointments made at the city level—two important powers. This might lead one to assume that the party is not directly involved in the nitty-gritty of a city's daily activities and problems.

Such a view was dispelled in a January 1981 speech by G. A. Aliev, then the First Party Secretary of Azerbaidzhan and a candidate member of the Politburo. In a scathing address delivered to the Baku party conference, he held the city's party committee responsible for serious shortcomings in the construction of housing and repairs, for providing poor consumer services—particularly the inadequate availability of food in stores, the chronic disruption of the public transportation system, and a poorly functioning health delivery service—for failure to protect the population against an increasing crime rate, and for ignoring corrupt practices such as the illegal selling of state-owned apartments by city officials.

For our purpose it was revealing that Aliev criticized by name the ministers of the petroleum-refining and petrochemical industries, the Azerbaidzhan railroad, and the ministry of industrial construction for their "irresponsible failure" to build housing for their workers. This, he declared,

> occurred because certain leaders are taking advantage of the new system of the single-developer . . . in Baku. They have ceased to build housing themselves and believe that their functions amount merely to putting capital investment at the disposal of the city soviet of Baku and that the latter should do the building. But other than *Glavbakstroi,* the Baku soviet has no construction subdivisions. Surely the leaders of the city of Baku know that we can't agree to this? Surely the ministry leaders realize that this is, at least, dishonest.[41]

This example is very instructive; it illustrates that even a Politburo member is relatively powerless when confronted by the self-interest of powerful ministries, and second, that a city, by establishing the office of a single-developer, can do itself harm and provide an excuse for ministries, which previously had used their construction base for building housing, to renege on that obligation. It also verifies the continuing dependency of many cities on enterprise capacities for constructing urban facilities.

The party leader's relationship with enterprises of ministries at both city and province level is that of economic coordinator. The party secretary and the plant director have a common interest in seeing that the monthly plan is fulfilled. Province secretaries are frequently in touch by phone with enterprises and will lobby (not always successfully) on their behalf with higher party authorities to rush shipments of materials and equipment to a factory. The province party committee will also pressure an enterprise director to request from his ministry funding for construction of housing, schools, and other urban construction.[42]

Ministries, for their part, feel that cities should provide these facilities from municipal funds. This is a major reason why ministries seek to enlarge enterprises in established cities. There they can piggyback on presently available city services and won't have to start from scratch, as is the case in new towns. This tendency has greatly contributed to unplanned city growth—plant expansion means more workers with families—invariably straining a city's services of housing, transportation, schools, and shops beyond its capacity.

City governments still are the weak sisters vis-à-vis the party and the enterprises, but compared to a quarter of a century ago many have made definite progress. Many now have an experienced staff of city planners, financial experts, architects, transportation, and other functional specialists and knowledgeable administrators. Many also have institutionalized the single-developer in charge of scheduling much construction. Cities also possess the legal power to regulate the expansion of enterprises belonging to ministries and the siting of new plants, but they still must tread carefully in this area.

In Novosibirsk, a city of 1.3 million, we were told by province and city officials in June 1981 that the province government (and presumably the party bureau) must approve the expansion of all plants. But when asked whether a ministry gets upset if its enterprise is turned down, the answer was that such a request is rarely refused.

The party has the political power, the city has the legal power, but the enterprises often are mightier because they have the economic and financial clout. As a general rule, both in the Soviet Union and in the United States, those running the economy are frequently more powerful than the politicians.

The Contemporary Soviet City: Three Typologies

The USSR can be viewed as having three types of cities:

1. *The enterprise city* is a company town writ large, where one or several factories belonging to industrial ministries finance all municipal services. The city soviet and its departments serve primarily as the administrative arms of enterprises. They have little political leverage. An enterprise can legally be designated as the single-developer of a city. This makes the director the de jure as well as the de facto boss of the municipality. Over 1,000 new industrial towns were built in the Soviet era, and most were initially organized along these lines. An example is the city of Rustavi in the Georgian Republic, which was founded in the midforties. Two factories, a metallurgical plant and a chemical combine, are its chief employers. The chairman of the city soviet, whom I interviewed in November 1974, was previously a deputy director of the metallurgical plant. The city's budget was completely dependent for its funding on these two enterprises.

The enterprise city faces serious problems when factories belonging to a number of different ministries control housing, heating, water supply, public transportation, and other urban services in different sections of town, using their own system of management. Consequently some sections of the city may have heat or water, while others may not. The Siberian city of Bratsk is such an example, which is not that uncommon. The city party committee and government should coordinate these services but are powerless to act.

". . . The city Soviets do not, as a rule, act as a single-developer during the intial stages of the construction of communities. They rarely achieve this position during the settlements' later development either," admitted *Pravda* on August 2, 1981. "Many ministries and departments will not concede even an iota of their rights," even when special instructions to do so exist. . . . Dozens of organizations put up a city or a settlement, but no one is willing to take full responsibility for carrying out a multifaceted, difficult program. Everyone works for himself. As a result, things get so confused that abnormal situations frequently arise. Under such circumstances comprehensive urban planning cannot take place."[43]

2. *The bureaucratic-political city* is found in larger, older municipalities.

Some are operationally close to the company town model because of their continued financial dependency on enterprises belonging to ministries. Many factories control and administer various urban services, and their directors specify the amount to be spent on new housing, schools, clinics, and shops. They, and not the local soviet, determine the sitings of new plants and the expansion of existing ones. But at the same time, the city has made progress in shifting some of the responsibility for civil construction to the city's single-developer and the transfer of some municipal services to city agencies. Moscow and other large cities in the 1950s were in this position, while many of the Johnny-come-lately cities, whose populations have burgeoned in the last two decades, are now there.

Those cities in the middle age of their development have, over a period of time, gradually accumulated in their bureaucratic struggle with powerful enterprises more power and responsibility for providing basic services, although they are still not financially independent to shape their own destiny—a common problem shared with most cities in the world. Even the most politically influential cities cannot prevent powerful sponsors—the armed forces, the security police, and certain ministries—from bypassing the single-developer to build or expand their own facilities. Even Moscow, which is the leader in urban development, still has some industrial plants that expand their premises despite a long-standing ordinance prohibiting such actions; and numerous enterprises belonging to sundry ministries, which have been ordered to move out because of their emissions' harmful effect on the city's air quality, have not only refused to relocate but have even increased their work force.[44] And in a number of the capital's districts, the majority of stores, preschool institutions, and housing still belongs to and is administered by ministerial enterprises.[45]

3. *The party-government city* is an ideal type, in the Weberian sense, and does not as yet exist. But the potential for it is there. Moscow, Leningrad, and certain capitals of republics are moving, albeit slowly, in that direction. If the party-government city came into being, it would mean that the city fathers had freed themselves from the tutelage of enterprise control. Ministries and enterprises would still make financial contributions for municipal services, but they would be funneled solely through the city's single-developer. Enterprises would have transferred ownership of their housing, preschool centers, clinics, stores, etc., to the city government. Instead of domination by agents of central ministries, control over cities would be exercised by superior party and government bodies at the district, province, republic, and all-union levels.

Will cities have traded in one master for another? Would this finally assure comprehensive urban planning? One speculation is that the bureaucratic-political battlefield over the funding and control of cities would be reshaped and acted out by party and governmental bodies primarily along hierarchical lines. The contemporary soviet city might then be better planned, but it would not be permitted greater autonomy in its decision-making process.

Notes

[1] *Naselenie SSSR 1973* (Moscow, 1975), 26-35; *Narodnoe khoziaistvo v 1980 g.* (Moscow, 1981), 7, 18-26; hereafter *Narkhoz.*

[2]Konstantin M. Simis, *Secrets of a Corrupt Society* (London, 1982), 128-29.

[3]V. Perevedentsev, "People, Reproduction and Family," *Sotsiologicheskie issledovaniia*, 2 (February 1982), translated in *Current Digest of the Soviet Press*, *34*, 19 (July 6, 1982), 5; hereafter *CD*.

[4]*Trud* (January 29, 1982); *CD*, *34*, 8 (March 24, 1982), 7.

[5]The percentage of manual work in industry was provided by L. I. Brezhnev, *Pravda* (November 17, 1981); *CD*, *33*, 46 (December 16, 1981), 5. The rest is from Y. L. Manevich, "The Rational Utilization of Manpower," *Voprosy ekonomiki*, 9 (September, 1981), 5; *CD*, *34*, 6 (March 24, 1982), 5, except for the labor turnover figures, which were calculated by Isaak Kaplan (private communication).

[6]Henry W. Morton, "What Have Soviet Leaders Done About the Housing Crisis?" in Henry W. Morton and Rudolf L. Tökes, eds., *Soviet Politics and Society in the 1970's* (New York, 1974), 170.

[7]*Narkhoz 1980*, 7, 392.

[8]*Pravda* (December 2, 1980); *CD*, *32*, 48 (December 31, 1980), 3.

[9]I am indebted to Norton E. Long for bringing the concept of pricing to my attention.

[10]*Narkhoz 1980*, 393.

[11]Ibid., 105.

[12]*Pravda* (November 17, 1981); *CD*, *33*, 46 (December 16, 1981), 3.

[13]*Literaturnaia gazeta*, 13 (1981), mentioned in Keith Bush, "Retail Prices in Moscow and Four Western Cities, March, 1982," *Special Radio Free Europe Research Report* (1982), 5.

[14]Gertrude E. Schroeder and Elizabeth Denton, "An Index of Consumption in the USSR," *USSR: Measure of Economic Growth and Development, 1950-1980* (Washington, D.C., 1982), 325.

[15]Gertrude E. Schroeder and Barbara Severin, "Soviet Consumption and Income Policies in Perspective," *The Soviet Economy in a New Perspective* (Washington, D.C., 1976), 621-23.

[16]*New York Times* (January 15, 1982).

[17]*Ekonomika i organizatsiia promyshlennogo proizvodstva*, 6 (June 1982); *CD*, , 31 (September 1, 1982), 6.

[18]*New York Times* (January 15, 1982).

[19]Ibid.

[20]Ibid. (January 9, 1983).

[21]*Radio Liberty Research Report*, 118/22 (March 12, 1982).

[22]Ibid., 215/82 (May 25, 1982).

[23]*Sotsiologicheskaia industriia* (September, 1982); *CD*, *34*, 42 (November 12, 1982), 21.

[24]*New York Times* (December 28, 1981).

[25]The resolution appeared in *Pravda* (December 21, 1979); *CD*, *30*, 51 (January 17, 1980), 17; Brezhnev's statement was reported in *Pravda* (November 1, 1982); *CD*, *34*, 44 (December 11, 1982), 9.

[26]*Radio Liberty Research Report*, 308/82 (August 19, 1982).

[27]*Ekonomika i organizatsiia promyshlennogo proizvodstva*, 6 (June, 1982); *CD*, *34*, 31 (September 1, 1982). The phrase "conditions of unstable supply" is a code for lack of food in stores.

[28]Elizabeth Denton, "Soviet Consumer Trends and Prospects," *Soviet Economy in a Time of Change* (Washington, D.C., 1979), 765.

[29]*Radio Liberty Research Report*, 255/82 (June 24, 1982).

[30]Anatoly Kapp, "Housing and the Masses," Occasional Paper 149, Kennan Institute

for Advanced Russian Studies (Washington, D.C., 1981), 12, 16-19.

[31]Robert J. Osborn, *Soviet Social Policies* (Homewood, Ill., 1970), 222.

[32]William Taubman, *Governing Soviet Cities* (New York, 1973), 108.

[33]*Sotsiologicheskie issledovaniia*, 1 (January-March 1982); *CD*, *34*, 10 (April 7, 1982), 7.

[34]Taubman, 105.

[35]The party resolution appeared in *Pravda* (March 14, 1971), and the government decree was published in *Izvestia* (March 20, 1971). For the 1978 citation see *Izvestia* (March 24, 1978); *CD*, *30*, 12 (April 19, 1978), 20.

[36]Ibid.

[37]For a more detailed explanation, see Henry W. Morton, "L'application de la réform en U.S.S.R., perspectives et problèmes: le cas du logement," *Revue d'études comparatives est-ouest*, *12*, 3 (September 1981), 75-78.

[38]*Izvestia* (March 29, 1981); *CD*, *33*, 13 (April 29, 1981), 11.

[39]Taubman, 6.

[40]Ibid., 48.

[41]*Bakinskii rabochii* (January 10, 1981), translated in *JPRS*, 77553 (March 10, 1981), 30-40.

[42]Jerry F. Hough, *The Soviet Prefects* (Cambridge, 1969), *passim*.

[43]*Pravda* (August 2, 1981), *CD*, *33*, 31 (September 2, 1981), 8-9.

[44]*Izvestia* (March 24, 1982); *CD*, *34*, 12 (April 21, 1982), 22.

[45]*Gorodskoe khoziaistvo Moskvy*, 2 (February 1979), 21-22.

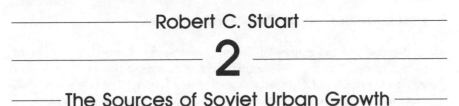

Robert C. Stuart

2

The Sources of Soviet Urban Growth

Introduction

The process of urbanization as a concomitant to the more general process of economic development has always been of great interest to the social analyst. Urban growth in the planned socialist economic system of the Soviet Union is of interest for a host of traditional reasons. It is also of interest, however, for the light that it might shed on the nature of the urbanization process under differing conditions, in particular under differing political and economic systems and with differing policy objectives.

The comparative analysis of urbanization patterns in socialist and nonsocialist economic systems has been limited in the past for a number of cogent reasons. In the Soviet case the relevant data have not been available, and until recently (the early 1960s) there was minimal published Soviet research on the question. With a lack of both primary and secondary materials, Western research on Soviet urbanization was understandably limited.

In a modest but important way, these facts have changed in recent years. Soviet data are now more readily available, and Soviet researchers are themselves publishing numerous studies on the general topic of urbanization in the Soviet Union.[1] In addition, Western studies now permit us to examine the nature of the Soviet urban sector and to consider the possibility that there is an urbanization process and result unique to the planned socialist economy.[2]

This chapter will explore three main issues. Section I will be devoted to a general summary of the Soviet urban growth experience. In Section II we will examine the sources of urban growth, beginning with an examination of the natural growth of population residing in Soviet urban areas, with special emphasis on the *rate* of natural population increase and the factors that have influenced this rate. Thereafter we will turn to an examination of rural-urban migration as a factor contributing to Soviet urban growth. Once again, our central interest will be the rate of migration and the forces that have influenced the migration streams. Finally, Section III will be devoted to some general conclusions about the Soviet urban growth experience, its past, present, and future.

I. Soviet Urban Growth: Past Trends

Both the rate and the pattern of urban growth in the Soviet Union since the implementation of a centrally planned socialist economic system in 1928 are in large part the result of two broad and interrelated forces.[3] The first and overriding factor has been the nature of Soviet rapid industrialization and in particular the organizational arrangements and policies utilized to achieve a high level of industrial development. The second factor influencing, in particular, the *pattern* of Soviet urbanization has been the large and highly diversified nature of the Soviet landscape, including natural differences, climatic forces, mineral deposits, and so on.

By most standards the Soviet Union is a country that has undergone both industrialization and urbanization at a relatively rapid rate to become, at the present time, a highly urbanized society. The Soviet urban sector has grown as a result of migration into urban areas from rural areas, as a result of the natural increase of the population residing in urban areas, and as a result of changes in the Soviet norms for the classification of urban areas.

According to official Soviet statistics and definitions, 82 percent of the population lived in rural areas, while only 18 percent lived in urban areas as of 1917.[4] By the year 1929, the beginning of collectivization and the Soviet industrialization drive, the comparable figures for rural and urban residence were 81 and 19 percent respectively. By 1980, however, 63 percent of the Soviet population resided in urban areas, while 37 percent lived in rural areas. This relatively rapid pace of movement into and growth of urban areas and the mechanisms used to direct and to control the process have created problems for the Soviet urban sector. The process of urbanization and the problems and solutions that it has spawned are the central focus of this essay.

While the growth of Soviet urban areas has been a concomitant of Soviet industrialization in general, the sharp regional diversity of this industrialization can also be observed in the regional diversity of Soviet urbanization.

For example, if one examines urbanization differentials at the republic level as of 1979, the following contrasts can be noted.[5] In Tadzhikistan, one of the less developed republics, 65 percent of the population was rural and 35 percent urban as of 1979. For the same year Estonia (one of the most developed republics) had an urban-rural population balance roughly the reverse of that observed in Tadzhikistan, with 70 percent of the population residing in urban areas and 30 percent residing in rural areas. This diversity of urbanization reflects both the nature of the Soviet industrialization experience and Soviet regional diversity in terms of natural conditions, historical experience, ethnicity, and so on. Such diversity would also be evident if one were to examine Soviet urbanization in more broadly defined regions such as Central Asia, Siberia, and the Far East as opposed to the political-administrative units (the republics).

Although it has been argued that prerevolutionary *levels* of urbanization were about "normal" for the accompanying level of economic development, it is apparent that much of the urbanization in the Soviet Union has taken place since the introduction of a socialist political system and, notably, national economic planning and the collectivization of agriculture in 1928.[6] Thus when examining Soviet urbanization patterns, it is interesting to ask to what extent the observed patterns differ from those of nonsocialist and/or nonplanned economic systems, and to what degree particular Soviet organizational arrangements and policies have been influential in explaining these observed patterns. Put another way, are the main features of the process of urbanization typical of all economic systems, or is the process of urbanization in planned socialist economic systems, as exemplified by the Soviet Union, unique in some dimensions?

In part the answer to this question may depend on the perspective from which the observer views the urbanization process.

Using a general Marxist-Leninist framework, Soviet authors view urbanization as an inevitable and desirable concomitant of industrialization.[7] Thus the urbanization process and its end result are viewed as a positive development both for the individual and for society as a whole. At the same time, Soviet economists, sociologists, demographers, and others have done considerable work on the problems of the Soviet urban sector. This literature focuses on questions of optimal city size, labor force availability and distribution, the availability of city services, problems related to housing, and so on. There is considerable discussion about the forces that influence the *rate* and *pattern* of urbanization and, above all, how planners can influence these forces in an era when the use of direct administrative controls seems to be declining.

Western analysis of the Soviet urbanization process is a relatively recent phenomenon, dating for the most part from the mid-1960s, or since the availability of census and other relevant data. What emerges from this analysis?

It is reasonable to generalize that Western students of Soviet development generally view the urbanization process as being broadly similar to that found in other nonsocialist countries, though with certain exceptions. The similarities are that the Soviet Union, like other developing countries, has experienced substantial growth of the urban sector, the result being a net of cities similar to those found elsewhere.[8]

The dissimilarities seem to be a lower *level* of urbanization than that experienced in market systems of comparable development (a point to which we will return) and differences in the mechanisms used to govern and hence to regulate the growth of Soviet cities.

In recent years the growth of Soviet medium and large cities would seem to have been very rapid.[9] A summary picture of the growth of Soviet medium and large cities is presented in Table 1. Let us consider this picture in two dimensions, the first being similarities with the Western experience, the second focusing on differences.

Considering the average annual percentage increase in the size of the cities listed in Table 1, it is quite clear that there have been sharp differences. Some cities, like Dushanbe, Erevan, Kishinev, Minsk, and Frunze, have grown rapidly. But overall, how rapid has the rate of Soviet urbanization been?

We have already noted that between 1929 and 1980, the proportion of the

Table 1
Selected Characteristics of Major Soviet Cities

City	Population 1959	Population 1970	Population 1980	Average annual percentage increase 1959-80
Alma Ata	456,481	729,633	932,000	9.47
Ashkhabad	169,935	253,118	321,000	8.08
Baku	967,615	1,265,515	1,571,000	5.66
Vilnius	236,078	372,100	492,000	9.85
Gorky	940,761	1,170,133	1,358,000	4.03
Dushanbe	227,137	373,885	509,000	11.28
Erevan	493,494	766,705	1,050,000	10.25
Kiev	1,109,840	1,631,908	2,192,000	8.86
Kishinev	216,005	356,382	527,000	13.08
Kuibyshev	806,356	1,044,849	1,226,000	4.73
Leningrad	3,321,196	3,949,501	4,638,000	3.60
Minsk	509,489	916,949	1,309,000	14.26
Moscow	6,044,144	7,061,008	8,099,000	3.09
Novosibirsk	885,045	1,160,963	1,328,000	4.54
Riga	580,428	731,831	843,000	4.11
Sverdlovsk	778,602	1,025,045	1,225,000	5.21
Tallin	281,714	362,706	450,000	5.43
Tashkent	926,744	1,384,509	1,821,000	8.77
Tbilisi	702,768	889,020	1,083,700	4.92
Frunze	219,711	430,618	543,000	13.37
Kharkov	952,560	1,222,852	1,464,000	4.88

Sources: *Itogi vsesoiuznoi perepisi naseleniia 1970 goda*, 1 (Moscow, 1972), table 3; *Narodnoe khoziaistvo SSSR v 1979 g.* (Moscow, 1980, 12-28).

Soviet population defined as urban grew from 19 to 63 percent. This represents an average annual growth of roughly 0.86 percent. Most Western students of the Soviet urbanization process would characterize this as quite rapid. However, as we have suggested in Note 9, a firm conclusion to this question should await a careful comparative study of urbanization rates under controlled conditions, in particular controlling for factors such as the level of economic development, definitional differences, and so on.

It may be worth noting, however, that quite apart from formal statistical comparisons, the growth rates of the cities listed in Table 1 must be viewed as rapid insofar as the process must have placed great stress on the ability of the Soviet system and its available resources to provide the needed housing, transportation, medical, and other urban facilities. This sort of pressure has been a major factor facing the Soviet urban planner.

From yet another perspective, the observed differential growth rates reflect particular Soviet conditions, such as the level of economic development of the region in which a particular city is located, the importance of the city in terms of the growth of industrial production activity, its importance as an actual or potential administrative/service center, and so on.

Turning to a different facet of measurement, a comparison of contemporary *levels* of urbanization with levels observed in nonsocialist economic systems suggests that relative to the Soviet level of economic development (as measured by gross national product per capita), the Soviet Union has relatively *low* levels of urbanization.[10] In this context it has been argued that Soviet planners, recognizing that rapid urbanization has both benefits and costs, have deliberately followed a policy of limiting the rate of urban growth below a rate that might be observed under different policies and a different economic regime. Why might such a pattern be followed? It could be a distinctive model of socialist urbanization, as part of the planned socialist economic system and/or policies designed explicitly to limit the growth of the urban sector. The latter might be pursued for a number of reasons, not the least important of which are the perceived ills of rapid urbanization in less developed market economies.

In the Soviet case one can observe policies that would seem to be designed to limit the rate at which the urban sector expands. For example, population mobility has doubtless been limited to some degree by the internal passport system, the employment and registration requirements, and the *propiska* system requiring official permission to remain in large Soviet cities. Furthermore, it has been argued that Soviet planners have deliberately followed a policy of capital intensity in urban areas, thus limiting the demand for labor there.[11] Put another way, there has been a tendency to substitute capital for labor where possible, and thus to limit the extent to which support services for labor (housing, transportation, and so on) are needed. Thus, despite the commonly held Western view that describes overstaffing and redundancy of labor in Soviet industrial enterprises, when measured statistically, the Soviet industrial establishment tends to be capital intensive.

Socialist urbanization patterns in general, and the Soviet urbanization case in particular, require additional empirical research. However, future research may show that despite the attempt to control the growth of the urban sector and given varying degrees of success with such controls, urban growth in the Soviet Union has simply been unable to keep pace with the rapid rate of industrial growth during periods when the latter was receiving major emphasis, for example, the 1930s. Thus, to the extent that Soviet industrialization was urban based, that system, with limited resources available for any particular activity, simply could not (or chose not to) build housing, transportation, and other urban support services at a rate sufficient to offset the inflow of population into the industrial establishment of the urban areas, the result being limited gains in the *per capita* availability of urban services. One could argue that the policies to limit the rate of growth of the urban sector, to the extent that this was intended, may have been partially effective insofar as they made it possible for the Soviet Union to avoid the *extremes* of rapid urbanization, for example, massive urban unemployment and associated poverty. At the same time, however, one could argue that these negative features of overly rapid industrialization did appear in another way in the Soviet case, for example, crowded housing conditions with several unrelated families sharing an apartment and facilities.

Thus far we have focused attention on the overall measurement of the pace of Soviet urbanization and the comparison of that pace with other cases. What have been the major *sources* of growth for the Soviet urban sector?

II. The Sources of Soviet Urban Growth

Although regional differentials in the Soviet urbanization process have been important, between 1929 and 1980 for the county as a whole, the urban sector grew by roughly 166 million persons. This represents an average annual increase in the urban population of roughly 3.25 million persons. As we noted at the outset, this expansion of urban population has been the result of three main factors: first, the movement of population from rural to urban areas; second, the natural increase of population resulting from the greater magnitude of births over deaths in urban areas; and finally, the administrative reclassification of rural areas into urban areas.

As the evidence in Table 2 suggests, migration from rural to urban areas has been the dominant portion of urban growth, although in recent years there has been a shift away from migration toward natural growth as an explanatory factor. As the urbanization process slows down, natural growth will become a larger

Table 2
Sources of Soviet Urban Growth
(percentages)

	1927-38	1938-58	1959-69	1970-79
Natural growth	18	20	40	44
Reclassification	19	18	14	
Rural to urban migration	63	62	46	56

Source: B. S. Khorev, *Problemy gorodov* (Moscow, 1975); Theodore Shabad, "News Notes," *Soviet Geography* (September 1979), 445-46, and personal communication with the author. Emigration from the Soviet Union is estimated by Theodore Shabad to be 0.2 million for the period 1970-79.

share of a smaller total. It should be emphasized that the sources of urban growth differ considerably from one region to another in the Soviet Union. Thus in recent years urban growth has been closely related to industrial growth, for example, in the automotive and energy fields. We turn now to an examination of natural population growth in Soviet urban areas.

The Natural Rate of Growth of the Population

In recent years a substantial portion of Soviet Urban growth has come about from natural expansion, that is, the excess of births over deaths in urban areas. At the same time, there has been concern and discussion in the Soviet Union regarding Soviet population dynamics in general and urban population dynamics in particular.[12] The pattern of Soviet urban birth and death rates can be summarized as follows: Throughout the period of rapid industrial development and urbanization, both the birth rate and the death rate have fallen as one would expect. Since the 1950s the death rate has been fairly stable (though slightly higher in the 1970s than in the 1960s), while the birth rate continued to fall and finally to stabilize in the 1970s.

The net impact of these trends has been a substantial slowing of the rate of growth of the Soviet population from roughly 17 per thousand in the 1950s to roughly 8 per thousand in the 1970s.[13] The pattern of change in urban areas is much the same, although the birth rate has generally been lower in the urban sector. According to preliminary results of the 1979 census, however, the migration of young people from rural to urban areas has changed urban birth rates such that the urban and rural rates of natural increase are now similar at 8.8 and 8.5 respectively. In addition, there are sharp regional differentials. For example, in 1979 the natural rate of population increase varied from a low of 1.0 per thousand in Latvia (a relatively developed region) to a high of 30.1 per thousand in Tadzhikistan (a less developed region). A picture of Soviet urban demographic trends can be assembled on the basis of the selected demographic data in Table 3. A number of observations seem pertinent.

First, as might be anticipated, there is substantially less variation in the death rates than in the birth rates. In fact, the death rates would appear to be positively correlated with the degree to which the republic is urban, being lowest in Tadzhikistan and highest in Latvia.

Second, it would seem that birth rates are inversely related to the degree of urbanization. Thus birth rates are generally lower in the most urbanized republics, for example, Latvia and the RSFSR, and much higher in the least urbanized republics, like Uzbekistan and Tadzhikistan.

Third, cities generally have a lower birth rate than the overall birth rates of the republics in which they are located. To some degree this reflects the generally lower urban as opposed to rural birth rates, although in Table 3 the republic data include both rural and urban, and the urban data are only for selected cities. Also, there are some interesting exceptions to this pattern. For example, the birth rate of Minsk in 1980 was higher than the birth rate of Belorussia for the same year,

Table 3
Natural Population Growth: Selected Cities and Republics of the USSR
(rates per 1,000 population)

Unit	Percent of unit population urban: 1980	Birth rate 1980	Death rate 1980	Natural growth of population		
				1980	1970	1960
USSR	63	18.2	10.1	8.1	9.2	17.8
RSFSR	70	15.8	10.8	5.0	5.9	15.8
Leningrad	100*	13.4	11.4	2.0	3.4	6.4
Moscow	100	13.2	11.8	1.4	2.3	6.9
Novosibirsk	100	15.4	9.3	6.1	7.3	na
Kuibyshev	100	13.9	10.1	3.8	6.5	na
Latvia	69	13.7	112.7	1.0	3.3	6.7
Riga	100	12.5	11.1	1.4	3.7	na
Ukraine	62	14.7	11.1	3.6	6.4	13.6
Kiev	100	15.6	8.2	7.4	8.4	10.6
Kharkov	100	14.8	10.2	3.6	6.5	na
Belorussia	56	15.8	9.5	6.3	7.6	17.8
Minsk	100	18.6	5.4	13.2	13.5	na
Kazakhstan	54	24.0	7.7	16.3	17.4	30.5
Alma Ata	100	17.3	9.1	8.2	9.0	na
Georgia	52	17.9	8.3	9.6	11.9	18.2
Tbilisi	100	16.1	8.1	8.0	10.0	na
Uzbekistan	41	34.4	7.0	27.4	28.1	33.9
Tashkent	100	19.2	7.9	11.3	13.4	na
Tadzhikistan	35	37.8	7.7	30.1	28.4	28.4
Dushanbe	100	21.9	6.8	15.1	15.2	na

Sources: Compiled from official Soviet statistics in *Narodnoe khoziaistvo SSSR* (various volumes), *Vestnik statistiki* (various issues).
*Cities are assumed to be 100 percent urban.

possibly in part explained by the fact that in recent years Minsk has been one of the most rapidly growing cities in the Soviet Union. It may be that a city undergoing rapid growth has, at any point in time, a substantial portion of the population consisting of recent migrants from rural areas. In this context the myriad of factors that tend to promote higher birth rates in rural areas may operate for some period of time after migrants have moved from rural to urban areas.

Fourth, the size factor is important. There is an inverse relationship between the birth rate and the size of the city. Larger cities are older cities, and all of the forces that contribute to lower birth rates in urban areas have been at work for longer periods of time.

Fifth, the pattern of a steadily declining birth rate for the Soviet Union as a whole is also evident for the urban sector. For the cities included in Table 3, all have experienced a declining birth rate, although with substantial variations. The decline for Dushanbe has been minimal, while for Moscow and Leningrad it has been sharp.

Finally, it is worth noting that the trends outlined above are important but in most cases not pervasive. The reader should be aware that any particular demographic observation, for example, birth rates, is a function of a number of interrelated forces, all of which must be considered and controlled if a useful analysis of causal forces is to be generated.

For the urban sector as well as the economy as a whole, the immediate and important implication of the slow rate of growth of the population is a very slow rate of growth of the labor force. While the consequences of this fact for the urban labor force will be dealt with elsewhere in this volume, it is important to note here that the focus of discussion in the Soviet Union and Eastern Europe is fertility and specifically the forces underlying fertility decline.

Thus far we have focused on changes in the Soviet urban population in very general terms, examining the death rate, the birth rate, and the resulting rate of population growth. We have noted the importance of a decline in the birth rate— that is, the number of children born per 1,000 population. A more precise way to examine this side of the population equation is to consider the concept of fertility, or the rate at which children are born to women of childbearing age.

Broadly speaking, a decline in fertility may come from two sources. First, there may be a decrease in the number of women in their childbearing and especially the prime childbearing years. Second, those who are in the childbearing years may decide, for a broad variety of reasons, to have fewer children. Since the 1950s the actual number of live births has changed very little in the Soviet Union. For example, in 1950 there were 4,805,000 live births, and in 1979 there were 4,807,000. While this represents a declining birth *rate* in percentage terms (the same number of children born annually to a larger eligible female population), of greater interest is the fact that it also represents a reduction in *fertility.* Specifically, this means that there has been a persistent pattern of women having fewer and fewer children, and thus average family size declines. This pattern is especially pronounced in large cities like Moscow and Leningrad, though the reader should be aware of three problems of measurement. First, to examine these trends carefully, one needs much better data on *net* reproduction, that is, the rate at which women of childbearing age in fact bear children. Second, it is important to note that there are important regional differentials, not just between urban and rural areas but also between areas such as the Russian Republic and Central Asia. Finally, it may be that the decline in fertility has ceased or even been reversed, in part a function of the growth in fertility of those women in the earlier range of the childbearing years.[14]

The forces that account for population change are generally very complex. In the case of a developing country, decreases in the death rate are generally identified with improvements in the delivery of health care, a subject discussed separately in this book. However, changes in the birth rate are generally related to a large number of factors, thus making it difficult to isolate and to identify specific causes in particular cases. What can be said about fertility in the Soviet case?

In a recent study of Soviet population policies, Jeff Chinn identifies three broad areas of focus: economic factors, administrative-judicial factors, and finally ideological factors.[15] In general, Soviet policies increasingly focus on means to increase fertility. For example, there is considerable emphasis on the development of child-care facilities, financial incentives to have children (liberalization of paid leaves for working women who have children), awards for motherhood (especially for those having large families), and a propaganda line emphasizing the desirability of having children.

Soviet researchers have devoted considerable effort to survey research to understand the basis of declining fertility and to develop policies to counter what is seen as an undesirable trend. At the same time, Western research on fertility in general and Soviet urban fertility in particular recognizes, along with the Soviet research, that fertility rates are the result of a complex net of interacting forces, often difficult to isolate one from another.

In the Soviet Union most women work. While this provides more family income for expenditures on everything (including the raising of children), it also leaves less *time* available for raising a family. The scarcity of time to be spent in the home can be partially offset by the use of modern home aids, for example, automatic dishwashers, microwave ovens, and so on. The Soviets lag in the develoment of these sorts of devices. In addition, while the Soviets stress the need for education and the necessity and desirability of women working, entry into the labor force and increasing levels of education are positively correlated, while both are negatively correlated with the fertility rate. Moreover, the typical Soviet urban family has a limited amount of living space, frequently utilized on a shared basis, and this probably is a negative influence on fertility. While great emphasis is placed on Soviet development of child-care facilities, their numbers are inadequate, and the use of grandparents as live-in child care presents many problems for the Soviet family, such as severe pressure on living space, the potential for conflict arising from differences in values, etc. At the same time, limited housing space has been viewed as a factor inhibiting the growth of the typical Soviet

family, although recent evidence seems to suggest that housing is not that important as a negative influence on family growth.[16]

In future years Soviet urban growth resulting from net reproduction of the
urban population will constitute a smaller share of urban growth. The result, the
aging of the urban population that is already in progress, will serve as a severe
constraint on urban labor supply while at the same time presenting new demands
on the urban service sector.

Reproduction of the population within the urban sector is only one source of
urban population growth. The second important component, to which we now
turn, is migration, or the movement of population from rural to urban areas.

Rural-Urban Migration and
Soviet Urban Growth

Rural-to-urban migration is one component of the more general process of
population mobility. Normally, one considers rural-urban migration on a net
basis, that is, arrivals into a city from a rural area minus departures from the city
to the rural area. One might be interested in such a movement in very general
terms (for example, its magnitude) or, more specifically, in the place of origin and
the place of destination. In either case rural-urban migration is usually defined on
the basis of a *change of residence*, thus excluding other interesting patterns of
movement from rural to urban areas like commuting to work.[17]

In recent years Soviet scholars have devoted considerable attention to the
study of rural-urban migration. In addition, the first statistical compilation of
Soviet internal migration (including rural-urban migration) appeared in the 1970
Soviet census.[18] This material has facilitated Western analysis of Soviet rural-
urban migration, the result being a preliminary yet informative view of past
patterns and trends. What is the nature of rural-urban migration in the Soviet
Union? To what extent do Soviet patterns of migration differ from those observed
elsewhere?

First, migration from rural to urban areas is typically a sequential process.
Thus the initial movement is from a rural area to a small town. The second stage
of the movement is from the small town to a larger city.

Second, Soviet rural-urban migration patterns can be explained rather well
in terms of traditional approaches to the study of population migration. Although
the nature of Soviet data limits the extent to which sophisticated statistical techniques can be utilized, nevertheless simple analysis suggests that the relative
attractiveness of the sending and receiving areas and the characteristics of the
potential migrant help us to understand why migration takes place.[19]

For example, Soviet attitude surveys have shown that Soviet rural dwellers
generally have a very negative view of the possibility of career advancement
within the rural sector. Thus it is not surprising that a significant portion of Soviet
rural-urban migration is accounted for by those who are relatively young, both
male and female.[20]

Furthermore, wages have been shown to be important in the migration decision. Rural wages are typically viewed as being relatively low, while urban wages are viewed as being relatively high, despite sometimes significant cost-of-living differences. Thus there tends to be empirical support for the concept of a "push" factor out of rural areas and a "pull" factor into urban areas.[21]

The urban sector is thus seen as more attractive for both short-term gain and for long-term career advancement. Both factors are more important for those who have obtained some form of education (for example, technical education) that facilitates migration.

But to what extent has Soviet population mobility in general, and rural-urban migration in particular, been constrained by administrative means? For example, internal mobility in the Soviet Union requires an internal passport, a document for many years denied collective farmers as a group. To take another case, there has always existed a formal mechanism for the organized recruitment of labor force (*orgnabor*) where it proves necessary, for example, in rural areas during the harvest. To take yet another case, there is the so-called "closed city" network, where a number of preconditions must be met before residence in a city is possible.[22] For example, it is very difficult to obtain the necessary permission (a document called a *propiska*) to gain permanent entry into the city.

Given the pressure for migration from rural to urban areas for quite traditional reasons, and given the constraints imposed on mobility, do we see a contradiction? Can potential Soviet migrants become actual migrants in order to pursue the personal gains they perceive as attainable through residence in urban areas?

The evidence suggests that while administrative controls have been important for *labor allocation* in the past, their role in this respect in controlling Soviet population movement, especially since the 1950s, has declined significantly.[23] Although the earlier use of administrative methods for the redistribution of population in general and the labor force in particular has not been fully documented, nevertheless the process seems to have been important. However, Soviet authors now argue strongly in favor of an incentive system to achieve the desired labor force and population objectives. Indeed, much Soviet literature is devoted to the question of determining the appropriate set of incentives for a particular task, for example, the attraction and retention of labor force and population in a particular region, such as Siberia.

In the more common case, for example, the movement of a rural dweller into a medium-sized Soviet city, barriers certainly exist, although informal procedures seem adequate for circumventing the restrictions where the drive for relocation is sufficiently strong. What sort of barriers are faced by the Soviet rural dweller wishing to migrate to a city or by the resident of a small city who wants to move to a larger city?

Housing has clearly served as a constraint on the rate of growth of Soviet cities.[24] However, the reasons for this sort of limitation are less clear. Is the rate at which the urban housing stock expanded consciously controlled as a mechanism to limit urban growth, or is it simply a matter of limited resources that can be devoted to housing expansion, or are both forces at work? Although massive amounts of urban housing have been constructed, the inflow of migrants from rural areas has generally outstripped the growth of housing, thus limiting the growth of housing on a per capita basis and leaving a strong and persistent excess demand for urban housing. Furthermore, studies have shown that new entrants into Soviet cities do not find separate dwellings but rather enter into a slow process of assimilation, living with others and gradually improving their living condition over time.[25] Thus one must conclude that resource limitations have constrained the growth of the urban housing stock and that housing has become a control factor, especially for some cities where additional rapid expansion is not desired by the planners.

A recent study by the author examining migration into large Soviet cities provides empirical support for the above views, and especially for the crucial role played by housing.[26] Thus in general the availability of housing is central to an understanding of Soviet city growth. Moreover, the movement into Soviet cities is sensitive both to the general availability of housing (that is, cities with a long-term record of better availability of housing are more attractive) and also *annual increases* in the volume of housing available. This evidence provides some support for the commonly held view that Soviet citizens are very eager to enter Soviet cities, and that there may be a backlog of potential migrants, with housing serving as one type of constraint on entry.[27]

On balance, then, it would seem that the sorts of factors that make Soviet cities attractive to rural dwellers are not substantially different from those that prevailed historically in other countries. What, then, is the difference in the Soviet case?

Although we lack in-depth empirical analysis of the role of administrative controls in Soviet population mobility, one could probably suggest the following: The apparent contradiction between rapid rural-to-urban movement and effective administrative controls to limit this movement can be explained by the fact that both the attractions and the job possibilities for potential migrants have created great pressures on Soviet cities. Controls have been used and have in part been successful in limiting urban expansion within the reasonable confines of expanding city services, for example, housing, retail trade, and transportation. The net result has been expansion of the Soviet urban sector at a rate apparently quite rapid by international historical standards, but not at a rate such that significant urban unemployment would result. This pressure has, however, resulted in a very slow rate of growth of *per capita* urban services. This in turn has probably been a major factor explaining the declining fertility in the urban sector.

III. Soviet Urban Growth:
Patterns and Prospects

At the outset we noted that in-depth interest in and analysis of the Soviet urban economy by both Soviet and Western researchers is a phenomenon of the past two decades. Although we have not considered the minor matter of urban classification as a contributor to Soviet urban change, we have examined both rural-to-urban and natural population growth in urban areas as two dominant factors explaining Soviet urban growth.

The dynamics of the Soviet urban population can be understood in terms of the basic forces that traditionally influence population, particularly urban population, growth. In addition to disruptive forces such as World War II, Soviet urban fertility has declined. This decline, in conjunction with a leveling of the urban death rate, has led to a decline in the rate of reproduction of the urban population. In an economy with very high rates of labor force participation by both males and females and a continuing need for expansion of the labor force, this fertility decline is in part understandable, yet unattractive. While Soviet policies have been directed toward increasing fertility (monetary incentives, child-care facilities, awards, etc.), the traditional Soviet emphasis on expanding educational attainment and participation have been counterproductive insofar as fertility is concerned. In part, and despite pronatalist policies, Soviet expectations for the urban population are not in harmony with what we know about Soviet urban fertility patterns and the forces influencing those observed patterns. Furthermore, given the traditionally rather slow change in population variables, one cannot expect significant modifications in these patterns in the near future.

We know that as a component of Soviet urban growth, rural-urban migration has been a major, though recently declining, factor. Moreover, although the *rate* of movement into Soviet cities is generally thought to have been high, we can make two important reservations. First, it is uneven by time period, having been highest in the early industrialization and collectivization period of the 1930s. Second, one's conclusion about the rate of rural-urban migration might be tempered somewhat if comparisons with other countries were made, controlling for other crucial factors like the prevailing *level* of economic development.

Turning to the forces that *influence* migration, once again a reasonable though imperfect picture emerges. We have observed, for instance, that traditional explanations for rural-urban migration serve rather well to explain migration in the Soviet case. Potential rural-to-urban migrants become actual migrants because they expect a better life for themselves and their children, including long-term career achievement, better rewards in the short term, and the cultural advantages of the urban setting. On the other hand, there have been forces limiting the extent to which potential migrants can in fact achieve their expectations. These forces include direct administrative measures such as residency requirements for cities, the possibility that state policies (for example, limiting the need for labor in urban industrial production) operate to limit migration, and finally, outright limitations on the ability of the state to provide necessary urban amenities. Thus the picture that emerges is a persistent and strong urge by rural dwellers to move to urban areas, an urge that is constrained by a number of planned and nonplanned factors. However, the ingenuity of the potential migrant and the inability of the planners to exert total control lead to a migration stream probably rather larger than it might otherwise be in the case of total control. Thus there is no real contradiction between possible limitations on migration set up by the state and the apparently rapid rate of migration out of rural areas.

While the above picture is probably reasonable, additional research is needed. Generally speaking, the limitations on available data preclude the sort of sophisticated migration analysis that can be done in other countries. Analyses by Soviet researchers provide survey studies of the motives of potential and actual migrants, but the data for empirical verification are absent. Regional differentials, for example, for cost of living, generally known to be very important in the analysis of migration, cannot be quantified in the Soviet case with any degree of sophistication. Thus our analysis of migration patterns is simplistic and based on highly aggregated data.

Beyond the analysis of the forces influencing rural-urban migration in the Soviet Union, it is necessary to analyze such trends in comparison to those in other countries, and to do so controlling for important country differences like level of economic development. Only then can we know if the *rate* of rural-urban migration in the Soviet Union has actually been high in a comparative historical context. Finally, we need direct and empirical investigation of Soviet economic policies and the extent to which these policies have been designed and in fact have been effective in manipulating migration patterns.

Notes

[1]Useful Russian sources include B. S. Khorev, *Problemy gorodov*, 2nd ed. (Moscow, 1975); Iu. L. Pivovarov (ed.), *Problemy sovremennoi urbanizatsii* (Moscow, 1972); Iu. L. Pivovarov, *Sovremennaia urbanizatsiia* (Moscow, 1976); E. S. Demidenko, *Demografischeskie problemy i perspektivy bol'shikh gorodov* (Moscow, 1980).

[2]See, for example, the argument in Gur Ofer, "Economizing on Urbanization in Socialist Countries: Historical Necessity or Socialist Strategy?" in Alan A. Brown and Egon Neuberger (eds.), *Internal Migration: A Comparative Perspective* (New York, 1977), 277-303. Additional Western studies are listed in the bibliography.

[3]Chauncey D. Harris, *Cities of the Soviet Union* (Washington, 1972), Introduction.

[4]Data used here are from *Naselenie SSSR* (Moscow, 1975), 7; *Narodnoe khoziaistvo SSSR v 1978 g.* (Moscow, 1979), 7 (hereafter *Narkhoz*).

[5]Although the issue will not receive attention in this chapter, the reader should be aware that the units for which data are generally available in the Soviet case (for example, the union republics) are extremely heterogeneous in many dimensions. Thus for measurement purposes, the problem of defining an appropriate unit of observation is a very difficult task. Data on rural-urban population distribution are from *Narkhoz*, various issues.

[6]For a longer perspective, see Robert A. Lewis and Richard F. Rowland, "Urbaniztion in Russia and the USSR: 1897-1970," in Michael F. Hamm (ed.), *The City in Russian History* (Lexington, 1976).

[7]For a discussion of these issues, see Jeff Chinn, *Manipulating Soviet Population Resources* (New York, 1977), chap. 2.

[8]Reference here is to the notion that the size distribution of cities in the Soviet Union and cities elsewhere reveals broad similarities. For an examination of this question, see Chauncey D. Harris, *Cities of the Soviet Union*, chap. 5.

[9]Since we know with reasonable accuracy the rate at which the Soviet urban sector has grown, why can we not say with assurance whether this rate of growth has been high,

moderate, or slow? Most Western observers would probably argue that the rate of urban growth has been quite rapid. This view typically rests on the nature of the political and economic means used to generate urban growth, the relatively short span of years over which the bulk of Soviet urban growth has taken place (roughly since the 1920s), and finally, rough and partial comparisons between Soviet urban growth rates and those observed elsewhere. However, until a careful statistical study is made comparing Soviet and other urban growth rates, it would seem premature to attach a label to the Soviet case.

[10]Gur Ofer, "Industrial Structure, Urbanization, and the Growth Strategy of Socialist Countries," *Quarterly Journal of Economics*, *90* (May 1976), 219-44.

[11]Ibid.

[12]For a general discussion of Soviet population trends and associated manpower implications, see Murray Feshbach and Stephen Rapawy, "Soviet Population and Manpower Trends and Policies," in *Soviet Economy in a New Perspective* (Washington, D.C., 1976), 113-54; basic population projections can be found in Godfrey S. Baldwin, *Population Projections by Age and Sex: for the Republics and Major Economic Regions of the U.S.S.R. 1970 to 2000*, Series P-91, no. 26 (Washington, 1979); for recent evidence, see Stephen Rapawy and Godfrey Baldwin, "Demographic Trends in the Soviet Union: 1950–2000," in U.S. Congress, Joint Economic Committee, *Soviet Economy in the 1980's: Problems and Prospects*, part 2 (Washington, D.C., 1982), 265-96; Ann Goodman and Geoffrey Schleifer, "The Soviet Labor Market in the 1980's," in ibid., 323-48; for a historical analysis, see Ansley Coale, Barbara Anderson, and Erna Harm, *Human Fertility in Russia since the Nineteenth Century* (Princeton, 1979); recent Soviet works are discussed in Chinn; empirical evidence on fertility and labor force participation can be found in Paul R. Gregory, "Fertility and Labor Force Participation in the Soviet Union and Eastern Europe," *Review of Economics and Statistics* (February 1982), 18-31.

[13]For a discussion of recent evidence, see Andrew R. Bond and Paul E. Lydolph, "Soviet Population Change and City Growth 1970–79: A Preliminary Report," *Soviet Geography*, *20*, 8 (October 1979), 461-88.

[14]For a discussion of this issue, see Warren W. Eason, "Demographic Problems: Fertility" in *Soviet Economy in a New Perspective* (Washington, D.C., 1975), 155-61.

[15]Chinn.

[16]Gregory.

[17]Commuting has been a growing phenomenon in the Soviet Union, especially where one or more members of a rural family obtain attractive employment in an urban setting but maintain rural residence. For a discussion of this subject, see R. Fuchs and G. J. Demko, "Commuting in the USSR," *Soviet Geography: Review and Translation*, *19* (6), 363-72. There is a great deal of literature on the general topic of migration in the Soviet Union. A useful survey of the literature through the 1960s can be found in Robert A. Lewis, "The Postwar Study of Internal Migration in the USSR," *Soviet Geography: Review and Translation*, 10 (April 1969), 157-66; a useful Soviet survey can be found in V. Perevedentsev, "Sovremeniia migratsiia naseleniia," *Voprosy ekonomiki*, 5 (1973), 128-37; for a general discussion of migration in a regional context, see Peter J. Grandstaff, *Interregional Migration in the USSR: Economic Aspects, 1959-1970* (Durham, N.C., 1980).

[18]Soviet migration data can be found in *Itogi vsesoiuznoi perepisi naseleniia*, 2 (Moscow, 1974), *Naselenie SSSR*, and in various issues of *Vestnik statistiki*. Problems of Soviet migration data are discussed in Grandstaff.

[19]For a background discussion, see Grandstaff.

[20]For a useful analysis of youth migration, see David E. Powell, *Rural Youth Migration in the Soviet Union* (Washington, D.C., 1975).

[21]Empirial evidence is provided in Robert C. Stuart and Paul R. Gregory, "A Model of Soviet Rural-Urban Migration," *Economic Development and Cultural Change*, *26* (October 1977), 81-92.

[22]For a discussion of this issue within the specific context of controls over labor allocation, see Edmund Nash, "Recent Changes in Labor Controls in the Soviet Union," in *New Directions in the Soviet Economy*, part 3, *Human Resources* (Washington, D.C., 1966), 849-61; for a Soviet discussion of this issue, including some empirical evidence, see M. Ia. Sonin, *Vosproizvodstva rabochei sily v SSSR v balans truda* (Moscow, 1959).

[23]For example, the number of workers moved annually through *orgnabor* has declined. See Sonin and Nash.

[24]For discussion and analysis of the housing question, see Henry W. Morton: "The Soviet Quest for Better Housing—An Impossible Dream?" in *Soviet Economy in a Time of Change*, *1* (Washington, D.C., 1979), 790-810; "Housing Problems and Policies of Eastern Europe and the Soviet Union," *Studies in Comparative Communism*, *12* (Winter 1979), 300-321; "Who Gets What, When and How? Housing in the Soviet Union," *Soviet Studies*, *32* (April 1980), 235-59.

[25]See the discussion of migration in Mervyn Matthews, *Class and Society in Soviet Russia* (New York, 1972).

[26]Robert C. Stuart, "Migration and the Growth of Soviet Cities," *Handbook of East European Economics* (Munich, 1982), 253-71.

[27]The reader can observe that the pattern of migration from rural to urban areas in the Soviet Union differs in important ways from patterns found in developing countries using predominantly market economic systems. For example, in many countries of Latin America, one finds migration from rural to urban areas based on expectations of material gain. For many, material gain is not in fact realized, the evidence being a large pool of poor unemployed and improperly housed urban migrants. This extreme has been avoided by the Soviet Union, although during times of rural turmoil, for example, collectivization, administrative measures were necessary to limit rural outflow.

II

THE SOVIET URBAN SCENE

—— Henry J. Raimondo and Robert C. Stuart ——

3

—————— Financing Soviet Cities ——————

Introduction

Social scientists have long been interested in the nature of the urbanization process, specifically, the structure and functions of evolving cities. In recent years there has been a growing interest in the nature of urbanization in a comparative perspective, that is, under different political and economic systems. In part this interest stems from analysis of urbanization in less developed countries, but it also extends to a comparison of urbanization patterns in market capitalist systems and planned socialist systems.[1] The emphasis is on differential urbanization patterns and the influence of the political-economic system on such differentials.

This chapter adopts a comparative perspective to study one dimension of the urbanization process: city finances. The focus will be on the Soviet city experience as an example of planned socialism. Comparisons will be drawn with city financial patterns typically observed under market systems. While such comparisons are useful, the reader should be aware of the fact that since there has been only very limited analysis of the Soviet financial system, with only limited and incomplete financial statistics available, we must be content to examine broad and at times incomplete patterns.

This examination will be divided into five sections: (1) the Soviet urban budget process: basic features; (2) the Soviet urban budget process: recent developments; (3) Soviet city revenues and expenditures in the post-World War II period; (4) variations in Soviet city expenditures; and (5) conclusions. Throughout, the emphasis will be on the Soviet experience in financing cities to understand the problems that have arisen, the solutions which have been utilized, and the relevance of the Soviet case to our understanding of the contemporary urban experience.

The Soviet Urban Budget Process: Basic Features

The analysis of the financial arrangements of Soviet cities begins with an understanding of the more general features of the financial structure of the Soviet

The authors would like to thank Donna Bahry, Carol Lewis, Henry Morton, and Gertrude Schroeder for helpful comments on an earlier draft. The authors alone bear responsibility for the final product.

economic system. We will begin by considering some basic characteristics of the Soviet economy; the nature of the Soviet city budget process will then be outlined.

Throughout this chapter the Soviet Union will be treated as a centrally planned socialist economic system.[2] This classification implies that with only modest exceptions, property rights are held by the state and what is popularly described as public ownership of the means of production is dominant. Under this regime the disposition and utilization of property for the achievement of economic and social objectives are primarily a function of state organizations.

The mechanism for resource allocation in the Soviet Union is the national economic plan rather than a market mechanism typically found in a market capitalist economic system.[3] This means that the decisions on production, distribution, and ultimately economic growth will, in the Soviet case, be formulated within the state planning agency (*Gosplan*) and in varying time frames (five-year and one-year plans) will be executed by state-owned-and-operated enterprises through an administrative (ministerial) hierarchy.

The Soviet urban budget process closely reflects basic characteristics of the Soviet economic system that stem from state ownership and control of resources and resource utilization. What are these characteristics?

First, the Soviet economic system is organized along vertical (hierarchical) lines. The generation, distribution, and utilization of information for decision-making purposes take place to a large degree within a vertical chain of command between local, intermediate, and central economic and political units. Minimal emphasis is placed on horizontal flows of information (for example, from one enterprise to another), and those flows that do take place and that pertain to interenterprise relations tend to do so through the vertical chain of command of the plan, not through a decentralized market arrangement.[4]

Within a hierarchial organizational arrangement, the Soviet budget is described as a consolidated budget in which budget entries (incomes and expenditure) are combined for all levels in the hierarchy to form a single national budget.[5] Although there are a number of variations in practice, most budget consolidation takes place in the following manner: the city is under the jurisdiction of a province (*oblast*) which in turn is under the jurisdiction of a union republic, of which there are fifteeen. These fifteen union republics differ one from another in a number of dimensions and, above all, are political and administrative entities rather than economic entities in the sense of incorporating any economic uniformity.[6]

With such a high degree of aggregation of budget numbers, analysis is complicated. Instead of examining a particular expenditure for a particular city, one must generally be content with a much more general picture analyzing, for example, a particular expenditure category for the urban sector of a republic. At the same time, since revenues derive from all levels and are presented in aggregated form, it is generally not possible to assess who pays for what item in any particular budget. In addition, a considerable portion of urban spending does not flow through an urban budget since state-owned enterprises and other organizations such as ministries can and do provide urban services, such as housing for employees, transportation and water services, etc. In this important sense the city budget is not an inclusive document, thus making it difficult to know who pays for and hence controls urban services. However, a pattern can be observed in which new towns built under Soviet rule are in large part financed by one or more dominant enterprises. In contrast, older established cities, such as Moscow, Leningrad, and the capitals of republics, have a greater control over municipal spending.

Second, since the budget of a Soviet city is part of an oblast, union republic, and ultimately USSR national economic plan, the city budget is developed and implemented as an integral part of the national economic plan. Put another way, planning for a Soviet city is a basic part of the overall planning experience, at least to the extent that the city controls the monies. The integration of city planning into national economic planning is important both for the formulation and the execution of the plan.

When the city budget is formulated, the information on which it will be based, in particular the financial information, is provided by local units (cities) as a body of information that flows upwards through the hierarchy. The budget is then formulated at the upper levels of the hierarchy.

The budget after its formulation is passed down through the hierarchy to become a legally binding document. The exercise of control over execution is a matter of upper-level units supervising lower-level units.[7]

Third, in budget formulation as in plan formulation, basic rules and/or informal procedures familiar to the student of Soviet economic planning are operative. For example, the magnitude of the budget and specific categories within the budget are largely a function of incremental budgeting. For most items within the budget, the planned outlay (or income) for next year is based on the outlay (income) for this year plus some percentage increment. As in most cases where incremental budgeting is used, it is frequently difficult to know (in the Soviet case) the means by which the size of the increment is determined.[8] However, such a procedure tends to generate a good deal of stability over time in Soviet budgetary categories.

In addition to the rules governing budget increments, overall Soviet financial policy has tended to be very conservative in two important respects.[9] Income should cover outflow, and for the most part, no forms of deficit financing should be used. The Soviet city is no exception. City budgets are typically in balance or have a small surplus, and credit facilities are very limited.

As with the general planning process, the city budgetary process is neither as rigid nor as formal as the above rules and procedures might imply. It is well known that Soviet enterprise managers can and do enter into a bargaining process with their superiors when the plan (and hence managerial objectives) are being formulated. The same is true for the Soviet city and is reflected in recent changes in Soviet thinking about the operation of Soviet cities.

The Soviet Urban Budget Process:
Recent Trends

Recent Soviet literature on the financing of Soviet cities presents a number of themes familiar to the Western economist.

First, Soviet urbanists, like their Western counterparts, argue that the growth in demand for urban services has outpaced the growth of both central and local revenue sources with which to finance these growing demands.[10] This imbalance is in part attributed to growing demands being placed on the aggregate Soviet budget for expenditures such as space, military, and agriculture, all of which, it is argued, commanded less attention in the 1950s. In addition, the Soviet leadership remains enthusiastic about urban expansion in the East and the development of urban centers (for example, the "science cities") that have little or no local revenue base. Thus it is argued that in relation to the growth of demand, there is inadequate recognition of urban financing needs.

Second, Soviet organizational arrangements present an interesting jurisdictional problem. As we have already noted, Soviet enterprises contribute to the urban budget according to enterprise subordination, not enterprise location. Thus an industrial enterprise located in Kiev, for example, but operating under the jurisdiction of a republic ministry would contribute to the republic budget. Since there are transfers from upper- to lower-level budgets in the consolidated system, one might argue that the revenue collected is part of a single pie, and that in the end part of it goes to the budget of the city of Kiev. This argument would not be appealing in the West, and apparently it does not appeal to Soviet urban advocates, who argue that Soviet cities need to identify additional and stable revenue sources.[11] It is also argued that in cases such as the hypothetical one above, the interests of city and enterprise can be more harmoniously coordinated with a direct connection between the enterprise and the city budget. Interestingly enough, this argument is pervasive in recent Soviet urban literature in spite of the fact that enterprises already provide on their own account housing, child care, and other services to the community in which they are located.[12] The emphasis is on the need to decentralize both authority and responsibility to local soviets, a policy that has apparently met with little success.[13]

Third, examination of Soviet urban revenues and expenditures is complicated by the fact that local (urban) services are in part provided directly by enterprises, cooperatives, ministries, and other organizations, although there are no substantive data on the pattern of this expenditure.

The extent and manner in which urban industry, for example, finances urban services outside of the urban budget could vary in a number of dimensions, and especially from one urban jurisdiction to another. For example, since enterprise profits are used both for contributions to budgets and for enterprise financing of worker needs (such as housing), one might imagine that in regions where industry is on balance more profitable (for whatever reasons), enterprise contributions to the urban economy might be greater than in other, "poorer" regions, although there is no substantive evidence on this point. Although there has been a tendency to view state budgetary expenditure as representing state intentions in the urban sector, it is not known to what extent state variations may in fact be used to offset local variations. Given the substantial regional variations in profit rates (resulting in part from state pricing and other policies), differences in revenue availability and hence the volume and quality of enterprise-provided urban services could be substantial.

Fourth, it should come as no surpirse to the reader to learn that two-thirds of all Soviet urban services are provided to the recipient without any direct user charges.[14] For those services provided with a user charge, the charge is typically such that the producing organization incurs losses. In short, there are very few profit-making enterprises in the urban public service sector. Since the 1965 reform Soviet economists have increasingly argued that such a situation is undesirable on at least two fronts. First, the absence of a direct user charge (or one that does not cover costs) leads to unconstrained growth of demand for services in the face of limited resources. Second, it is argued that in the absence of profitability criteria, it is difficult to assess the effectiveness with which a particular service is being provided. Thus as profits are increasingly used as a mechanism of enterprise guidance *and* as a source of loal budgetary revenue, it is understandable that Soviet economists would argue for the implementation of user charges.

Fifth, in recent years there has been a changing picture on the revenue side of urban budgets. Soviet urban budget revenues are classified as *assigned* or *adjustment* revenues.[15] The former are derived from such sources as local taxes but are subject to year-to-year fluctuation. The latter are derived from state taxes and levies such as the turnover tax (basically a hidden sales tax). The recent emphasis on decentralization in combination with the declining importance of the turnover tax (a major source of budget revenue) has increased the relative importance of enterprise contributions, hence the jurisdictional problem already mentioned. But the potential importance of enterprise profits can be appreciated in the following context: between 1950 and 1975 the income of Soviet city budgets grew in the aggregate 8.2 times, but the sum of local taxes and levies grew only 48.3 percent.[16]

In another but important dimension, the forces discussed above in combination with the 1965 economic reform have brought new emphasis to the calculation of enterprise profits and the manner in which profits contribute to budgets. The general and oft-stated Soviet goal is a set of enterprise guidance rules such that urban interests, enterprise interests, and social interests are harmonized. Although the details are beyond the scope of the present essay, suffice it to say that enterprise profitability has taken on new importance, and price reform has been directed toward the achievement of several goals, one of which is the achievement of enterprise profitability.[17]

Rather than simply deductions from profits, since the reform of 1965 there has been a fixed charge on enterprise capital (*plata za fondy*) in addition to profit deductions and a fixed charge for enterprises in favorable conditions, as well as the so-called "free remainder" of profits (in essence, profits remaining after required deductions have been made), the latter being the single most important item. Roughly 60 percent of enterprise profits enter the state budget. In addition, payments from the charge on fixed capital are of growing importance, representing 1.2 percent of enterprise payments into *local* budgets in 1969, but growing to 16.8 percent by 1975.[18]

Finally, as we have noted, Soviet budget data are imperfect for the tasks at hand since they do not include all activities of the urban economy. On the expenditure side, the Soviet urban budget data include those expenditures channeled through and controlled by the city soviet. How inclusive are the official expenditure series? Although there may be regional and other variations, the official series include a substantial (though in some cases declining) share of total expenditures.[19] For example, for the total Soviet budget between 1950 and 1977, the share of *budgetary spending as a portion of total spending* for various categories has behaved as follows: social-cultural expenditures, 90.7 percent to 78.9 percent; education, 87.9 percent to 67.8 percent; and finally, health from 87.3 percent to 78.1 percent. A similar pattern can be observed in the case of budgetary expenditures on social-cultural categories in the Ukraine. Thus in this area budget spending as a portion of total spending declined from 67 percent in 1965 to 59 percent in 1970, remaining stable through the mid-1970s.

Thus official Soviet expenditure series represent a substantial share of total expenditures by category and must represent the perception of the Soviet leadership on necessary expenditures in each case. At the same time, it is possible that aggregate trends (as opposed to trends in state budgetary spending) may differ insofar as the nonbudget component of total spending may, for a particular item, behave differently than the budget component.

Soviet City Revenues and Expenditures

Thus far we have examined some of the important features of the Soviet budgetary system and trends in recent Soviet thinking on the financing of Soviet cities. We turn now to an examination of income and expenditure in the Soviet urban sector. Although we have observed that the official Soviet series on expenditure and income are not inclusive of all Soviet urban financial resources, these data capture the dominant components of Soviet urban finances in many categories. Our task is to determine the trends in Soviet urban income sources and expenditure categories, evaluate whether these trends are compatible with announced Soviet regional growth and equality goals, and speculate on the implications of these trends for future Soviet urban fiscal policies.

Tax objectives. Soviet tax policies try to guarantee a stable flow of revenues to support national policies, account for cost differences among plants which produce the same products, and be understandable, inexpensive to administer, and fair. These tax objectives are not unique to the Soviet Union.[20] The unique dimension is that the Soviet tax system favors indirect taxes. These taxes are hidden in daily economic transactions and are not paid in any one lump sum. This conceals not only the actual tax burden on the Soviet citizen but also the structure of the taxes. This concealment is important in an economic system that relies on differential wages to induce desired labor force responses. The Soviet city revenue system is designed around these features.

Revenue sources. The sources of revenue in a Soviet city budget reflect the peculiarities of the Soviet financial and economic system. During the post-World War II years three revenue sources have been dominant. They are described in order of importance.

The first revenue source is the turnover tax, a tax collected on a national basis.[21] In simple terms the turnover tax is levied on items entering into retail trade and represents the difference between the equilibrium price level (that is, the price that would equate supply and demand) and the cost of the item entering into retail trade. Cost, in Soviet accounting practice, is defined as the industrial branch average cost of production (basically labor plus materials) plus various small markups as the item in question proceeds through the distribution channel from the factory to wholesale and finally retail trade.

Western economists view the turnover tax as the least desirable form of sales tax. It arbitrarily discriminates against products that go through many stages of production and distribution, and it is "pyramided" from stage to stage of production. This raises the cost of the product.[22] Soviet economists favor the turnover tax because it conforms to the tax objectives mentioned earlier.

The second revenue source is profit deductions. Although economic reform has led to alterations in the precise rules for determining profit deductions, with the possible exception of a capital charge introduced in 1965, the essence of the system has not changed.[23] Under various jurisdictions state enterprises operating under the *khozraschet* system of management (literally "economic accountability") are encouraged to generate profits. The state sets the prices of inputs and outputs so that on average an enterprise will make planned profits. Part of these profits will be retained for use within the enterprise, while at the same time a part will be deducted for use in the state budget. The advantage of a profit deductions tax is that local administrators can adjust the level of the profit deductions to allow for the cost differences and internal investment needs of various enterprises.

The third revenue source is taxes on the population. These taxes are similar to income taxes in Western nations and are primarily levied on the urban population. The tax is deducted from wage or salary income. Its base is differentiated by marital status, family size, and source of income. The tax rate schedule is progressive.[24] The Soviet government is not eager to employ direct taxes, such as income taxes, whose impact may obviously reduce wage differentials between attractive jobs, industries, and regions and their less attractive counterparts.

In addition to these three major revenue sources, the Soviets levy taxes on enterprise income, use local taxes and fees, and sell state bonds and lotteries to finance their cities.

Data. City budget data were collected for 1950, 1960, 1968, and 1975, representing income flowing through the budget process. The last year is the most recent year the desired budget breakdowns were available. The source of data is the *Mestnye biudzhety* volumes for the appropriate years.

"City budget" is different than "local budget." City budget refers to the financial resources administered by an executive committee of a Soviet city. Budget data may not include all the resources spent in a Soviet city. Local budget refers to the financial resources allocated by all units below the republic level. Most of the cities in the Soviet Union used in this essay are located in the RSFSR and the Ukraine, although the data include cities in all fifteen republics.

Tax levels and changes. In order to show the tax trends in Soviet cities, data on city revenues for 1950, 1960, and 1975 were aggregated at the republic and the national level. We will discuss city budget trends at the national level and contrast them to city budget trends at the republic level for each of the fifteen republics. Table 1 shows the national results.

Soviet city revenues have grown significantly from 1950 to 1975, showing a 560.7 percent increase, or an average annual increase of 37.4 percent (in 1950: 2.3 billion rubles, and in 1975: 15.5 billion rubles). The turnover tax has outdistanced this rate of growth with an increase of 1,424.8 percent over the same period (in 1950: 0.43 billion rubles, and in 1975: 6.5 billion rubles). The result is that the turnover tax accounts for approximately 40 percent of total city revenues and is the dominant tax in Soviet city finances. Cities in only three republics—the Ukraine, Belorussia, and Kirghizia—show a decline in the share of city revenues raised by the turnover tax during the 1960 to 1968 period. This fact should not diminish the importance of this tax. Thirteen republics use the turnover tax as their primary revenue source for cities.

The profit deductions tax on enterprises has been the second most important source of city revenues. It has grown by 741.6 percent (in 1950: 0.52 billion rubles, and in 1975: 4.4 billion rubles). As a share of city revenue the profit deductions tax climbed from 22.2 percent in 1950 to 28.3 percent in 1975. At the republic level the trends in the tax have differed from the national figures. For example, in the 1960–68 period cities in only four republics—the Ukraine, Belorussia, Kirghizia, and Tadzhikistan—showed an increase in the share of revenues raised by this tax. For cities in the other eleven republics the share fell. Still, cities in ten republics make the profit deductions tax their third major source of city revenues.

The tax on enterprise income (for those enterprises contributing to city revenues) is the only city revenue source whose level declined, by 7.3 percent (in 1950: 0.18 billion rubles, and in 1975: 0.17 billion rubles). This tax has consistently ranked as the least productive source for cities. It contributed only 1.1 percent of city revenues in 1975, down from 7.84 percent in 1950. The low standing of this tax also holds at the republic level, although cities in only six republics—the RSFSR, the Ukraine, Belorussia, Uzbekistan, Georgia, and Latvia—have shown an actual decline in the tax revenue from 1950 to 1968. Cities in all fifteen republics rank the tax on enterprise income as the least productive source of city tax revenues.

From this declining city revenue source, we turn to another tax source that has grown faster than overall city revenues, namely, the tax on population. This tax, paid in various forms directly by people, has increased by 937.2 percent (in

Table 1

City Revenue in the Soviet Union for Selected Years

Source of revenue	Amount (thousand rubles)				% of revenue				Average annual % change	
	1950	1960	1968	1975	1950	1960	1968	1975	1950-60	1960-75
Total	2,349,900	6,143,090	10,845,216	15,525,800	100.00	100.00	100.00	100.00	16.1	10.2
Turnover tax	425,802	2,164,825	4,327,241	6,492,500	18.12	35.24	39.90	41.82	40.8	13.3
Profit deductions tax (local subordination)	521,678	1,760,610	3,125,591	4,390,200	22.20	28.66	28.82	28.28	23.7	10.0
Tax on enterprise income	184,232	307,769	110,621	170,800	7.84	5.01	1.02	1.10	74.0	− 3.0
State taxes on population	327,106	991,495	1,850,194	3,392,600	13.92	16.14	17.06	21.85	20.3	15.2
Local taxes and fees	524,733	524,620	674,572	778,500	22.33	8.54	6.22	5.01	NC	3.2
Other	366,349	393,771	756,997	301,200	15.59	6.41	6.98	1.94	.8	− 1.6

Sources: *Mestnye biudzhety SSSR*, 1970, and Poliak (1978).

1950: 0.32 billion rubles, and in 1975: 3.4 billion rubles). It has become the third most important city revenue source, accounting for 21.9 percent of revenues, up from 13.9 percent in 1950. At the republic level the trend for the tax on population is not as easy to summarize. In the 1950 to 1960 period, six republics—Belorussia, Uzbekistan, Moldavia, Kirghizia, Tadzhikistan, and Armenia—reduced the share of city revenues raised by this tax; and in the 1960 to 1968 period, cities in five republics—Uzbekistan, Georgia, Lithuania, Tadzhikistan, and Armenia—followed suit. Despite these changes in share, twelve republics use the tax on population as the second most important source of city revenue. The growth of this tax runs counter to the Soviets' preference for indirect taxes.

Local taxes and fees have also grown modestly, by 48.4 percent (in 1950: 0.52 billion rubles, and in 1975: 0.78 billion rubles). These taxes and fees accounted for 5.0 percent of city revenues in 1975, which is a steady decline from a share of 22.3 percent in 1950. This national trend holds for cities in the fifteen republics. The 5.0 percent share ranks local taxes and fees as the fourth source of city revenues. They rank fifth for cities in eight of the republics.

The last category of city revenue sources is a combination of state loans (bonds), state lottery, forest income, surplus, and miscellaneous items. In total this group has declined 182.2 percent (in 1950: 0.37 billion rubles, and in 1968: 0.30 billion rubles). Separately, state loans have fallen since 1950, while the state lottery has grown since 1960. This group ranks fifth as a source of city revenues, contributing 1.9 percent of the total. These national trends are generally consistent with trends at the republic level. Nine republics place this group as their fourth source of city revenue.

Four conclusions follow from these data:

1) While the fifteen Soviet republics generally reflect the national trends on level and changes in city revenue sources, there are differences across republics.

2) Soviet city revenues have grown substantially during the 1950 to 1975 period. From 1950 to 1960 the average annual increase was 16.1 percent, and from 1960 to 1975, 10.2 percent.

3) Turnover taxes, profit deductions, and taxes on the population showed increases above the national average in city revenues. Taxes on enterprise income and local taxes and fees declined in importance.

4) The city revenue systems in the Soviet Union appear to rely on indirect taxes, with the exception of the taxes on population, and to be proportional at best, or mildly regressive.[25]

If we exclude point 3, which deals with specific types of taxation in the Soviet Union, the remaining conclusions about city finances apply to market capitalist economies such as the United States. Under planned socialism and market capitalist economies there is diversity in the level and form of city finances; the pressure to raise more revenues for city operations exists; and cities use indirect, proportional (or regressive) taxes to finance themselves.

This last point brings out an additional comparison between the systems. In the market capitalist system politicians favor indirect taxes and taxes which tend to be less progressive than they appear to confuse the consumer-voter.[26] This same political motivation may be present in a planned socialist economy such as the Soviet Union.

Expenditure objectives. The earlier section on the Soviet budgetary process pointed out three features that influence city expenditures, namely, vertical economic organization, integration of city spending with the national economic plan, and a set of informal procedures of operation (e.g., incremental budgeting). The resulting Soviet city budget should promote social homogeneity and balanced development.[27]

Expenditure categories. A high degree of aggregation of expenditure categories makes it difficult to analyze specific uses of budget funds. The bulk of expenditures fall within one of the following three categories. They are presented in order of importance.

First, the category *city economy* includes capital and current outlays on the physical plant of the city; for example, repairs to buildings and road maintenance.

Second, *social-cultural* expenditures include urban services: for example, education (e.g., kindergartens, day-care centers, public school through the middle level, libraries, museums), health (e.g., hospitals, sanitation and prevention centers, and ambulances), and social insurance (e.g., housing for the elderly, rehabilitation programs, pensions and grants).

Third, *administration* expenditures are a separate though relatively small budget item. They include office upkeep, business trips, equipping and repairing buildings that house administration units.

Expenditure levels and changes. In order to show the expenditure trends in Soviet cities, data on city expenditures for 1950, 1960, 1968, and 1975 were aggregated at the republic and the national level. Table 2 shows the national results.

Soviet city expenditures have grown from 1950 to 1975, showing a 690.3 percent increase, or an average annual increase of 27.6 percent (in 1958: 2.3 billion rubles, and in 1975: 17.8 billion rubles). The city economy category has grown even faster, 1,217.9 percent (in 1950: 0.55 billion rubles, and in 1975: 7.3 billion rubles). It made up 40.7 percent of the city expenditures in 1975. City economy expenditures are lumpy by nature; that is, they come in waves largely due to the inclusion of capital outlays. This helps explain why this category increased as a share of city expenditures from 1950 to 1960, declined from 1960 to 1968, and increased again from 1968 to 1975.

These national trends reflect the republic trends. For cities in fourteen republics (the exception: Armenia), city economy expenditures grew faster than total expenditures. In eleven republics this category ranks first. For cities in thirteen republics the city economy grew in the 1950 to 1960 period and declined in the 1960 to 1968 period.

Social-cultural expenditures as a group dominate Soviet city expenditures, with 56.5 percent of the city budget in 1975. Usually they are divided into education, health, and social insurance. Education is the second most important category. It has increased by 597.9 percent (in 1950: 0.74 billion rubles, and in 1975: 5.1 billion rubles). Education accounted for 28.8 percent of the city budget in 1975. Unlike city economy expenditures, education decreased as a share of the city budget from 1950 to 1960, increased from 1960 to 1968, and decreased from 1968 to 1975.

The cities in the republics follow these trends except for Tadzhikistan, which places education first in its 1968 budget, and Belorussia, Moldavia, Tadzhikistan, and Armenia, where increases in education outstrip increases in total expenditures.

Health expenditures have also grown, but not as fast as total expenditures. This category is up 466.8 percent (in 1950: 0.85 billion rubles, and in 1975: 4.8 billion rubles). Its share of city expenditures decreased from 1950 to 1960, increased from 1960 to 1968, and decreased from 1968 to 1975. It was 26.9 percent in 1975, the third major category. The cities in the republics conform to these trends. However, cities in six republics—Kazakhstan, Azerbaidzhan, Lithuania, Moldavia, Tadzhikistan, and Armenia—have experienced different patterns in the share of the city expenditures allocated to health than the national figures show.

The last social-cultural item, social insurance, is a small portion of the budget. Its 1975 share was 0.79 percent, making it the sixth expenditure category. It has grown 514.3 percent (in 1959: 0.02 billion rubles, and in 1975: 0.14 billion rubles). Generally the cities in the republics reveal similar trends.

Administration is another small budget item. Its 1975 share was 0.90 percent, a steady decline from 1950. Yet administration expenditures have grown 236.8 percent (in 1950: 0.08 billion rubles, and in 1975: 0.16 billion rubles). It ranks as the fifth major expenditure category. Once again, the cities in the republics show the same trends.

Four conclusions follow from these data:

1) While the fifteen republics generally reflect the national trends, diversity in expenditures exists despite the integrated budget and the promotion of social homogeneity and balanced growth.

2) Soviet city expenditures are growing. During the 1950 to 1960 period, the average annual rate was 19.08; and during the 1950 to 1975 period, 11.45 percent. This corresponds to the revenue trends for the same time periods.

3) Combined social-cultural expenditures dominate city expenditures. If these are disaggregated, city economy ranks first and education second. Administration expenditures rank fifth and have steadily declined.

Table 2

City Expenditures in the Soviet Union for Selected Years

Expenditure categories	Amount (thousand rubles)				% of expenditure				Average annual % change	
	1950	1960	1968	1975	1950	1960	1968	1975	1950-60	1960-75
Total	2,258,354	6,566,195	11,722,572	17,847,600	100.00	100.00	100.00	100.00	19.08	11.45
City economy	550,587	2,912,764	4,373,692	7,256,400	24.38	44.36	37.31	40.66	42.90	9.94
Social-cultural	1,607,045	3,532,613	7,121,463	10,083,900	71.16	53.80	60.75	56.50	11.98	12.36
Education and science	736,901	1,707,211	3,664,476	5,142,500	32.63	26.00	31.26	28.81	13.17	13.41
Health and physical culture	846,883	1,776,156	3,365,550	4,799,800	37.50	27.05	28.71	26.89	10.973	11.35
Social insurance	23,035	49,933	89,092	141,500	1.02	0.73	0.76	.79	11.68	12.23
Administration	82,882	83,391	109,020	160,700	3.67	1.27	0.93	.90	.06	6.18
Other	17,163	36,771	116,053	346,600	0.76	0.56	0.99	1.94	11.42	56.17

Sources: *Mestnye biudzhety SSSR*, 1970, and Poliak (1978).

4) Soviet city spending consists of expenditures that appear to
be redistributive within a city. This must be tempered by the
fact that spending differences across cities exist which may
be prorich.

This last point will be discussed further in the next section.

Variations in Soviet City Expenditures

The summaries of Soviet city revenues and expenditures point to the similarities
in city budgets across republics. In almost every fiscal category there were
exceptions. We turn now to an analysis of the expenditure variations across
republics and suggest factors that may be associated with these variations.

Expenditure variations. An examination of city expenditure variation in the
Soviet Union would include two dimensions of the expenditure decisions: the
level of per capita expenditures, and the *growth* in per capita expenditures.

The first dimension—the level—would be measured by calculating the
unweighted national per capita expenditures in 1975. This figure is 122.7 rubles
per person, representing total city budgetary expenditure divided by city population for 1975. The per capita spending in each of the fifteen republics is indexed
to this figure. For example, cities in the RSFSR spent 122.0 rubles per person in
1975, or 99 percent of the national average—$(122.0/122.7) \times 100 = 99$. Each
republic above the national average is placed in the "high" spending cateogry;
those below, in the "low" spending category. There are seven republics in the
former and eight in the latter.

The second dimension—the growth—would be measured by calculating the
unweighted national growth in per capita city spending from 1958 to 1975. This
figure is 157.7 percent. Again, the per capita city spending growth in each of the
fifteen republics is indexed to this figure. For example, cities in the RSFSR
increased per capita spending from 1958 to 1975 by 137.4 percent, or 88 percent
of the national growth rate—$(137.4/157.7) \times 100 = 88$. Each republic above the
national average is placed in the "rising" category; those below, in the "falling"
category. There are ten republics in the former and five in the latter. Table 3
displays the fifteen republics by this two-dimensional measure. The first number
is the relative *level of per capita spending*, and the second number is the *relative
growth of per capita spending*. Cities in three republics—Moldavia, Georgia, and
Latvia—are in the "high and falling" category; cities in two republics—the
RSFSR and Tadzhikistan—are in the "low and falling" category; cities in four
republics—Armenia, Estonia, Lithuania, and Uzbekistan—are in the "high and
rising" category; and cities in six republics—Belorussia, Azerbaidzhan, Turk-
menia, Kirghizia, Kazakhstan, and the Ukraine—are in the "low and rising"
category.

Despite the Soviet objectives of social homogeneity and balanced growth,
city expenditure differences exist across republics. Past research has identified
some of the determinants of spending in planned socialist economies and capital-

ist market economies.[28] We now identify factors which may influence city expenditures.

Factors associated with city expenditures. This section has selected seven variables that have been found in the analysis of market systems to help in the explanation of observed variations in city expenditures. These factors, associated historically with variations in city expenditures, are correlated with per capita Soviet city expenditures for 1958, 1968, and 1975. The variables and their hypothesized correlation relationships are:

a) Per capita income, as measured by the relative national income by republic: The Soviet city finances services with revenues raised by direct and/or indirect taxation. Per capita income indicates the average individual's willingness and ability to pay these taxes. It is a demand-side variable. Per capita public service expenditures are positively related to per capita income levels. Marxian economics would deny utility, and therefore the willingness of the individual to pay for public services would not be stressed. Income as a measure of ability to pay would still be useful.

b) Population and population change, as measured by population level and growth. As the size of a city changes, the demand for and the level of city services should change. Per capita city services are positively related to population and population change. In the Soviet case there is some evidence that Soviet planners are trying to control Soviet city size.[29] One method of discouraging the growth in city size is to restrict the growth of city services. If this objective holds, these two variables may be negatively associated with per capita city expenditures.

Table 3
A Two-Dimensional Measure of Relative City
Expenditure Variations by Republic

High and falling	*High and rising*
Moldavia 116/97	Armenia 125/111
Georgia 111/92	Estonia 119/102
Latvia 102/69	Lithuania 111/101
	Uzbekistan 102/124
Low and falling	*Low and rising*
RSFSR 99/88	Belorussia 100/101
Tadzhikistan 83/72	Azerbaidzhan 96/103
	Turkmenia 93/111
	Kirghizistan 83/116
	Kazakhstan 82/135
	Ukraine 77/105

Source: Computed by the authors from Tables 1 and 2 and Soviet census volumes.

c) Education, as measured by the number of persons per 1,000 (ten years or older) who have higher and secondary education (complete or incomplete): Education is a demand-side variable. As an individual's educational level improves, the person has traditionally demanded more city services for himself and others. A positive relationship with per capita city expenditures is expected.

d) Dependency, as measured by the percent of the population below 16 years old and above 59 years old: These age groups are traditionally high consumers of city services (e.g., education and health). Many of the services these age groups consume are redistributive in nature. Therefore if a Soviet city is concerned with these groups, per capita city expenditures should be positively related with dependency.

e) Living space, as measured by square meters of housing space per capita: The square meters per person may indicate the density in the city. If it falls, the density is increasing. This is usually associated with increased demand and cost of providing city services. Therefore the expected relationship between living space and per capita city expenditures is negative.

f) City hardship, as measured by a composite index number that indicates the degree of lack of education, dependency, and crowded living space: Each of these three variables measures a dimension of social distress. If city government attempts to ameliorate these conditions, there would be a positive association between per capita city expenditures and city hardship. Since the Soviets are interested in social homogeneity and balanced growth, we would expect this positive relationship.

Results. Table 4 presents the correlations of these seven variables and per capita city expenditures for 1958, 1968, and 1975. Any interpretation of simple correlations of city expenditure data aggregated at the republic level is speculative. The data do not indicate who benefits from the spending. Some interesting patterns do emerge, however.

The signs of the variables often change across years. This is also true of the magnitudes in almost every case. These changes indicate a shift in Soviet city spending policies. In 1958 per capita city expenditures are associated with relatively well-off cities. The positive association of per capita city expenditures with (ranked by size of correlates) living space (0.547), per capita income (0.459), and education (0.084) argues for the spending–well-off cities relationship. It is not surprising to find a negative association between per capita city expenditures and dependency (-0.314) and the city hardship index (-0.449). This merely reenforces our conclusions. The population variable and population change variables have negative correlates (-0.025 and -0.395, respectively). This relationship might imply a Soviet desire to restrict city growth.

The data for 1968 show a change in Soviet city spending policies. In 1968 per capita city expenditures are associated with relatively distressed cities. The positive association of per capita city expenditures with city hardship (0.145) and dependency (0.457) argues for the spending–distressed city relationship. This is reenforced by the negative association of per capita city expenditures with living space (-0.048) and per capita income (-0.036). Also, the negative association between per capita city expenditures and population size (-0.283) argues for the continued policy of limiting size. Notice that there is now a positive correlate for change in city population size.

The data for 1975 show a mix of the 1958 and the 1968 patterns. Although this is a simplification, it is *as if* Soviet city spending patterns served well-off cities in 1958, distressed cities in 1968, and some elements of both in 1975. For example, in 1975 per capita expenditure was associated with dependency (−0.172), living space (0.359), and hardship (−0.156) in the same way as it was in 1958.

Table 4
Correlates of Per Capita Soviet City Expenditures, by Republic—1958, 1968, and 1975*

| | Per capita Soviet city expenditures | | |
Characteristics**	1958	1968	1975
Income	0.459	−0.036	−0.060
Population	−0.025	−0.283	−0.160
Population change	−0.395	0.125	0.273
Education	0.084	0.002	−0.008
Dependency	−0.314	0.457	−0.172
Living space	0.547	−0.048	0.359
Hardship	−0.449	0.145	−0.156

*This table shows the correlation between per capita Soviet city (budgetary) expenditures and a number of characteristics typically associated with variations in per capita city expenditures in market economies.

**Income data are from Gertrude E. Schroeder, "Soviet Wage and Income Policies in Regional Perspective," *Association for Comparative Economic Studies Bulletin*, 16 (Fall 1974), 3-20, and Gertrude E. Schroeder, "Soviet Regional Development Policies in Perspective," NATO, *The USSR in the 1980s* (Brussels, 1978), 125-40. Other data are from the Soviet census volumes, statistical handbooks, and *Vestnik statistiki*.

Alternatively, in 1975 per capita expenditure was associated with per capita income (−0.161) and change in population (0.273), as it was in 1968. In all years per capita expenditure was negatively associated with population.

This section adds to the four conclusions reached in the previous section on Soviet city expenditures. The additions are that factors similar to those in market capitalist economies influence Soviet city spending; and while speculative in nature, an interpretation of city spending patterns emerges. In 1958 well-off cities are favored; in 1968 distressed cities are favored; and in 1975 a blend of these policies is apparent.[30]

Conclusions

This essay discusses Soviet city finances with two objectives: to describe tax methods, expenditures categories, fiscal trends, and expenditure variations in Soviet cities, and to compare Soviet (planned socialist economy) with United States (market capitalist economy) city finances whenever possible.

Using city budget data aggregated at the republic level, the chapter draws specific conclusions about Soviet city revenue and expenditure patterns. These conclusions centered on the dramatic growth in city revenues (particularly the turnover tax, profit deductions, and the tax on population) and city expenditures (particularly the city economy, education, and health); on the reliance on indirect, regressive (or at best proportional) texes to finance city services; and on the variability of city expenditure levels around the nation associated with such factors as per capita income, population, population change, education, dependency, living space, and city hardship. This analysis has been based on urban budgetary income and expenditure. While the essay examines nonbudgetary urban financing, no attempt is made to incorporate this nonbudget income and expenditure in our statistical compilations. Thus we have examined state priorities as reflected in state budgetary decisions. Since state-budgeted resources represent the bulk of Soviet urban income and expenditures, the inclusion of the nonbudgetary resources may temper, but not reverse, our conclusions.

The surprise is that these conclusions (excluding the Soviet specifics) can also be made about cities in the United States as well as other countries with planned socialist and market capitalist economic systems. One Soviet specific finding, though speculative, presents an issue for future research. Soviet city expenditures policies appear to have shifted from 1958 to 1968 to 1975. Unlike 1958, there was increasing emphasis on distressed cities in 1968 and a blurring of policy objectives in 1975.

Notes

[1] See, for example, Gur Ofer, "Economizing on Urbanization in Socialist Countries: Historical Necessity or Socialist Strategy?" in Alan A. Brown and Egon Neuberger (eds.), *Internal Migration: A Comparative Perspective* (New York, 1977), 277-303; Gur Ofer, "Industrial Structure, Urbanization, and the Growth Strategy of Socialist Countries," *Quarterly Journal of Economics*, *90* (May 1976), 219-43; for general background, see James H. Bater, *The Soviet City* (London, 1980); Chauncey D. Harris, *Cities of the Soviet Union* (Washington, D.C., 1972).

[2] For an elaboration of this classification, see Paul R. Gregory and Robert C. Stuart, *Comparative Economic Systems* (Boston, 1981), chap. 1.

[3] For a discussion of the organization and planning of the Soviet economy, see Paul R. Gregory and Robert C. Stuart, *Soviet Economic Structure and Performance*, 2nd ed. (New York, 1981), chap. 5.

[4] For example, if the output of one enterprise is to be sold to another enterprise (an intermediate good), the arrangements would traditionally be developed through and implemented by the plan rather than a simple direct contact between the two firms.

[5] For a general treatment of the Soviet budgetary process, see Gregory and Stuart, *Soviet Economic Structure and Performance*, chap. 5; for background on Soviet urban management, see Carol W. Lewis and Stephen Sternheimer, *Soviet Urban Management: With Comparisons to the United States* (New York, 1979); for a detailed discussion of the budget process as it pertains to Soviet cities, see Carol Weiss Lewis, *The Budgetary*

Process in Soviet Cities (New York, 1976).

[6]When analyzing the Soviet Union in a regional perspective, the selection of an appropriate unit of observation is very difficult since the fifteen union republics represent a substantial degree of diversity and varying degrees of aggregation. At lesser levels of aggregation (the raion, for example) necessary data are frequently unavailable. In particular, it must be remembered that the republics differ in many important dimensions. The Baltic republics are small and relatively highly developed. The Central Asian republics are relatively poor. The Russian Republic, in terms of land area and population, is large and dominant. Indeed, the Russian Republic and the Ukraine account for a large share of the total Soviet urban population.

[7]The subordination of Soviet cities can vary. For a more detailed discussion, see Carol Weiss Lewis, chap. 2.

[8]In Soviet planning procedures this is frequently described as the *ratchet* process.

[9]For a discussion of the Soviet financial system, see, for example, George Garvy, *Money, Financial Flows, and Credit in the Soviet Union* (Cambridge, Mass., 1977); O. Kuschpeta, *The Banking and Credit System of the USSR* (Leiden and Boston, 1978).

[10]See, for example, G. B. Poliak, *Biudzhet goroda* (Moscow, 1978).

[11]See, for example, T. A. Tokareva, "Mestnye biudzhety na sovremennom etape," *Finansy SSSR*, 4 (April 1979), 29-34; Ia. B. Khesin, *Puti povysheniia ustoichivosti dokhodnoi bazy mestnykh biudzhetov* (Moscow, 1976); N. M. Kabrel'ian, B. I. Kulabukhov, and L. N. Kudriavtseva, "Iz praktiki regulirovaniia mestnykh biudzhetov Donetskoi oblasti," *Finansy SSSR*, 4 (April 1977), 81-84.

[12]Soviet enterprises and other organizations retain a portion of their profits for expenditure on social-cultural categories. Although there are no systematic data available on the expenditure of these funds, fragmentary evidence would suggest that for some categories, for example, expenditures on housing or on child-care facilities, enterprise (that is nonbudget) spending can be important.

[13]For an assessment, see Carol W. Lewis, "The Economic Functions of Local Soviets," paper presented at the Second World Congress on Soviet and East European Studies, Garmisch, 1980.

[14]Poliak, 15-16.

[15]For a useful discussion, see Carol Weiss Lewis.

[16]Poliak, 27. A user charge would mean that for use of a service there would be a direct payment by the recipient.

[17]The complications of Soviet pricing policies are examined in Morris Bornstein, "Soviet Price Policy in the 1970's," *Soviet Economy in a New Perspective* (Washington, D.C., 1976), 17-66.

[18]Poliak, 107. A useful survey can be found in National Foreign Assessment Center, *The Soviet State Budget Since 1965* (Washington, D.C., 1977).

[19]These data are from the official Soviet statistical handbooks. The authors are indebted to Donna Bahry for pointing out this means to examine total vis-à-vis state budgetary spending patterns. For a discussion of this problem, see Donna Bahry, "Measuring Communist Priorities," *Comparative Political Studies* 3 (October 1980), 267-92.

[20]Franklyn D. Holzman, *Soviet Taxation* (Cambridge, Mass., 1955), part 1.

[21]For a detailed discussion of the turnover tax, see Gregory and Stuart, *Soviet Economic Structure and Performance*, 158-59.

[22]Richard A. Musgrave and Peggy B. Musgrave, *Public Finance in Theory and Practice* (New York 1980), 442-63.

[23]All Soviet enterprises are budget financed. If a firm incurs losses, in a sense it receives a subsidy from the state budget. However, for an enterprise making profits, part of

the profit will remain within the enterprise for such purposes as decentralized investment, bonuses, and cultural expenditures, the remainder being directed into the state budget. The most important change (since 1965) is the introduction of a fixed charge on capital.

[24]Holzman, chap. 8.

[25]Holzman, chaps. 10 and 11.

[26]Randell Bartlett, *Economic Foundations of Political Power* (New York, 1973), chap. 10.

[27]There is considerble debate in the literature as to the objectives of Soviet regional policies and the extent to which objectives have in fact been achieved. Our concern here is limited to an examination of regional differences in *state budgetary spending* in the urban sector. For a background discussion, see Carol Weiss Lewis, "Politics and the Budget in Soviet Cities" (unpublished Ph.D. dissertation, Princeton University, 1975), 121-62; for a general treatment of the regional question, see, for example, V. N. Bandera and Z. L. Melnyk (eds.), *The Soviet Economy in Regional Perspective* (New York, 1973); for a recent appraisal, see Gertrude E. Schroeder, "Soviet Regional Development Policies in Perspective," in *The USSR in the 1980s* (Brussels, 1978), 125-41. Data used are in money terms. Most indicators would suggest that there has been minimal overt inflation in the Soviet Union during the years under consideration.

[28]For the socialist planned economies, see Frederic L. Pryor, *Public Expenditures in Communist and Capitalist Nations* (London, 1968), and Lewis and Sternheimer, chap. 4. For the market capitalist economies, see Glenn Fisher, "Determinants of State and Local Government Expenditures," *National Tax Journal*, 17 (March 1965), 75-85; James C. Ohls and Terence J. Wales, "Supply and Demand for State and Local Services," *Review of Economics and Statistics*, 54 (November 1972), 424-30.

[29]This argument is advanced in Gur Ofer: *The Service Sector in Soviet Economic Growth* (Cambridge, Mass., 1973), and "Industrial Structure."

[30]A similar ambivalence toward central cities is shown in intergovernmental grant policy in the United States. In the 1961-70 period grants were clearly directed to distressed central cities, and in the 1971-77 period grants were distributed to serve both distressed cities and their well-off counterparts. See Henry J. Raimondo, "Central City Isolation and Intergovernmental Grants, 1961-77," *Growth and Change*, 13 (January 1982), 26-36.

4

The Soviet Urban Labor Supply

For the directors of the Soviet economic system, no goal is more important than economic growth. There was a day when Soviet achievements were the envy of other growth-minded nations. But today, the withered pace of growth and the possibility that even more deceleration may bring internal stringency hardly make the Soviet Union an object of envy.[1] A major reason for past growth was a large pool of labor that was available to be tapped. This source of abundant labor has disappeared, not only for short-term needs but also for the rest of this century. In addition there are a number of constraints which prevent Soviet planners from rectifying this situation.

This chapter will analyze the labor force problems that exist within urban areas. The discussion will encompass all places defined by the Soviets as urban, which includes urban settlements with only a few thousand people as well as the major cities with more than a million population.

This essay will examine the labor force shortage of Soviet cities from two broad perspectives. The first is the demographic problems of Soviet cities. In this instance the stresses arise from the general decline in the supply of able-bodied workers (ages 16-59 for men, 16-55 for women), the differential birth rates of various nationality groups in the USSR, and the perverse age structure of Soviet cities. The second major group of labor supply problems falls under an umbrella that might be called allocative inefficiencies. This means that there are certain systemic and behavioral problems that create unnecessary shortages. That is, a better allocation of labor could increase the available labor input in Soviet cities. These problems include, but are not limited to, labor turnover, the weaknesses of central planning, the immobility of certain nationality groups, and the health of the Soviet people. Finally, there is an assessment of Soviet ability to maintain the high labor force participation rates of women and an analysis of the potential for increasing the size of the labor pool through an increase in part-time work.

It will be shown that the long-run labor supply picture in the USSR is bleak. The burden will be placed on Soviet planners to adopt policies that will lead to the improved utilization of the existing labor force, such as, for example, increases in capital investment to raise labor productivity. Even under realistic assumptions about what Soviet planners can do over the next decade, the effects on the productivity of land, labor, and capital may not be very great. Ultimately, the constraint of shrinking numbers and systemic deficiencies will be more powerful determinants of the limits of Soviet growth in the future.

Demogaphic Problems

All estimates of Soviet population growth predict declining additions to the labor force. For the period 1981–85, it is projected that the average annual increase in the able-bodied population will be 0.3 percent, one-fifth of what it was in the previous five-year period and about one-sixth what it was during the period 1971–75.[2] Soviet forecasts confirm the gloomy prospects for the labor force through this century. Given the low crude birth rates of the past and their persistence up to the present at a low level, Soviet research predicts that during the period 1986–2001 there will be no increase in the size of the labor force, in contrast to labor force additions of 30 million during the period 1971–86.[3] It is only in the second half of the 1990s that the labor force will experience positive additions.[4]

Compounding this trend is the fact that Soviet society has become increasingly urban. In 1961, 50 percent of the population was urban, in 1971 it was 57 percent urban, and in 1981 that figure was 63 percent.[5] The importance of this is that the birth rate in urban areas is always lower than rural birth rates. For example, since 1965 the birth rate in urban areas has ranged between 15.3 and 17.0 per 1,000 population, while in rural areas the range was 18.7–21.1 per 1,000 population for the same period.[6] The birth rates in the largest cities of the country are even lower than for urban areas in general. This is especially true for Moscow and Leningrad. In 1973 in Moscow the crude birth rate was only 12.4 per 1,000.[7] The combination of a relative shift in the population to cities and the lower birth rates in urban areas has therefore had a negative impact on the growth of the urban labor force.

In addition, there is a lower than average increase in the population of the republics that are the most heavily urbanized, while the largest increases in the population come from those republics that are the least urbanized. For example, from 1959 to 1970 the total Soviet population grew by 15.8 percent. But the population in Central Asia grew by 50 percent, with a birth rate twice as high as the rate in the Slavic and Baltic Republics.[8] While the urban population as a percent of the total population in the slow-growing Slavic and Baltic republics was 65.1 percent in 1979, in the considerably faster-growing Central Asian republics the comparable figure was 43.4 percent.[9]

One estimate is that by the year 2000, Central Asia will account for 50 percent of total population growth in the USSR.[10] While a massive movement of Soviet Central Asian Muslims to the cities of the western part of the USSR could help relieve the labor shortage, for several reasons beyond ethnicity and favorable climate, such a migration is unlikely to occur during the 1980s.[11] First of all, the differential in earnings between Central Asian farmers and nonagricultural workers in the Russian Republic is too small to produce high levels of migration. Second, despite high rates of population growth, Central Asian cities are also plagued with a labor shortage. Third, recent investment policy provides for funding of new projects where there is a population surplus with the goal of utilizing local resources, including an increase in labor participation rates where they are low. These policies tend to encourage investment in Central Asia and therefore an increased likelihood that migration to the most labor-starved cities in other parts of the country will not take place. Finally, plans for irrigating Central Asian land will increase the demand for local labor.

Migration

This raises the question of whether Soviet planners can look to migration out of rural areas into the cities as a means of augmenting the urban labor force.[12] During the early years of the Soviet period, migration of the rural population was the dominant source of growth of the urban population. Thus from 1927 to 1938 rural migration accounted for 62.7 percent of urban population growth, while the natural increase of the population accounted for 17.8 percent of it. During the period 1959–69, the importance of migration as a source of urban growth declined to 45.6 percent, and natural increase accounted for 40.5 percent. In sheer numbers agriculture still has a surplus; about 25 percent of the Soviet labor force is in agriculture, as compared to about 4 percent in the United States. However, it is unlikely that planners can look to the rural population as a significant source of urban labor in the future. This is due to the fact that the age composition of the countryside has changed in a perverse direction. The proportion of the young has declined, while the percentage of older age groups has risen. For example, in 1970 the proportion of people aged 20-29 years was 9.6 percent, down from 16.7 percent in 1959, while the share of agricultural workers aged 55-69 years rose to 13.2 percent in 1970 from 1959's figure of 10.7 percent. The older workers are not mobile and are generally poorly educated. Thus even if they were willing to move, their benefit to an urban labor force is of doubtful value. Moreover, there is a strong desire on the part of Soviet planners to keep rural youth in the countryside since they are being equipped with skills associated with the mechanization of agriculture.

The Aging of the Urban Population

This leads us to another problem adversely affecting the urban labor supply, namely, the aging of the Soviet population in general, and of urban areas in particular.[13] At the most basic level, the aging of the population can be seen by looking at the percentage of the population over the age of 60 years. It has increased from 9.4 percent of the total population in 1959 to 13.3 percent in 1974.[14] In 1970, 10.3 percent of the urban population was over 60, whereas 13.6 percent of the rural population was in this group, reflecting the earlier assertion of the extreme aging of the rural population. However, the problem is even worse in the large cities of the USSR. There are data from three major cities in the Russian Republic (Moscow, Leningrad, and Sverdlovsk) and five cities in the Ukraine (Kiev, Kharkov, Donetsk, Dnepropetrovsk, and Odessa) that confirm this phenomenon. In 1970, 15.2 percent of Moscow's population was over the age of 60, as opposed to 10.0 percent in 1959. Even more important, in 1970, 19.6 percent of the city's population was eligible for old-age pensions. In Leningrad in 1970, 21 percent of the population was over the age of 55, and the size of the group aged 60-69 had doubled since 1959.

Much the same pattern held true of Sverdlovsk and the Ukrainian cities. Given the fact that the population will continue to age and given the low birth rates that we have seen occur in urban areas, it is clear that there will continue to be an undesirable relationship between the proportion of the urban population that is likely to be in the labor force and the share that will be economically inactive. However, the unwillingness of Soviet authorities to publish the 1979 census prevents us from confirming this trend. As we will see below, Soviet planners are taking pains to recruit old-age pensioners into the labor force, and there is no doubt that this group is looked to as a means of dealing with the urban labor supply problem.

Urban Housing and the Labor Shortage

In both the case of migration and the aging of the population, the issue of housing availability must be taken into account. The fundamental reality of the Soviet urban housing situation is that there is an extreme shortage of apartments. This is important because even if migration should suddenly mushroom or if planners decided to conduct a campaign to import skilled industrial workers into the cities, there would be enormous difficulty in finding a place to live. For example, by the measure of number of households per 100 housing units, only Bulgaria had a worse ratio than the Soviet Union in a comparison of twenty-six Western countries and Eastern Europe.[15] Morton estimates there was a deficit of 9.6 million housing units in urban areas in 1970. At the end of 1974 fully 30 percent of Moscow's population lived in communal apartments. Moreover, at the end of 1977 only Estonia, Latvia, and Georgia had reached the figure of 9 square meters (100 square feet) of living space per person. The average for all urban residents in the USSR was 8.2 sq m. Thus the standard of 9 sq m per person, which is regarded as the desired minimum, has yet to be achieved. As of 1980, about 20 percent of the total urban population lived in communal apartments, suggesting some improvement in the urban housing problem.[16]

The Demographic Implications of
Soviet Health Problems

Another trend which adversely affects the urban labor supply is the serious health problems of the Soviet people. They are manifested notably, although not exclusively, in two ways: first, by the decline in the life expectancy of males and the leveling off of the figure for women, and second, by a rise in infant mortality. The recently revealed Soviet "health crisis" not only tends to aggravate the demographic trends discussed above but also affects the productivity of the existing labor force.[17]

Infant mortality rose by 36 percent from 1971 to 1976, and the Soviet infant mortality rate is at least double that of the U.S. rate. While the 1974 rural infant mortality rate (28.2 per 1,000 births) is higher than the urban rate (27.7), the difference is small. If the Soviet urban infant mortality rate had been at the level of U.S. rate (15.1), this would have added approximately 32,000 more infants to the Soviet urban population in 1974. In addition there has been a rise in the national crude death rate (CDR). It reached its lowest point of 7.1 per 1,000 population in 1963–65 and has not stopped rising since that time. In 1980 it had reached 10.3 per 1,000 population.[18] In the United States on the other hand, the CDR fell from 9.5 per 1,000 in 1960 to 8.7 per 1,000 population in 1979. The increase in the Soviet CDR during this period occurred in every age group. The implications are clear; in relative terms fewer workers are available in every age group.

Inefficiencies in the Allocation of Urban Labor

While the dynamics of the Soviet demographic profile make a major contribution to the urban labor shortage, the causes of this problem also emanate from a number of systemic phenomena. Thus, while the urban labor shortage is real from the perspective of the discrepancy between short-run demand and supply, to a certain extent the shortage results from the misallocation of the existing labor force. A more efficient allocation of labor would reduce the shortage.

At the end of 1930 the Soviets declared that they had eliminated unemployment, and in the subsequent fifty years plus they have never changed their position. It is indeed likely that the high unemployment levels periodically experienced in the West due to cyclical fluctuations in aggregate demand are in fact absent from the Soviet scene. Yet there are frictional, structural, and underemployment problems that alter the meaning of the Soviet claim of full employment.

Labor Turnover

The first of these problems is the extremely high level of labor turnover, or the number per 100 workers who either voluntarily quit their jobs or are fired because they violate work rules. From 1940 to 1956 Soviet workers were essentially frozen in their jobs and could only leave a post with official approval or through reassignment. Since 1956 it has been legal for workers to quit their jobs.[19] Over the last twenty-five years the annual turnover rate has been about 20 percent in industry and about 30 percent in construction.[20] This should be compared with a turnover rate of about 5 percent in West Germany[21] and a rate averaging 4.3 percent in the United States for the period 1959–80.[22] The loss of output due to labor turnover has been estimated by Soviet economists at 3–5 billion rubles a year.[23]

In the midseventies it was estimated that labor turnover created the equivalent of a loss of 400,000 workers for one year in the RSFSR, and for the USSR as a whole, turnover caused the loss of 1.5 million workers, which is the equivalent of 1.5 percent of the nonagricultural labor force.[24] The economic losses occur because: (1) people spend one to two months out of work before they take another job; (2) workers who are constantly changing jobs waste resources because, according to various Soviet sources, 40-75 percent of them change their occupations and thus forsake the previous training they received; and (3) productivity is 25-30 percent below normal levels in the period just before workers leave a job and during the first two months at a new position.[25]

Before leaving the turnover issue, it should be mentioned that while Soviet urban workers are free to leave their job, they may not be able to enter the city they most prefer. While large cities are viewed as the best place to live because of the availability of more goods, cultural amenities, and educational opportunities, people may not be able to obtain the residence permit (*propiska*) necessary to live in such a city. In order to receive the treasured permit one needs housing. As we saw earlier, Soviet cities are ill-equipped to handle migrants because of the housing shortage. As a result, as a matter of policy large cities are essentially closed to immigrants, especially Moscow.[26]

The Use of Redundant Labor

One of the dysfunctional manifestations of Soviet central planning and its reliance on output as the primary criterion for judging enterprise behavior is that there is little incentive to economize on the use of labor.[27] According to Gosplan the ratification of plans that called for the employment of 104.1 million workers in 1975 exceeded by 2.5 million the number of workers that should have been employed. There are several reasons why Soviet enterprises in effect hoard excess labor. First, factory managers are often called on to change the composition and size of their output targets during the plan year. If the enterprise is caught without the necessary additional labor, it faces the possibility of not fulfilling output plans and, as a consequence, losing the coveted bonuses that accompany success. Second, urban enterprises are annually called on to supply workers to collective and state farms to help with planting and harvesting. This also creates an incentive to maintain enough of a labor force at the factory so that production can withstand the temporary loss of workers to the countryside. Third, one of the chronic problems of the Soviet system is the inability to supply inputs evenly over the course of production periods. As a consequence of such interruptions there is often feverish production activity during the last ten days of the month, known as "storming," as well as at the end of the fiscal year and certain days designated for intense effort. Finally, as Berliner points out, the fact that Soviet workers can so easily leave their jobs creates excessive mobility. This was seen above when the problem of a high turnover rate was explored. As a result there is a powerful incentive to anticipate high quit rates by hoarding labor.[28]

Beginning in 1967 the Soviets conducted an interesting, albeit stunted, experiment known as the Shchekino method for dealing with the hoarding problem and raising labor productivity.[29] The system worked in the following way: the enterprise wage fund was frozen at a given level. When workers left the enterprise or were fired, the management was given the right to distribute the bulk of the earnings of former employees to those remaining at the enterprise with the intent of raising labor productivity and, as a by-product, releasing labor for other places in the economy. In fact, Soviet data show very good results as regards labor productivity and output at Shchekino. Yet the method never spread significantly, and only about 1,000-1,200 enterprises, an extremely small number of Soviet factories, ever came under the aegis of the method. Principally this is because the program was sabotaged when the USSR State Committee on Labor and Wages changed the rules of the game and eliminated the right to transfer wage savings to the enterprise's material incentive fund. In addition there is a complex set of procedures that management must go through before they can be transferred to the Shchekino system. In sum, the incentives to adopt this system are negligible at best.

One final structural issue should be mentioned. There are too many auxiliary workers in Soviet enterprises relative to the number of basic production workers.[30] Auxiliary workers include those who do repairs, transportation, and warehouse work. In the USSR it is estimated that there are 85 auxiliary workers for every 100 basic production workers. In the United States there are only 38 for every 100 production workers. Even if the productivity of Soviet workers was as high as U.S. workers, and it is considerably lower, labor productivity would be less because of the more than double need for auxiliary workers in Soviet enterprises. There is little doubt that this structural problem contributes to the shortage of urban labor.

Labor Exchanges

As we mentioned above, the Soviets declared the existence of full employment in 1930. As a result, they closed down all the labor exchanges since, by definition, there was no need for an organization to find jobs when there was no person without employment. But in 1969, apparently recognizing the need for some way of dealing with the urban labor supply problem, they opened up labor exchanges in nine cities of the RSFSR.[31] Six years later there was a labor exchange in 278 Soviet cities and an office in every city over 100,000 population in the RSFSR. In 1969, 128,000 registered with the exchanges, and five years later this number had increased to 1.2 million. In the same period 37 to 64 percent of those who registered at the exchanges found jobs. However, the impact of exchanges on total hiring appears to remain insignificant. In 1974 the percentage of people hired without the use of any organization (86) was the same as in 1968. However, the benefit of exchanges may well rest with the fact that they speed up the process of hiring and also create a better mesh between job openings and the unemployed.

The Participation of Women in the Labor Force

One of the major sources of urban labor has been the unusually high participation rates of married women. About 90 percent of able-bodied women in the USSR are in the work force, the highest figure in the world. A serious question must be raised as to whether this high allegiance to work can be maintained in the future. If not, then the problems we have sketched above will be aggravated.

The major issue is the level of family income. Will income beyond a certain level cause married women to leave the labor force? Lacking historical evidence on the correlation between participation rates and women's or family income, it is difficult to make any solid prediction. We know that in the midsixties the monthly income required for a family of four to have the basic material comforts was equal to the average wage of two full-time workers.[32] There is sufficient anecdotal evidence to indicate that Russians have hopes for consumption levels that exceed whatever "basic material comfort" might have meant in 1965.[33]

At any given level of job dissatisfaction, the marginal disutility of work rises as income rises, which may cause women to leave the labor force. This dissatisfaction can stem from several causes. First, there is the potential frustration of occupational segregation and the inability of women to enter occupations they view as desirable. Such segregation in the Soviet labor force has been well documented by a number of observers.[34] It has also been demonstrated that women work in the lowest paying areas of the economy.[35] A second source of dissatisfaction emerges from the judgments women make about their present work situation. One study of more than a thousand workers in Leningrad and Kostroma revealed that about one-fourth of the women were either "not satisfied" or were unsatisfied more often than not with their work. The main reasons for the dissatisfaction were the remoteness of their home from their place of work (29.3 percent), inconvenient shift (25.4 percent), and poor pay (15.1 percent).[36] In the United States about 2,000 job satisfaction surveys show a proportion of dissatisfied workers ranging from 10 to 21 percent.[37] A third source of frustration for women workers is the length of the workday. There is a well-known desire for part-time work which has been expressed any number of times in the press.[38] More will be said about this below.

Finally, there is the perpetual problem of child care and the disproportionate responsibility for performing this function borne by working mothers within the marriage. One aspect of the problem that has potentially negative implications for Soviet planners is in the child-care area, where the number of places in preschool institutions is either insufficient to handle the number of children in need of day care, or they are overcrowded.[39]

However, the case for maintenance of high female labor force participation seems persuasive. The first reason is that there is little evidence that future increases in income will not be accompanied by concomitantly rising expectations and future aspirations. In fact, the distance between attainment and aspirations could conceivably remain constant or even widen.[40] There is no a priori reason for expecting Soviet women to rush for home and hearth if family aspirations rise pari passu with income.

A second reason for supporting the hypothesis that the labor force participation rate of married women will remain constant is that there is a high correlation between the historical rise in the percentage of Soviet women working and the level of educational attainment.[41]

Third, if materialism drives the Soviet Union as it does Western countries, then we can look at the richest nations in the world to see what is likely to happen in the Soviet Union. If we look at the twenty-five nations with the highest per capita income and compare female participation rates in the 1960s and 1970s, in twenty of the countries, including the USSR, the labor force participation rate increased; in two other countries it remained the same; and in only three cases was there a decline in the labor force participation rate of women.[42]

Fourth, the direction of demographic trends suggests that (a) working women are less likely to have children, and (b) women do not want large families, a fact that also increases the convenience of remaining employed. Soviet data show a remarkable consistency in the inverse relationship between the birth rate and the percentage of women in the labor force of the union republics.[43] Additionally, there has been a continual decline in the percentage of families choosing to have a third child or more. In 1966, 38 percent of all births fell into this category, but this figure has declined in each subsequent year so that higher-order births in 1979 were only 23 percent of the total number born.[44]

Fifth, the high and rising divorce rate in the Soviet Union has a salutary effect in the short run. With the second highest divorce rate in the world at 3.6 per 1,000 population (next to the U.S. rate of 5.1 per 1,000), the pressure on single women, especially those with children, to remain in the labor force is quite strong. This is especially true of the urban areas. For example, in 1972, 86 percent of all the divorces in the country occurred in urban areas,[46] although only 59 percent of the population were urbanites. The highest divorce rates in the country are found in the major cities, Riga (6.7), Moscow (5.1), and Leningrad (5.6).[47] There is substantial evidence that divorce reduces the birth rate in the USSR[48] and therefore, in the long run, reduces the future labor pool.

When considering female labor force participation, one cannot ignore the factor of nationality. The percentage of able-bodied males in the labor force does not differ significantly among the fifteen republics that make up the USSR, but there are significant differences in female participation rates. About 94 percent of the women in the European republics are in the labor force, whereas in the Central Asian and Transcaucasian republics the participation rates are about 83 and 80 percent, respectively.[49] If any significant gains are to be made in adding to the urban labor force, they will have to come in the cities of the non-European republics.

Part-time Work

Notwithstanding the strong arguments for a continuation of the exceptionally high female labor force participation rate, there is pressure, particularly from women, for increasing the opportunities for part-time work. Indeed, the existence of part-time work represents a potential source for increasing the supply of urban labor. It will also be seen that while part-time employment represents a potential blessing for Soviet planners, it also has certain inherent drawbacks.

Soviet efforts at enlarging the labor pool through additional part-time workers are really a development of the last ten to fifteen years. Part-time work (*nepolnii rabochii den'*) is defined as an individual working less than the legal norm, where remuneration is proportional to the amount of time worked or is dependent on output produced.[50]

The amount of part-time work is relatively minuscule in the Soviet Union. For the nation as a whole, the proportion of all workers doing part-time work was 0.32 percent in 1974, 0.41 percent in 1976, and 0.32 percent in 1979. It was much higher in some of the service sectors of the economy: 1.02 percent in education and 1.9 percent in communications.[51] This is in vivid contrast to the United States, where the proportion of part-time workers (less than 35 hours work per week) has risen in the last two decades from 8 to 14 percent.[52] In 1961 part-time workers were about 9 percent of the total East German labor force.[53] In the Russian Republic in 1970, approximately 0.1 percent of all workers were employed at part-time work, a figure which rose by 1974 to 2.0 to 2.5 percent.[54]

A number of factors have contributed to keeping the use of part-time workers at a low level. A distinction has to be made between those already in the labor force as full-time workers who would like to become part-timers and those not currently in the labor force. From the point of view of economic planners, the latter group represents a welcome addition to their active labor resources. However, the idea that full-time workers might want to change their work status to part-time is a clear threat to the labor supply and the rate of economic growth. Soviet data show that if the government allowed 50 percent of the female labor force to have one additional free day every month, that would be the equivalent of an annual reduction of 950,000 workers for the USSR. A one-hour reduction of the workday of women would be the equivalent of an annual loss of 2.5 million workers.[55]

There are a number of reasons given by enterprise management for not increasing the availability of part-time work, but they all resolve to a concern for meeting the various plan targets. Most notably, labor productivity is often measured by dividing gross output by the average number of production personnel, and part-time personnel are counted in the same way as full-time employees.[56] This kind of accounting system creates a disincentive for management to hire part-timers since their presence can lower reported productivity. In addition, many enterprises have not set up part-time jobs or schedules that would accommodate part-time employment.[57]

In the household sector the major deterrent to the greater use of part-time work is, of course, the resulting decline in family income. The Soviet wage structure and its absolute level are designed to oblige both a husband and wife to work.

Having looked at the barriers that exist at the enterprise level and in the planning system, we turn now to examine why women want part-time work, how many of them want such work, and the socioeconomic groups from which they come. Two studies carried out about 1970 looked at what motivates women to work.[58] The results, shown in Table 1, are very similar. It is clear that the family's need for income is the overriding motive for working. Those who cited their need for independence (8.3 and 11.3 percent, respectively) are probably also associated, at least partially, with a desire for income.

Table 1
Urban Women's Motives for Working,
in %, circa 1970

	Iakova	Kharchev and Golod
Need for additional family income	53	53.5
Desire to be in a collective	24	21.5
Use of specialty for societal good	9	
Desire to be independent	8.3	
Desire to be independent of husband		11.4
Desire to participate in social labor		13.6

Sources: Z. A. Iakova, *Gorodskaia sem'ia* (Moscow, 1979), 50-51; A. G. Kharchev and S. I. Golod, *Professional'naia rabota zhenshchin i sem'ia* (Leningrad, 1971), 42.

A study was also conducted among part-time workers who had previously worked full-time. Somewhat more than half (53.3 percent) work because of the family's need for income; 32.1 percent because they want to work daily, function in a collective, or use their skills; and 12.1 percent were looking to acquire seniority to qualify for a pension.[59] Working women face different pressures than do men, all of which make part-time jobs more attractive to women. This is for two reasons: first, because of their responsibility for housework, and second, because of the presence of children. The importance of family obligations in reducing female participation in the labor force is verified by the fact that 61 percent of the nonworking women are under the age of 35.[60] It is contended that 8 to 9 percent of all able-bodied urban women are "lost" to the labor force because they have young children.[61] But the Estonian experience suggests the availability of part-time work attracts this group into the labor force. Within the Estonian Ministry of Light Industry, 74 percent of the part-time workers were women aged 21 to 40, and three-fourths of this group had shifted to a reduced work load because they had young children.[62] Nonetheless there is a fundamental and not adequately answered question: Would unemployed women with small children go to work faster if part-time work were readily available, or would they stay away from full-time work longer? At best, this is a difficult question to answer. The potential negative consequences of fewer full-time workers is probably a strong enough incentive for planners not to consider making part-time work more readily available.

We now consider the number of women who want to work part-time. Ninety percent of those who want part-time work in the Soviet Union are women.[62] Various Soviet studies confirm the strong interest in part-time work, although it is ambiguous whether the state would benefit. Some results suggest that individual welfare would be increased at the expense of the state's interest. For example, a survey of women workers in a Moscow watch factory and in a number of Moldavian enterprises revealed that about 6 to 12 percent of the women, mostly with either preschool or young school-age children, wanted to transfer to part-time work.[64] Among new brides 50 percent said they wanted to work part-time after the birth of their children.[65] In another group of nonworking women, 40 percent said they would be willing to take part-time work if it was offered to them, and another 16 percent said they would be willing to work at home. In half of these cases the women said their willingness to take part-time work was contingent on being able to place their children in a preschool establishment; another 9 percent said they needed a school with a prolonged day; and 27 percent said they needed a job nearer their home.[66] Thus a prerequisite for drawing women into employment is meeting their needs as mothers.

There is also some evidence for suggesting that the availability of part-time work benefits the state. Part-time working women were asked what they had planned to do if part-time work had not become available. Only 17 percent said they would have worked full-time, and 46 percent said they planned to stay out of the labor force. The study also indicated that about 70 percent of the women who formerly did full-time work and were currently doing part-time work would return to their previous work schedule. On the average, those women who leave full-time employment to care for an infant will do part-time work for four years and then return to full-time work.[67]

A second source for part-time work is old-age pensioners (OAPs). Those eligible for a pension are women over the age of 55 and men over the age of 59. The potential that the Soviets have in successfully recruiting OAPs continues to increase as the percentage of individuals of retirement age concomitantly increases. In 1950, 1960, and 1970 the proportion of the total population that had reached retirement age was 10.4, 12.4, and 15.4 percent, respectively. Estimates for 1980, 1990, and 2000 are 15.5, 17.6, and 19.2 percent.[68]

The proportion of working pensioners as a percentage of all pensioners has tended to move in response to the presence or absence of incentives in the pension system. As Table 2 shows, there was a dramatic decline after 1956 in the participation of OAPs in the labor force, which continued until 1965, when the participation rate began to rise steadily, so that by 1975 one-fourth of all OAPs were in the labor force.

The rise in participation rates is reflected in the increased relative importance of OAPs in the labor force. Table 3 shows that from 1960 to 1975, the percentage of OAPs in the total Soviet labor force rose from 0.8 to 4.3, constituting more than a fivefold increase. It should be pointed out that about 60 percent of recent retirees choose to remain in employment.[69] For purposes of analysis the watershed years are 1956, 1964, and 1970 because of the significant changes which took place in the pension law.

Table 2
Working Pensioners as a Percent of All Pensioners,
USSR, 1956-75 (full-time and part-time)

1956	59.0		1968	15.9
1957	28.6		1969	18.9
1958	19.2		1970	19.0
1959	15.1		1971	20.5
1960	11.7		1972	21.3
1964	10.1		1973	22.3
1965	12.5		1974	23.4
1966	14.0		1975	24.3
1967	15.2			

Sources: M. S. Lantsev, *Sotsial'noe obespechenie v SSSR* (Moscow, 1976), 127, 131 and 137.

Table 3
Old Age Pensioners as a Proportion of the
Total Soviet Labor Force, 1960-75

1960	0.8		1972	3.4
1965	1.3		1973	3.7
1970	2.8		1974	4.0
1971	3.2		1975	4.3

Sources: Table 1 and *Narodnoe khoziaistvo SSSR v 1975 g.* (Moscow, 1976), 531.

Further increases in the reward for continued employment may yield some benefits. In a study of nonworking OAPs, 24 percent indicated a desire to work part-time, 1.3 percent to work at home, and 9.9 percent would work full-time.[70] A more recent Belorussian study indicated that more than half of the employees who want to leave employment after receiving their pension could continue on the job if the work was part-time.[71]

While there are obvious increases in output to be gained by employing additional pensioners, there are certain productivity limitations. A 65-year-old person was usually educated somewhat before the period of World War II. Hence these individuals are the least skilled and educated part of the population, and their productivity is likely lower than workers educated in the post-Stalin era.

Student Workers

The final major group from which the Soviets can draw part-time workers is students. Their potential period of employment can be divided into work during the summer and work during the school year. In the past decade summer work appears to be numerically more important. In the early seventies most students in higher education institutions who worked usually did construction work in the countryside during the summer.[72] The summer of 1972 was the first one for which high school students were recruited. About three million worked for one month (July), usually on collective farms.[73]

The scant literature that exists on students working suggests that an inadequate effort has been made to recruit them for part-time work during the school year. In particular there are about six million full-time students, about equally divided between higher and technical higher education, who need money.[74] In fact, 75 percent of the students said that income was the main reason for doing part-time work. Half of all students are without a stipend during the school year, and some 13 percent have a family.[75] While Soviet higher education is nominally free, it is apparent that many need some sort of income if they are to survive financially while going to school.

It is certainly possible for the Soviets to increase the labor force by drawing additional workers into part-time work. However, it does not appear realistic to believe that significant inroads can be made on the urban labor shortage via this route. The labor force participation rate of women is already extremely high in urban areas. The only way that more women might be brought into the labor force would be if substantially greater investments were to be made in child-care facilities and in the production of home appliances to make it practical for more mothers of young children to work. There is some potential for increasing the share of OAPs in the labor force. However, there does not appear to be any published evidence as to how much more their activity rate can increase; there is certainly a maximum dictated by the state of health of the pensioners, which earlier evidence suggests is declining. Students currently are half of all part-time workers. In a nonagricultural labor force of 110 million, that would mean about 1.1 million students, or about 18 percent of the total, work part-time. If the employed student population were to rise to 25 percent of their present total number, then the number of full-time equivalents in the labor force would increase by 200,000. This appears to be the only group where major additions to the urban labor force can be made.

Commuters and Foreign Labor

There are two other alternatives used by other nations to expand their labor forces: commuting and the importation of foreign labor. Commuting is a technique that has been used to good advantage in many countries, including the USSR.[77] However, the evidence suggests that it is highly unlikely that the Soviets can stretch their use of commuting much further. This is due to the fact that commuting time and distances have continually increased as the resources in the areas most proximate to industrial centers were depleted. For example, in Moscow, which has a half-million in-commuters, it is not unusual for a worker to commute 35 to 40 miles to work. Even if the ring of feasible commuting could be extended, the negative consequences dampen the efficacy of such a goal. The results of travel fatigue are higher turnover, lower productivity, and more illness among long-distance commuters than among the general working population. The costs of commuting are not simply transferred to individual commuters; they redound to the state as well.

A policy to introduce foreign labor into the urban work force in a substantial way seems unlikely. It is only within the last decade that the Soviets have imported foreign workers into the general labor force.[78] They have used mainly East Europeans on such projects as the Orenburg pipeline. Outside of the bloc countries, only small numbers of workers have been used on specific projects such as the automobile factory at Togliatti. There are several problems that stand in the way of a greater use of foreign workers in urban areas. With respect to potential workers outside the bloc, there is the traditional Soviet xenophobia and the likely unwillingness to expose Soviet urbanites to "alien" ideas. Foreign labor is probably most appealing when it can be isolated from the indigenous population, something more difficult to do in cities than in rural areas. In addition it is not likely that planners would want to spend precious hard currency on workers' wages. Within the bloc the nonconvertibility of currency and the reluctance of others with labor supply problems are deterrents to making the flow of workers into the USSR an easy matter. As a result, the employment of foreign workers amounts to less than five one-hundredths of 1 percent, and the projections are that somewhere between 40,000 and 50,000 foreign workers will be employed on Soviet territory.[79]

Conclusion

We have come full circle to the original contention of this essay. It seems clear that Soviet planners have limited discretionary control over the urban labor force supply, given the current environment. We examined the labor shortage from two perspectives: the demographic constraints and the inefficient use of the existing urban labor supply.

From the demographic viewpoint all forecasts show declining additions to the Soviet labor force given the low birth rates of the past. This becomes even more aggravated given the lower birth rates that exist in urban areas relative to rural areas and the fact that the nation is becoming increasingly urbanized. Furthermore, population increases are taking place in the least urbanized republics, such as in Central Asia. All the evidence suggests that Central Asian Muslims are reluctant candidates for migration to urban areas. Indeed migration, which was such an important source of labor in Soviet cities during the early years of Soviet economic growth, has substantially declined in importance. This is due to the changing age structure of the rural population, which has aged and now encompasses both a less mobile and less well educated population. Even if migration should occur, the shortage of housing in Soviet cities would place a ceiling on the number who could feasibly be expected to move. The entire Soviet population has aged, but this is even more true of urban areas, especially the large urban centers. This has led to an increasing proportion of the urban population that will not be in the labor force.

Finally, Soviet health problems have affected the urban labor supply. These factors include falling life expectancy, a rise in infant mortality, and a rise in the crude death rate of all age groups, which means fewer workers in these groups.

Problems of inefficient resource allocation have compounded the demographic situation. Labor turnover is several times higher than in the United States or West Germany and costs the Soviet Union the equivalent of about 1.5 million workers a year. Soviet firms also retain a superfluous labor surplus, largely to cope with anticipated changes in the assortment plans and for periods of intense production activity. Soviet factories maintain a higher than desirable ratio of auxiliary to production workers. This relationship lowers the productivity of the labor force.

Part-time work is a little-used mechanism for coping with the urban shortage. Overwhelmingly, it is women who want such work, but Soviet figures indicate that the offering of part-time work on a broad scale to this group would reduce the female labor supply. The incentive system has been changed to draw old-age pensioners into the labor force, and the Soviets have succeeded here. It is possible, however, that they have reached the upper limit of the numbers that can be persuaded to continue working. The possibility of increasing the number of commuters seems very limited, and the use of extensive foreign labor appears to be out of the question.

These factors all converge to place a low ceiling on economic growth, with all the attendant negative outcomes that implies for the welfare of Soviet citizens and national security concerns.

Notes

[1]See Seweryn Bialer, "The Politics of Stringency in the USSR," *Problems of Communism* (May-June 1980), 19-33, and Abram Bergson, "Soviet Economic Slowdown and the 1981–85 Plan," *Problems of Communism* (May-June 1981), 24-36.

[2]Murray Feshbach, "The Structure and Composition of the Industrial Labor Force," in Arcadius Kahan and Blair A. Ruble (eds.), *Industrial Labor in the U.S.S.R.* (New York, 1979), 5.

[3]*Nash sovremennik* (June 1975), trans. in *Current Digest of the Soviet Press*, 32 (September 3, 1975), 1-5 (hereafter *CD*).

[4]Feshbach, 5.

[5]*Narodnoe khoziaistvo SSSR v 1980 g.*, 7 (hereafter *Narkhoz*).

[6]*Narkhoz 1970*, 48; *Narkhoz 1980*, 31.

[7]*Literaturnaia gazeta* (April 30, 1975); *CD*, 27, 18 (May 28, 1975), 1-4.

[8]Alfred J. DiMaio, Jr., "The Soviet Union and Population: Theory, Problems, and Population Policy," *Comparative Political Studies*, *13*, 1 (April 1980), 117. The Central Asian republics are the Uzbek, Kazakh, Kirghiz, Tadzhik, and Turkmen. The Slavic republics are Russia, the Ukraine, and Belorussia, and the Baltic republics are Latvia, Lithuania, and Estonia.

[9]Ibid., 119.

[10]Michael Rywkin, "Central Asia and Soviet Manpower," *Problems of Communism* (January-February 1979), 3.

[11]This discussion is drawn from Murray Feshbach, "Prospects for Outmigration from Central Asia and Kazakhstan in the Next Decade," *Soviet Economy in a Time of Change* (Washington, D.C., 1979), 656-89.

[12]The discussion on migration is drawn from Anatolii Vasilevich Topilin, *The Territorial Redistribution of Labor Resources in the USSR*, trans. in *Problems of Economics* (May 1980), 43-49.

[13]Unless otherwise noted, the discussion on the aging in Soviet cities is from Jeff Chinn, *Manipulating Soviet Population Resources* (New York, 1977), 56-66.

[14]*Narkhoz 1974*, 33.

[15]The empirical data in this section are drawn from Henry W. Morton, "The Soviet Quest for Better Housing—An Impossible Dream?" *Soviet Economy in a Time of Change*, 797.

[16]*Narkhoz 1980*, 392.

[17]The discussion about the Soviet health situation is drawn from Christopher Davis and Murray Feshbach, *Rising Infant Mortality in the U.S.S.R. in the 1970's*, U.S. Bureau of the Census, series P-95, 74 (September 1980), and Nick Eberstadt, "The Health Crisis in the USSR," *New York Review of Books* (February 19, 1981), 23-31.

[18]*Narkhoz 1980*, 31.

[19]Feshbach, 9.

[20]*Narkhoz*, various years.

[21]Wolfgang Teckenberg, "Labour Turnover and Job Satisfaction: Indicators of Industrial Conflict in the USSR?" *Soviet Studies*, *30*, 2 (April 1978), 194.

[22]*Employment and Training Report of the President* (Washington, D.C., 1981), 224.

[23]Teckenberg, 195.

[24]This discussion of labor turnover is drawn from David E. Powell, "Labor Turnover in the Soviet Union," *Slavic Review* (June 1977), 272-73.

[25]Ibid., 271-73.

[26]David A. Dyker, "Planning and the Worker," in Leonard Schapiro and Joseph Godson (eds.), *The Soviet Worker: Illusions and Realities* (New York, 1981), 40; Henry W. Morton, "Who Gets What, When and How? Housing in the Soviet Union," *Soviet Studies*, *32*, 2 (April 1980), 237-39.

[27]This discussion is drawn from E. L. Manevich, "Manpower Shortages and Reserves," *Problems of Economics* (December 1978), 4, 6-7.

[28]Joseph Berliner, *The Innovation Decision in Soviet Industry* (Cambridge 1976), 166; the quit rate is the percentage of the labor force quitting a job.

[29]The discussion of the Shchekino method is drawn from *Sovetskaia Estonia* (September 18, 1968), *CD*, *20*, 40 (October 23, 1968), 13; *Pravda* (March 28-29, 1977), *CD*, *29*, 13 (April 27, 1977), 14-16; *Pravda* (July 26, 1978), *CD*, *20*, 30 (August 23, 1978), 24; Manevich, 9-10.

[30]This discussion is from Feshbach, 8, and Manevich, 7.

[31]On the subject of labor exchanges, see Phillip Grossman, "The Soviet Government's Role in Allocating Industrial Labor," in Kahan and Ruble, 52, and Dyker, 42-43.

[32]G. S. Sarkisian and N. P. Kuznetsova, *Potrebnosti i dokhod sem'i* (Moscow, 1967), 56, 66.

[33]See, for example, Hedrick Smith, *The Russians* (New York, 1976), passim.

[34]See, for example, Gail Warshofsky Lapidus, "Occupational Segregation and Public Policy: A Comparative Analysis of American and Soviet Patterns," *Signs*, *1*, 3, part 2 (Spring 1976), 119-36.

[35]William Moskoff, "An Estimate of the Soviet Male-Female Income Gap," *The ACES Bulletin*, *16*, 2 (Fall 1974), 21-31.

[36]A. G. Kharchev and S. I. Golod, *Professional'naia rabota zhenshchin i sem'ia* (Leningrad, 1971), 45.

[37]Cited in Sanford Cohen, *Issues in Labor Policy* (Columbus, Ohio, 1977), 82.

[38]*Pravda* (January 3, 1975), *CD*, *27*, 5 (February 26, 1975), 23-24.

[39]*Pravda* (September 26, 1976), *CD*, *27*, 39 (October 27, 1976), 3; *Pravda* (April 5, 1974), *CD*, *26*, 14 (May 1, 1974), 9-10.

[40]The full implications of this possibility have been set forth in Julian L. Simon, "Interpersonal Welfare Comparisons Can Be Made—And Used for Redistribution Decisions," *Kyklos*, 24 (1974), 69.

[41]*Zhurnalist* (March 1975), *CD*, *27*, 23 (July 2, 1975), 9-10; Gail Warshofsky Lapidus, "USSR Women at Work: Changing Patterns," *Industrial Relations*, *14*, 2 (May 1975), 182.

[42]*The Morgan Guaranty Survey* (February 1978), 8; *ILO Yearbook of Labour Statistics* (Geneva), 1970 and 1977.

[43]*Narkhoz za 60 let* (1977), 70, 470.

[44]*Narkhoz 1979*, 37.

[45]*Narkhoz 1979*, 2; *Statistical Abstract of the United States* (Washington, D.C., 1979), 60.

[46]Iu. A. Korolev, *Brak i razvod* (Moscow, 1978), 186.

[47]L. V. Chuiko, *Braki i razvody* (Moscow, 1975), 131.

[48]Jeff Chinn, *Manipulating Soviet Population Resources* (London, 1977) 112-14.

[49]Steven Rapawy, *Estimates and Projections of the Labor Force and Civilian Employment in the U.S.S.R. 1950 to 1990*, U.S. Department of Commerce (September 1976), 7.

[50]"O metodischeskikh rekomendatsiiakh po izucheniiu istochnikov i vozmozhnostei privlecheniia naseleniia na rabotu s nepolnym rabochim vremenem," *Normativnye akty po ispol'zovanii trudovykh resursov* (Moscow, 1972), 578.

[51]I. Golubeva and L. Kuleshova, "Ispol'zovanie rezhimov nepolnogo rabochego vremeni i optimizatsiia uchastiia zhenshchin v proizvodstve," *Sotsialisticheskii trud*, 4 (1978), 106; T. Skal'berg, E. Martirosian, and L. Kuleshova, "Rabota s nepolnym rabochim dnem—vazhnoe sredstvo privlecheniia trudovykh resursov," *Sotsialisticheskii trud*, 2 (1977), 105.

[52]*Employment and Training Report of the President* (1978), 85.

[53]Skal'berg et al., 103.

[54]A. E. Kotliar and S. Ia. Turchaninova, *Zaniatost' zhenshchin v proizvodstve* (Moscow, 1975), 102.

[55]A. M. Iuk, *Trud zhenshchiny i sem'ia* (Minsk, 1975), 123.

[56]*Izvestia* (April 13, 1972), *CD*, *24*, 15 (May 10, 1972), 19.

[57]*Sovetskoe gosudarstvo i pravo* (October 1970), *CD*, *28*, 45 (December 8, 1976), 22.

[58]Z. A. Iakova, *Gorodskaia sem'ia* (Moscow, 1979), 50-51; Kharchev and Golod, 42.

[59]A. Novitskii and M. Babkina, "Part-time Work and Employment," *Problems of Economics*, *16*, 9 (January 1974), 45.

[60]Golubeva and Kuleshova, 107.

[61]*Nedelia* (August 8-14, 1977), *24*, 32 (September 7, 1977), 5-6.

[62]Skal'berg et al., 105.

[63]Kotliar and Turchaninova, 98.

[64]Ibid., 99.

[65]L. Anikeeva and L. Shokhina, "Zhenshchiny s det'mi i nadomny trud," in *Zhenschiny na rabote i doma* (Moscow, 1978), 49.

[66]Golubeva and Kuleshova, 106.

[67]Ibid.

[68]Murray Feshbach and Steven Rapawy, "Soviet Population and Manpower Trends and Policies," *Soviet Economy in a New Perspective* (Washington, D.C., 1976), 115.

[69]*Izvestia* (January 6, 1976), *CD*, *28*, 1 (February 4, 1976), 18.

[70]Novitskii and Babkina, 42.

[71]*Izvestia* (July 26, 1977), *CD*, *29*, 30 (August 24, 1977), 16.

[72]"Studentam, ubiraiuschim urozhai," *Trud* (June 30, 1972), 14.

[73]Iu. Viktorov,"Tretii i semestr studentov," *Trud* (July 23, 1971), 1.

[74]A. Novichev, "I student i dvornik," *Literaturnaia gazeta* (August 30, 1978), 12.

[75]Novitskii and Babkina, 46.

[76]Ibid., 45-66.

[77]The discussion of commuting is drawn from Roland J. Fuchs and George J. Demko, "Commuting in the USSR," *Soviet Geography: Review and Translation, 19*, 6 (June 1978), 363-72.

[78]For material relating to the use of foreign labor within the USSR, see Feshbach and Rapawy, "Soviet Population and Manpower Trends and Policies," 128-30; Friedrich Levcik, "Migration and Employment of Foreign Workers in Comecon Countries and Their Problems," *Eastern European Economics 16*, 1 (Fall 1977), 3-33.

[79]Levcik, 14, 16-17.

——————————————Peter H. Juviler——————————————

5

——The Urban Family and the Soviet State:——
——————————Emerging Contours of a——————————
——————————Demographic Policy——————————

City Progress and Problems

Marxist and Soviet theorists share the widespread Western prourbanism also expressed in Lenin's oft-quoted view that "cities are the center of a people's economic, political, and cultural life and the leaders of progress."[1]

Whatever their own conceptions of progress may be, villagers in European parts of the USSR tend to share this positive view of cities. Parents surveyed in Briansk Province "would rather send a son or daughter to the city at any price than see them remain in their native village . . . more than 80 percent of the parents polled, . . . believe that their children are better off seeking their 'fortune' in the city."[2]

Cities, especially the big ones of a half million, million, or more population, have led the way in postwar recovery toward "higher standards of living, more free time, more opportunity for cultural activities, and an individual's well-rounded development."[3] They are the best place, it would seem, for parents to carry out their obligation "to raise worthy members of a socialist society"[4] and to meet the needs of economic development for new cadres to carry on the "scientific and technological revolution." But as A. G. Kharchev and other specialists on the family point out, "The progress of science and technology has at the same time engendered consequences not only favoring the family, but some also complicating its stabilization and creating a number of contradictions and difficulties. . . ."[5] The symptoms of this are lower birth rates and higher divorce rates than the government would like to see. The contributions of family instability and infertility to the long-standing demographic problem of labor shortages are amplified by regional demographic maldistribution and recent rises in mortality, especially of infants and males. Soviet demographers are straightforward about the fact that urban families are at the center of a demographic shortfall of growing urgency centered on the large cities but spreading beyond them, featuring

> a decline in birth rates, a change to preference for a
> family with one or two children, the aging of the population,
> an increased male mortality rate, changes in marital
> structure, a rise in divorce, etc. One may assume that it is in
> large cities that standards of demographic behavior form
> which then spread to other types of settlement.[6]

I am indebted to Professor Robert Osborn and the editors for their comments on the draft of this chapter.

Soviet experts on population and the family debated for years whether the lower birth rates and higher divorce rates posed a problem and what should be done about it. The disagreement apparently continues.[7] But an official policy has emerged for now, at least. The future labor supply *is* considered threatened; the family infertility, instability, and recently growing mortality are documented; but these "contradictions and difficulties," as Kharchev called them, are depicted as not inherent in socialist urbanization and surmountable under conditions of Soviet socialism. To overcome them, it is acknowledged, will take "a comparatively long time and an active and effective demographic policy."[8]

What has been happening to the urban family, its background, and governmental responses to it are the topics of this chapter.

Infertility and instability are not new in the Soviet urban family. They caused the Stalinist regime to launch the first Soviet pronatalist drive, a heavily compulsive one. It emerged in 1936 and 1944 as a ban on both abortions and legal recognition of extramarital paternity, even when acknowledged by the father, plus very difficult and expensive divorce procedures, tinged with pittances to unwed mothers, allowances and awards to mothers of large families topped by the order of "Mother Heroine," and more day-care places. Post-Stalin legislation between 1955 and 1974 lifted the abortion ban, simplified divorce, recognized extramarital paternal responsibility under some conditions, and continued to emphasize parental and spousal responsibility to try to "strengthen the family" while increasing family welfare through expanded pensions, leaves, allowances, and day care. But all these welfare measures were piecemeal doses and not a new, sharp wave of pronatalism as under Stalin.[9]

This chapter proceeds now to recapitulate recent trends in urban and rural birth rates. There follows a sketch of regional variations and patterns of migration and population distribution; mortality rates in the context of the urban environment; and the transformation of the family during urbanization, with its special impact on women. What have been the regime's responses to family breakdown and unfavorable demographic trends? Has it adopted a comprehensive new family and demographic policy? What are the prospects for the success of new regime measures and their implications for the frequently shifting relationship between the urban family and the Soviet state?

Urbanization and Birth Rates

During six decades of the USSR the share of urbanites in the populace has gone from about 18 to 63 percent, as Table 1 shows. Birth rates, too, fell steadily from a recorded peak of 44 in 1936 to a low point of 17 in 1969 and a plateau of about 18 in the 1970s and early 1980s. As in other developed countries, industrialization and urbanization have taken the Soviet Union from high birth rates and mortality to low birth rates and mortality, with an overall plunge in natural increase (the increase due to the surplus of births over deaths).[10]

Lacking huge foreign immigration, as in the United States, or vast reserves of foreign "guest workers," as in Western Europe, industrial and accompanying urban growth in the USSR have had to draw on the once-overpopulated villages.

Table 1

Russian and Soviet Vital Statistics

Year	Births	Deaths	Natural increase	Urban births	Rural births	Ratio: rural to urban births	Fertility		ratio: rural/urban	Population		% urban
							urban	rural		urban (mil.)	rural (mil.)	
1913	45.5	29.1	16.4	30.2	48.4	1.62				28.3	130.7	18
1926	44.0	20.3	23.7	34.1	46.1	1.35						
1937	38.7	18.9	19.8									
1940	31.2	18.0	13.2	30.5	31.5	1.03				63.1	131.0	33
1950	26.7	9.7	17.0	26.0	27.1	1.04				69.4	109.1	39
1960	24.9	7.1	17.8	21.9	27.8	1.27				103.6	108.8	49
1965	18.4	7.3	11.1	16.1	21.1	1.31	57[a]	90.4[a]	1.59	120.7	108.9	53
1969	17.0	8.1	8.9	15.6	18.7	1.20	55.7[b]	82.3[b]	1.48	132.9	106.6	55
1970	17.4	8.2	9.2	16.4	18.7	1.14	57.1[c]	83.5[c]	1.46	136.0	105.7	56
1975	18.1	9.3	8.8	17.2	19.6	1.14	59.3[d]	86.6[d]	1.46	151.9	101.4	60
1979	18.2	10.1	8.1	17.0	20.4	1.20	60.5[e]	91.9[e]	1.52	163.6	98.8	62
1980	18.3	10.3	8.0	17.0	20.4	1.20				168.9	97.7	63

Note: For fertility, the rates show live births per 1,000 women aged 15-49. Years for births, deaths, and natural increases are selected. Urban and rural births, 1937, not available. Ratios are calculated. All years except 1926 and 1937 within contemporary boundaries of the USSR. a. for 1965-66. b. for 1969-70. c. for 1970-71. d. for 1975-76. e. for 1979-80.

Sources: *Narodnoe khoziaistvo SSSR v 1972 godu* (Moscow, 1973), 7, 46, 47; *Narodnoe khoziaistvo SSSR v 1980 godu* (Moscow, 1981), 7, 31; *Vestnik statistiki*, 12 (1971), 74; 12 (1973), 75; 12 (1977), 75; 1 (1981), 71.

The exit of young people caused an aging population, with lower birth rates than otherwise would have been recorded. The political violence of civil war and famine, the devastating collectivization of agriculture, and World War II took their deep, unfathomable toll.[11] Rural birth rates fell sharply after the 1920s to the urban level or perhaps below—we may never know. Scant breakdowns of rural and urban birth rates show that by 1940 the rural level was only 3 percent above the urban. After World War II rural birth rates kept falling but still drew ahead of urban ones. The roughly 20 percent spread in rural and urban birth rates distorts the demographic picture as much as it reveals it.

Young rural families remain considerably larger and more fertile than their urban counterparts are. Since 1965, as the data of Table 1 show, both urban and rural fertility have held up when measured in numbers of children born per 1,000 women 15 to 49 years old. Village mothers tend to have about 50 percent more children than do city ones. This is concealed by the aging of the rural population owing to emigration to the city.[12] The average rural birth rates are lower than rural fertility. But they are still higher than urban rates, concealing the fact that, also owing to emigration from villages to towns, the villages over vast areas of the USSR are losing population while the cities grow, even if at a diminished pace. Between 1965 and 1979 the rural population *dropped* by 10.2 million and the urban population rose 42.5 million.[13] City growth from migration has as a rule substantially exceeded growth from births.[14]

Rural-urban migration has changed the share of persons living in urban families from less than half of all persons living with their families in 1959 to 60 percent, as Table 2 shows. The ratio of urban to rural family dwellers has nearly doubled. By 1981 nearly two-thirds of close to 70 million Soviet families (66.3 million in 1979) and over 63 percent of all Soviet people lived in urban areas.[15]

Urban areas range from small new settlements huddled around construction sites to centuries-old cities, many now agglomerations. These large cities of a half-million and more are growing at faster rates than are small cities, despite governmental restraints implemented through the system of internal passports and police residence permits.[16] Moscow's population has doubled since 1939, to 8,203,000 on January 1, 1980.[17]

Table 2
The Proportion of Urban and Rural Family Members in the Total of All Family Members Living with Their Families (percent) in 1959, 1970 and 1979 (percent)

Year	Urban family members	Rural family members	Ratio of urban to rural family members
1959	47	53	.89
1970	55	45	1.22
1979	60	40	1.50

Sources: Calculated from (1959) *Itogi vsesoiuznoi perepisi naseleniia 1959 goda: SSSR* (svodnyui tom)(Moscow, 1962), 240; (1970) *Itogi vsesoiuznoi perepisi naseleniia 1970 goda.* VII (Moscow, 1974), 186; *Vestnik statistiki*, 12 (1980), 59.

Alongside the economic and social effects of the Soviet Union's industrial and political revolutions, then, urbanization through migration is closely associated with the declines in Soviet family fertility and the emergence of the one- or two-child family as the norm over much of the USSR.

Regional Variations

Both regional patterns of birth rates and the directions in which families and single persons choose to migrate contribute to a population distribution which adds to the effect of the present labor shortages. The republics with lowest birth rates, as Table 3 shows, are the most industrialized and labor-short and have hinterlands with the lowest rural birth rates and the greatest depletion of population. Small families predominate in the roughly 80 percent of the population concentrated in the republics of low and moderate birth rates.[18] The regional maldistribution (economically speaking) of population depletion and plenty shows up in Table 3. Moving from low to moderate and high birth rates, birth rates in republic capitals increase; but the birth rates in the republics as a whole increase very much more, from slightly higher than their capital's (or even less in Belorussia and the Ukraine) to between 50 and 70 percent higher in Central Asia, where the surplus population is least needed and least likely to migrate out of villages.[19] Currently the issue is unresolved of whether to bring more industry to Central Asia or to try to lure Central Asians to where industry is now located. This is quite apart from the still unclear political implications of the steady increase in the percentage of Moslem (origin) population and the steady decrease in the percentage of Russian and other European nationalities.[20]

Table 3
Birthrates by Union Republics and Capitals, 1980.
(in live births per their 1,000 inhabitants)

| | Low birthrates | | | Moderate birthrates | | | High birthrates | |
	republic	capital		republic	capital		republic	capital
RSFSR	15.9	13.6	Kazakhstan	23.8	17.8	Uzbekistan	33.8	19.2
Ukraine	14.8	15.6	Azerbaidzhan	25.2	18.5	Kirghizia	29.6	19.8
Belorussian	16.0	18.8	Moldavia	20.0	18.2	Tadzhikistan	37.0	21.9
Georgia	17.7	15.1	Armenia	22.7	19.6	Turkmenia	34.3	22.4
Lithuania	14.0	12.9						
Latvia	14.0	12.9						
Estonia	15.0	14.6						

Sources: *Vestnik statistiki*, 12 (1981), 63 (capitals); *Narodnoe khoziaistvo SSSR v 1980 godu* (Moscow, 1981), 33 (republics).

The regional flow of migration does not compensate for this regional maldistribution of fertility to the satisfaction of the Soviet leadership. Brezhnev, briefed with information from demographers, whom, we shall see, he had put to pondering demographic policy, pointed out to the Twenty-sixth Party Congress in 1981 what many delegates must already have known about migration: that "people prefer to move from north to south and from east to west, although rational distribution of productive resources requires movement in the opposite direction," while "on the contrary, there is a surplus population in Central Asia and a number of districts of Kazakhstan," which is staying put.[21]

Mortality in the Urban Environment

Socialist urbanization means, according to the Communist Party's "Manifesto of Developed Communism," following the example of the big cities.[22] They have been pulling ever farther ahead of the lower-priority backwater towns in available housing, medical facilities, libraries, movie house seats, and per capita retail trade[23]—ahead of those old Russian towns that Konstantin Paustovsky once lovingly described as "almost always very pretty, these cities, picturesque, cozy, full of healing peace and quiet."[24] They have moved ahead also, though, as the Soviet sources tell us, in the damaging strain and pollution of city life, apparently contributing substantially to recent rises in mortality rates.

Mortality rates dropped for many years along with birth rates. But then in the mid-1960s adult mortality began to increase until, according to the statistics for 1975-76, mortality, in rates of death per 1,000 persons in a given age group, had risen for every age group except 15-19. Mortality, which had been 3.9 per 1,000 for persons aged 40 to 44 in 1965-66, reached 5.3 per 1,000 in 1975-76. No more age-specific mortality figures have appeared since then.[25]

Infant mortality (death rates of newborn children up to one year old per 1,000 live births) began to rise after 1971. That year it was at a reported low of 22.9, down from 181.5 in 1940. By 1974 it was up to 27.9.[26] After 1974 publication of infant mortality rates stopped. They have been estimated by Davis and Feshbach at 31.1 in 1976, more than twice the U.S. rate. A Soviet official in charge of demographic statistics for the State Planning Commission attributed rises in reported infant mortality to improved statistical reporting, especially from border areas like Central Asia. But his figure, 28 since 1978, is still far higher than are rates of most developed countries. Moreover, Soviet figures actually need to be multiplied by 1.144 to make them comparable with figures from other countries using an international standard definition of infant mortality.[27] Whatever grief and losses infant mortality has caused, they are small numerically compared with the millions of intentional family limitations by abortion (see p. 93).

What has mortality to do with the demographic behavior of the urban family?

First, secular increases in mortality, both infant and adult, such as have occurred recently in the USSR, even if below the estimates just cited, are unprecedented in industrialized countries. They may signal a decline in family health and medical care. According to a Soviet source, infant mortality rates are "leading indicators of a county's health . . . social and economic development, its people's material well-being and state of medical care, especially for children and mothers."[28] Second, although infant mortality is higher in rural areas than in cities and in non-European areas than in European ones, available Soviet data indicate that the recent increases in mortality of infants and adults originated primarily in urban areas.[29] The increases have to do with the physical environment of the urban family, its way of life, and the medical care available to it, judging from both Western and Soviet comment.

Environmental pollution associated with industrial areas and cities has been especially harmful during the flu epidemics of the sort that hit the USSR annually during the 1970s. Pollution increases the possibility that flu will turn into pneumonia, the chief killer of infants.[30] A Soviet survey of city-dwelling parents' responses to their children's illnesses concluded that the frequent illnesses of the first child, aggravated by pollution, drain the health, strength, and patience of parents, especially of the mothers, on whom falls the main onus of nursing the sick children, and may discourage them from having any more children.[31]

A new form of pollution is low-level atomic radiation. There is no consensus on what level of radiation harms people.[32] But one U.S. researcher has concluded from regional infant mortality data abroad and in the United States that low-level atomic radiation fallout, such as from atomic power plant leaks like the one at Three Mile Island on March 28, 1979, increases infant mortality. (Damage to the fetal thyroid caused by radioactive iodine from fallout tends to slow growth of the fetus, thus increasing the chances of a newborn baby's death.) He points out the coincidence between rises in Soviet atomic power plant capacity since 1969 and infant mortality year by year. If this finding is correct, atomic fallout from nuclear power will be demographically significant for Soviet cities and their surrounding regions. The installed capacity of atomic power plants close to cities in European Russia increased twenty-two times between 1969 and 1979.[33] The present generating capacity of Soviet atomic power plants is slated to triple during the Eleventh Five-Year Plan, 1981–85, with plants springing up like mushrooms across the country.[34] No mass "antinuke" movements can exist in the USSR; no outcry against the possible perils of atomic power has been tolerated. But leading Soviet texts on urban problems time and again list "ionizing radiation" or "new sources of energy" among such hazards associated with environmental damage as birth defects, genetic mutations, and infant mortality.[35]

Ideologically, the Soviets treat environmental hazards to the urban family in the USSR as temporary "survivals" not inherent in socialism.[36] The empirical part of Soviet analyses of urban life is much franker. Deterioration of the urban environment is depicted by M. S. Bednyi, a pioneer in Soviet medical demography, as having contributed to such existing "serious population problems" as maldistribution and slow growth. Virtually every Soviet work on urban ecology now cites health hazards in urban life: the pace, strain, pollution, injuries, and bad habits of sedentary work, eating, and hard drinking. Cardiovascular diseases, hypertension, chemical poisoning, cancer, and traumas associated with the urban environment as well as with aging have relaced the once rampant infectious diseases like polio, typhus, and cholera as leading killers and maimers. Dr. Bednyi pleads urgently for stronger measures to protect present and future generations from the health damage that can be inflicted by an otherwise progressive "scientific and technological revolution":

> Chemicalization, automatization, automobilization, the deterioration of the natural environment, radiation, the quickening rhythms and tempos of life, information and psychological overloads, and many other factors accompanying the scientific and technological revolution very obviously call for countermeasures.[37]

This is because, Bednyi says, they have "an exceptionally powerful and all-embracing effect on the health of the entire population."[38] Rising rates of mental illness and congenital diseases as well as of mortality all appear to be associated with the health hazards of industrialization.[39]

Males, according to Soviet findings, are especially vulnerable to the health hazards of urban industrialization, be it due to their lower resistance than that of females, the nature of their work, or their heavy drinking and its consequences of liver and other ailments as well as drink-connected injuries and deaths.[40] The gap between women's and men's life expectancies widened from 7.4 years in 1958–59 to 10 years in 1970. Life expectancy was 64 for men but 74 for women in 1971–72, the last years for which figures have been published.[41] Bednyi estimates that 7.9 years of the ten-year gap between male and female life expectancies are environmentally caused; only 2.1 years of the difference in life expectancies may be attributed to biological differences between the sexes.[42]

Male mortality is emerging not only as a direct drain on labor power but also as a factor lowering family fertility, which is the reason for mentioning it here. Thus A. G. Volkov, head of the Department of Demography of the Research Institute of the Central Statistical Administration, reports 23.2 million marriages between 1970 and 1979 and 6.8 million divorces. But the increase in married couples between 1970 and 1979 was less than the difference between marriages and divorces by eight million, which thus is the number of marriages broken up by death of a spouse. Twice as many male spouses died as female, or 5.3 million males. Thus deaths of male spouses alone rivaled divorces as a breaker of families.[43] Many of the deaths of spouses occurred during child-bearing periods. Moreover, as will be discussed under "Divorce" (see p. 95), wives are much less likely to remarry than are husbands.

Alcoholism is rising among women as well as among men as a demographically significant factor in parents' way of life. Alcohol abuse is associated with birth defects and infant mortality and probably plays a significant part in their recent rises. Lack of data in the past has prevented conclusions about women's smoking,[44] but it too may well contribute to the rise. Recently a Soviet medical researcher wrote about women's smoking that "mothers who smoke give birth to twice as many babies who weigh under 2.5 kilograms as do nonsmoking mothers. Doctors usually wear themselves out with these babies, who are weak and vulnerable.'' He reports that men smokers outnumber women 63 to 31 among workers and 57 to 36 among middle-level professional employees, but that women smokers outnumber men now by 46 to 31 at the higher professional levels.[45] The number of women working at these higher professional and higher smoking levels increased 63 percent during the 1970s.[46]

Changes in parents' living patterns may contribute to increases in infant mortality and birth defects. As more housing becomes available, more grandparents live apart from their children and grandchildren. Increasingly, day care replaces *babushka*. Every year recently about 500,000 more children have been going to nurseries and kindergartens, for one reason or another.[47] This shift from home care to day care increases the probability of disease and death because infection rates are higher among day-care children than they are among children tended at home.

A move among mothers from breast to formula feeding has appeared that also apparently raises risks of infant illness due to contamination of the bottle feed, of malnutrition because of defective formula, and therefore of infections, especially respiratory ones. Such infections, plus the complications caused by pollution and in conjunction with the flu epidemics already mentioned, contribute to rising infant mortality.

Of great importance here, most likely, is the poor and apparently deteriorating quality of Soviet health care, evidence of which abounds for the English-speaking reader in the translations from Soviet reports carried by the *Current Digest of the Soviet Press*.[48] Brezhnev gave high-level substance to this evidence at the Twenty-sixth Party Congress. He noted, alongside gains, instances of personnel shortages, especially shortages of nurses and orderlies, obsolete equipment, lack of medicine, lags in hospital construction, the inattentiveness of ''certain medical personnel,'' and their ''violation of their medical obligations.''[49]

The Family Transformed

Urbanization has transformed the Soviet family itself as well as its environment, although not according to the original radical communist blueprints that would have stripped the family of its social functions. The key continuity with the old days is that reproduction still involves the responsibilities of child rearing. But the material and psychological sides of the family—its economy, values, and motivations—have changed drastically along with urbanization, and in ways which underlie, as in other industrialized countries, the slump in birth rates depicted in Table 1. As a Soviet sociologist puts it, two-thirds of the Soviet populace live in urban areas, and one-third in big cities. And it is on conditions there that the natural increase in the Soviet population will increasingly depend and hence the availability of much needed labor resources. Yet urban families most frequently have only one child. Their small size and the resultant shortfalls in population reproduction among urban families reflect the basic economic and psychological changes brought about by industrialization and urbanization.[50]

During the course of this century the three generations of the formerly extended Soviet family have lost their binding economic value to one another.[51] A combination of industrialization and coercion have taken away the family workshop, the family store, the family business, and the family farm (save for the subsidiary garden plot). The generations are drawn apart as parents and children go to work or train away from home. Grandparents get retirement pensions. The family as a whole looks to the public sector for support—legal or illegal. This is not to say that there are no support functions within the family, such as feeding, clothing, child support—some enforced by law. It means, rather, that children have become consumers rather than helpers. Their grandparents and parents form no working unit. The ties remain; grandparents often help their own children cope as parents, but from the greater distance of a separate dwelling. The traditional values supportive of large and stable families prevail only among non-Europeans, concentrated in Central Asia and parts of the Caucasus and the RSFSR.

Family values have changed most of all among women. Their determination, in European parts of the USSR, to limit themelves typically to one or two children shows up in their steady resort to abortions, the main form of contraception in the USSR. Western estimates have placed Soviet abortion rates at 2.5 to 3 per live birth for the USSR as a whole in 1965 and about 2.2 per live birth in 1973, or 10 million abortions for 4.5 million live births. This is the highest rate in the world.[52]

Moreover, during the five-year plans, women's education and employment have reached levels on a par with men's, in terms of numbers if not of job status.[53] And the higher the rate of women's employment, the lower birth rates have dropped. Women work outside the home not only because many have to but also because by now most women want to, savoring their development and associations at work and their financial independence as well. The process would appear irreversible, at least in the near future.[54]

Family sizes are smallest among people with the most education, skill, and mobility, living in the largest industrial and cultural centers. Over and again Soviet demographers depict these urbanites as the best equipped culturally but the least likely to raise children for the future society. They are nowhere near reproducing themselves.[55] The average number of children born to a sample of women of child-bearing age in Kazan was 2.2 for women with up to seven grades of schooling, 1.59 for women with higher education, and 1.46 for women with advanced degrees.[56] The number of children already born and expected by families in the USSR averages about 2.4; in Moscow, though, it is 1.6, Leningrad 1.7, Minsk 2.1, and Tashkent 2.8 (but it is 6.1 in the villages of Uzbekistan outside Tashkent).[57] Census data for 1979 on the fertility of women of various educational levels, for the USSR and the union republics, fully confirm this inverse relation between education and willingness to have children.[58]

Women's taxing "second shift" as the main homemakers confronts them daily with the inadequacies of services for the family. As Table 4 shows, plans for appliance repairs, laundering, and dry cleaning get fulfilled, but largely in services to institutional customers rather than to individual families. Topping the list of twenty stated causes of dissatisfaction with the environment in the city of Kazan (population 607,000 in 1959 and 1,002,000 in 1980) were availability of food (71.1 percent of respondents dissatisfied), mass transit (60.53 percent), urban maintenance of greenery, roads, and housing (57.56 percent), the variety and quality of dining services (53.08 percent), and the quality of work done by tailors, laundries, cleaners, etc. (35.1 percent).[59]

Table 4
Percent Fulfillment of Annual Plan (1) and Percent of Services Rendered to Individual Customers (2), Selected Republic Capitals, 1978

	Repair of appliances		Repair of radio and TV		Dry cleaning and dyeing		Laundry	
	1	2	1	2	1	2	1	2
Moscow	100.3	33.3	104.4	76.1	100.4	93.4	100.3	40.3
Kiev	102.7	17.0	100.1	28.9	103.2	92.5	92.7	33.6
Tashkent	103.5	54.9	102.3	40.8	100.4	80.7	1201.2	9.9
Dushanbe	120.6	66.5	148.7	44.8	24.5	79.6	112.2	7.6
Riga	111.9	25.6	102.2	38.0	101.9	86.1	94.8	31.3

Sources: *Vestnik statistiki*, 12 (1981), 63 (capitals); *Narodnoe khoziaistvo SSSR v 1980 godu* (Moscow, 1981), 33 (republics).

Atommash, an atomic power plant equipment factory, provides an example of everyday difficulties for families even at important sites. The construction of the factory, in Volgodonsk, Rostov Province, has been lagging behind schedule. But construction of preschool institutions, stores, public dining rooms, schools, Pioneer camps, and other services has lagged another 70 percent more behind the lagging rates of plant building. *Pravda* correspondents report that a family lives in Volgodonsk not as in a city but as in "a vast dormitory. Everyday amenities have not been provided." Volgodonsk had 26,000 inhabitants and "all the necessities of life" before construction of Atommash. "Today the population here is almost 150,000, and it is no longer a city but a clump of residential buildings." The number of social, cultural, and service institutions is so small that there are lines of people at all points from morning to evening. The deputy personnel director gave an example of the reasons for high labor turnover at the plant: why during the first three months of 1981, 4,977 people arrived at the construction project and almost 3,000 left. Five years before, a highly skilled worker brought his family to Volgodonsk, on doctors' recommendation, so that his sickly son could recuperate in a better climate. The son is in robust health. But his wife is unhappy. She still could not go to work because "the child couldn't be placed in a kindergarten, the school was also crowded, there was no Young Pioneer camp, and none was envisaged." So the family moved somewhere else where "daily living conditions were better suited to modern people." The plant lost a valuable worker.

Though kindergarten groups in Volgodonsk are twice as large as the health norm, there are still 7,000 children waiting to get in. Medical services are below par. There is hardly more than one movie theater seat for every ten needed.

The government rule is that for a set amount of housing, a set norm of service facilities, of amenities of everyday life, must be provided. But in Volgodonsk, as in many other cities, this has not happened. Rather, appropriations for such amenities were cut by tens of millions of rubles in the last five-year plan. No funds at all were planned for consumer services; cultural, trade, and public dining amenities; Young Pioneer camps or food distribution; laundries; semifinished food shops; ice cream production, etc. The USSR Ministry of Power and Electrification is the contractor for the plant and runs it. But it has agreed to allocate only 85 million of the estimated 120-150 million rubles needed to build amenities. This means that the disproportion will not be eliminated; on the contrary, the situation will worsen.[60]

Given wives' already heavy share of homemaking, it would not be surprising if many wives in developing industrial areas, like the disillusioned wife in Volgodonsk, vote for a move. Nationwide, though, even in the long-developed big cities, women feel particularly severely the consequences of family responsibilities, especially after the birth of the first child. Husbands have nearly twice the spare time women do for study and leisure pursuits; "lack of spare time naturally reflects on the quality of family upbringing of children and works to the detriment of the cultural development of married working women," their chance to study for advancement, and their health.[61] Working mothers suffer heightened fatigue both at home and on the job. Sickness rates among working mothers are two and a half times those among working men.[62]

As a result, working mothers tend to fall steadily behind men in professional advancement and postgraduate education. At higher levels of achievement and pay, women are dramatically underrepresented.[63]

Divorce

The situation in families has involved a rising incidence of volatile marital relations along with urbanization. Divorce rates vary, of course, with region, age, and ethnic makeup. They tripled for the USSR under the legislation of 1944, partly because of a more liberal interpretation after Stalin's death, from 0.4 divorces per 1,000 population in 1950 to 1.3 in 1960, and from 1.7 to 3.8 in Moscow and 1.5 to 3.0 in Leningrad. Still, the 1944 procedures remained long, complex, and costly—in two courts, with a 50-200-ruble divorce registration fee and a publication of notice required between courts, at the cost of 40 rubles plus an additional wait.[64] A 1965 reform moved the entire proceeding into one people's court, eliminating the fee and wait for publication. This had much to do, ZAGS (civil registration) people told this writer, with the increase in divorce rates from 1.6 to 1965 to 2.8 in 1966.

These officials, and the sociologists citing low Soviet rates as signs of socialism's superiority, must have been surprised when divorce rates for the USSR increased from 2.6 in 1970 to much higher levels: 3.5 in 1977, 1978, and 1980 and 3.6 in 1979.[65] Divorce rates rose more slowly for the major cities in 1970–80 than for the USSR as a whole, as Table 5 shows. They actually fell in Riga and Moscow. Except for the capitals of the Caucasian republics, all rates listed exceeded national averages. Rates in the Central Asian capitals of Dushanbe, Frunze, Ashkhabad, and Tashkent were among the closest to the national rate. Rates fell between 1979 and 1980 in all the cities listed (except for Tallin, Sverdlovsk, Minsk, and Perm), paralleling the drop in rates for the country as a whole. Villagers had one-sixth of all Soviet divorces in 1979, with 38 percent of the population. Rural divorce rates, then, are one-third the urban rates. An urban family is three times more likely to break up through divorce than a rural family is (of 951,161 divorces in 1979, 792,134 were in urban families and 159,027 in rural). These national figures conceal sharp regional differences. Very low divorce rates prevail in Central Asian villages and in the Caucasus, and rates closer to urban ones in villages of European parts of the USSR, especially around large cities, where "city norms of marital behavior are spreading to the rural population."[66]

Soviet experts on the family interpret the divorce rate increases as a sign of greater family instability that has troubling implications not only for children's upbringing but also for the demographic situation in the USSR. An estimated 70 to 80 percent of divorcing spouses are of child-bearing ages 20 to 40.[67] Soviet demographers estimate that about 15 percent fewer children will be born because of family breakup, owing to divorces and to spouses' deaths (predominantly male spouses' mortality) during child-bearing ages, than if the marriages had lasted beyond these ages. It is particularly hard for older women in the USSR, as in many other countries, to find a husband. Fewer than half of divorced Soviet women remarry. The chances that a divorced Soviet woman will remarry are one-third the chance of a divorced husband's remarrying.[68]

Family strains symptomized by divorces may act to deter a husband or a wife from having a child or another one. The wife wonders if she will have to raise the child alone. The husband ponders child support payments he may have to make.[69]

Women have taken a clear lead in initiating divorces. Two out of three divorces are initiated by women; three-quarters of the women petitioning have minor children.[70] But they would rather go it alone or, in relatively few cases, with someone else. In part this is because women are more independent with their separate incomes now that they work outside the home. Spouses thus value marriage economically and morally less than did spouses of earlier times.

The family revolution in functions and values has also brought on other kinds of instability during the decades of high-tempo industrialization and severe

Table 5
Divorce Rates in Republic Capitals (Republics in Parentheses) and Cities
with over One Million Inhabitants in 1980 (Divorces per 1000 inhabitants)

City	Year			
	1970	1977	1979	1980
Alma Ata (Kazakh)	4.7	6.5	6.8	6.7
Novosibirsk	5.1	6.1	6.4	6.3
Riga (Latvian)	6.7	6.3	6.4	6.3
Leningrad	5.7	6.0	6.1	5.9
Omsk	—	5.4	5.7	5.6
Donetsk	—	—	5.5	5.4
Kuibyshev	4.4	5.4	5.7	5.4
Tallin (Estonian)	4.8	5.2	5.2	5.4
Kiev (Ukrainian)	5.2	5.3	5.4	5.3
Moscow (Russian)	5.6	5.3	5.5	5.3
Kishinev (Moldavian)	4.9	5.4	5.4	5.2
Dnepropetrovsk	—	5.5	5.3	5.1
Kharkov	5.1	5.3	5.6	5.1
Cheliabinsk	—	5.2	5.2	5.1
Sverdlovsk	4.4	5.1	4.8	4.9
Minsk (Belorussian)	3.5	4.1	4.5	4.7
Kazan	—	—	4.6	4.5
Gorky	4.1	4.6	4.3	4.3
Dushanbe (Tadzhik)	3.2	3.9	4.6	4.3
Perm	—	—	4.1	4.3
Ufa	—	—	—	4.2
Frunze (Kirghiz)	3.9	4.5	4.6	4.2
Askhabad (Turkmen)	3.4	4.1	4.3	3.8
Vilnius (Lithuanian)	3.8	4.5	4.1	3.8
Tashkent (Uzbek)	3.8	3.4	3.9	3.6
Baku (Azerbaidzhan)	3.3	2.9	2.9	2.5
Tbilisi (Georgian)	2.8	3.0	2.9	2.9
Erevan (Armenian)	2.1	1.9	2.1	2.0
USSR	2.6	3.5	3.6	3.5

Note: blank entries indicate city did not yet have a million inhabitants.
Sources: 1970: *Vestnik statistiki*, 11 (1971), 90.
1977: *Vestnik statistiki*, 11 (1978), 87.
1979: *Vestnik statistiki*, 12 (1980), 67.
1980: *Vestnik statistiki*, 12 (1981), 62.

restrictions on religious influence. Women these days are making greater demands than their mothers did for equality in family burdens, decency and sobriety on the part of their husbands, and emotional support. They have more options and make more demands than their mothers and grandmothers did.[71] As illiteracy and cultural backwardness were eliminated, traditional values also disappeared, leaving a "vacuum" of family standards.[72] Also, the move from village to city and the breakup of extended families, sped up by the increased availability of separate housing for the older and younger generations, eliminated the social controls and supports that in the villages once helped keep couples together.[73]

All these material and psychological aspects of urbanization in the USSR have changed the quality of family life and reduced the size and stability of the family. Small, unstable, demographically worrisome families are becoming the norm in the cities and are approaching this norm in the hinterlands of the cities in European parts of the USSR.

Adopting a Demographic Policy

The Soviet regime reacted cautiously during the 1970s to the appearance of statistics detailing this shortfall in the performance of the urban family. Specialists debated whether present economic sacrifices were worth any possible future gains that might flow from a pronatalist effort.[74] The regime gradually took increasing note of the demographic side of the regional labor shortages plaguing the economy and threatening worse bottlenecks as the large older "shift" moved into retirement and the meager younger contingent from after the postwar baby boom took its place. So cautious was the regime and so evident was the economic squeeze on investment and the military in the beleaguered economy that an active pronatalist policy would entail, that it was plausible to predict regime inactivity in this sphere.[75] Nevertheless the regime has now adopted a fairly vigorous pronatalist policy.

What we do not know is how far the regime will carry its pronatalist policy. It is of such recent vintage, and leadership changes in the USSR create such uncertainties, that prediction now would be rash. I shall merely summarize what seems to have emerged in the way of a demographic policy during the early 1980s.

At the Twenty-fourth Party Congress in 1971, Brezhnev demanded "forecasts of the growth of the country's population" to help long-term planning. Measures with pronatalist potential ordered by the congress and implemented during the Ninth Five-Year Plan, 1971–75, included extension of the 112-day paid maternity leave to mothers who worked less than a year, two million more preschool places, and a virtual antipoverty measure of an allowance of 12 rubles a month for each child up to eight years old in families where per capita income is less than 50 rubles a month.[76]

Birth rates had stopped falling by the Twenty-fifth Party Congress in 1976. But longer-range demographic problems and regional shortages still loomed. Brezhnev told scientists "not to lose sight of the problems of the environment and of population problems, which have become aggravated lately.'' He called on the scientists "to work out an effective demographic policy" as "one of the important tasks for the whole complex of natural and social sciences."[77] Several proposals from pronatalist demographers found their way into congress directives for the Tenth Five-Year Plan, 1976–80: an optional, partly paid one-year maternity leave and part-time work or work at home for mothers. But these directives were not implemented as scheduled. The regime was apparently not yet ready to add to the budget expenditures beyond existing social welfare measures like maternity leaves and allowances, preschool expansion, survivors', old age, and disability benefits, and so forth.[78]

But Brezhnev and his advisers were not done with the issue. He told the October 1976 Plenum of the Central Committee that population problems "have become more urgent recently and require an effective demographic policy."[79] The new Soviet Constitution of 1977 contains a familiar article (35) on equal rights for women and the ensuring of these rights by various legal, educational, and health measures, plus "providing conditions enabling mothers to work; by legal protection and material and moral support for mothers and children, including paid leaves and other benefits for pregnant and working mothers, and gradual reduction of working time for mothers with small children." Additionally, the Constitution mentions the family for the first time, and at some length:

> Article 53. The family is under the protection of
> the state. Marriage is based on the free consent of the woman
> and the man; spouses are completely equal in their fam-
> ily relations.
> The state helps the family by providing and ex-
> panding a comprehensive system of child-care institutions,
> by organizing and improving communal services and
> public catering, by paying grants upon birth of a child, by
> providing children's allowances and benefits for large
> families, and other forms of family allowances and
> assistance. . . .
>
> Article 66. Citizens of the USSR are obliged to
> concern themselves with the upbringing of their children, to
> prepare them for socially useful work, and to raise them
> as worthy members of socialist society. Children are obliged
> to care for their parents and help them.

Neither the obligations of the government nor those of spouses, parents, and children proclaimed in the Constitution have legal force; but they represent more or less the activist family policy of the regime (less in terms of real equality for women and of effective control over upbringing) and are implemented in family, welfare, labor, and administrative law.

By 1981 constitutional provisions were receiving additional practical expression. Regime responses to demographic strains became more specific, urgent, and comprehensive. Brezhnev gave the first Central Committee report to a party congress ever to detail population problems. Besides his emphasis on population maldistribution already cited, Brezhnev highlighted the family:

> In accordance with the instructions of the Twenty-fifth Party Congress, the Central Committee has given serious attention to working out and implementing an effective demographic policy and to recently aggravated population problems. The main path to their solution is to take better care of the family, young couples, and above all women (*Applause*).[80]

The Twenty-sixth Congress Guidelines (1981) for the Economic and Social Development of the USSR during the Eleventh Five-Year Plan, 1981–85, expanded on Brezhnev, proclaiming a policy

> to help strengthen the family as a most important cell of Soviet society; to create optimum conditions for women to combine motherhood with an active working career; to improve social support of children and the incapacitated; to implement a system of measures to increase people's life expectancy and ability to work and to strengthen their health.[81]

This congress produced the first comprehensive new pronatalist policy since Stalin's partially dismantled mix of compulsion (the abortion bans, divorce restraints, and bans on extramarital paternity rights) and aid to large families and unwed mothers. The 1981 guidelines ranged from new leaves and grants to health-care improvements to cut down the troubling level of mortality.

A second aspect of this program is its compromise on women's equality. Traditionalist proposals in the USSR would have women paid to stay home and raise more children. Egalitarian, or as U.S. feminists call them, androgynous, proposals would have men share women's burdens and women, men's opportunities. Men's obligation to help is being propagated through some trade union channels as part of the "communist way of life,"[82] but this has resulted in no concrete policy, such as paternity leaves as well as maternity leaves, or a national campaign to raise the consciousness of nonhelpful husbands. A third, compromise path, one adopted at the Twenty-sixth Congress, aims to "create optimum conditions for women to combine motherhood with an active working career."[83]

The Incentives Package

The compromise on women's rights was spelled out in the congress Guidelines and implementing party government decrees summarized in the press in March 1981.[84] Allowances to unwed mothers were raised on December 1, 1981, from 5 to 20 rubles a month and granted for a longer period: until the child reaches age 16 not 12 (or to age 18 for students without stipends). Vague wording in the March 1981 decree calls for "the widespread dissemination" of an option for working mothers to work a partial day or partial week, on a flexible schedule, or to work at home. "Beginning in 1981," working women with two or more children up to age 12 are to receive three extra days' vacation up to twenty-eight calendar days, first call on vacation scheduling at a convenient time, plus the option of two weeks more unpaid leave if the administration agrees and production conditions permit. During the Eleventh Five-Year Plan, paid leave to care for a sick child will increase from ten to fourteen days, the extra four days payable at 50 percent of the current allowance. Mothers who have raised five children to eight years old or one invalid child are to receive a pension, even without the required work seniority, when they reach 55 if they worked no fewer than five years, three of them continuously up to the time they apply for the pension, beginning November 1, 1981. These measures are to apply equally and simultaneously across the USSR, as (or if) they are implemented.

Many other parts of the new policy package of incentives to women reflect another aspect of the policy besides the compromise on women's roles inherent in it; that is, several provisions are clearly differentiated by region. To this day some "scholars"—and who knows, maybe regional leaders too—have opposed a differentiated demographic policy as a "violation of the rights of certain nationalities or rights of inhabitants of regions," that is, as discrimination against the recipients of unequal benefits. The rationale of the differentiation, according to the director of the Institute of Sociological Research of the USSR Academy of Sciences, is that differentiation makes for a "flexible" policy, one that takes into account regional differences in way of life and birth rates, such as the spread of birth rates per 1,000 inhabitants between the low of 14 in Latvia and the high of 37 in Tadzhikistan, where it does not need stimulating.[85]

Thus women are receiving the option of a partly paid maternity leave until the child's first birthday (in addition to the 112-day maternity leave), and that leave has been introduced, as the congress ordered, "by stages, region by region." The progression seems to be from regions of lowest birth rates or population crisis, through, finally, to regions of high birth rates and a surplus population. Also, the areas of most urgent concern feature higher leave pay. Leave pay is 50 rubles in the Far East, Siberia, and the northern regions (Karelian and Komi Autonomous Republics, Archangel and Murmansk Provinces, and depleted old northwest Russia—Vologda, Novgorod, and Pskov Provinces, demographic disaster areas due to migration to cities). The leave was ordered introduced in these regions on November 1, 1981. It was to be introduced in the rest of the RSFSR, the Ukraine, Belorussia, Moldavia, and the Baltic republics on November 1, 1982, at 35 rubles a month, and in the Caucasus and Central Asia on November 1, 1983, also at 35 rubles a month. An optional extra six months of unpaid leave without loss of seniority is to be introduced on the same regional schedule. Eventually the unpaid leave is to be a full twelve months. Further increases in leaves and allowances are, the congress said, to be introduced during the Twelfth Five-Year Plan.

The 1981 package leaves in effect the 1947 family allowance scale held over from Stalin's time, which favored large families and, therefore, high-fertility areas like Central Asia. Upon the birth of the living child indicated, the mother receives the following lump sum and monthly payments:[86]

	3rd	4th	5th	6th	7th	8th	9th	10th	11th+
Lump sum	20	65	85	100	125	125	175	175	250
Monthly	—	4	6	7	10	10	12.5	12.5	15

The 1981 package introduced lump sum grants of 50 rubles for the first child, 100 for the second and third, leaving other payments the same as above, thus adding an incentive of sorts for small families, too, and inherently also balancing what had been a one-sided flow of grants to high birth-rate areas like Central Asia and the Caucasus, especially as rates fell in the Western USSR. The regional differentiation inherent in the emphasis on small families with the new grants is augmented by a schedule of introduction that follows the schedule for the part-paid leaves, beginning with the Far East, Siberia, and the northern regions, etc. In another pattern of differentiation the 2.5 million new day-care places called for in the Eleventh Five-Year Plan were to be distributed so as "to end the shortages in regions with high employment of women."

    One purpose of the prenatalist measures is to help young couples get started in life. The family life of young people begins immediately with serious strains in many cases because of difficulties with housing. According to Soviet surveys, more than half of all young couples start out living with the parents of one of them, about a quarter live by themselves in an apartment, and more than 5 percent must go on living in dormitories. The congress Guidelines for the Eleventh Five-Year Plan seem to have had this in mind in directing that families with children and newlyweds get preferred access to housing, although by an unspecified date. Similarly the drafters of a decree effective April 1, 1982, had the housing difficulties of urban families in mind. As of that date employees of Soviet enterprises and other agencies, including collective farms, in the same priority regions just listed are to receive interest-free loans of 1,500 rubles after the birth of their first child and if they are under 30 years old, have good references, and one of them has worked at the lending organization at least two years. The purpose of the loan is to help them get better living conditions by building a house, buying a coop apartment or furniture, or such. The loan is repayable in eight years, but it is reduced 200 rubles for the second child and 300 rubles more for the third child. Loan eligibility begins in the lower priority regions from April 1, 1983, and April 1, 1984.[87]

Persuasion and Compulsion

The pronatalist campaign aims at consciousness as well as the pocketbook. According to the congress Guidelines, more literature is to be published on "questions of demography, the family, marital sex, the upbringing of children, improving health, and so forth," so as "to strengthen the family as one of the highest moral values of socialist society."

Measures "to strengthen the family" and to increase the number of married couples by reducing the single population and heading off divorces began long before the Twenty-sixth Congress of 1981. They have included get-acquainted services for helping to put single people in touch with one another.

But such services suffer from the shortage of single men as compared with single women and from the desire of many men to take advantage of their "sellers' market" to go for the younger women, as sadly and hilariously portrayed in the film *Moscow Does Not Believe in Tears*. But get-acquainted services and Palace of Culture evenings for "People over Thirty" gain ever wider endorsement.[88] Here is a sample entry from a get-acquainted column of a Riga newspaper, *Rigas Bolls*:

> People say I am a kind woman, with a nice figure.
> I look younger than my thirty-eight years; five feet six, high-
> er education. I am seeking a life companion, forty-five
> or younger, who loves nature and children, has a sense of
> humor, doesn't drink; education unimportant.[89]

A second way marriage is promoted as an institution in the USSR is the Family Service, a self-supporting organization for counselling fiancees and married couples on psychological, sexual, medical, legal, and other matters. Moscow, Leningrad, and several other larger cities are developing the Family Service.[90] But all this is sorely hampered by the lack of trained specialists on marital matters, a dearth of consultants and lecturers, and a lack of research to guide existing, often underqualified personnel.[91] The deputy head of the Moscow City school system looks out from her post in the city soviet and sees the years go by without a solution to the matter of sex education. The Moscow City Soviet had organized talks on sex education two years before for older students in a few schools. "But where are the programs? Where are the textbooks?" she asked. "A member of our Social Council wrote a book on sexology that is being published in Estonia and Hungary, but it is not yet available in Russian."[92]

Divorces in the USSR have become routine, especially when uncontested. Uncontested divorces not involving minor children go straight to ZAGS, the civil registry agency. Contested divorces and uncontested divorces involving minor children or property, support, or custody disputes must receive Poeple's Court Approval before they can be finalized by registration at ZAGS. Court divorce procedure involves a preparatory stage giving the court the option of setting delays totaling up to six months if reconciliation seems possible and a hearing stage in People's Court during which the court grants a divorce on finding "that further cohabitation of the spouses and the preservation of their family have become impossible." So fast and easy in fact have court divorces been that even couples supposed to get ZAGS divorces manage illegally to take their petitions to court (say, by cooking up a dispute) because of the three-month waiting period for

ZAGS divorces.[93] The USSR Supreme Court issued a decree on November 18, 1980, referring to the rising divorce rates, deploring judicial casualness in divorce cases, and ordering judges to take reconciliation proceedings seriously and to grant divorces only when careful inquiry convinces the court that the family has suffered an irreversible breakup.[94] There appears to be little agreement among legal scholars about the effectiveness of refusing divorces, but more agreement about the desirability of exploring fully the possibilities of reconciliation and the cooling-off periods of delay associated with it, especially in the case of young couples.[95] Jurists of the USSR Supreme Court and the USSR Ministry of Justice have echoed the Supreme Court's demand that trial courts try harder to "strengthen the family" by making full use of the reconciliation procedures under divorce law.[96] Without changing divorce law on the books, the regime could order that law interpreted in an even more restrictive way so as to lower the official rates of registered divorce. Whether this will happen, and if it does, whether it will change the actual rate of family breakup, is another and complex question. Laws work most consistently when they reflect widely held values. No indication exists now that present widely held values about marriage and divorce will support a judicial and administrative campaign to lower divorce rates.

Once a modern state intervenes to regulate family life, as well as manipulate it via incentives, compulsion enters in. Compulsion is inherent in the legal enforcement of family rights and obligations, from child and spousal support to parental duties and the protection of the child. In some ways the Soviet government uses less compulsion, say, on divorces and abortions than do many other countries. In other ways the Soviet government is especially compulsive: for example, on parents' liability and possible loss of parental rights for deviations from "communist morality" in the religious or political atmosphere of the home, on which narrow limits of tolerance exist in the USSR.[97] All signs and hints point away from a return to a ban on nonmedical abortions.[98] But any but a short-term prediction would be rash, especially in this time of transition for the USSR.

Conclusion

As in other industrialized countries, economic development and urbanization, plus medical advances originating in urban centers, have taken what is now the USSR from an era of high birth rates, mortality, and population growth, stable families, and low divorce rates to relatively low birth rates, mortality, and high divorce rates, the highest in the world after those of the United States. Possibilities of zero population growth are alluded to in Soviet analyses, and one Western estimate presents the possibility of zero population growth or population decline in the USSR by the twenty-first century.[99]

Again, the transformation of the family under these conditions has been similar to that in other industrialized countries, very broadly speaking: the loss of productive functions and separation of work from the home, but not housework; the changing economic and emotional value of family members one to the other; women's going out to work and the conflicts of role their double burden entails;

the lower value put on marriage and large families and the consequences of women's greater independence in their readiness to leave unsatisfactory family situations more quickly than was the case in preurban and less urbanized families.[100]

Distinctive aspects of the Soviet context stand out alongside the familiar ones. Demographically, population problems are shaped by the particular ethnic patterns in the USSR and the difficulties with housing, food, and amenities in many labor-short regions, prompting migration away from instead of into them. Population surpluses and population shortages just do not fit. And there is no politically or geographically feasible source of mass foreign labor, or "guest workers," such as bailed Western Europe out in economically happier days of growth. Also, political and managerial aspects of the Soviet economic system require full employment for legitimacy and discourage labor-saving innovations on a scale that would end the labor shortage in the immediate future. Over the longer run, changes may become imperative and possible. But this discussion illustrates that demographic "problems" are not independent of factors lying beyond the family.

Another of the contextual factors has been rising mortality and the set of circumstances underlying it, harmful to the family, especially the urban family and to its capacity and desire to have children. The rising Soviet mortality rates and the environmental damage to family life they betoken should serve as a warning to other developed countries seeking to cut corners on medical and social services and living standards.

An active, pronatalist demographic policy is not peculiar to the Soviet Union. In fact, with Western Europe and Eastern European communist countries in mind, one can say that the Soviet regime has come rather late to contemplate large expenditures on a coherent demographic policy.[101] Ever since Stalinist days the regime has been profamily and has favored high population growth. Over the years it has passed piecemeal reforms to help working mothers and families. But having dismantled the coercive sides, or most of them, of Stalin's pronatalism, it launched no new grand policy until 1981, after years of careful consultation and choosing among priorities. So far, compulsion does not figure in the new program.

One should not of course mistake proclamations and phrases about the Soviet "effective demographic policy" for substance. But contrary to most expectations, an attempt at such a policy has been decreed, and again contrary to expectations, it is being implemented.

One part of the program is a birth-stimulation package of incentives differentially allotted to favor small families generally as regards shares of the new incentive monies, and labor-short and population-depleted regions in particular. The old grants to mothers of large families and medals to Mother Heroines, etc., continue, predominantly in Central Asia. The program is broad in its total content of new and existing measures, ranging from longer maternity leaves and new family allowances to efforts to head off hasty divorce and to provide families with information and counseling that might help preserve them, as well as to bring more of the growing number of single people together to form new families.

But the program is broader and more comprehensive than it is deep. The incentives are modest, such as the 35- or 50-ruble maternity leave pay and the 50- and 100-ruble lump sum payments, if taken as additional motivators to have children. Expenditures listed in the Soviet state budget of 1980, before the new package, for maternity grants, payments to single mothers and mothers with large families, and for children in low-income families totaled 3.021 billion rubles.[102] The incentives package of 1981, and some pension increases also ordered, will "improve the material position" of 4.5 million families with children, it is reported, and 14 million pensioners, at an overall annual cost of 2.5 billion rubles. When pension payments are subtracted, this cannot leave a princely sum for birth stimulation.[103] As it is now, or was in 1980, pensions for old age, survivors, and permanent disability totalled 33.323 billion rubles, up nearly 10 percent from 30.601 billion rubles in 1979. The increase in pension payments just due to aging and other population changes far exceeded, then, any incentive package for birth stimulation in 1981.[104]

So on the scale of the individual family, compared with the cost of raising a child, or on the scale of national totals, the birth-stimulation program is comprehensive—made up of new and existing measures to "strengthen" and stabilize and enlarge families—but as yet relatively shallow. One study has shown, for example, that the new 1,500-ruble credits for young parents, interest-free, are modest when compared both with those said to have been successful in East Germany and with the costs and difficulties of buying housing space in the USSR.[105] Additionally, whatever the relative size of new family allowances and benefits, the money coming with them is only as good as the ruble's power to purchase needed food, clothing, and services in a system characterized by shortage.[106]

Other Soviet opinion and a study by the U.S. researcher Jeff Chinn indicate that rising living standards and help to the family, even if significant by today's levels, could be negated by family expectations that rise even faster than their material positions improve. All in all, if birth stimulation incentives do have some impact, it may be at an unaffordable cost.[107]

Beyond the material realm, some Soviet demographers find from their surveys that spousal needs and choices about how many children to have lie beyond the reach of birth-stimulation measures: "many families won't react to stimulating birth rates and motherhood because, first, they don't feel the need for a second or third child, and second, because a certain proportion of spouses lack confidence in the stability of their marital relations."[108]

For all its limitations, the incentive package to stimulate births is farther along than is the twin task laid down in 1981 of ameliorating the entire urban environment, from availability of foodstuffs and services to curbing pollution and improving health care.

So far, new countermeasures against environmental damage to health and rising mortality have been minimal. The Twenty-sixth Congress Guidelines of 1981 ordered improvements during the 1981–85 plan in day-care facilities and orphanages, by improving diets with 10-15 percent more food and by better trained and rewarded staffs. Up to 1981, however, expenditures for health care have risen slowly and annually take an ever smaller share of the national budget of the USSR.[109] Yet eliminating environmentally connected disease and death will be many times more costly, Soviet opinion notes, than was eliminating infectious diseases like smallpox or typhus.[110] Environmental protection laws get ignored or resisted (sound familiar?).[111] All in all, it appears from Soviet comment that environmental dangers are mounting faster than resources are being made available to deal with them.[112]

More attention, it would seem, should be paid to the "reserves" hidden in untapped male help in the home. Consciousness raising for real equality is only beginning. The party leadership, unlike Cuba's Fidel Castro in 1975, has publicly skirted the issue. It has also ignored suggestions that everyday services be handed over, in part at least, to smaller private or cooperative enterprises that would have more accessibility, flexibility, and incentive to tailor, launder, repair, clean, and cook well.[113]

Surely I do not have to go any farther to show that the state of the urban family in the USSR and its fertility and stability over the next few decades depend on many and complicated occurrences in policy and the urban environment as well as in the psychology of the family itself. For example, might not spouses turn inward and have more children if their rising expectations finally are confounded, and if a career, either for men or women, holds fewer or changing advantages? One can only speculate about such important sides of family life. Indeed, demography is and must be an inexact science. "Practice has still very limited scientific knowledge on which to draw," says a Soviet sociological journal; and that knowledge will guide policymakers to knowledge of "what demographic policy will work, how moral and legal norms influence family behavior, how public opinion will react to changes occurring in the position of women and in relations between the sexes, and how various forms of social control affect individual behavior."[114]

Given this understanding of the complexity of spousal and parental motivations among advisers to the Soviet leaders, they must indeed be very concerned about population trends associated with the predominance of the urban family over much of the USSR if they are committing themselves to the long-term allocation of more resources, though moderate by some standards, and to the tricky business of getting women (and to a lesser extent their husbands) to have more children than they do now. Ultimately, intuition says, the solutions to demographic problems will be economic and administrative, meaning vast and systemic changes in labor utilization and technology, as well as management; or they will occur in the medium run, finding ways to tap the human resources of the non-European, high-fertility parts of the USSR where urban family values are still alien.

Notes

[1]*Polnoe sobranie sochinenii*, 5th ed. (Moscow, 1961), 341; Jeff Chinn, *Manipulating Soviet Population Resources* (New York, 1977), 12-16; G. M. Romanenkova, "Sotsial'no-ekonomicheskie faktory demograficheskogo razvitiia krupnogo goroda," in N. A.

Tolokontseva and G. M. Romanenkova, *Demografiia i ekologiia krupnogo goroda* (Leningrad, 1980), 7.

[2]L. Noskov, "Young People Enter Life: Find Work in Your Native Village," *Sel'skaia zhizn'* (May 29, 1981), 3; abstr. in *Current Digest of the Soviet Press, 33,* 24 (July 15, 1981), 15 (hereafter *CD*).

[3]E. K. Vasileva, *Obraz zhizni gorodskoi sem'i* (Moscow, 1981), 5.

[4]"Fundamentals of Marriage and Family Law of the USSR and Union Republics," June 27, 1968, in *Vedomosti Verkhovnogo Soveta SSSR, 27* (1968), item 241, Article 18, as revised by edict of October 9, 1979; ibid., *42* (1979), item 696.

[5]A. G. Kharchev, *Brak i sem'ia v SSSR* (Moscow, 1979), 3.

[6]N. E. Chistiakova, "Vosproizvodstva naseleniia," in Tolokontseva and Romanenkova, 22.

[7]Jeffrey W. Hahn, "Soviet Demographic Dilemmas," *Problems of Communism* (September-October 1981), 56-61; David Heer, "Soviet Population Policy: Four Model Futures," in Helen Desfosses (ed.), *Soviet Population Policy: Conflicts and Constraints* (New York, 1981), 124-54; Alfred DiMaio, Jr., "Contemporary Soviet Population Problems," ibid., 16-43.

[8]Kharchev, 3.

[9]Rudolf Schlesinger (ed.), *Changing Attitudes in Soviet Russia: The Family in the U.S.S.R.; Documents and Readings* (London, 1949); Peter H. Juviler, "Family Reforms on the Road to Communism," in Peter H. Juviler and Henry W. Morton (eds.), *Soviet Policy Making: Studies of Communism in Transition* (New York, 1967), 29-60; Yuri I. Luryi, *Soviet Family Law* (Buffalo, 1980); John F. Besemeres, *Socialist Population Politics* (White Plains, 1980), 43-116; David M. Heer, "Population Policy," in Jerry G. Pankhurst and Michael Paul Sacks (eds.), *Contemporary Soviet Society* (New York, 1980), 63-87.

[10]S. I. Bruk, *Naseleniia mira: etno-demograficheskii spravochnik* (Moscow, 1981), 11-28.

[11]Frank Lorimer, *The Population of the Soviet Union: History and Prospects* (Geneva, 1946), 41-43; Peter H. Juviler, *Revolutionary Law and Order: Politics and Social Change in the USSR* (New York: 1976), 64.

[12]Chinn, 22-35.

[13]*Narodnoe khoziaistvo SSSR 1980* (Moscow, 1981), 7 (hereinafter *Narkhoz*).

[14]*Vestnik statistiki*, 9 (1975), 91 (the last year for urban migration data). On the rural side, a rare glimpse of the deepening rural population crisis in the Russian USSR non-black-earth region is provided by the separate rural and urban vital statistics for the USSR published for 1971–72 in *Vestnik statistiki*, 12 (1973), 80. From its totals of births and deaths for urban and rural population and from population figures in *Narkhoz 1972*, 7, and birth rate figures, ibid., 47, it is possible to calculate rates of death and natural increase:

	Births		Deaths		Natural increase	
	urban	rural	urban	rural	urban	rural
1971	16.9	19.2	7.6	9.2	9.3	10.0
1972	16.9	19.0	7.7	9.7	9.2	9.3

and to see how migration causes aging of the rural population, higher death rates, and a natural increase leveling down to and maybe below the urban level, despite greater female fertility in the villages (see Table 1). Rural extremes range from -1.0 natural increase in Kalinin Province of northwestern Russia to $+29$ (!) in the Tadzhik republic (even higher in Tadzhik villages, if data were available). *Vestnik statistiki*, 12 (1973), 76-79. National rural death rates were not published after the 1972 figures. On the urban side, figures below show that Minsk's natural increase is much higher than is Moscow's. Still even in Minsk, as in Moscow (even if to a lesser extent), net in-migration accounts for a majority of the city's growth. Estimated from the population and natural increase figure, Moscow's population of 8,203,000 on January 1, 1981, was 104,000 greater than a year before, with only 15,388 of that increase due to an excess of births over deaths, or natural increase, the rest being due to mechanical increase, net in-migration. Minsk, a city of 1,333,000 on January 1, 1981, had grown 38,000 in a year, 17,482 owing to natural increase, the rest due to mechanical increase. *Narkhoz 1980*, 21; *Narkhoz 1979*, 23; *Vestnik statistiki*, 12 (1981), 63.

[15]*Vestnik statistiki*, 13 (1980), 69; *Narkhoz 1979*, 7, 35; *Narkhoz 1980*, 7.

[16]On the passport system, see Victor Zaslavsky and Yuri Luryi, "The Passport System in the USSR and Changes in Soviet Society," *Soviet Union*, 6, part 2 (1979), 137-53. On urban growth, see *Narkhoz 1979*, 18-30, *Narkhoz 1922-1972* (Moscow, 1972), 1, 19, 21, 23; Romanenkova, 17; G. M. Romanenkova, "Sotsial'no-ekonomicheskie posledstviia demograficheskogo razvitiia," in Tolokontseva and Romanenkova, 43; E. S. Demidenko, *Demograficheskie problemy i perspektivy bol'shikh gorodov (urbanizatsiia pri sotsializme)* (Moscow, 1980), 115, 119; A. Golovin, "Migratsionnye protsessy," in Tolokontseva and Romanenkova, 29.

[17]*Narkhoz 1959* (Moscow, 1960), 35; *Narkhoz 1980*, 21.

[18]*Narkhoz 1979 godu*, 37; *Narkhoz 1960* (Moscow, 1961), 60; Romanenkova, 16.

[19]Europeans made up the overwhelming majority of total persons changing their residence in 1970. *Vestnik statistiki*, 2 (1973), 85.

[20]Murray Feshbach, "Between the Lines of the 1979 Soviet Census," *Problems of Communism* (January-February 1982), 29-35; Bessemeres, 57-83; Seweryn Bialer, *Stalin's Successors: Leadership, Stability and Change in the Soviet Union* (New York, 1980), 290-91; Jerry F. Hough, *Soviet Leadership in Transition* (Washington, D.C., 1980), 11-12, 30-31, 33, 35, 65, 137; Michael Rywkin, *Moscow's Muslim Challenge: Soviet Central Asia* (Armonk, 1982).

[21]*Pravda* (February 24, 1981).

[22]*Kommunist*, 7 (1976), 17, quoted in Demidenko, 80-81.

[23]N. A. Aitov, "O dal'neishem sovershenstvovanii sotsial'nogo planirovaniia i upravleniia," *Sotsiologicheskie issledovaniia*, 1 (1981), 47; Golovin, "Migratsionnye protsessy," Tolkontseva and Romanenkova, 29.

[24]"Sud'ba malenkovogo goroda. Pis'mo iz Tarusy," *Pravda* (July 16, 1965), quoted in Demidenko, 131.

[25]*Narkhoz 1974* (Moscow, 1975), 47; *Narkhoz 1976* (Moscow, 1977), 73; complete tables for 1958-59 to 1975-76 in Davis and Feshbach, 2.

[26]*Narkhoz 1974*, 44.

[27]Estimates of rising mortality are from Davis and Feshbach, 3-6, 23. Serge Schmemann reported on the interpretation of Alexander I. Smirnov, of USSR Gosplan, in *The New York Times*, June 21, 1981 and the *International Herald Tribune*, June 23, 1981.

[28]V. Petukhov and O. Nikolaev, "Nekotorye sovremennye problemy okhrany zdorov'ia detei," in D. I. Valentei et al. (eds.), *Podrastaiushchee pokolenie* (Moscow, 1981), 35.

[29]Davis and Feshbach, 8, 23.

[30]N. A. Tolokontseva and N. V. Zazanov, "Faktory, predeliaiushchic sostoianie zdorov'ia naseleniia," Tolokontseva and Romanenkova, 105, 121.

[31]Ibid., 4.

[32]Mary McNeal (ed.), *Environment and Health* (Washington, 1981), 65-69.

[33]Ernest J. Sternglass: "The Lethal Path of T.M.I. Fallout," *The Nation* (March 7, 1981), 273; *Secret Fallout* (New York, 1981).

[34]"Osnovnye napravleniia ekonomicheskogo i sotsial'nogo razvitiia SSSR na 1981–1985 gody i na period do 1990 goda," *Pravda* (March 5, 1981); S. Bogatko and M. Kriukov, "Behind the Decisions of the Twenty-Sixth CPSU Congress: Atommash," *Pravda* (July 11, 1981); *CD, 33*, 28 (August 12, 1981), 6.

[35]N. A. Tolokontseva and N. V. Bazanov, "Oznovnye osobennosti i nekotorye tendentsii izucheniia zdorov'ia gorozhan," Tolokontseva and Romanenkova, 118; V. A. Perepelkina, "Adaptatsiia cheloveka v usloviiakh krupnogo goroda," ibid., 38; ibid., 5; M. S. Bednyi, *Mediko-demograficheskoe izuchenie naseleniia* (Moscow, 1979), 128.

[36]Demidenko, 66.

[37]Bednyi, 71. See also Tolokontseva and Romanenkova, 4-6; G. M. Romanenkova, "Sotsial'no-ekonomicheskie faktory," 16; Demidenko, 116-17.

[38]Bednyi, 5, 77.

[39]Ibid., 139.

[40]Tolokontseva and Bazanov, 116-17.

[41]*Narkhoz 1979*, 436.

[42]Bednyi, 150; *Narkhoz 1960*, 62.

[43]A. F. Volkov, "Sem'ia kak faktor izucheniia demograficheskoi situatsii," *Sotsiologicheskie issledovaniia*, 1 (1981), 35, 39.

[44]This survey of possible contributors to rises in infant mortality in the USSR is based on Davis and Feshbach, 17-20, unless otherwise noted.

[45]F. Uglov, "All-Powerful Cigarette?—The Battle with It Isn't Simple, but It's Imperative for the Sake of Everyone's Health," *Komsomol'skaia pravda*, February 13, 1981; *CD, 33*, 7 (March 18, 1981), 13.

[46]*Narkhoz 1979*, 398.

[47]Ibid., 59.

[48]A sampling of Soviet press coverage on medical care such as regularly translated in *CD* appears in Jan S. Adams et al., *The USSR Today: Current Readings from the Soviet Press*, 4th ed. (Columbus, Ohio, 1977), 99-105. See also Davis and Feshbach, 20-22, and Mark Field's chapter in this book.

[49]*Pravda* (February 24, 1981).

[50]A. B. Baranov, *Sotsial'no-demograficheskoe razvitie krupnogo goroda* (Moscow, 1981), 8-9.

[51]L. E. Darskii, "Sotsial'no-demograficheskie issledovaniia problem rozhdaemosti," *Sotsiologicheskie issledovaniia*, 3 (1979), 13-15.

[52]Chinn, 110; Christopher Davis and Murray Feshbach, *Rising Infant Mortality in the U.S.S.R.* (Washington, D.C., September 1980), 13. Jancar, 52, 70, cites an estimate by Henry P. David: 1.6 abortions per live birth in 1960 and 2.5-3.0 in 1965; and by the Population Council: 10 million abortions per 4.5 million live births in 1973. Davis and Feshbach cite the estimate of Tietze and Borgaarts for the Population Council of 2.5 abortions per live birth in 1965–66 and the figures, apparently from a national sample survey in a medical book published 1976, of 3.2 per live birth in 1962, increasing to 4.0 per birth in six for every woman in the USSR. Davis and Feshbach, 13.

[53]V. Z. Rogovin, *Sotsial'naia politika v razvitom sotsialisticheskom obshchestve: napravlenie, tendentsii, problemy* (Moscow, 1980), 178; N. K. Morozova, "Problemy vzaimosviazi zaniatosti zhenshchin i rozhdaemosti," Tolokontseva and Romanenkova, 65; *Zhenshchiny v SSSR: statisticheskie materialy* (Moscow, 1981), 8.

[54]V. A. Sysenko, *Ustoichivost' braka: problemy, faktory, usloviia* (Moscow, 1981), 74-88.

⁵⁵Darskii, 10-13; see also Z. I. Fainburg, "Emotsional'no-kul'turnye faktory funkt-sionirovaniia sem'i," *Sotsiologicheskie issledovaniia*, 1 (1981), 144.

⁵⁶V. O. Rukavishnikov, *Naselenie goroda: sotsial'nyi sostav, naselenie, otsenka gorodskoi sredy* (Moscow, 1980), 72.

⁵⁷Fainburg, 10-11; Chistiakova, 28.

⁵⁸*Vestnik statistiki*, 1 (1982), 60.

⁵⁹Rukavishnikov, 74.

⁶⁰Bogatko and Kriukov, 6-7. All quotations are from ibid.

⁶¹V. A. Sysenko, 42; E. K. Vasil'eva, *Obraz zhizni gorodskoi sem'i* (Moscow, 1981), 75-85.

⁶²Iu. B. Riurikov, "Deti i obshchestvo," *Voprosy filosofii*, 4 (1977), 111-21.

⁶³N. K. Morozova, "Problemy vzaimosviazi zaniatnosti zhenshchin i rozhdaemosti," Tolokontseva and Romanenkova, 62-68; *Zhenshchiny v SSSR: statisticheskie materialy* (Moscow, 1981), 10; T. N. Sidorova, *Trud i sovremennaia zhenshchina: opyt sotsiologicheskogo issledovaniia* (Moscow, 1981), 8, 25-27, 44, 90, 130.

⁶⁴Peter Juviler, "Marriage and Divorce," *Survey*, 48 (1963), 104-17.

⁶⁵*Narkhoz 1979*, 35; *Narkhoz 1980*, 30.

⁶⁶Volkov, 38.

⁶⁷S. I. Gusev, "Rassmotrenie sudami del o rastorzhenii braka," *Sovetskoe gosudarstvo i pravo*, 6 (1981), 52, and figures of the same order in Sysenko, 139.

⁶⁸Volkov, 39-40.

⁶⁹Sysenko, 106-7; Chinn, 110.

⁷⁰Fainburg, 145-46; Gusev, 51-52; Sysenko, 6, 37.

⁷¹Peter Juviler, "The Soviet Family in Post-Stalin Perspective," in Stephen F. Cohen, Alexander Rabinowitch, and Robert Sharlet (eds.), *The Soviet Union since Stalin* (Bloomington, 1980), 227-51.

⁷²A. G. Kharchev and M. S. Matskovskii, *Sovremennaia sem'ia i ee problemy: sotsial'no-demograficheskoe issledovanie* (Moscow, 1978), 54.

⁷³Kharchev, 171.

⁷⁴See Note 8; Darskii, 16-17.

⁷⁵Heer, 149-50.

⁷⁶Richard Bessel (comp.), *Current Soviet Policies VI. The Documentary Record of the 24th Congress of the Communist Party of the Soviet Union* (Columbus, Ohio, 1973), 19, 26, 163.

⁷⁷Rebecca Gruliow (comp.), *Current Soviet Policies VII. The Documentary Record of the 25th Congress of the Communist Party of the Soviet Union* (Columbus, Ohio, 1976), 20, 115.

⁷⁸Alastair McAuley, *Economic Welfare in the Soviet Union: Poverty, Living Standards, and Inequality* (Madison, Wis., 1979), 70-98.

⁷⁹*Pravda* (October 26, 1976).

⁸⁰*Pravda* (February 24, 1981).

⁸¹*Pravda* (March 5, 1981).

⁸²See the work of a researcher for the trade unions, T. N. Sidorova, *Trud i sovremennaia zhenshchina: opyt sotsiologicheskogo issledovaniia* (Moscow, 1981).

⁸³On three approaches to women's role in the USSR, see Gail Warshofsky Lapidus, *Women in Soviet Society: Equality, Development, and Social Change* (Berkeley, 1978).

⁸⁴*Izvestia* (March 31, 1981); *Pravda* (September 6, 1981).

⁸⁵T. Riabushkin, "Demograficheskaia politika v svete reshenii XXVI s"ezda KPSS," *Vestnik statistiki*, 2 (1982), 7.

⁸⁶*Okhrana detstva v SSSR* (Moscow, 1979), 188.

[87]Sergei Voronitsyn, "Interest-Free Loans for Young Married Couples in the USSR," *Radio Liberty Research Bulletin*, RL 156/82 (April 7, 1982), 1-2.

[88]Iu. A. Korolev, "Effektivnost' brachno-semeinogo zakonadtel'stva: opyt sotsiologicheskogo podkhoda k analizu iuridicheskoi problemy," *Sotsiologicheskie issledovaniia*, 1 (1981), 77; "Vazhnaia problema sovetskoi sotsiologicheskoi nauki," ibid., 2 (1979), 5; Volkov.

[89]"Solving Soviet Family Problems: Divorce, Remarriage, and Alienated Youth," excerpted from *Nedelia* (January 12-18, 1981), in *World Press Review* (April 1981), 36.

[90]"Vazhnaia problema," 5.

[91]"Solving Soviet Family Problems," 36.

[92]Ibid.

[93]"Fundamentals of Marriage and Family Law of the USSR and Union Republics, June 27, 1968," *Vedomosti Verkhovnogo Suda SSSR*, 27 (1968), item 241, Article 14; Luryi, 53-63; a translation of the "Fundamentals" can be found in William E. Butler, *The Soviet Legal System: Selected Contemporary Legislation and Documents* (Dobbs Ferry, N.Y., 1978), 455.

[94]"Report and Directive of the USSR Supreme Court Plenum," *Biulleten' Verkhovnogo Suda SSSR*, 1 (1981), 3-6, 12-17.

[95]"Rassmotrenie del o rastorzhenii braka (obzor sudebnoi praktiki)," ibid., 2 (1982), 15-24, S. Ia. Palestina, "Effektivnost' norm o rassmotrenii braka," *Pravovedenie*, 4 (1981), 27-36.

[96]Gusev, 53-54; N. Baskatov and N. Nikol'skaia, "Aktivno sodeistvovat' ukrepleniiu sem'i," *Sovetskaia iustitsiia*, 5 (1981), 5-7.

[97]Peter H. Juviler, "Law and the Delinquent Family," in Donald D. Barry, George Ginsburgs, and Peter B. Maggs (eds.), *Soviet Law After Stalin. Part II. Social Engineering through Law* (The Netherlands, 1978), 213-28.

[98]Riabushkin, 7; G. I. Litvinova and B. Ts. Urlanis, "Demograficheskaia politika Sovetskogo Soiuza," *Sovetskoe gosudarstvo i pravo*, 3 (1982), 38.

[99]*United Nations Demographic Yearbook 1979* (New York, 1980), 157, 485-87, Note 10.

[100]See Note 54.

[101]Heer and Jancar, passim.

[102]*Vestnik statistiki*, 2 (1982), 79.

[103]Ibid., and *Pravda* (September 6, 1981).

[104]*Vestnik statistiki*, 2 (1982), 79.

[105]Voronitsyn, 1-2.

[106]G. Sarkisian, "What Does Well-Being Mean to the Soviet People?" *Nauka i zhizn'*, 12 (1981), transl. in *Reprints from the Soviet Press*, *34*, 3 (February 15, 1982), 14.

[107]Chinn, 2-4, 52-55, 70-129.

[108]Sysenko, 10.

[109]*Narkhoz 1980*, 523; *Pravda* (November 18, 1981).

[110]Bednyi.

[111]Arkadii Vaksberg, "Courtroom Sketch: Break," *Literaturnaia gazeta* (June 3, 1981); *CD*, *33*, 18 (June 3, 1981), 3-4.

[112]Demidenko, *Demograficheskie problemy*, 118-19; Bednyi, 78.

[113]Iu. G. Te, "O povyshenii sotsial'noi effektivnoti bytovogo obsluzhivaniia naseleniia," *Sotsiologicheskie issledovaniia*, 1 (1981), 121.

[114]"Vazhnaia problema," 8-9.

——————————— Louise I. Shelley ———————————

6

——————— Urbanization and Crime: ———————
——————— The Soviet Experience ———————

Introduction

The course of urbanization in the USSR differs from that observed in most other countries. The developed countries of Western Europe, North America, Japan, and Australia did nothing to stem the flow of rural emigrants into urban areas. The cities of the developing countries of Latin America, Asia, and Africa are presently overwhelmed by the problems created by new urban residents as millions of people have abandoned their traditional agricultural homelands and have flocked into cities unable to provide jobs or social services to these new urban residents.[1] The Soviet Union has tried to control the process of urbanization during much of the sixty-five years of the Soviet period, which has resulted in an urban environment that differs in many respects from that observed in most other developed and developing countries.

The unique process of Soviet urbanization has produced crime patterns that are different from those observed in other societies. The Soviet Union has not found the key to the resolution of its crime problems, but the controls that it has placed over the process of urbanization have produced a distribution of crime among cities that is unique in the world. In the rest of the world the crime rate is directly correlated with the level of urbanization. The Soviet Union also conforms to the internationally established correlation between the level of urbanization and the recorded crime rates. But in other counties the largest cities, on average, have the highest crime rates, while small cities are spared the crime problems associated with large metropolitan areas. Whereas in the Soviet Union the largest cities have proportionally less crime per resident than do medium-sized ones. This is a consequence, in part, of the steps taken by Soviet authorities starting in the late 1920s and early 1930s to control the process of urbanization and industrialization.

Historical Background

Soviet authorities did not immediately enact policies to control the process of urbanization. Unfortunately, like most of the other countries in the world, they were forced to learn the hard way about the criminological consequences of urban development. But while the Soviet authorities could not immediately rectify the damage done by the influx of large numbers of immigrants from rural areas in the early 1920s, the lessons that they learned from this period were applied already in the second decade of Soviet rule, when they chose to enact population controls that would limit residential mobility within the society.

The Soviet Union was not immediately faced with the problem of urban growth in the immediate postrevolutionary period. The outbreak of the Civil War and the chaos brought by the revolution resulted in serious food shortages that were particularly acute in urban areas. In the first few years of the Soviet period there was even an exodus from urban to rural areas as individuals sought to be nearer the limited food supply.

With the introduction of Lenin's New Economic Policy (NEP) in 1921 the national economy stabilized and reconstruction began. Cities once again became potential sources of employment. Rural-urban migration quickened even though not all migrants were able to secure jobs. Unemployment and other difficulties notwithstanding, the 1926 census indicates that 5.6 out of the 26.3 million urban population arrived in the city sometime during the preceding six years.[2]

The consequences of the influx of large numbers of rural emigrants to ill-prepared cities were quite devastating, especially to the largest cities, Moscow and Leningrad. Residential conditions were terrible, food supplies were inadequate, family life suffered, and the crime rate rose significantly.[3]

The crime rate grew annually, and the growth rates for female and juvenile offenders were even more remarkable than those observed for the population as a whole.[4] Gangs of homeless youth wandered through the cities, terrorizing the population and committing major property and violent crimes.[5] The revolution had not brought the new Soviet man but instead had yielded a decline in moral conduct. Scholars studying the crime problem recommended solutions based on increased controls over the population. Such suggestions were not original to these scholars but were based on the population controls in force during the tsarist period. Criminologists of the period recommended the registration of criminals, and some even went so far as to suggest the introduction of a system of internal documentation to monitor the movements of the population.[6] Before such an encompassing scheme was ultimately adopted in the early 1930s, certain more focused control measures were applied to the criminal population. A detailed census of the prison population was conducted in conjunction with the national census of 1926.[7] Measures of restraint were used against criminals residing in major urban centers in the late 1920s, as those offenders who were deemed a threat to the social order of these cities were forced to resettle permanently in secondary urban centers and rural areas.[8]

The manipulation of the process of urbanization initially affected only the criminal populations of major urban centers, but by the early 1930s more encompassing measures were introduced that affected the lives of the rest of the Soviet population and the course of Soviet urbanization. The impetus for these more extensive measures of population control was not solely the result of the urban crime problem, but the calls of criminologists for tighter controls over individual movement and residence surely found a receptive ear in a leadership that was looking for ways to insure the supply of individuals necessary for its industrialization drive and to successfully mount a purge against political enemies. As Soviet authorities needed to insure a work force for their industrial sites, they could no longer permit free choice of residence within the country. In addition, documentation of all Soviet citizens made it easier for the police to locate individuals sought for arrest. The effect of such measures was to slow the rate of growth of such cities as Moscow, Leningrad, and Kiev and to divert rural emigrants to secondary cities and new industrial centers.

Population Controls

The elaborate mechanism needed to control the movements of the entire Soviet population was initiated in the early 1930s with the introduction of the internal passport. The internal passport that must be carried at all times by Soviet citizens sixteen and older reduced the mobility of the population. Prior to the issuance of these passports in 1932,[9] Soviet citizens could reside in a city or town of their choice and could travel freely without documents. After the introduction of the passport system the mobility of urban residents was limited and that of peasants was almost completely curtailed. From the 1930s to the late 1970s, collective farm workers were not authorized to receive passports and only recently have become eligible to get them, a right that as yet has not been fully realized. The failure to issue the agricultural population internal passports helped control rural-to-urban migration. Agricultural workers could leave their farms for short visits only with great difficulty; movement to urban areas was achieved only after overcoming greater impediments. Passes from the local village councils are still needed for travel from the collective farm for more than a month.[10] Departure from a collective farm and permanent resettlement in an urban area are more difficult and are an option available almost solely to the youthful population.

Young men who are drafted into army service and individuals eligible for higher education do have an opportunity to leave the collective farms. Youths, after army service, volunteer for jobs on construction sites in the far east and far north, where they receive internal passports. Similarly, collective farm workers who are admitted to institutions of higher learning are assigned work upon graduation and rarely are forced to return to the agricultural community where they were born and raised. In the nearly fifty years since the internal passport was introduced, the adult population on collective farms has moved with less facility from their place of residence to urban areas. The manipulation of the process of urbanization thus shifts rural emigration away from the largest cities that are customarily the ultimate destination for emigrants from rural areas in other societies. The internal passport system limits the rate of urbanization in Soviet society. As a result of this population control and the rapid growth of industrial production, Soviet urban conditions are very different from those observed in developing countries today and in the past century, as these societies are and were not able to control movement from rural to urban areas nor to provide employment for all their new urban settlers.

The registration system or system of *"propiska"* that was adopted in the early 1930s in conjunction with the passport system has helped control the distribution of the population among urban centers. Each passport indicates the place where the individual is registered to live or his *"propiska."* To obtain residence permission in a major urban center, an individual must be born there, marry someone with a right to live in the city, or be offered employment that carries with it a residence permit. High party and cultural positions as well as jobs in the police and security police are among the categories of employment that carry with them permission to live in a major urban center such as Moscow, Leningrad, and Kiev.

The passport and registration systems have not been extremely effective in redirecting internal immigration, a fact acknowledged by Soviet scholars.

> Measures of planning organs to limit the growth of cities
> in practice have turned out inadequate. During the 1960s the
> growth of the population in large cities made up 75 per-
> cent of the entire growth of the city population. . . . If more
> effective measures are not taken to lower the population
> growth of large cities due to migration, then by 1990, in this
> writer's opinion, about three-fourths of the entire urban
> population of the country will be concentrated in the fifty
> largest urban centers.[11]

Even though these control measures have not fully realized their objective, they have managed to divert some of the rural-to-urban migration away from the major Soviet cities.

Areas of Recent Settlement

Soviet immigrants to new communities arrive in urban areas that are able to provide for their basic needs. New urban areas provide jobs, housing, albeit inferior, and some social and medical facilities. The residential situation of these new immigrants is very different from that of new urban immigrants in industrializing countries in the past or the present century. Recent urban arrivals in nineteenth-century Europe faced the horrible conditions graphically described by Engels in *The Condition of the Working Class in England*. Rural emigrants in the third world today often face conditions that are comparable if not worse than the environment described by Engels. The environment encountered by recent settlers in new Soviet urban communities may, however, be inferior to that of recent rural emigrants to the established cities of the industrialized nations.

The areas where the recently urbanized work force settles are by no means problem free. Soviet scholars point out that the residential conditions of their new urban settlers are inferior to those of more long-term residents in these same urban communities.[12] Migrants are often forced to live in large, impersonal dormitories. Recreational facilities are limited, and social services are often strained beyond capacity. Moreover, the centralized planning of the industrialization process often results in new urban settlements that are overwhelmingly male or female, thereby reducing social opportunities for the young and nubile work force. These problems produce a residential environment that is less than ideal for the new urban settlers, but it is certainly preferable to the conditions that are faced by most recent urban immigrants in the industrializing world today.

Soviet manipulation of the industrialization process has resulted in fewer urban problems than in societies that have failed to interfere in the process of urbanization, yet Soviet authorities have not been able to avoid all the adjustment problems of individuals unaccustomed to life in urban areas. Former rural residents, accustomed to living in a protected, extended family and to knowing the fellow residents of their community, find it difficult to adjust to the impersonal conditions of the urban environment.[13] Without the support and guidance of their families and with the increased temptations of urban life, many recent urban settlers commit antisocial acts. Many of them would not have perpetrated criminal acts if they still resided in their home communities and did not have the increased opportunities to commit crime.

Individual adjustment problems and the conditions of urban life, rather than the process of urbanization, appear to be the reason that urban areas in the USSR have significantly more crime than rural areas. The fact that urban areas in the Soviet Union have 40 percent more crime than rural areas[14] shows the limitations of the controls over the process of societal modernization. The Soviet Union has, however, escaped the very high crime rates and rapid growth rates of crime that are characteristic of the cities of developing countries that have failed to control the urbanization process. But the new and expanding cities of the Soviet Union have much higher crime rates than the older established cities that have restricted the flow of new residents. Control of the rate and spatial distribution of urbanization has thus limited the growth of crime, but it has failed to eliminate the crime problems associated with urbanization. Urban crime remains a serious problem in the USSR because the Soviet Union has not fully succeeded in eliminating the problems of personal adjustment associated with rural-to-urban migration.

Crime Data

The conclusions reached here on the effect of the manipulation of urbanization on rates of crime are based on an analysis of Soviet criminological research and on interviews with Soviet émigré lawyers. The research was conducted by a large group of Soviet researchers employed by universities, institutes, and the research arms of the police and the procuracy in the western republics of the USSR. These scholars had access to the police, procuratorial, and court statistics that are considered state secrets and are consequently not published. The data available to these trusted scholars share some of the same problems of comparable American data. Crime statistics collection is not centralized but provided by different local authorities that have a vested interest in showing to the party bureaucracy their ability to control crime.[15] Therefore Soviet police, like their counterparts elsewhere in the world, reduce the number of crimes registered to exaggerate their success in controlling crime and solving criminal cases.

The research on urban crime was conducted by scholars who not only had access to available data but were authorized to collect the data necessary for their analysis. They use the data as indicators of national crime trends rather than as concrete statements of absolute crime rates. Therefore, although there are distortions in the data used by Soviet scholars, the generalizations that they draw are based on distinctive trends instead of small statistical variations. Therefore the significant differences they found between urban and rural crime rates and the crime rates among different-sized cities are too great to be attributed solely to statistical error or the falsification of police reports. Not only are the differences observed significant, but the researchers studying the impact of urban conditions on crime are sensitive to the possible sources of error. Therefore, although it is not possible to confirm the scholar's conclusions by examining the original data, the sophistication of the researchers and the consistency of their findings suggest that the research that provides the basis of this paper's conclusions is sound.

Soviet scholars are careful to present their results without exaggerating their findings. But having only limited familiarity with foreign criminological literature and crime problems, they often fail to see the full implications of their research findings. Unaware that other societies have not been as successful in controlling the process of modernization as the USSR, they do not realize that their findings on urban criminality are a distinct case study of the impact of the manipulation of urbanization on the extent and distribution of urban crime.

Urban vs. Rural Crime

Urbanization has had a negative effect on criminality nationally. Proportionately more crime per capita has been perpetrated in cities than in rural areas before and ever since the revolution. The continuing urbanization of Soviet society has even broadened the gap between urban and rural crime rates. The crime rates of urban areas have increased, particularly in the remote areas of the country and in the new cities that cannot afford to be selective about the individuals to whom they grant residence permits. As so much of the male youthful work force, the group most likely to commit crimes, has found ways to leave the countryside, the crime rates of rural areas have dropped, whereas the process of urbanization has led to even higher rates of urban crime. In the 1970s 40 percent more crime was committed in urban than in rural areas, but only slightly more than half the Soviet population lived in urban rather than in rural areas (106 million rural versus 135 million urban inhabitants).[16]

Crime in Established Urban Areas

The impact of urban growth on crime is evident not only in terms of broad national figures but also in regions that have experienced particularly rapid and intensive urbanization. The highest rates of criminality are observed in the most urban republics. In the period 1963–66 the ten republics with the highest levels of crime were regions with the highest level of urbanization. Estonia and Latvia, republics with high crime rates, are 65 and 62 percent urbanized, respectively.[17]

Their crime problems were exacerbated in the 1970s as both these republics experienced a rapid and significant influx of Russians into their republic capitals. Neither Tallin nor Riga are *rezhimnyi* cities, large established cities allowed to control urban growth, which means that neither city can select the residents it chooses to register. Estonia, particularly in the pre-Olympic period, was forced to accept many Slavic settlers because it did not have a work force sufficiently large to construct the sports facilities and accommodations necessary for the expected tourists. In addition, individuals released from labor camps, usually of Slavic background, were settled in Estonia to promote Russification and to provide an additional work force for factories and construction trusts. The city of Tallin was unprepared for such a massive influx of new residents and had neither the housing nor the expanded social services necessary to accommodate these people. Work sites were able to absorb a few released offenders, but the release of large numbers of excriminals to one enterprise strained the capacities of the workers and the administration to exercise a beneficial influence over the released offenders. While Riga provided a slightly less hostile environment to the new Slavic settlers, it still lacked the social resources necessary to absorb the large population influx. It is hardly surprising that the crime statistics of these two republics reveal that it is the non-Estonian and the non-Latvian migrants into their republic capitals, many with criminal backgrounds, who were responsible for much of the recent growth in urban criminality.[18] The experience of Latvia and Estonia indicates that nationality policies have compounded the criminological problems that accompany the process of urbanization.

The problems of urban growth in Latvia and Estonia are, however, less pronounced than in the new and expanding cities of the Soviet east because the two old Baltic cities there have established infrastructures, and a strong Germanic tradition of societal order endures. Even though the rate of population influx strained these cities' capacities to absorb newcomers, the generally law-abiding nature of the established community did much to ease the problems caused by this large and unexpected population movement. But newly established communities lack the buffer of a long-term resident population to ease the strains of rapid urbanization. Therefore the new cities of the Soviet Union have much more severe crime problems than those experienced by Riga and Tallin. In the new communities the permanent residents have lower rates of criminality than those who had arrived more recently,[19] but the composite crime rate of the two groups is higher than the population of established cities (see Table 1), where the long-term resident population has significantly lower crime rates than the recent arrivals.

Table 1
Conviction Rates for American and Soviet Cities

USSR	Conviction rate per 100,000 population	USA	Conviction rate per 100,000 population
Soviet cities over 1.5 million, (Moscow, Leningrad, Kiev) 1969	442		
Soviet cities with population under 0.5 million, 1973 (Tartu, Tobolsk, Vladivostok, secondary cities of Latvia)	500	American cities, 1977 (2,925 cities with total population of 39 million)	
USSR, (national average) 1976	1,045		2,573

The newly established cities of the far eastern RSFSR, eastern and western Siberia, and Belorussia not only have the highest crime rates but the greatest increases in criminality. In some of these areas the crime rate has increased at a greater rate than the population,[20] an increase attributable, in large part, to the migrants. For these reasons the secondary cities of the Soviet Union have higher crime rates than the established cities of Slavic Russia that are permitted to maintain strict controls over the nature of their permanent population.

Kiev and Leningrad, cities with low rates of population growth, have lower crime rates (see Table 1) than secondary Russian cities like Tobolsk, which has grown rapidly in recent years.[21] The stability of a Soviet city's population, and not its size, appears to be more significant in determining its level of criminality. Port cities, for this reason, like their counterparts elsewhere in the world, have higher crime rates than their degree of urbanization might suggest. This is true of Riga and Tallin and is further accentuated in the larger ports of the south and east.

The crime rate of Odessa is heightened not only by a lively second economy that increases arrests for all categories of economic crime but by a high rate of prostitution that contributes to a high rate of property crime. The presence of a large number of transient sailors also affects the crime rate of nearby Baku, where even the constraints of a traditional Moslem society are insufficient to combat the temptations of easy money. An émigré who worked closely with the juvenile division of the Baku police and was briefed on the crime problems of the youthful population reported that about 40 percent of the juveniles of Azerbaidzhani and Slavic nationalities were involved in a broad range of property crimes and prostitution, often facilitated by the presence of large numbers of both foreign and domestic sailors. The crime problems of these southwestern port cities are considerably less than the eastern port of Vladivostok. The high crime rate of Vladivostok, reported to be the highest in the USSR,[22] is aggravated not only by its transient maritime population but by the fact that the *primorskii* (coastal) *krai*, an area along the East coast inhabited by over 1.5 million residents, is a favorite settlement area for convicts released from nearby labor camps. The presence of both a large offender population as well as an unstable population creates an environment where it is unsafe to appear on the streets past dusk.

Crime in Recently Urbanized Areas

While the port cities of the Soviet Union represent individual cases of high crime rates, the majority of cities with the highest crime rates are concentrated in the interior of the country, in areas that have only recently been urbanized. It is these remote areas with severe climates that have traditionally been unable to attract residents voluntarily. In tsarist times the remote areas of Siberia were used as places of exile for political offenders, but in the Soviet period these lands have been the home to labor camps and the new industrial cities. Soviet authorities have tried to attract a labor force to these remote cities voluntarily through propaganda campaigns and wage differentials; but despite the extensive financial investment in these new cities, Soviet leaders have not been successful in encouraging voluntary population movement in this direction. Therefore, as Soviet industrial plans demanded development in the remote regions of Siberia and farther east, laborers have been directed since the late 1930s to specific projects in these areas where they have had to stay "until permission to depart was granted or until directed elsewhere."[23] The cities of the far east and far north have gained inhabitants not only by providing financial incentives for workers and by directing population movements but also by encouraging released inmates to settle in areas close to their former labor camps.

Released offenders with multiple convictions or who served sentences for serious crimes are severely limited in their choice of residence.[24] They cannot reside in major cities or certain desirable districts or regions. Since the newly established cities that are located near the labor camps require additional laborers to meet their industrial plans, they are forced to offer residence permits to these undesirable individuals because they cannot attract enough needed manpower voluntarily. Therefore, since the early 1950s, when large numbers of offenders were released from Stalinist labor camps and had no choice but to settle in the neighboring cities, crime rates have been extremely high in these industrial small and medium-sized cities. One former procuratorial investigator, employed in Khabarovsk during much of the 1950s, reported on the impact of these recent releases on the local crime rate. There were many nights of his investigatorial career when three or four corpses of murdered individuals were discovered. So many murders were committed that he rarely had time to investigate the scores of other serious offenses that were also most often committed by recent releasees from labor camps.

Therefore it is hardly surprising that when serious criminological research was resumed in the 1960s, Soviet scholars of crime learned that it was the remote and recently settled areas of the USSR that had the highest crime rates. While Soviet authorities planned employment and housing for new settlers to the new cities of the far east and far north, all they could attract were former labor camp inmates and former rural residents settling down after army service. It is therefore hardly surprising that the remote oblasts of Tiumen, Magadan, Kamchatka, Yakutsk, Tuvin, Komi, Krasnoyarsk, and Primorskii, which needed new urban inhabitants and would accept all potential residents, had the highest crime rates of the RSFSR.[25] In the mid-1970s Soviet scholars confirmed the unique position of these areas, but more recent data are not available. The planning of the urbanization process meant that the large and desirable cities were the beneficiaries of the planning process, but the new and remote towns bore the criminogenic costs of the temporal and spatial control of urban development. The oblasts (regions) that were spared the influx of these undesirable new settlers also escaped much of the republic's criminality. For in the twenty RSFSR oblasts with the smallest population influx, thirteen regions were in the lower half of all RSFSR oblasts in their rates of criminality.[26] Soviet urban planning thus has not led to positive results for all cities.

Planned urban growth affects the distribution of crime not only among cities but also within cities. Soviet authorities, through their planning apparatus and their controls over the extent and locale of urban settlement, should be able to prevent the high concentration of crime in certain city neighborhoods. As there is no independent housing construction, Soviet planners determine both the type and location of new apartment buildings. The *militsiia*, or police authorities, control the registration of all individuals within cities. No one can move into the city or change his residence without the permission of the police. Therefore Soviet authorities should be able to insure that neighborhoods with traditionally high rates of crime do not receive individuals prone to criminal activity and that new areas of construction are not populated by too many youthful males, the group most likely to engage in crime. Despite the fact that Soviet authorities have control over entry into cities and settlement patterns within cities, neither in established nor newly founded cities have Soviet officials been able to reduce significantly the crime rates associated with certain traditionally crime-ridden neighborhoods or with the neighborhoods recently populated by urban migrants. Therefore, in city areas populated by the criminal element, the young male working class and recent rural emigrants, crime rates are high despite Soviet efforts to control the urban environments.

Soviet crime studies attempt to map the patterns of crime within the city. They show that crime is concentrated in the older sections of the city that have traditionally had high rates of crime, as well as in the new housing tracts where residents lack a sense of community and are unaccustomed to the ways of urban life.[27] The housing shortage in the USSR has made it impossible to destroy areas with very substandard housing that have traditionally been the home of the criminal population. Therefore, in the older established cities the neighborhoods that could have provided the setting for Gorky's *Lower Depth* are still often inhabited by the descendants of the denizens of this mythical flophouse. These individuals still contribute excessively to the crime rate of their community, as they did in the first decades of the Soviet period.

Rural emigrants are frequently the inhabitants of the new housing built on the fringes of older established cities and are the core of the residential neighborhoods of newly established cities. Some long-term urban residents move into this new housing, but much of the new apartment construction in both new and established cities is inhabited by recent urban immigrants. These new urban settlers, unaccustomed to urban and apartment living, find it difficult to adjust to the demands of this new way of life. The impersonal new neighborhoods contribute to the poor adjustment of the new settler, producing not only high rates of divorce and alcoholism but also crime. The perpetrators of these criminal acts rarely have criminal records and might often have lived law-abiding lives but for their inability to cope with their new residential environment.

Even though certain old deteriorated neighborhoods and new residential apartment complexes in large cities have higher crime rates than other city regions, large Soviet cities have been reasonably successful in controlling their overall crime rates. As a result of the exile of serious offenders from urban areas and the restraints on admission of youthful males into cities, large Soviet cities have fewer potential criminals than corresponding-sized cities in other countries. It is the smaller, newly established cities with large numbers of rural emigrants residing in impersonal apartment complexes that contribute disproportionately to the Soviet Union's crime rate. Whereas the small and medium-sized new cities have the highest crime rates in the USSR, the large older cities are not entirely spared the problem of youthful male criminality despite the fact that severe limitations are placed on the admittance of youthful males to major urban centers.

Transients and Urban Crime

Urban areas, despite their restrictions on settlers, are nevertheless in need of a youthful male work force. The youths who are denied registration permits in cities settle instead in the communities that surround all major urban centers. These residents are often forced to commute as much as four hours daily to and from the city to attend school or work. While traveling, they often drink excessively and make the acquaintance of parasites and recidivists. Under their influence they often commit criminal acts in the city rather than in the residential communities. The contribution of these youths to crime is so significant that in large cities like Leningrad and Moscow, a large proportion of the crime is attributable to them.[28]

Another major source of urban criminality in major Soviet cities is people who come into the city not on a regular basis as commuters but to shop and make transport connections. These are people who come from smaller cities and often collective farms, and they are rarely criminals at home. But since the peasants lack the internal passports necessary to register in hotels and the transients with passports often lack the money and the "know-how" to bribe their way into a hotel, many are forced to stay overnight in railway stations. Tired and confused, they often commit minor forms of criminality, particularly hooliganism, at or near railway stations. Despite particular police vigilance at train stations, Soviet authorities have been unable to prevent the concentration of urban crime at and around the terminals.

Conclusion

The controls over the course of urban development as well as the rapid industrial development of the USSR have not created a national crime rate significantly different from that of other developed countries at a time when one might expect higher rates due to the development of many new cities. While comparisons cannot be made of urban crime rates, national figures reveal that the USSR in 1976 had approximately 1,060 convictions per 100,000 population.[29] (However, the discrepancy that exists between crimes reported and actual convictions suggests that the Soviet Union has a crime rate at least one and a half times as great.) United Nations crime figures for the developed countries for the period 1970-75 reveal that the composite rate for the developed countries was 1,835 offenses per 100,000.[30]

But the Soviet Union does have a distinctive distribution of urban crime. Medium-sized cities (populations under 500,000), particularly in the Slavic regions of the country, have been able to rid themselves of undesirable criminal elements and to be selective in those to whom they choose to grant residence permits. Medium-sized port cities, new industrial centers, and republic capitals subject to Russification have higher than anticipated crime rates. Port cities with highly transient populations, new cities in remote areas populated by large numbers of youthful male emigrants from rural areas, and Baltic cities being Russified by undesirable Slavic elements also have higher crime rates than the largest cities. Therefore, in the Soviet Union, although the level of urbanization is directly correlated with the crime rate, the largest cities do not have the highest crime rates.

The crime that is committed in the largest cities is perpetrated primarily by transients and commuters to the city who violate the law either near railway stations or on the city outskirts. The same demographic traits that characterize the criminal population of established cities contribute to the extraordinarily high rates of crime recorded in the medium-sized cities of the USSR.

Soviet urban crime patterns differ from those observed in other societies because of features unique to the Soviet development process. While the redirection of rural emigrants away from the major urban centers has improved the crime problem of the largest cities, it has aggravated the crime problems of areas of recent settlement. Urban crime rates reflect not only the channeling of immigrants but the nature of the housing conditions, social amenities, and the population in the area where they settle. While most urban areas suffer from the influx of large numbers of rural emigrants, areas with more settled populations, few transients, and a balanced sexual ratio suffer less.

New urban residents turn to crime because of personal adjustment problems as well as conditions unique to the urban environment. The greater opportunities to commit crime as well as increased exposure to material goods serve as stimuli for crime commission. But certain features unique to Soviet society either aggravate or reduce the likelihood of crime commission. Soviet postrelease programs for exconvicts have been successful in certain Baltic areas because of national (ethnic) self-interest; but in urban areas with already high crime rates, the practice of entrusting the released convict to the worker collective is of limited use. The Soviet planning process that has created new cities of predominantly one sex has also created urban communities with abnormally high crime and illegitimacy rates. The crime rates of large established cities are also affected by the unique features of the Soviet development process, as their crime problems can be attributed in large part to commuting youth and transients.

Soviet attempts to redirect urban growth have not proved to be a panacea for urban crime. Urban residents, particularly recent arrivals, commit crimes because of the opportunities of city life as well as their personal adjustment problems. The unique features of the Soviet development process have merely shifted urban crime from primary to secondary cities. Soviet cities, like their counterparts in the rest of the world, still contribute disproportionately to their nation's crime.

Notes

[1]M. B. Clinard and D. J. Abbott, *Crime in Developing Countries* (New York, 1973); Louise I. Shelley, *Crime and Modernization* (Carbondale, 1981).

[2]James H. Bater, *The Soviet City* (London, 1980), 60.

[3]M. F. Teodorovich, "Zhilishchnye usloviia i prestupnost'," *Voprosy izucheniia prestupnosti na Severnom Kavkaze*, 3-4 (1928), 29-61.

[4]D. P. Rodin, "Prestupnost' muzhchin, zhenshchin i nesovershennoletnikh v 1922 godu," *Bulleten' tsentral'nogo statisticheskogo upravleniia*, 5735 (October 25, 1923), 67-76.

[5]See Peter H. Juviler, "Contradictions of Revolution: Juvenile Crime and Rehabilitation," paper presented at the conference, "The Origins of Russian Culture," Kennan Institute, May 18-19, 1981.

[6]S. N. Krenev, "Prestupnost' po Leningradskoi gubernii," *Administrativnyi vestnik*, 2 (1927, 49-52; S. M. Potapov, "Nauchnye metody bor'by s prestupnost'iu," *Administrativnyi vestnik*, 12 (1927), 45-48.

[7]A. G. Beloborodov (ed.), *Sovremennaia prestupnost'* (Moscow, 1927).

[8]See N. F. Kuznetsova (ed.), *Sravenitel'noe kriminologicheskoe issledovanie prestupnosti v Moskve v 1923 i 1968-1969 gg.* (Moscow, 1971).

[9]Bater, 57-58; Mervyn Matthews, *Class and Society in Soviet Russia* (New York, 1972), 53-54.

[10]Matthews, 54.

[11]E. S. Demidenko, *Demograficheskie problemy i perspektivy bol'shikh gorodov* (Moscow, 1980), 115.

[12]M. M. Babaev and Iu. M. Antonian, "Sotsial'naia sreda i lichnost' prestupnikov-

migrantov i postoiannykh zhitelei,'' *Voprosy bor'by s prestupnost'iu*, 22 (1975), 12.

[13]Ibid., 13.

[14]Walter Connor, *Deviance in Soviet Society* (New York, 1972), 174-75.

[15]Peter H. Juviler, *Revolutionary Law and Order* (New York, 1976), 133.

[16]Bater, 66-69.

[17]A. F. Sokolov, ''Urbanizatsiia i nekotorye voprosy bor'by s prestupnost'iu,'' *Sbornik uchenykh trudov: Problemy sovetskogo ugolovnogo prava i kriminologiia* (Sverdlovsk), 28 (1973), 151.

[18]V. Sveics, ''Criminality in Riga: Russian and Latvian,'' presented at the Fifth Conference on Baltic studies in Stockholm, June 14-17, 1979.

[19]Babaev and Antonian.

[20]N. N. Kondrashkov, ''Analiz raionnoi statistiki prestupnosti,'' *Voprosy preduprezhdeniia prestupnosti*, 3 (1966), 35-46.

[21]M. M. Babaev, ''Kriminologicheskaia otsenka sotsial'no-ekonomicheskikh i demograficheskikh faktorov,'' *Sovetskoe gosudarstvo i pravo*, 6 (1972), 98.

[22]Soviet dissertation defense at the Criminal Law Department, Law Faculty, Moscow State University, Moscow, Spring 1975.

[23]Bater, 57.

[24]Leon Lipson and Valery Chalidze (eds.), ''Documents,'' *Papers on Soviet Law*, 1 (1977), 185-86.

[25]M. M. Babaev, ''Krimonologicheskie issledovaniia problem migratsii naseleniia,'' *Sovetskoe gosudarstvo i pravo*, 3 (1968), 88.

[26]Ibid., 88-89.

[27]R. S. Mogilevskii and Iu. A. Suslov, ''Gorodskaia prestupnost' kak ob''ekt kriminologicheskikh issledovanii,'' *Pravovedenie*, 5 (1973), 114.

[28]O. V. Derviz, ''Rabota ili ucheba vne mesta postoiannogo zhitel'stva—odin iz faktorov prestupnosti nesovershennoletnikh,'' in N. P. Kan and M. D. Shargorodskii (eds.), *Prestupnost' i ee preduprezhdenie* (Leningrad, 1966), 65-70.

[29]Calculated from a table given in Fredrick Neznanskii, ''Statistika prestupnosti v SSSR,'' *Posev*, 5 (1979), 47.

[30]''United Nations Crime Survey (1977)'' in L. Shelley (ed.), *Readings in Comparative Criminology* (Carbondale, 1981), 162.

PART
III

SOVIET URBAN SERVICES

Mark G. Field

7

Soviet Urban Health Services: Some Problems and Their Sources

Introduction

"Ah, yes, but what of socialized medicine?" is the conventional and traditional counter to almost any critique of Soviet reality. Free care thus emerges as one of the few redeeming cases on an otherwise bleak landscape and is often held as a positive achievement, an important social invention, a distinct and pioneering Soviet contribution. Indeed, it would be fair to state that the *principle* of free and universally accessible medical services at the expenses of society as pioneered by the Soviet Union has gained full acceptance among the Soviet population,[1] and probably elsewhere. The Soviet implementation of that principle has sometimes been held by outside observers, such as the eminent medical historian Henry Sigersist,[2] as a model worthy of study, if not emulation, by other nations.

The principle derives from the idea that health is such an important component of the human condition that (just like education) it cannot be left to the vagaries of the market place, the individual's ability to pay for it, or social origins and position. Thus medical care, which in an earlier age was considered an item of personal consumption, which one bought if one could afford it or went without if one could not or received as charity, has been replaced by the concept of a personal right, an entitlement. And if Mussolini was said to have made the trains run on time, Stalin may well deserve the credit for having presided over the development of Soviet socialized medicine. His successors have not altered that blueprint, only expanded the size of the enterprise.

The mention of Stalin and medicine in the same breath confronts us, however, with a paradox: the very essence of state-provided medical care flies against all our commonsense assumptions about the nature of a totalitarian society, either of the Stalinesque type or its authoritarian versions under both Khrushchev and Brezhnev. Medicine embodies a profound humanitarian concern and tradition about helping the sick, the wounded, the suffering. It evokes images of white coats, of hospitals and clinics, of devoted personnel struggling to help, to comfort, to heal. A Soviet-type society, on the other hand, almost by definition, seems to be congenitally unable to care for the individual, to be concerned about his or her suffering, welfare, or well-being. It evokes a completely different series of images, of cruelties and inhumanity, perhaps best epitomized by the *Gulag Archipelago*. How do we reconcile that contradiction?

A plausible way to do so is to examine the impact of illness, or morbidity,[3] and mortality in two interrelated but distinct ways: (1) its effect, often devastating, on the individual in suffering, dependency, in the anxiety it arouses because of its close association with death, and often its social and financial costs; (2) the impact it has on the social system, if we conceive of that as a structure of roles individuals are expected to perform as part of their position or status. The first point can be called an "expressive" concern; the second one an "instrumental" or "functional" concern. It is that second concern which, to my mind, provides an important explanatory key to an understanding of the Soviet health system. Thus while the Soviet regime has not been particularly worried about the expressive impact of illness, it has shown awareness, at least in the past, that health was an important *natural resource* of society, and illness (as well as premature mortality), a critical threat to that resource. Obsessed as the Soviet leaders have been since the inception of the five-year plans with production and productivity, they reasoned that a nation could not industrialize and militarize with a population and a labor force that were subject to high rates of debility, morbidity, and (premature) mortality. Thus the principle of universal entitlement to health care, which has such a strong ideological appeal because of its humanitarian aspect, must also be seen as contributing, in a functional way, to the strength of society, regardless of its political nature. This calculus is not different, after all, from that of providing the military with a medical corps to protect, maintain, repair, and enhance the working and fighting capacity of its personnel.

The burden of this essay is not so much the *principle* on which Soviet socialized medicine rests, nor even the rationale behind it, but rather the manner in which it is being carried out. William Knaus, an observer of the Soviet medical scene, an American physician who has familiarity with the subject, summed up his and others' judgment by referring to ". . . as either an enormous success or colossal failure." He went on to state that it was truly both:

> As a national program aimed at conserving scarce resources while providing basic services, it is a qualified success. From the perspective of a patient in need of special attention or individual emphasis it is frequently a failure.[4]

It is not my intent now to provide an assessment of that "success-failure." A definitive judgment is difficult to make, if not impossible, unless specified for the different types of populations in the Soviet Union. Rather I will concentrate on Soviet urban health services, in line with my mandate but in full consciousness that an overall view of the Soviet health system must take into consideration that sizable proportion of the population that still lives in the countryside, and for whom the provision of health services has been particularly poor.

Inasmuch as current demographic trends suggest the increasing urbanization of the Soviet population, one may surmise that the differential between urban and rural health services will gradually decrease, though not completely disappear, in the future. There is also evidence that the rural population, given the failure of the health system to reach into the villages, increasingly makes use of urban health facilities. This then reinforces the validity of examining urban health services as prototypical for the entire society, as reflective of basic problems, and as suggestive of future trends.

The "Charter" of Soviet Socialized Medicine

At the most general level, the present Soviet Constitution states that each Soviet citizen is *entitled*, among other things, to qualified medical care in case of illness, and at no cost to him or her.[5] The implementation of that most general entitlement is via "Soviet socialized medicine," usually described as a socialist system of governmental and community or collective measures having as their general purpose the prevention and the treatment of illness, the provision of healthy working and living conditions, and the achievement of a high level of work capacity and long life expectancy.[6] As such the system has several well-defined formal characteristics that serve as bridges between that generalized statement of intent and the organization and management of health services:

1. Public health and personal medical care are a state matter and responsibility and a function of the government;
2. The development of all public health and medical measures takes place within the framework of a single plan;
3. The health system is centralized and standardized;
4. Health care and allied services are made available to the population at no direct cost at the time of service;
5. Prevention stands at the core of the Soviet health system;
6. The system embodies unity of theory and practice;
7. The health system belongs to the people, and the people must help and support it—for example, through volunteer activities;
8. Health services are provided on a priority basis.

A few brief comments on some of these principles and operational characteristics are in order.

It should first be noted that the health system is not only a *responsibility* of society and of the state, it is also an *instrumentality* in the hands of the polity in the pursuit of *its* goals and programs. Such a pursuit might be incompatible with a private health care system unresponsive to governmental priorities. And furthermore, it would also be incompatible with a strong and relatively autonomous medical profession oriented both to the expressive welfare of the population and to its own power and privileges. It is therefore not surprising that there is no "medical profession" in the Soviet Union in the sense of a relatively independent corporate group entitled to organize its members and to take "political" stands, as the case might be, for or against governmental policy. Whatever one's view of the American Medical Association or other similar associations in the West, there is no equivalent in the Soviet Union. Doctors are state functionaries, with all that this implies.

Equally important as part of the control of the polity over the health system is that the system is financed by the state treasury. Thus, by contrast with the United States, it is possible to determine fairly accurately what percentage of the Gross National Product and of the national, republic, and lower administrative budgets will be allocated to health care. It is possible for the Soviets to keep the salaries of their health personnel at a very low level even when compared to other occupations in the Soviet Union, let alone physicians' incomes in the West. The Soviet health system may be defined as labor, and not capital, intensive—in that labor is cheap, equipment and medical technology expensive.

The Soviet health system is basically a prepaid or prospective payment scheme, which is considerably cheaper to operate than a reimbursement (retrospective) or insurance system in which services are rendered by providers and bills then submitted. The latter feature can inflate health care costs, as it has in Western Europe and in the United States. And it is true that with some exceptions, the Soviet citizen does not pay for services at the time such services are performed. Soviet propaganda stresses, time and again, that it is the government that provides health care to its people almost as an act of generosity (compared to the parsimony of capitalistic systems). But the fact of the matter is that these services *are* paid by the citizens themselves through taxations and levies, in the same way as health fringe benefits paid by employers in the United States eventually mean reduction in discretionary incomes. There is, moreover, increased evidence that the system of "free" medical care in the Soviet Union is, to some degree, a myth, not only because nothing is free but because, as we shall see later on, most Soviet citizens feel it is necessary to give private additional payments to physicians, nurses, and hospital attendants to get better attention or attention at all. It is of course impossible to calculate what these "under the table" payments amount to and how much of the Gross National Product they represent. What we know, however, is that in the last few years, the estimate is that the percentage of the GNP *officially* allocated to the health care system, or the percentage of the national budgets going into this area, has gone down by more than 20 percent.

Taking budgetary figures first: in 1950, 5.2 percent of total budgetary allocations went to health protection; this rose to 6.6 percent for 1960 and 1965, but by 1978 the figure had fallen to 5.2, the same as in 1950.[7] Estimates of GNP and percentages allocated to health have been made both in rubles and in dollars by Edwards, Hughes, and Noren.[8] They are shown in Table 1.

The figures in parentheses refer to percentage of GNP allocated to health. Whether calculated in rubles or dollars, the estimates also indicate a decrease by more than 20 percent between 1955 and 1977, though absolute figures have more than doubled.

The realization that in the last decade or so infant mortality in the Soviet

Table 1
Soviet GNP and Health Expenditures, 1955-77

	1955	*(%)*	*1965*	*(%)*	*1975*	*(%)*	*1976*	*(%)*	*1977*	*(%)*
	Billions 1976 rubles									
GNP	174	(100)	304	(100)	456	(100)	505	(100)	533	(100)
Health	5	(29)	8	(2.6)	11	(2.3)	11	(2.2)	11	(2.1)
	Billions 1976 dollars									
GNP	464	(100)	793	(100)	1202	(100)	1253	(100)	1294	(100)
Health	45	(9.7)	69	(8.7)	94	(7.8)	96	(7.7)	97	(7.5)

Union had gone up by more than 25 percent has prompted some observers (see Note 6) to tie part of that rise to a decrease or a degradation in the health care system, though it is difficult to prove it definitely.[9]

Finally, the idea of a priority provision of health services might surprise those who are still under the impression that Soviet society is an egalitarian system. I shall deal in greater detail with the stratification of Soviet society and the parallel stratification in the provision of medical services in the next section. All I can say at this point is that there is not a single health system equally available to all (for example, like the British National Health Service) but a variety of health systems that deal with different populations and/or administrations. I suppose that one might argue that eventually they are all under the umbrella, supervision, or inspiration of the USSR Ministry of *Health Protection*.[10]

Soviet Clinical Practices: Medicine, Society, and Culture

Although the basic problems posed by morbidity and early mortality are truly a universal of the human condition, the variety of responses has been enormous throughout the ages and cross-culturally. And yet the development of science and of technology, and their application to morbid states, has tended to introduce an element of uniformity. As a consequence, the health system may be seen as the resultant of at least two forces, sometimes in conflict with each other: (1) particularistic sociocultural features and (2) universalistic elements of science and technology. It is still very much of a moot point whether in the process of societal evolution, one of these two elements will become dominant. Certainly the idea of convergence and of modernity would have us believe that contemporary societies are becoming increasingly alike because they are all affected by the universal elements of science and technology. These elements, in turn, shape social organization and affect cultural patterns so that, for example, a factory is a factory regardless of where it is located. And by the same token, we could argue that a hospital, given contemporary medical technology, is increasingly likely to be similarly organized and managed whether in Sweden, the USSR, France, or Nigeria. Or that antibiotics will be the treatment of choice for certain types of infection anywhere in the world. And yet, it seems to me, that particularistic sociocultural factors, because they have behind them the force of history and tradition, shape and reshape, interpret and reinterpret the universalistic aspects of modern science and technology. If we fail to recognize the significance of these particularistic elements, we shall miss an important explanatory mechanism. A balanced view of the Soviet health system (or any other, for that matter) thus partakes of both universalistic aspects of contemporary medicine *and* peculiar features of Soviet society, history, culture, politics, traditions, economic resources, and institutions. A Soviet hospital is as much, or even more, a distinctly Soviet entity as a medical one.

Compared to most societies, the Soviet Union is a closed system. Since Stalin died, a great deal has been and can be learned from Soviet sources. This requires diligent research and patience, and the nuggets of insights in the area of health services are still rare or episodic.[11] It is therefore fortunate that the recent publication of the book by Knaus to which I have already referred, *Inside Russian Medicine*, provides important and rare views into the actual practice of medicine in the Soviet Union. It complements and fleshes out the glimpses of that system one may gather from Soviet official discussions on the subject, whether in the specialized literature or in the general press such as *Izvestia*, *Pravda*, and particularly *Literaturnaia gazeta*, which likes to pursue such issues as medical care or the supply of pharmaceuticals and to invite readers to send in comments. Knaus's book is not by far a systematic treatment. Rather it consists of a series of vignettes about aspects of the Soviet system, impressions gathered during several sojourns in the Soviet Union when he was responsible for the health of American State Department guides accompanying exhibits under the Cultural Exchange Program.[12] I will rely a great deal on Knaus's materials because they provide important views usually not available to outsiders of Soviet urban clinical medicine, of medical practices, and of hospitals. Admittedly these views may seem overcritical and based on limited contacts and experiences. They are those of a Western physician accustomed to working in a high-technology atmosphere and in conditions that simply cannot be matched in the Soviet Union, except perhaps in facilities reserved for the elites. And yet most of his observations are confirmed, time and again, in the Soviet sources already mentioned and are not simply "muckraking," a view held, for example, by Patrick Storey.[13] Knaus's report was perhaps most useful in focusing on certain aspects of the Soviet health system and in adding the eyewitness dimension.

Soviet Socialized Medicine in Practice

I have selected a few themes that, I believe, illustrate the proposition spelled out in the early part of this chapter: that the Soviet health system cannot be understood or analyzed simply in the universalistic terms of medicine as applied science and technology. Rather it is an amalgam of these characteristics and of the distinct patterns of everyday Soviet life, the scarcities, the bureaucracy, the officiousness of state employees, the absurdities of formal rules, the inequities, and so on which permeate it from top to bottom and from side to side.

Stratification

Ever since Stalin called for the elimination of egalitarianism as a leftist or infantile deviation in the early 1930s, Soviet society has spawned an elaborate system of rankings, of distinctions between who is very important, important, and not important.[14] The provision of health services also follows quite closely this differentiation. The Soviet health system is divided, broadly speaking, into two unequal categories: the territorial and the closed networks. The territorial network is available to the general population, with primary access determined by residence. The closed networks, on the other hand, are reserved for special groups. At the lowest level are the medical facilities reserved for workers of enterprises with over a certain number of personnel, where access depends on the job or position held.

Next there are the special facilities of certain agencies or ministries, such as the armed forces, the Ministry of Internal Affairs, the railroads. Another network is reserved for members of the intellectual elites, such as members of the Academy of Sciences, the Union of Soviet Writers, artists of the first rank, and so on. Finally, at the apex of the Soviet medical (and sociopolitical) pyramid are the complex of medical institutions, rest homes, sanatoria, and dispensaries reserved exclusively for the members of the Kremlin elite and their families, and which precisely parallel the other perquisites of rank such as private *dachas*, chauffeured limousines, seaside vacation homes, restricted special stores, and so on. This is sometimes referred to as the Fourth Administration of the Ministry of Health Protection. I would like to call this network of specialized health care units the *Medical Archipelago*.

Just as there are in all Soviet cities, in railroad stations, and in other places special detention facilities for prisoners, there are in all Soviet cities specialized clinics and hospitals where the elites can receive medical care protected from scrutiny. These facilities may be free standing, or they may be restricted sections of general hospitals.[15] In that respect they resemble, to some extent, the private wings of American hospitals or amenity beds in Great Britain, reserved for those who want more privacy, more luxury, and in fact better and more attentive medical care. The major distinction, however, is that Soviet members of the establishment do not personally pay for these facilities but receive care there as a perquisite of rank, paid by the state, paid in fact by the taxes of ordinary citizens who must content themselves with run-of-the-mill hospitals and clinics.[16]

Needless to say, these clinics and hospitals are better equipped than those of the ordinary networks. In case certain blood tests cannot be performed in the Soviet Union, blood samples are routinely flown to a laboratory in Helsinki, and results flown back to Moscow, according to Knaus. Even within the Kremlin polyclinic, distinctions are made by rank:

> Deputy ministers and persons of lower rank are seen in
> regular private cubicles, but ministers have special examin-
> ing rooms. . . . There are carpets on the floor, book-
> cases, a leather couch, and heavy red drapes over the win-
> dows. It is like a living room, not a clinic.[17]

Equipment, drugs, procedures not available in the Soviet Union are import-ed from abroad, either from the satellite countries or from the West if necessary. In some instances top specialists are invited to come to the Soviet Union to consult on important cases or, as the case might be, to operate.[18] There are apparently differences of opinion in the USSR on the quality of physicians who practice on the members of the Soviet upper classes: some view them as political appointees who are mediocre doctors; others feel that top-ranking members of the medical profession either work there or are invited to consult. I am inclined to believe that elites as a rule prefer expert professionals to politically reliable hacks. I see no reason that Soviet officials are different, particularly when their health and well-being are involved. Indeed, Lenin, who was no fool, would bear me out on this. In a letter he wrote to Gorky in 1913, he stated: "God save us from doctor-comrades in general, and doctor-Bolsheviks in particular! But really, in 99 cases out of 100, doctor-comrades are asses. . . . I assure you that except in trivial cases, one should be treated by men of first-class reputation."[19] "Special care for special people" is thus part of the reward and privilege structure of Soviet society. In *The First Circle* Solzhenitsyn noted this by describing how Alevtina Nikanorovna, a member of the elite, saw it:

> . . . Whoever had status was assured of good health. All
> you had to do was telephone some famous professor, best of
> all some laureate of the Stalin Prize; he would write out
> a prescription and any coronary occlusion would instantly
> disappear. You could always afford to go to the best
> sanitarium. She and her husband were not afraid of illness.[20]

It may be useful to reflect that this consciousness of ranks and differences between important and unimportant persons extends even to the ordinary hospi-tals. A shock of recognition will surely come to those who know of the existence, in Soviet cities, of center lanes on all main arteries where official cars can speed while all the other traffic waits. Here is the situation in Moscow City Hospital No. 68:

> The patients usually walked close to the wall, moving
> slowly and keeping their hands in the pockets of their robes.
> The center was kept clear for physicians, nurses and
> visitors who walked quickly, arms swinging freely, talking
> loudly.[21]

In conclusion, the question we may then ask ourselves is: to what degree does this stratification in access to medical care pose a "functional" problem to Soviet society? If we assume that health care has some impact on morbidity and mortality, then the fact that the great majority of the population gets second- or third-rate care must have some "functional" impact.

Bureaucracy

There is no reason to believe that the Soviet health care system is immune to the bureaucratization of Soviet life. In fact, the bureaucratization of medicine and particularly hospital care is a worldwide phenomenon that has resulted from increased size, specialization, the need for coordination and integration, and third-party payments. But there seems to be a special quality to the impact of bureaucratization in Soviet medicine which magnifies a general phenomenon: it is the deprofessionalization of medical services, the unwillingness of individuals to make personal decisions and shoulder personal responsibilities, and a tendency to practice medicine "by the numbers" that make the accommodation of special situations, including emergencies, often difficult. Apparently, most everything in the health system is routinized and proceeds according to officially established and rigid norms. Thus physicians and other health personnel are expected to work a specific number of hours per day and to see a specific number of patients per hour, the number varying with the specialty. What this encourages is a segmental sense of responsibility, a nine-to-five mentality. Soviet physicians will not hesitate to leave their workplace at the end of their duty time, even though there may still be patients waiting to see them. They assume that someone else will take care of them or that the patients will come back the next day.[22]

The existence of bureaucratic practices and attitudes in the health care system is not, of course, a state secret. Time and again, the Soviet press, particularly in such outlets as *Literaturnaia gazeta*, has reported complaints received by readers about the rigidities of health institutions.[23] Hospitals, for example, will not admit new patients after a specified hour in midafternoon. After 3 p.m. in Irkutsk, for instance, all emergency admissions are referred to a single designated city hospital.[24] Every disease is tariffed as to the number of hospitalization days permitted, and indeed mandatory (a delivery is usually nine days; an appendectomy is ten days; a hysterectomy is two weeks). Even if the patient is well enough to be discharged earlier, this may not be allowed.[25] Knaus reports that to order a radio-isotope scan of the liver in Kishinev (Moldavian Republic) requires five separate forms, the approval of six persons, and a ten-day wait.[26] Hospitals are assigned "death quotas," and investigations will follow if they exceed these quotas. The upshot: hospitals will often refuse to admit terminally ill patients, their families being encouraged to take them home so they will die there.[27] Patients will be subjected to routine procedures whether they need them or not because those are the regulations.[28] Very often these bureaucratic routines degenerate into a mere and meaningless ritual. For example, the belief persists that infections are brought into the hospital from the outside. Visitors are forbidden to retain their coats while in the hospital; and the rules are that books and news-papers cannot ever be placed on a bed for fear of infection, "never mind if the sheets have not been changed for a week."[29] While these silly and meaningless rules are ferociously enforced, sterility is poorly observed in operating rooms and in disregard of the fact that most infections originate *within* the hospital. As a result, the incidence of postoperative infections is very high, affecting about one-third of patients operated on. In fact most physicians with whom Knaus discussed the infection problem preferred comparing their incidence of postoperative infec-tions with that found in developing countries, such as Afghanistan, rather than with the United States or other developed countries.[30]

Bureaucratically determined instructions overload physicians in outpatient clinics, thereby reducing the time available for patients who really need to see a doctor. Thus, according to an article in *Literaturnaia gazeta*,

> . . . only one-third of patients (at the polyclinic) had
> come for their initial appointment. The rest were there for
> follow-ups. Only a few needed to see a doctor on that
> particular day: their appointments had all been made in ac-
> cordance with the instruction. If it were not for this in-
> struction . . . a polyclinic physician would have half as
> many patients . . . in some cases only one-third. Hence
> the doctor could give each of them 15 or even 20 minutes,
> instead of just 7 . . . we must place more faith in the
> physician and not force his actions into a Procrustean bed of
> instructions. . . .[31]

There is nothing particularly lethal about Soviet bureaucratic routines in hotels, in dining rooms, in railroad stations, in housing offices, in retail stores and governmental offices. They are the annoyances of daily life in the Soviet Union. But the existence of the very same phenomena in the health system, where one deals with human lives, with suffering and iatrogenic problems, suggests that deeply ingrained bureaucratic patterns cause more than irritation.

Falsification

The tradition of falsification, of eyewash, of dissimulation, or Potemkin villages and *Dead Souls*, is an old one, inherited from the Russian past; it is alive and well today in the Soviet medical system. This is why one must, when approaching Soviet statistical data about health, use a large grain of Siberian salt. There are, for instance, apparently quotas for all types of operations, and these quotas are always met—on paper at least. If the number of operations, let's say appendectomies, falls below the expectations, more cases are "invented" to fill the quota. The same applies to hospital occupancy rates. If they were to go down, then budgets and supplies might be curtailed the next fiscal year. And so high occupancy rates are routinely reported, whatever the situation.[32]

Thus the hospital director or manager plays the game in the same way as the industrial manager.[33] It is not unusual, nor seen as improper, to request twice as many supplies as needed (and to document that need) since the director knows that he will be lucky to get half. And as Knaus remarks, "such false reporting (in the medical area) has never been considered dishonest . . . the easiest way to stay out of trouble is to do exactly what is expected."[34] Here again we are dealing with a phenomenon that is common in Soviet life, and publicly acknowledged as such. Thus a few years back Dr. Boris Petrovskii, then Health Minister of the USSR, mentioned that hospitals had been built to be attached to stations for emergency care, and he mentioned that they had been established in more than sixty cities. "However," he added, "in some cities they exist only formally."[35] By this Petrovskii meant they exist only on paper.

The Soviet Union is proud of its system of preventive examinations or *dispensarizatsiia*. Here again, quotas of examined patients may be met through the expedient of filling forms without actually examining patients. The results of these ghost examinations are aggregated and published as another example of the preventive orientation of Soviet medicine.[36] If sometimes the facts are too unpleasant or too embarrassing, their publication is simply discontinued. This is, for example, true of the already noted increase in infant mortality. At first the data were reported routinely, then only selectively, and then after 1974, infant mortality statistics ceased being publicly reported. This hardly means that there is no more infant mortality in the Soviet Union. On the contrary, it suggests that it has increased or remained comparatively high. Indeed, in a rare confirmation, Dr. Alexander Smirnov, of the State Planning Commission, reported in the course of a press conference in June 1981 in Moscow that the infant mortality rate from 1978 to 1980 and later was about 28, i.e., not lower than the last statistics officially published by the Soviet Union valid for 1974 (27.9).[37]

Given the bureaucratic nature of the Soviet health system, it may be posited that the widespread misreporting of information and statistical data can only have a deleterious effect on the general provision of health services. So far, only one redeeming aspect of that feature of the system has been identified: in some instances (as is also true in industry, as reported by Berliner) such fudging or shady practices may be "functional" in that they permit managers of health institutions to fulfill their mandates better than if they went by the book.

Doctor-Patient and Nurse-Patient Relationships

One of the greatest advantages of a system of socialized medicine, the Soviets repeat *ad infinitum*, is that it has removed the "capitalistic cash nexus" between the doctor and the patient. The latter is not seen as a source of profit or income, and the physician is free to practice the best medicine he or she can without regard to either the income or the financial position of the patient. This is well and good in theory: the practice, however, appears to be somewhat different.

The general impression that emerges from outside observers, as well as from the Soviet sources themselves (see Note 23), is the frequent lack of sensitivity toward patient feelings and emotions displayed by Soviet physicians. This lack of sensitivity probably has many roots, but anyone who has dealt with officials in the Soviet Union can well appreciate that this pattern is not unique with doctors. As mentioned earlier, it is true that there is little relationship between income (or better, salary) and medical practices. The Soviet doctor knows that patients will be there, and he will be paid whatever he does or does not do (except for the grossest infractions—and even then personal responsibility is minimized). This certainly can lead to the opportunity to devote oneself exclusively to the patient's welfare.

The evidence, however, is that the situation in Soviet medicine encourages indifference, "formalism," and the nine-to-five attitude referred to earlier. There is indeed little incentive, except a personal one, to be gentle and considerate with patients (except when they are willing to pay money or give gifts—as we shall see when we discuss the "second economy"). Furthermore, there is evidence that future physicians receive (or received in the past) very little orientation and training in medical psychology. According to Pavel Beilin, writing in the *Literaturnaia gazeta*,

> Until recently, medical psychology and psychotherapy in
> fact were not taught. . . . Recently they started to teach them
> but much too little. In all, 19 hours were allocated to
> medical psychology out of 7,800 hours. In other words, for
> knowledge of the body—7,781 hours, for knowledge of
> the soul (*dusha*)— . . . 19.[38]

The impression is that hospital physicians, in particular, tend to be brusque with patients, that most physicians regard patients as little children who do not understand anything about their health or their bodies. Natalia Gorbanevskaia, a dissident who was forcibly put into a mental hospital, remarked about the "attitude so common among our doctors that the patient is completely in their power and that he must be treated like a silly baby with neither mind nor will of his own; I used to think that this attitude was common only among psychiatrists, but it seems this is not so."[39]

The brusqueness and the patronization mentioned earlier tend to be exhibited more often in hospitals than in outpatient clinics, where patients and doctors have a steadier relationship, as we shall see. Hospital physicians do not expect to see the patient again as they are often rotated. Patients tend to be processed rather than treated as human beings with their full quotas of fears, anxieties, and emotions. In a survey of two thousand letters written by patients in Kiev and reported in the *Literaturnaia gazeta*, one of the major themes was the insensitivity of Soviet doctors, who themselves feel frustrated, hampered by the bureaucracy, by the lack of supplies, alternative treatment possibilities, and so on. In that survey one doctor was reported to have said to a patient: "You have a stomach ulcer and diabetes. You will not survive an operation. I simply do not know what to do with you."[40] In another survey, conducted in Kiev to which I have already referred (see Note 11), one patient was told by the doctor: "You are 76 years old.

The average life expectancy is 68. What are you complaining about?'' or ''You should have come a year and a half ago. Now it is already (too) late.''

This attitude is also extended to relatives of patients. They are often treated in perhaps the same way as those who inquire at the police stations about a spouse or relative: with indifference, condescension, if not cruelty. It is no wonder that the hospital is generally feared as it was in the United States a century ago. And that fear comes not only from the knowledge of rough and impersonal handling by indifferent staff, but also because, as we shall see, the quality of care and the lack of supplies and equipment may make a hospital stay an episode dangerous to life and health, as well as to one's emotional stability. And the use of mental hospitals to incarcerate dissidents only emphasizes the similarities with prisons.

Given the social distance that exists between hospital doctor and patient, the accepted view is that one does not question the judgment of a doctor: to do so would be *nekul'turno*, an act of arrogance. This attitude is, of course, cultivated by the doctors and nurses, as would any bureaucrats since it makes their life and work easier.

Patients are referred to hospitals by their outpatient doctors. These outpatient doctors have no say or control over the care of their hospitalized patients because of the institutional separation between the outpatient polyclinic and the inpatient hospital.

Generally speaking, the relationship between the polyclinic physician and patients is a considerably closer one because they stay together for much longer periods of time. Indeed, a patient is assigned to a doctor on the basis of residence, and that doctor serves as a general practitioner.[41] But even this is subject to some qualification. According to Paikin and Silina, one-third of outpatient practitioners have held their job for less than one year. Only 3 to 10 percent of all such doctors have worked at the same place for more than ten years.[42] Still the general life situation, income, and other conditions of everyday existence are so similar between the average patient and the polyclinic doctor that the social distance is reduced. Most Soviet *vrachi*, particularly the *terapevty*, practice a kind of relaxed, comforting, commonsense, low-technology type of medicine, on the assumption that most conditions will get better anyway, that a few conditions are referable to specialists, and the rest are beyond remedy. Thus if time is available, a physician's visit may approach a kind of social chitchat. However, when the waiting lines are long, little time is left, and most of that is eaten up by the writing of forms and other bureaucratic requirements. ''I go through my appointments without looking up,'' a physician admits. She has thirty-six patients to examine in four hours. When does she get any time to look up? On the average she has seven minutes per patient. Sometimes she does not even get seven, as she is interrupted by other physicians who drop into her office.[43] In fact, it is probably true that while paying lip service to the patient, the Soviets do not consider patient satisfaction as important in evaluating medical services.[44] These are ''expressive'' frills the system is not particularly concerned with.

Relationships between patients and nurses appear worse than between doctors and patients in the hospital. Generally speaking, Soviet nurses are poorly educated and trained, do not have the prestige and power of physicians, and take their frustrations and helplessness out on the patients. I think that anyone who has dealt with service employees and other white-collar workers in Soviet administrative offices (at the post office, at a hotel, in stores, at Intourist, and so on) will recognize that the officiousness of the nurse is not unique. There is no one she can boss but the patients. "Stop being a child," a nurse was reported yelling at an elderly patient who had dissolved into tears after being told he needed a serious operation. The better or more capable nurses aspire not to stay in nursing but to move upward and to become physicians themselves. In fact, Soviet hospital nursing still partakes of an attitude that it is not quite a respectable job,[45] a view that was prevalent in the West about a century earlier.

I shall deal later on with the concept of the second "economy." But it is not surprising, given the situation described here, including the relatively low incomes of health personnel, that patients should try with money and gifts to secure a more personal attitude from such personnel, thereby negating to some extent the advantage of "free" medical care.

The Hospitals

The Soviet Union has more hospital beds per capita than the United States, and indeed most countries. The general impression, however, is that there is very little in these hospitals, in terms of equipment and medical technology, besides these beds. One reason that could be adduced for the large supply of beds is that housing conditions are such that it is most difficult to keep a sick person at home. This may be the reason that compared to the situation in the United States, patients stay for longer periods in Soviet hospitals and tend to be hospitalized more frequently. One might say that many Soviet hospitals are dormitories for individuals who do not feel well. Whereas American hospitals have been accused of doing too much for patients, the reverse situation seems to obtain for Soviet hospitals. Knaus reports that one-third of Soviet hospitals do not have adequate laboratories for blood transfusion, and when laboratories exist they are frequently closed, particularly at night and on weekends.

Many hospitals are located in old, dilapidated buildings; and although adequate as dormitories or hotels, they are hardly the kind of facility that has become commonplace in the West. The Botkin Hospital in Moscow, consisting of prerevolutionary and more recent buildings, is fairly well-known because Westerners are sometimes hospitalized there. In the Botkin, as in most older Soviet hospitals, toilet facilities are primitive (see Note 15). On David's (a hospitalized American) floor there were three toilets for seventy-six men. These had no seats and, unless one brought a morning copy of *Pravda*, no toilet paper. Compounding the problem, the Soviets dispense enemas as readily as American hospitals give back rubs. The toilets are always in use and frequently overflow, constantly covering the bathroom floor with a sticky mixture of urine and feces.

If this is the case for a Moscow hospital that admits foreigners, one can well imagine the situation in other hospitals, particularly outside of the capital. It is therefore not surprising that for most Soviet citizens the hospital is a place to keep away from, if at all possible, justifying its Russian etymological root of *bol'*, i.e., pain or suffering. The care is often primitive; operations are performed without the required sterility precautions; the equipment and the supplies often short or not available. Knaus even reports the amazing fact that apparently the Soviet Union does not manufacture wheelchairs. When patients cannot move on their own, they are placed on litters or stretchers. The diet in Soviet hospitals is skimpy and monotonous, and it is customary for relatives or friends to bring food or send food parcels to the patients. It is not unknown for the staff to appropriate food destined for patients, as is sometimes done in prisons.[47]

It is true, of course, that American hospitals (and American medicine) have been accused of being crisis oriented, obsessed with technology, depersonalized, and expensive; and the accusation is well justified. American hospitals often do too much, which sometimes leads to problems and errors as well as unneeded services and surgery. But in the Soviet system the reverse situation seems to obtain. Thus

> The condition of the patient's cardiovascular system is
> not fully evaluated prior to surgery, and he goes into shock
> on the operating table. A blood transfusion is not prop-
> erly matched, and the recipient has a seizure. Blood tests
> monitoring white blood cells are not done frequently
> enough, and a life threatening infection develops. All of
> these errors can, and do, occur in American hospitals,
> but from unofficial estimates, from a review of the Soviet
> medical literature, and from conversations with Soviet
> physicians, they are likely to happen in the USSR. . . . The
> seriously ill Soviet patient is afraid . . . he knows that
> the Soviet hospital system has the same problems as the fac-
> tory where he works, the stores where he shops, the
> transportation system he uses.[48]

I think that the above remarks will be sufficient to again convey the idea that the Soviet hospital, while it partakes of many of the universal characteristics of hospitals around the world, is also a *Soviet* institution. And therefore if we were to project our mental image of a Western or American hospital as we know and have experienced it (whether it be a community hospital or a large teaching university one) and assume that the Soviet hospital corresponds to that image, we would be off the mark.

Biomedical Technology

I have suggested that the Soviet medical system, by contrast with Western and American ones, tends to be labor rather than capital intensive. Depending on one's viewpoint, particularly if one finds Western health care depersonalized, inhuman, and alienative of the patient, this labor intensity is potentially positive. And in some instances it certainly is. Figures suggest that Soviet patients have many more visits to the physician in the polyclinic and more hospitalization episodes than their American counterparts. But in the final analysis, modern medicine based on the application of science and technology is more than the laying of the hands and the sympathetic listening of the therapist: it must, *and the Soviet health system is in principle dedicated to this proposition*, have at its disposal the necessary equipment and supplies to practice medicine according to the state of the art. And here again, anyone familiar with Soviet production, particularly of consumer goods and their distribution, will find an answer to the supply of medical equipment. That supply obeys the same general rules; and given the fact that the health system is not a high-priority area, it suffers the same shortages and erratic distribution as the rest of the consumer economy.

A few years ago Raymond Bauer and I were asked to do a comparative study of the Soviet and the American pharmaceutical system. The study was prompted by the many justified criticisms addressed at the profit-making American pharmaceutical industry and the high cost of drugs at the time of purchase. In fact, the Soviet system of pharmaceutical research, testing, development and distribution, and information in *principle* resembled the blueprint that critics of the American situation advocated: a "rational" and integrated government-run system that would eliminate needless duplications, avoid excessive costs, be sensitive to demand, and refrain from the excesses in marketing and advertising epitomized, particularly, by the American detail men used by pharmaceutical houses to peddle their wares to physicians.

A review of Soviet materials revealed an extremely inefficient system, riddled by bureaucracy, poor quality, and severe problems in production, shortages, distribution, retailing, and informing physicians about new items.[49] Altogether, the American system could be described as relatively expensive at the point of purchase but efficient in supplying American patients and hospitals with precisely what was prescribed when it was needed. The Soviet system, although drug retail prices were relatively low, was one in which the patient very often was unable to obtain prescription and nonprescription items, or only with difficulty. Complaints were voiced, time and again, that not only were pharmaceuticals not available but even the simplest items of medical care—bandages, absorbent cotton, aspirins, thermometers, iodine, and so on—were difficult to procure.

It is my impression that since the early 1970s no miracle has happened, and the supply of pharmaceuticals and of medical equipment remains deficient, erratic, short. For example, *Pravda* in 1978 published a response by the USSR Deputy Health Minister A. I. Burnazian to letters from readers complaining about the work of the pharmaceutical system. He acknowledged that in spite of some improvements, there were still many deficiencies in all aspects of the pharmaceutical system, from production to distribution, retailing, and informing physicians.[50] As a result, as we shall see below, there is a black or gray market in drugs unavailable either for purchase in pharmacies or for use by physicians within hospitals.

The shortage in equipment for hospitals is also a problem. It is twofold: (1) not enough money is available to hospitals to purchase the equipment; and (2) even if the money is available, often the equipment is not available, or if available, of poor quality and often unusable. Knaus notes time and again how poorly supplied Soviet hospitals are whether it be in transfusion, in x-ray equipment and film, or in equipment to save premature babies. Thus even Moscow, a city of seven million inhabitants with the most sophisticated medical care available in the USSR, has *only one* hospital that specializes in treating premature births.[51] Respirators are not only used to save infants, they also take over when a person can no longer breathe because of disease or drugs. According to Soviet projections, there are only one-fourth as many respirators produced as needed, and a third of them are broken. Soviet engineers used German and Swedish models. But the Soviet version is shoddy, poorly machined, the bolts do not fit, and plastic knobs, when broken, cannot be replaced. In addition, controls on these machines are often improperly calibrated, and patients receive too much or too little ventilation.[52]

These shortcomings affect not only clinical medicine but also prevention, and this in a system that proclaims prevention as its keystone. For example, a lack of laboratory facilities to detect streptococcal infections leads to rheumatic diseases and constitutes a definite health risk for thousands of Soviet children.

Granted that in the West we often do too much. But if too much is a problem, it is a problem of cutting down already available (and often profitable) services and supplies. Too little, on the other hand, is a more difficult problem to solve, particularly under Soviet conditions, given the limited resources available. This can easily lead to manifold negative, if not tragic, personal consequences. Let's hear from a surgeon working in a town near Khabarovsk who unloaded his frustrations on Dr. Knaus. After complaining that he operated for three months with his bare hands because there was a delay in getting rubber gloves manufactured,

> we once ran out of vascular sutures. One night a young
> boy came in after falling off a tractor. His popliteal artery
> was ripped open. If I'd had some vascular suture I'd
> have been able to save his leg. As it was, I had to cut off his
> leg! Nine years old and with only one leg.[53]

Year after year the same complaints are voiced in letters to the editor and in "investigative" articles that confirm such complaints. They usually reveal the incredibly inefficient manner in which medical supplies and pharamceuticals are produced; and like peeling an endless onion, those reporters who try to get at the root cause always discover another link in the chain of events that accounts for the problems. Responsible officials, against whom public anger can be directed, are identified. Fines are imposed, but to no avail, particularly since they do not come out of the pockets of the "guilty." To take one report from many, there is in Kuibyshev "complete disorganization in the pharamaceutical supply . . . a doctor writes a prescription, and it is not available in the pharmacy." Cases like this are in the hundreds, while letters, telegrams, telephone calls, teletype messages are exchanged, all to no avail.[54]

Needless to add that these shortages and this shoddiness, which parallel the general supply of most consumer goods, are unlikely to be found in the health system reserved for the elites.

The "Second Economy"

Increased attention has been paid recently in the West to the phenomenon of the "second" economy in the Soviet Union. This formally illegal private economy and corruption exist because of the ubiquitous shortages in most consumer goods (including food) on the Soviet marketplace. I have no intention of describing the second economy (it was well done by Grossman)[55] except to note that it is in essence a black or gray market system, that it deals in goods, supplies, and services not usually available in stores or markets, and that it contributes to an inflation of costs since those engaged in it use it to derive personal profits. In some instances it consists of a barter arrangement, as when a shop girl will sell goods only to friends who have something in return to sell to her. Items are stolen from state stores, factories, and supply depots and privately sold to individuals. Money is offered as a bribe to obtain goods or services that normally should be available without such an enticement, and so on.

The second economy also affects the health care system, particularly since health care is a poorly financed item in Soviet society. It has become a normal procedure to give medical and nursing personnel either money or gifts to secure more personalized attention.

I think it is perfectly understandable, given the importance that illness or suffering plays in a person's life, that some attempt be made by the patient to motivate the physician to do his best or to do something extra. And given the general bureaucratic indifference of Soviet employees, this attitude is not surprising. This is, I believe, reinforced by the fact that Soviet physicians and health personnel are paid, as mentioned earlier, very little. Craig Whitney reported the case of a physician who took a high-paying job in a medical laboratory as a senior researcher. She wanted to go back to her job as a general practitioner, even with a loss of about $150 per month in salary, because her patients who were sales clerks would sell her items of clothing at the normal price. Now, the doctor reported, she has to pay the clerks double to get them.[56]

By the same token, a physician can exchange professional services for food, particularly meat, which is not generally available in stores.[57] It is *not* illegal for a Soviet physician to have a private practice, and indeed tax rates (which are incidentally quite high[58]) have been published for physicians and dentists in private practice. It can be surmised that it is the desire for privacy and the hope for better and more personalized care that will impel a patient to see a physician privately and pay the extra amount. Thus a private abortion costs about 40 to 50 rubles, as against the fee of 5 rubles in a public clinic; a visit to a professor of medicine may cost up to 150 rubles.[59] Here is a young man reporting how his father's illness had cost the family most of its savings:

> First it was 100 rubles to get him admitted to a small
> room in Botkin (hospital). Twenty rubles a day for the

nurse—my father was old and couldn't control his bow-
els very well. Then 350 rubles so that a certain professor
performed the surgery. . . . The antibiotics were another
two or three hundred rubles. In the end, however, all of it
was wasted. . . . Father developed an infection and
died.[60]

The existence of bribery and corruption is not, of course, a secret to anyone
who lives in the Soviet Union. From time to time items appear in the press
reporting cases and deploring the practice, all apparently to no effect since the
practice is widespread, if not universal. One letter to *Literaturnaia gazeta*, for
example, excoriated the practice of

. . . collections . . . from patients for gifts to doctors.
These may not be crimes, but they are immoral acts. Repeated directives condemning them apparently have been insufficient. I propose a law providing severe penalties for
presenting gifts . . . to doctors even out of the best of
motives. The subtle extortion from patients, in violation of
the Hippocratic oath, is worst of all.

This letter was published as part of a long-term series of articles and letters on the
question of gifts, bribes, and tips.[61]

In the wake of shakeups in the Azerbaidzhan Republic, *Bakinskii rabochii*
reported widespread corruption in the organs of health (embezzlement, bribery,
extortion, use of official position for mercenary purposes, etc.), including the
hoarding of medicines and their resale at high prices.[62] It also reported, in
another article, that there are frequent cases in which surgeons will not begin
even an urgent operation until they have met with the patient's relatives and
agreed on a fee. ". . . a number of hospitals have even established unofficial but
fixed rates for a number of types of treatment, especially surgery. . . ."[63]

Given past experience and continuing shortages, it is very unlikely that
Draconian laws, directives, resolutions, edicts, and indignant letters and articles
in the press will have much effect on these practices. In a system where the
director of a medical school (in Georgia) was sent to jail for fifteen years in 1976
because 170 from a class of 200 medical students had been admitted through
bribes (see Note 50); or where students who had never been to medical school
requested and obtained admission as pseudotransfers into the second-year class
through the use of forged certificates,[64] there is little chance that such practices
will be eliminated in the near future.

In the hospitals nurses and attendants also have to be bribed or paid money
to get sheets changed, a bed pan, a back rub, narcotics, and other services.
Indeed, patients who go to the hospitals come armed with a sheaf of ruble notes.
Those who do not know this practice suffer the consequences, as did an American
tourist who broke her hip. She spent "four days lying in her excrement, grossly
mistreated and abused."[65]

Pharmaceuticals also fall into the channels of the second economy. It is not unusual for patients to be approached by suppliers of black market drugs who will sell them at a multiple of the original price, as noted earlier. In some instances physicians instruct patients (or their relatives) about the black market, where to obtain the drugs, so that they will bring them to the hospital for administration. Comparing the George Washington Hospital with the Botkin Hospital in Moscow, Knaus noted that the GWH lists sixty-seven antibiotics in its formulary: the Botkin lists eight, of which only four are routinely available.[66]

Given the erratic nature of medical supplies, it is not unusual for hospitals to engage in barter or exchange in order to maintain their inventory. If one hospital has an extra supply of, let's say, sutures, it will cast around other hospitals to see whether it could not exchange them for items in short supply, syringes for example. At the same time, should excess supplies be available, some of them may well make their way onto the black market.[67]

It might be noted that this pattern of trading, of adjusting supply and demand, is in no way peculiar to the medical system: it is an accepted practice, as mentioned earlier, in Soviet industry. Without it industrial and medical performance would be even worse than it is.

The upshot of this is that the claim of *besplatno*, of free and high-quality medical care, often sounds, if one may be forgiven the expression, like a sick joke. Here again the Soviet health system is affected, in almost its entirety, by the larger patterns and problems that characterize and plague Soviet society and its economy. The time may well come when the health authorities, recognizing the pervasiveness and the universal nature of the problem, will officially sanction extra payments for medical care if, as the formula might state, people are willing, able, and eager to pay for such services. I have already mentioned the private practice of medicine. There are also the so-called "paying polyclinics" where, for a rather modest fee, patients may avail themselves of the services and consultations of physicians, many of whom are better qualified than those found in the free polyclinics. But as far as I can judge, these polyclinics, which are perfectly legal, have not received much support from the health authorities, though they do seem to provide important services.[68] Thus the very same forces of the market mechanisms the system of socialized medicine was to eliminate have found their way back into the practice of medicine, either to counteract bureaucratic depersonalization and indifference or to secure a better deal in a shortage situation.

The Quality of Care

It is in the light of the above elements that one can make some impressionistic judgments on that most difficult and elusive concept, the quality of care. It is clear that the Soviet approach to health care, so far, has been a quantitative, labor-intensive one. With its plethora of physicians and hospital beds, Soviet medicine appears, on first blush, impressive; and it has indeed impressed many Western and other visitors, particularly when they are shown statistical tables of progress made since the revolution, both in personnel and in facilities. And it is possible that in a truly dialectical sense, increased quantitative changes lead to qualitative ones.

Yet a closer examination of clinical practices suggests that the quality of care is low when using, as a measuring rod, Western Europe and the United States. Indeed, in some instances it resembles what one witnesses in the lesser developed countries (recall, for example, the earlier reference to Afghanistan). And the level of infant mortality is certainly not what one might expect of a highly industrialized nation, with an economy that in size alone is second only to the United States, a nation that pioneered a national system of socialized medicine. Thus with the exception of the elites for whom the best is available or imported, the population in general receives a kind of mass medical care, with little attention to detail, quality, and personal feelings and emotions.

This does not mean that it has to continue to be a low-quality operation. It may very well improve as the Soviet leadership and the health authorities increasingly realize how backward their system really is in comparison to what it could be. This will require important changes in the structure of the health system, and in the motivation and the attitudes of health personnel, as well as significantly larger budgetary allocations. The way in which the Soviet economy has developed in the last few years, and the increased defense investments the Soviets have made since the midsixties, make a reordering of priorities and a significant increase in the quality of medical care, at this historical juncture, most unlikely. Indeed, the reverse seems to be in the cards, if the rising death rates in the Soviet Union are any indication.[69]

Conclusions

I started with the proposition that from society's viewpoint, the primary functional problem caused by morbidity and premature mortality was their impact on the social role-performance capacity of individual members of society. In that respect health can be seen as a natural resource; and the medical knowledge and techniques devised by man, as well as the specialization of roles and organizations to deal with the sick, as specific responses to the threat posed by disease and early death. This in no way invalidates the individual or expressive concern which is the epicenter of clinical medicine, nor the personal and emotional impact of illness on the person, which often is devastating (including, of course, the realization that illness prevents one from performing one's social responsibilities and affects one's self-image).

The rise of medicine as an applied science and technology in the nineteenth century has led, in the last hundred years, to the emergence of a "health system," complex, sophisticated, expensive, but overall more successful in dealing with the morbidity and early mortality threat than any other approach in the past: hence its visibility and its legitimacy.

To a large extent, the Soviet health system shares many of the features of such systems in other contemporary industrial societies.

Given the priority arrangements of Soviet society and its total resources, the fraction of the GNP allowed to flow into the health system is considerably smaller than that in the United States, and recently it has decreased; at the present time my estimate is that it is only one-third of the American corresponding investment, though this is only a very rough guess. Monies that flow into it through the second economy would lead to an upward revision of that estimate.

But alongside these elements, the Soviet health system is permeated by its Soviet (and some would add, its Russian) nature. We must therefore talk about Soviet medicine as a distinctive way in which the universal elements of medical care and knowledge are applied in a specific national and historical setting. It would be foolish to argue that there are no problems in Soviet medicine that could not be solved through the infusion of a few billion rubles. We have not solved many of our own medical problems by throwing money at them in the United States. Certainly some additional appropriations would help, but not necessarily to the degree we might expect. For example, one of the perennial complaints of the Health Ministry is that budgetary appropriations and allocations to build or repair hospitals are not used by health authorities: in many instances construction workers, building materials, and supplies are not available even with money. And if the Soviet medical equipment industry does not produce certain types of sutures, antibiotics, or respirators, the availability of money per se will not help (unless these items are purchased abroad). Thus the problems of the Soviet medical system are the general problems of Soviet society, and solutions to the former are not possible without solving the latter.

This view is also compatible with the increased recognition that the activities of the health system per se and of medical practitioners have but a relatively modest impact on morbidity and mortality. Of greater import, it is claimed, are changes in the economic level of society, reduction of family size, improvement in housing, education, nutrition, general sanitation, and well-being.[70]

When I am asked to summarize the main problems of Soviet urban health services, I could very easily list some of the major ones: lack of sufficient funding, lack of equipment and medical supplies, demographic changes in the direction of an older population (with higher morbidity problems), declines in fertility and in the natural increase in the population.[71] But at the same time, I have become increasingly convinced that the health of a population is also affected by nonmedical measures and factors. There is thus increased skepticism in the West about the nature of the health system, its misplaced priorities, its reliance on technology and gadgetry that is often of dubious clinical value, and particularly its escalating costs, which are seen as only marginally affecting the health of the population.

Given the above argument, the conclusion from the Western experience would be to downsize the health system, to decapitalize it, to increase its labor intensity, and to deal with morbidity and premature mortality through nonmedical, social, and welfare measures that in the long run might have a more beneficial impact on the health and the well-being of the population. It is interesting in this respect that the Soviet Union seems to have followed this path, at least insofar as the health system is concerned, and was able to do so because of its tight control over it.

By this I mean decreased shares of budgetary allocations to health. But I doubt that this was the result of a deliberate policy on the part of the leadership to shift resources from health to other areas that would better contribute to the well-being of the population. Rather, I suspect, the savings were swallowed by other, less benign components of the Soviet budget such as the military in an increasingly costly effort to maintain parity with the United States. This shift, I also would further suspect, may also account for *part* of the increase in the crude mortality rate, and perhaps even more specifically in the mortality rate of that population most at risk, infants under the age of one.[72]

It is in the light of such findings (about mortality) that it has become fashionable to speak of a "health crisis" in the Soviet Union.[73] In my view it is more than simply that: the crisis in health may well reflect deeper systemic problems in the society, its political system, and its economy. Improvements in the health status of the population will thus depend on measures aimed not only at the system of socialized medicine but also at the general standard of living of the entire population, including those who live at or below the poverty line. McAuley estimated that by the end of the 1960s, in spite of efforts to raise the floor below which people would not be allowed to sink, about 35 to 40 percent of the population were "poor" according to the criteria established by the Soviets themselves.[74] And we know that poverty is associated with illness and premature mortality. And it may well be that it is that population which, with its high rates of morbidity and mortality, is pushing national rates to such a level that the authorities are reluctant to publish statistics.

And finally, to go back to that more narrow assessment of success and failure of the health system per se, it may well be that functionally or instrumentally the Soviet health system has produced important and beneficial quantitative changes that have yielded impressive statistical averages. This often means that the individualistic and expressive (or emotional) needs of individual patients get short shrift. But this is also why the implementation of the blueprint of socialized medicine in its Soviet form has found little favor among outside observers for whom the patient, rather than patients, is still the central concern of clinical medicine.

Notes

[1]Mark G. Field, "Former Soviet Citizens' Attitudes Toward the Soviet, the German and the American Medical Systems," *American Sociological Review*, 20 (December 1955), 674-79.

[2]Henry E. Sigersist: *Socialized Medicine in the Soviet Union* (New York, 1937); *Medicine and Health in the Soviet Union* (New York, 1947).

[3]Morbidity is a generic term denoting illness, trauma, disease, i.e., any impairment to the health of individuals. Premature or early mortality refers to deaths considered to have occurred before a "normal" or "natural" life span. Morbidity and premature mortality are the central concerns of medicine and public health.

[4]William A. Knaus, M.D., *Inside Russian Medicine* (New York, 1981), 356-57. I have made rather extensive use of this recently published book because it contains insights on Soviet medicine not usually available to outsiders.

[5]Article 42 of the Constitution states: "Citizens of the USSR have the right to health protection. This right is ensured by free, qualified medical care provided by state health institutions; by extension of the network of therapeutic and health-building institutions; by the development and improvement of safety and hygiene in industry; by carrying out broad prophylactic measures; by measures to improve the environment; by special care for the health of youth, including prohibition of child labor, excluding the work done by children as part of the school curriculum; and by developing research to prevent and reduce the incidence of disease and ensure citizens a long and active life" (adopted in 1977).

[6]Mark G. Field, *Soviet Socialized Medicine* (New York, 1967), 42-48.

[7]Christopher Davis and Murray Feshbach, *Rising Infant Mortality in the U.S.S.R. in the 1970's* (Washington, D.C., 1980), 30.

[8]Imogene Edwards, Margaret Hughes, and James Noren, "U.S. and U.S.S.R.: Comparisions of GNP," in *Soviet Economy in a Time of Change* (Washington, D.C., 1979), *1*, 369-99.

[9]The relationship between health system resources and activities and infant mortality (or mortality in general) is not a direct one. Infant mortality, generally speaking, is affected by both medical and nonmedical factors, the latter having a greater effect than the former. By nonmedical factors are meant general economic well-being, housing conditions, food supply and nutrition, family organization and stability, prematurity, and so on.

[10]This is a literal translation of the word *zdravookhranenie*. Thus the ministry is neither a Health Ministry nor a Ministry of Public Health in the strict sense of these words. Its overall responsibility is the health of the population, and it thus embraces, under the same administrative roof, clinical (or medical) *and* preventive (public health) services.

[11]I was taken to task violently by the Soviets two decades ago because I had utilized displaced persons to gain some ideas about what the practice of medicine had been (from the patient's viewpoint) in the forties. Having met, at long last, the person who had criticized me as well as his colleagues at the Semashko Institute in Moscow, and having established a face-to-face relationship with them, I proposed (by letter) that the very same questionnaires I had administered to the displaced persons be utilized by them to carry out a survey of patient satisfaction in clinics and hospitals, thereby securing an unbiased sample. The answer that came back, six months later, was that essentially the research I proposed was not needed since they had an excellent idea of how people felt regarding their health care from discussions, newspaper articles, television programs, and so forth. The real reason for that refusal, one may surmise, is that the results of such questionnaires would have revealed a picture of dissatisfaction that hardly coincides with the rosy descriptions served by Soviet propaganda. More recently, however, attempts have been made to survey patients on their experiences at the clinic. For example, the following questions were asked anonymously of patients in Kiev: 1. Did you feel better after seeing the physician? 2. Do you trust your physician? 3. Would you like to be treated by another physician? 4. How do you assess the results and the course of treatment? See Pavel Beilin, "Live (*zhivaia*) Medical Soul," *Meditsinskaia gazeta*, October 16, 1981, 4.

[12]The assignments of a physician to such groups resulted from the earlier death of a guide from a botched appendectomy.

[13]Cited in Constance Holden, "Health Care in the Soviet Union," *Science*, 212, *1092* (September 4, 1981).

[14]See, for example, Walter D. Connor, *Socialism, Politics and Equality* (New York, 1979); Mervyn Matthews, *Class and Society in Soviet Russia* (New York, 1972); Frank Parkin, *Class Inequality and Political Order* (New York, 1971).

[15]In Moscow the Kremlin polyclinic is on Kalinin Prospekt; in Leningrad, near the Neva River and the Winter Palace; in Irkutsk it is a pink and white four-story building

surrounded by large shade trees and protected by a high iron fence. See Knaus, "Special Care for Special People," 299 ff.

[16]A Hungarian sociologist colleague, who occupied an important position in the Hungarian Academy of Sciences, told me that at one time he needed some elective surgery. He went to the hospital, asking that he be given a private room that would permit him to work quietly, adding that he was ready and prepared to pay for the cost of such a luxury. He got his private room but was unable to pay for it as there was no mechanism to compute and receive such payment. He added that, in fact, his private accommodations were paid by those in the public wards. (Personal communication.)

[17]See Knaus, 300.

[18]Thus Dr. Michael DeBakey was asked to come to Moscow first to consult, and later to operate, on Mstislav Keldish, the president of the Soviet Academy of Sciences (1972 and 1973). In 1979 Warren Zapol of the Massachusetts General Hospital was summoned to the Soviet Union to operate on the eldest daughter of Dr. Vladimir Burakovskii, an internationally known cardiovascular surgeon and director of the Bakulev Institute of Cardiovascular Surgery (ibid., 303-12). This was widely reported in the Soviet press as an example of Soviet-American medical cooperation, but no reference was made to the identity of the patient.

[19]Letter to Gorky, November 1913, in Bertram Wolfe, *Three Who Made a Revolution* (New York, 1964), 613.

[20]Alexander I. Solzhenitsyn, *The First Circle* (New York, 1968), 346. I am indebted to Walter Connor for bringing this to my attention in his book, Note 14, 258.

[21]Knaus, 144.

[22]Knaus, 104 and 125.

[23]See, for example, the letter of G. Kozhukhantseva, "The Human Factor," *Literaturnaia gazeta*, December 14, 1977, in which she complains bitterly about being refused attention by a physician in a nearby clinic after she had fallen and hurt her back, and the pain and suffering she had to endure to reach another clinic where a traumatologist was available.

[24]Knaus, 20-22.

[25]Ibid., 107.

[26]Ibid.

[27]Ibid., 108, 271.

[28]Ibid., 104.

[29]Ibid., 141.

[30]Ibid., 137.

[31]"The Sector Physician," *Literaturnaia gazeta*, September 27, 1978, trans. in *Current Digest of the Soviet Press*, 30, *40* (November 1, 1978), 5 (hereafter *CD*).

[32]Knaus, 108.

[33]Joseph S. Berliner, *Factory and Manager in the U.S.S.R.* (Cambridge, 1956).

[34]Knaus, 108.

[35]"High Duty of Physicians," *Izvestia*, February 24, 1977, 5.

[36]Knaus, 83.

[37]Serge Schmemann, "Soviets Affirm Rise in Infant Mortality," *New York Times*, June 21, 1981, 15.

[38]"The Human Factor," written as a commentary on the Kozhukhantseva letter, Note 23, *Literaturnaia gazeta*, December 14, 1977.

[39]*Abuse of Psychiatry for Political Repression in the Soviet Union* (Washington, D.C., 1972), 130.

[40]See Note 31.

[41]That physician is called an *uchastkovii vrach* or microdistrict physician. In most instances that physician by training is a generalist, called in Russian a *terapevt*. Although technically a *terapevt* is considered a specialized physician, in fact he or she is the nearest equivalent to a general practitioner. Thus Soviet physicians who do not become specialists (surgeons, oncologists, psychiatrists, etc.) remain *terapevty*.

[42]See Note 31.

[43]Knaus, 345.

[44]Ibid., 146.

[45]Ibid., 125.

[46]Ibid., 123.

[47]"In a number of medical institutions in Baku, Kirovabad, Agdam, Yevlakh and other cities and districts in the republics cases have come to light of . . . the misappropriation of food intended for persons undergoing inpatient treatment," the Aberdaidzhan Communist Party Central Committee, *Bakinskii rabochii*, June 16, 1979, 2; *CD*, 40, *31* (August 29, 1979).

[48]Knaus, 116-17.

[49]Raymond A. Bauer and Mark G. Field, *The Soviet and the American Pharmaceutical Systems: Some Paradoxical Contrasts* (Cambridge, 1962); Mark G. Field, *The Soviet Pharmaceutical System: Administration and Operations—1966* (Cambridge, 1966); Mark G. Field, with Natasha Lissman, *The Soviet Pharmaceutical System Revisited: Developments 1965-1972* (New York, 1972).

[50]"A Person Goes to the Drug-store," *Pravda*, May 21, 1978, 3; *CD*, 50, *20* (June 14, 1979), 20.

[51]Knaus, 107 and 212.

[52]Ibid., 110. Knaus also cites the *Bulletin ispolitel'nogo komiteta Moskovskogo gorodskogo soveta deputatov trudiaschikhsia* (February 1976), which details the scandalous situation regarding the equipment of Moscow hospitals.

[53]Ibid., 333.

[54]"The Fine (Does Not Come) Out of One's Pocket," *Meditsinskaia gazeta*, September 16, 1981, 2.

[55]For details see Gregory Grossman, "Notes on the Illegal Private Economy and Corruption," *Soviet Economy in a Time of Change* (Washington, D.C., 1979), 834-55.

[56]Craig Whitney, "In Soviet Bribes Help to Get a Car, Get an Apartment, and Get Ahead," *New York Times*, May 7, 1978, 1, 22.

[57]David K. Shipler, "Soviet Medicine Mixes Inconsistency with Diversity," *New York Times*, June 26, 1977.

[58]The tax on a net income of 1,800 per year is 422.20 rubles, or about 23 percent, with 40 percent on amounts above 1,800, 46.5 percent above 2,400, reaching 69 percent on amounts above 7,000 rubles. Cited in Grossman, 835, note 3.

[59]Knaus, 330.

[60]Ibid., 136.

[61]"The Debatable and the Indisputable," *Literaturnaia gazeta*, January 5, 1977; *CD*, 29, *2* (February 9, 1977), 16.

[62]See Note 47.

[63]"Combat the Antipodes of Communist Morality," *Bakinskii rabochii*, January 23, 1979; *CD*, 31, *4* (February 21, 1979), 13.

[64]S. Bablumian, "Face to Face with the Law: Pseudo-students," *Izvestia*, September 11, 1981, 6.

[65]Shipler.

[66]Ibid., 128.

[67]Ibid., 129.

[68]"If the Patient Came from Verkhoiansk," *Literaturnaia gazeta*, December 28, 1977, *CD*, 29, *52* (January 25, 1978), 11.

[69]Richard Cooper, "Rising Death Rates in the Soviet Union," *New England Journal of Medicine*, 304 (May 21, 1981), 1259-65.

[70]See, for example, the work of Thomas McKeown in England and of John McKinlay in the United States.

[71]See, for example, V. A. Miniaev, L. V. Poliakov, N. S. Sokolova, and E. A. Boiarinova, "Medical Aspects of Demographic Policy in the Conditions of the Large City," *Sovetskoe zdravookhranenie*, 3 (1981), 7-11.

[72]And to add a gloomy comparative note, should the present social policies of the Reagan administration be carried out to their logical conclusions, I would not be at all surprised to see within a year or two an upward swing, for example, in the black, Hispanic, and poor-white American infant mortality. For example, see Bernard Weintraub, "Don't Throw the Baby with the Medicaid-Medicare Bath Water," *New York Times* (July 22, 1981), 22.

[73]Nick Eberstadt, "The Health Crisis in the U.S.S.R.," *New York Review of Books* (February 19, 1981).

[74]Alastair McAuley, *Economic Welfare in the Soviet Union: Poverty, Living Standards and Inequality* (Madison, 1979), 70.

Richard B. Dobson

8

Soviet Education: Problems and Policies in the Urban Context

It is difficult to do justice to problems of urban educational policy in a single chapter, if only because the Soviet educational system has a complex organizational structure and performs diverse functions. Since 1973 all children have been required to complete eight years of schooling in the "general-education school," which offers academic training in standard subjects along with courses designed to foster civic competence and preparation for work. The public school is also charged with political and moral socialization—with instilling the norms of "communist morality," patriotism, and devotion to the Soviet regime and with transmitting a "materialistic" Marxist-Leninist world view. It further contributes to social and cultural integration by giving all students training in Russian, the *lingua franca* of this ethnically diverse society where Russians now constitute less than half of the school-age population. The influence of the school thus radiates outward, touching most aspects of urban life—the family, the work force, official and informal youth groups, even citizens' political attitudes and behavior, moral standards, and leisure-time pursuits.

The range of educational "problems" is correspondingly broad. Plant managers, for instance, regularly comment in the press on inadequacies in the schools' labor training. Party and Komsomol (Young Communist League) officials fire off salvos against shortcomings in political and atheistic upbringing. Educational administrators worry about curricular reforms and staffing, while teachers complain about shortages of textbooks and problems of discipline. For their part, parents voice concern about problems relating to their children's progress in school—excessive amounts of homework, grading practices, and the like. This chapter will concentrate on the issues that relate most directly to the urban environment. We will begin by reviewing general policy, types of schools,

The research reported in this chapter was supported by a National Fellowship from the Hoover Institution (1980–81) and a visiting fellowship from the Kennan Institute for Advanced Russian Studies (April 1981). I also wish to express my appreciation to Murray Feshbach of Georgetown University and the staff of the Foreign Demographic Analysis Division, U.S. Bureau of the Census, for help in locating materials; to Robert J. Osborn and the editors for their comments on an earlier draft; and to the Department of Sociology and Institute for Research on Educational Finance and Governance, Stanford University, for additional assistance.

problems of administration, and social differences in access. In the second part we will look more closely at variations among urban day, evening, and correspondence general-education schools, as well as the "second economy" in education. The last section will explore three areas of particular concern to party and educational officials—reforms of the academic program and the maintenance of scholastic standards, youth problems affecting the schools, and recent efforts to improve labor training.

The Structure of the Educational System

In the past three decades the overriding objective of Soviet educational policy has been "universal secondary education"—that is, to ensure that every youngster completes the equivalent of a ten-year secondary education. This policy, according to official spokesmen, is motivated by economic, political, and social imperatives. It is believed that a well-educated work force is essential for economic growth and innovation, that the requirements for civic competence are rising, and that all citizens should enjoy the right to secondary schooling. Accordingly, many small schools have been consolidated into larger units; teachers' qualifications have been raised; and more and more students have been enrolled in "complete secondary" schools that combine grades one through ten in a single building. (These contrast with the primary and eight-year institutions, whose students must enroll in another school to advance to a higher grade.) Between 1950 and 1980 the proportion of all day students attending ten-year schools rose from less than a third to four-fifths. Even more striking is the growth in secondary-school graduations. From 284,000 in 1950, the number of students who graduated from the tenth (or eleventh) grade of day, evening, or correspondence schools rose dramatically to a million in 1960, 2.6 million in 1970, and nearly 4 million in 1980.[1]

Before proceeding we must step back for a moment to gain a view of the overall dimensions of the educational system. Table 1 presents summary statistics on the number of schools, enrollments, and graduations for the years 1965–80. Basically, the system consists of a "trunk"—the general-education school—from which more specialized institutions branch out. In 1980 there were 145,000 day schools with a combined enrollment of 39.5 million students; an additional 4.7 million youngsters were enrolled in evening or extramural general-education classes. Aside from these schools, there are three types of institutions which give training in specific occupational specialties:

1) The vocational-technical schools (*professional'no-tekhnicheskie uchilishcha*, abbreviated PTUs) train skilled workers in particular trades through courses that normally last one to four years. In view of the economy's need for skilled workers, the government has given high priority to expanding and upgrading the PTUs. Between 1965 and 1980, as Table 1 indicates, nearly 3,000 new PTUs were opened, so that by 1980, the country's 7,242 PTUs had a total enrollment of 3.6 million, well over twice as many as in 1965. Since 1969, most PTUs have been converted into "secondary vocational-technical schools"

Table 1
Number of Schools, Enrollments, and Graduations, USSR, 1965-80

	1965	1970	1975	1980
Number of schools				
General-education	214,000	190,000	164,000	145,000
Vocational-technical*	4,319	5,351	6,272	7,242
Specialized secondary	3,820	4,223	4,302	4,383
Higher	756	805	856	883
Number of students (in thousands)				
General-education				
day	43,410	45,448	42,611	39,546
evening-correspondence	4,845	3,745	4,983	4,729
Vocational-technical**	1,701	2,591	3,381	3,971
Specialized secondary**	3,659	4,388	4,525	4,612
Higher**	3,861	4,581	4,854	5,235
Number of graduates (in thousands)				
General-education†				
day	913	1,968	2,716	2,728
evening-correspondence	427	613	848	1,238
Vocational-technical**	1,100	1,638	2,094	2,430
Specialized secondary**	622	1,033	1,157	1,275
Higher**	404	631	713	817

Sources: *Narodnoe khoziaistvo SSSR v 1980 g.* (Moscow 1981), 372, 374, 455-56, 458, 462, 469.
*Number of schools in 1966, 1971, 1976, and 1981.
**Full-time, evening, and correpondence divisions.
†Graduates of the tenth or eleventh grade. Although the standard "complete secondary" curriculum consists of ten grades, evening and correspondence schools, as well as day schools in the Baltic republics, have eleven grades.

(SPTUs), whose curriculum combines vocational training with general education. In 1980 more than half of the students attended SPTUs, and an additional one out of five was studying at a technical school (*technicheskoe uchilishche*) designed for those who have already completed a secondary education.

2) The 4,383 specialized secondary institutions (*srednie spetsial'nye uchebnye zavedeniia*) train middle-level white-collar personnel or highly skilled workers, such as technicians, nurses, and elementary-school teachers. These

schools, which recruit either eighth- or tenth-grade graduates of the general-education school, had a combined enrollment in 1980 of 4.6 million students, most of whom attend technical schools known as "technicums." Three out of five students were studying full-time; the remainder attended evening or extra-mural classes.

3) Further up the educational ladder are the 883 higher educational institu-tions (*vysshie uchebnye zavedeniia*, abbreviated VUZy) which train professional workers in specialties requiring advanced training, such as engineers, doctors, secondary-school teachers, and agronomists. Only young people who have al-ready completed a ten-year secondary education are eligible to compete for admission. Most VUZy are highly specialized institutes with a technical profile. Of the 5.2 million students enrolled in higher education in 1980, 57 percent attended full-time programs, which normally run for five years; the others attended night classes or extension-correspondence courses, which usually take at least one additional year to complete.

Though the great majority of young people now complete secondary educa-tion, not all do so by graduating from the tenth (or eleventh) grade of the general-education school. Differentiation is introduced upon completion of the eighth grade, the legal minimum, when students are fifteen or sixteen years old. At that juncture an adolescent must decide whether to continue in the upper grades of the general-education school, compete for admission to a specialized secondary educational institution, enroll in a PTU, or enter the work force. For every 100 young people who graduated from the eighth grade at the beginning of the 1980s, slightly more than 60 continued in the ninth grade of the day school; 20 entered secondary vocational-technical schools (SPTUs); 10 gained admission to special-ized secondary educational institutions; and 8 continued their secondary educa-tion through night or correspondence general-education classes while holding down a job or learning a trade.[2] (In the large European industrial cities, the proportion entering PTUs exceeds the national average.)

Most of the specialized institutions are situated in towns—especially the metropolitan areas. The extreme case is Moscow, which as the Soviet Union's capital and largest city possesses—in addition to its 1,033 general-education schools—140 specialized secondary educational institutions, 113 SPTUs, 74 institutes, and the country's major university. As of 1978 Moscow had more than 1.6 million students: 736,000 youngsters attending the day schools, 97,000 studying in evening classes, 66,000 attending SPTUs, 216,000 enrolled in spe-cialized secondary educational institutions, and 632,000 pursuing college studies.[3]

This concentration of educational institutions, coupled with the nature of the towns' economy, accounts for the high educational level of the urban labor force. According to the 1979 census, one out of every ten persons employed in the Soviet economy had completed a higher education. Yet in the major cities the proportion of college graduates was much higher—one out of five in Leningrad, Minsk, Vilnius, Baku, and Tashkent; one out of four in Moscow, Kiev, and

Erevan; and an extraordinary one out of three in Tbilisi, capital of the Georgian republic.[4] In turn, this highly educated work force makes possible the cities' preeminence in scientific work, industrial production, and culture and contributes to urbanites' relatively high standard of living.

Problems of Administration, Planning, and Coordination

The various types of schools fall under separate jurisdictions. The general-education schools are administered by the USSR Ministry of Education (*Ministerstvo prosveshcheniia SSSR*) and comparable ministries within each republic, which establish general policies and basic norms governing teacher-student ratios, curricula, textbooks, and examinations. Departments of education attached to the soviet executive committees at the province, city, and district levels are responsible for the implementation of policies, hiring of teachers, siting of new schools, and so on. Falling under the jurisdiction of the USSR State Committee for Vocational-Technical Education, comparable committees at the republic level, and branch ministries related to the schools' particular specialization (heavy industry, construction, agriculture, etc.), the PTUs also are administered by committees subordinated to the province, city, or district soviet executive committees. The specialized secondary and higher educational institutions are both administered by the USSR Ministry of Higher and Specialized Secondary Education, republic ministries of the same designation, and branch ministries that relate to the particular school's specialization.[5]

These diverse jurisdictions create difficulties for planning and coordination at the municipal level. Though it is impossible to explore this matter in any detail here, a few comments regarding implementation of the plans to expand the network of trade schools will illustrate the problems. Time and again, the PTUs' ambitious enrollment targets have not been met. To correct this, the Council of Ministers in each republic was instructed to approve uniform plans for the number of eighth-grade graduates who would continue in the ninth grade or enter the vocational schools or technicums. But because of its interest in maintaining its own enrollments, as F. R. Filippov points out, the general-education school has been slow to cooperate: "a reduction in the number of ninth-graders endangers the teachers' normal teaching load, requires changes in the school's staff and in the principals' and vice-principals' salaries, and most important, elicits censure as well as various administrative measures from the public education authorities, who are struggling to draw most students into the ninth grade of the general-education school."[6]

To make matters worse, the general-education school still directs its least-desirable students to the PTUs—just when the government is doing its utmost to raise their prestige. Since 1970 thousands of angry parents have written letters to the press, complaining that school authorities withhold documents needed for eighth-grade graduates to enroll in other schools or refuse to admit students with low or average marks into the ninth grade. Despite repeated denunciations of unwarranted "administrative selection," the practice goes on.[7] Looking into this matter in 1980, for instance, correspondents from *Sovetskaia Rossiia* found that after the eighth grade, "an entirely unexpected criterion for selection comes to the foreground: academic performance."

"No 3s [average grades] on your [eighth-grade] certificate and irreproachable discipline? In that case you can hope [to continue in the ninth grade] because the school will have less trouble with you in the remaining two grades.

You have an average grade, and it was necessary to summon your parents to the school? Then, it's better that you go to a PTU."

However, in our official discussions, no one—from school teachers to the assistant minister of education— was willing to acknowledge even the most general features of such selection's existence. It's a thankless task—to prove what everyone knows. But all the same . . .

In 1979, as in preceding years, those who entered PTUs were for the most part youngsters with average grades, "C-students" [*troechniki*]. In Perm Province they accounted for 84 percent of the entering students; in Sverdlovsk Province, 81 percent; in Cheliabinsk Province, 86 percent.[8]

Problems of coordination extend beyond the rivalry between the regular school and the PTU. Responsibility for the fulfillment of plans for the training of young workers lies with the committees for vocational-technical education, but investments are provided by the branch ministries and departments, which have considerable discretion in the placement of PTUs and by no means always complete their construction plans on time.[9] Furthermore, towns and cities where the ministries have chosen to build PTUs usually are experiencing not only a manpower shortage but also a decline in secondary school graduations (a consequence of an earlier drop in the number of births). Thus "where there are lots of trade schools, there are more and more vacant lathes and school desks; but in places where there are not enough schools, eighth- and tenth-grade graduates are available in abundance."[10] The imbalance is especially marked in Central Asia, where relatively few PTUs have been constructed. Paradoxically, despite the region's rapidly growing rural population, industrial enterprises in many Central Asian cities suffer a chronic labor shortage; they therefore import skilled workers from Siberian and European towns, where workers are already in short supply.[11]

Social Background and Educational Attainment

The parents' complaints about "administrative selection" touch on a sensitive issue connected with the differentiated structure. Parents are, of course, aware that their children's future status depends heavily on the education they receive. The universities and institutes prepare young people for what Soviet scholars call "upper-echelon intelligentsia" positions, or what we would loosely term upper-middle-class professions, whereas the technicums and other specialized secondary educational institutions turn out middle-level white-collar workers, "semiprofessionals." (These two groups of skilled mental workers constitute, in Soviet parlance, the "intelligentsia.") The vocational-technical schools replenish the working class by providing training in the blue-collar trades.

In theory the Soviet educational system provides all youngsters with free access to any type of education that they wish to pursue. None of the state institutions charges fees for tuition, and most full-time students who attend technicums, institutes, and universities receive stipends that help to cover their living costs. Yet choice is limited by the number of openings available; especially in the more prestigious college specialties there are far more applicants than can be accepted. Soviet sociological studies show that a student's social background affects academic performance, as well as career choice. Children from "middle-class" (that is, "intelligentsia") families tend to earn higher marks in school. They also overwhelmingly elect to continue in the upper grades of the day school—the route that affords the best prospects for college entry. Because of greater support from their families, their higher academic performance, and the superior educational resources that they enjoy, the intelligentsia's children are, on the average, at least four times as likely as urban workers' offspring to pursue full-time study in higher education two years after leaving the eighth grade. The more prestigious college specialties—for example, the natural sciences or medicine—draw most of their students from the intelligentsia.[12]

Children of blue-collar workers are much more likely than the intelligentsia's offspring to enroll in trade schools or technicums, where together with children of farm workers and the least-skilled white-collar workers, they typically constitute 80-98 percent of the enrollment. The PTUs, in particular, have long suffered a reputation as a refuge for the urban adolescents with the weakest academic records, young people "from the sticks," and troublemakers. The stereotype clearly had some basis. Among students accepted by Moscow PTUs in 1966, "almost one-third were characterized by antisocial behavior (had been taken into custody by the police, been entered on the books at juvenile detention centers, or committed crimes and been convicted)."[13] By converting the PTUs into secondary schools, the government has hoped to improve their academic standards, enhance their reputation, and gain a better mix of students.

The Urban General-Education School

The remainder of this chapter will focus on the urban general-education school, which in 1980 enrolled 22.1 million youngsters in its full-time programs. Beginning at the age of seven, children are expected to attend the school in whose residential recruitment area (*raion obsluzhivaniia*) they live; in towns this area generally coincides with the microdistrict (*mikroraion*), the territory allocated to a school for recruiting pupils for the first three grades. Most enter school after having spent one or more years in a kindergarten, which at the beginning of the

1980s enrolled two and a half times as large a share of the towns' children as compared with rural youngsters. Some nine out of ten urban day students attend "complete secondary" schools, whose average enrollment (880 in 1975) is roughly twice that of the average rural ten-year school. These large urban schools are generally better equipped with science laboratories, libraries, and sports facilities than the rural schools are, and their teachers typically have higher qualifications. A quarter of the urban day students attend afterschool "extended-day" programs that combine extracurricular activities (sports, excursions, crafts) with supervised study. (Schools run six days a week. Consequently the school day is shorter than under a five-day system.) These programs are especially popular with the working parents of younger schoolchildren.[14]

In a number of important respects, the general-education school differs from the American public school. Instruction is provided in some sixty languages spoken by various nationalities. (Children who are not in Russian classes study Russian as a second language.) At the same time, the school curriculum is basically uniform throughout the country. With the exception of a few "options" that supplement the standard curriculum in grades 7-10, students have little choice in what they study. Beyond this the Soviet school relies more heavily than the American on rote learning and memorization (though attempts have been made to change this) and puts less of a premium on independent thought. On the whole, relations between students and teachers are more formal and authoritarian than in the United States. Students show deference by standing when the teacher enters the class and rarely challenge the teacher's opinion. They are also required to wear uniforms. Furthermore, political and moral upbringing is far more explicit, consistent, and pervasive than that conducted in American schools. In comparing schools in the two countries, Susan Jacoby found Soviet schools to be more like the parochial schools that she attended as a child than American public schools: "Both were deeply concerned with perpetuating an ideology as well as transmitting knowledge; both were more interested in obtaining 'right' answers than questioning minds; both set strict standards of conduct for their students; both adopted certain authoritarian tactics in the classroom, at least partly because of severe overcrowding."[15]

Unlike many American schools, the Soviet school does not commonly practice "tracking" by dividing students according to ability or curriculum. Since the CPSU Central Committee's authoritative denunciation of ability testing in 1936, IQ tests have been banned from Soviet schools. The official educational philosophy regards all children, except the severely handicapped, as being able to master the standard curriculum and advance in step with their peers. When a student falls behind, failure is not attributed to lack of innate ability but rather to laziness, poor study habits, shortcomings on the part of the teacher, or insufficient parental support.

Furthermore, the academic program is generally more rigorous than the American. In the first grade of a Russian school, children devote half of their class time to Russian language study (twelve hours per week), a quarter to mathematics, and the remainder to labor training, physical education, art, music, and singing. In the fourth grade, the first year of the secondary cycle, students begin "departmentalized" instruction, and the balance begins to shift toward science and mathematics, subjects that receive by far the greatest attention in the upper grades. In the course of ten years of schooling, students cover three years of arithmetic (grades 1-3), two years of arithmetic combined with algebra (grades 4-5), five years of algebra (grades 6-10), ten years of geometry, and two years of calculus (grades 9-10). In addition, they take five years of physics, four years of chemistry, a year of astronomy, four and a half years of biology, five years of geography, and three years of mechanical drawing! Thus the Soviet secondary-school graduate receives far more training in mathematics and the natural sciences than does the typical American high school graduate. In fact, Izaak Wirszup, a professor of mathematics at the University of Chicago, argues that the differences are "so great that comparisons are meaningless."[16] Though the differences in requirements are certainly striking, Soviet schools also have had serious difficulties in maintaining academic standards, a point we shall return to later.

Differences among Urban Schools

Notwithstanding the basically uniform curriculum, Soviet schools differ significantly in their academic quality and social composition—especially, as we shall see, in the case of "special-profile" schools that have been established for "gifted" children. One source of differentiation is the language of instruction, which is associated with ethnic variations that color all aspects of school life. Since by law parents may choose to send their children to Russian-language or native-language schools, urban areas with ethnically mixed populations provide instruction in various languages either in separate institutions or in parallel tracks within the same school. Yet, particularly in the southern regions inhabited by traditionally Islamic peoples, the native-language schools are often regarded as inferior to the Russian schools. Because of the advantages that mastery of Russian confers and the Russian schools' better reputation, many non-Russian parents prefer to send their children to Russian schools.[17]

Furthermore, though residential segregation along social-economic lines is less pronounced than in most American cities, it nonetheless leaves its imprint on the schools' academic quality and climate. Schools located in industrial areas have large contingents of working-class children; on the other hand, schools in districts where research institutes and higher educational institutions are concentrated—for example, Moscow's Novocheremushkin district or the Vake district at the center of Tbilisi—have student bodies composed heavily of college-educated professionals' children. These variations in the schools' composition in turn affect their quality, for the better-qualified teachers are attracted to the "middle-class" schools, where they find the students brighter, better-motivated, and less disorderly. Like upper-middle-class parents in Los Angeles or New York, the more highly educated Soviet parents commonly cite the percentage of a school's graduates who enter college as a yardstick of its quality and take pains to enroll their children in the better-caliber schools—even if it means having to travel to the other side of town to work.

The distinctive Soviet policy of *shefstvo*, or "sponsorship," often reinforces these differences among urban schools. According to educational law, each general-education school is sponsored by an enterprise, organization, or farm that assists the school by repairing buildings, equipping classrooms, organizing labor training, and arranging extracurricular activities. This policy places some responsibility for equipping the schools in the hands of individuals who have a stake in them, helps acquaint students with the everyday activities of parents and other working adults, and serves as a means for enterprises to recruit young workers. In Kiev, for instance, where two secondary schools with a "trade emphasis" are sponsored by the Central Department Store, the students not only meet with the store's employees for labor lessons at school, but they participate in a wide range of activities, including joint entertainment evenings and vacations at its camp. After graduating, many become sales personnel themselves. In this way *shefstvo* gives each school distinguishing features. Some patrons are more affluent than others (hence better able to equip the schools); and through labor training and extracurricular activities, the sponsors mold the students' attitudes and ambitions. A school under the patronage of a research institute or university usually has quite a different character from one sponsored by a machine-building plant or a department store.[18]

Special-Profile Schools

Urban schools' academic quality and climate depend not only on the language of instruction, locale, composition of the student bodies, and characteristics of the sponsoring enterprises. Possessing an importance far greater than their numbers are the "special-profile" general-education schools that give advanced training in academic subjects such as mathematics, physics, computer science, or chemistry, as well as in foreign languages. Throughout the country, approximately a thousand such schools have been established by the republic ministries of education as a means of providing accelerated training for talented students. Many *spets-shkoly*, as they are commonly called, are sponsored by research institutes and higher educational institutions; and a select few—notably, the physics and mathematics boarding schools—are actually administered by universities, where most of their graduates matriculate. Admission is usually on a competitive basis. The universities' schools select students through academic competitions called "olympiads" in which thousands of young people compete. Most, however, select their students from an urban area (not necessarily the microdistrict) through achievement tests or informal assessments. Essentially, these are college-preparatory institutions whose teaching staffs are more qualified and whose standards are higher than those of the regular schools. Not only do almost all students aspire to higher education, but most graduates perform exceptionally well on the entrance examinations given by universities and institutes. As a rule, some 65-99 percent of the graduates go directly from secondary school to college—a decided contrast to the one-out-of-four chances of the average urban secondary-school graduate.[19]

Since the *spets-shkoly* are concentrated in major urban centers, they are much more accessible to the young people living there. Whereas the special physics and mathematics boarding school at Leningrad University is the only one of its kind for a vast territory containing 4,000 schools and a population of some 22 million, for instance, Leningrad city had no fewer than 57 special schools in the early 1970s: ten for mathematics, seven for physics, three for chemistry, and two for the humanities, plus thirty-five foreign-language schools. Nearly one out of ten "complete secondary" schools in Moscow and Leningrad has a foreign-language profile; and as one journalist remarked, an urban district without one is considered "substandard."[20]

Owing to their superior academic training and high prestige, *spets-shkoly* are especially popular among urban upper-middle-class parents, whose children are far more heavily represented in the special than the regular schools. In Ufa, for example, the sociologist L. G. Zemtsov found that children from the intelligentsia accounted for three out of four students enrolled in a foreign-language school but made up only a third of those attending the regular school in the same neighborhood.[21] Because the intelligentsia's children so often predominate and set the tone, the *spets-shkoly* are sometimes attacked for "elitism," for violating egalitarian values. Critics contend, not without reason, that ambitious parents use "connections" to get their children enrolled or provide them with the childhood tutoring that will guarantee admission. Sounding much like an American opponent of high school "tracking," Zemtsov goes on to observe that

> students enrolled in schools for the gifted often relate to
> the other children who are "unworthy" with evident superi-
> ority and contrast themselves with their age-mates, con-
> sidering the latter as "dull" and "ordinary." On the other
> hand, children who are studying in the regular schools
> and classes consider themselves deficient and second-class.
> The cultivation of inordinate pretensions among some
> and the violation of the feeling of self-respect among others
> can in no way correspond with the norms of communist
> morality. We equally have no need for an "elite" and for a
> faceless grey mass of "common," mediocre people.[22]

Evening and Correspondence General-Education Schools

At the other extreme, in terms of quality, are the evening and correspondence classes attended by young people who have not completed a secondary education. Under the slogan "A Secondary Education for Every Young Worker!" enrollments have been increased sharply. Of the 5 million young workers enrolled in part-time classes in 1980, approximately half attended evening classes; the remainder pursued correspondence studies. Eleventh-grade graduates of these schools numbered 1.2 million in 1980—nearly a third of the total number of general-education school graduates.[23]

It has been extremely difficult to maintain academic standards in the part-time programs. Drawn disproportionately from socially disadvantaged families, often poorly motivated and academically weak, the students face the added difficulty of pursuing studies at the end of a day's work. Nor surprisingly, absenteeism is rampant, and the number of dropouts is also high (half a million annually at the end of the 1970s). The state of affairs described by correspondents from *Uchitel'skaia gazeta* in Dubossary District, a major industrial region in Moldavia, is far from unusual:

> A. F. Kholban, a history teacher, says, "At the beginning of the school year all the classes at the dormitory were taught in the evening. Because there was a sharp drop in their numbers, we had to switch to a correspondence school arrangement. . . . Both attendance and grades are very low. We often go around the dormitory and beg the pupils to come downstairs one flight—to class. . . ."
>
> With the enterprise's uneven work pace, the labor turnover, the manpower shortage and the lack of a system of material and nonmaterial incentives, what happens is that the instructional process becomes virtually unmanageable.
>
> Poor attendance also inevitably results in a low caliber of learning.
>
> "If we could just get the attendance under control," one of the night-school teachers said pensively. "But we haven't been able to. You come to class and two people are there. It demoralizes you. But you begin. And just as you reach the most poetic moment of your narrative, the door opens and two more pupils come in. You look, and by the end of class you have seven. The next class period you come with the continuation of the topic you began, and none of the same pupils [is] there."
>
> How do the night schools get out of this situation? Sometimes by the simplest and most unpedagogical method—by disregarding absences and recording grades for nonexistent answers.[24]

In 1980, when People's Control Committees and various financial agencies investigated some 800 night schools in various parts of the country, they found serious shortcomings to be the rule rather than the exception. In a number of areas public education departments had inflated enrollment figures by 50 to 100 percent in order to meet goals laid down by the ministry. Having been "recruited" by schools and enterprises eager to fulfill enrollment quotas, a large share of the students had no clear idea why they should get an education. At many schools only 10 to 20 percent regularly attended classes, but most nonetheless managed to graduate.[25]

To improve the schools, teachers are urged to give individual attention to students (many of whom are acknowledged to be "difficult") and to pack as much work as possible into the class sessions so that homework assignments can be minimized. The course structure is being streamlined so that upper-grade students will have to study only four or five subjects at the same time, and students will be permitted to pass examinations at the end of the year, instead of having to wait until the end of the eleventh grade. To provide an incentive, furthermore, schools are encouraged to arrange instruction so that workers can raise their skill grade—and so earn higher pay—while completing their secondary schooling.[26]

Urban Education's "Second Economy"

Aside from the state-administered schools, a thriving "second economy" exists in Soviet cities, where tens of thousands of young people turn to private tutors to bone up for college entrance examinations. As one villager observed in writing to *Literaturnaia gazeta*, private tutoring has become a common feature of urban life:

> When I come to the city, I often see announcements
> glued on special boards: "I give lessons in physics, apply at
> the following address . . ."; "I give lessons in chemis-
> try for applicants to institute . . ."; "I am looking for a tu-
> tor in . . . ." The pages of the city newspapers are also
> full of such notices. A strange feeling is created. It seems,
> then, that the skills you received in school are something
> unreal, while for "cash" they'll force authentic knowledge
> into your head, and then you'll definitely get into an
> institute.[27]

Since the late 1960s, not only have more and more young people hired coaches, but the scale of the private teachers' operations has expanded. In some large cities individual tutors have given way to groups referred to as "firms" that employ receptionists and advertisers and rent out several rooms for their classes.[28]

Given the demand, private instruction can be a lucrative business. In 1980 a correspondent from the newspaper *Sovetskaia Rossiia* responded to one of the countless advertisements displayed in Moscow. The tutor he contacted invited him to join fifteen other students for a ten-day series of four-hour lessons—at a cost of five rubles per hour. For an additional fee of 150 rubles, the tutor promised to guarantee admission, explaining that colleagues on the admissions committee would accept all applicants whose names he submitted. By charging the sixteen students in one of his classes five rubles per hour, plus the additional fee for "guaranteed admission," the man could bring in 5,600 rubles for ten weeks' work—more than twice as much as the average worker makes during an entire year![29]

Official spokesmen deplore the use of private tutors because it reflects poorly on the quality of teaching in the public schools and represents a form of capitalist enterprise that should have no place in a socialist state. The sharpest criticism, however, is levied on the grounds that tutoring deepens inequality of educational opportunity—that it "disrupts and counteracts the state's social policy in education."[30] Indeed, Soviet sociologists' studies show unmistakably that urban youth from well-to-do intelligentsia families are the principal beneficiaries of this "second economy." According to a 1974 survey of first-year college students in Kharkov, for example, scarcely any students from farm workers' homes had used tutors to prepare for the entrance examinations, but 11 percent of the urban workers' offspring, 20 percent of the white-collar workers' children, and fully 69 percent of the students from the intelligentsia had.[31]

Maintaining that private instruction violates the principle of free public education, the Russian Ministry of Education instructed service firms in June 1969 *not* to provide tutors to parents wishing to give their children additional instruction.[32] Because this ban achieved little success, however, some cities adopted a different tactic—they established their own tutoring services in an attempt to run the private teachers from the market by undercutting their charges. According to one enthusiastic report, the tutors employed by the Express Service organization in Riga have been so successful that they have eliminated the market for private coaches in Latvia's capital.[33] Furthermore, as Minister of Education Prokof'ev points out, universities and institutes can help to combat private tutoring by providing college-preparatory classes for a modest fee.[34]

Problems Facing the Urban Schools

The Academic Program

In the mid-1960s, recognizing the importance of intellectual creativity for scientific-technological innovation and the challenge posed by the post-Sputnik curricular reforms in the United States, Soviet authorities launched a major effort to make the curriculum more intellectually demanding. The Academy of Pedagogical Sciences appointed special commissions to revise course formats and textbooks so that they would promote independent thought rather than passive learning. The mathematics program, much like the "new math" in American schools, stressed mastery of concepts rather than routine computations. Yet, as in the United States, the reforms created new problems. For example, the eighth-grade physics text introduced in 1970 lacked methodological recommendations, leaving teachers bewildered about how best to teach unfamiliar materials and concepts; students' interest in physics plummeted.[35] More general problems are summed up by Izaak Wirszup:

> [T]he new mathematics program, especially in combina-
> tion with demanding science courses, has in many respects
> overburdened the Soviet educational system: students
> have been overworked, many teachers have been exposed to
> nearly insurmountable hardships, and parents have been
> dissatisfied. The program exposed and aggravated the differ-
> ences in cultural levels and educational standards exist-
> ing, first, between metropolitan and rural areas, and, second,
> between the western Soviet Union and the eastern
> (Asian) republics, at a time when authorities were priding
> themselves on narrowing these gaps.[36]

In 1977, taking account of these shortcomings, the CPSU Central Committee and USSR Council of Ministers mandated a thorough review of all school curricula and of mathematics in particular. Superfluous material was to be deleted and concepts simplified.[37] "The orientation toward maximum difficulty has not justified itself in the schools' work," the late A. I. Danilov, the Russian Republic's minister of education, emphasized. "It has led to the same results as its opposite—the orientation toward minimum complexity. Both ultimately engender idleness in schoolchildren, loss of interest in education and in discipline. . . ."[38] However, the preparation of new texts has been impeded by infighting among scholars and educators who disagree over the best approach. In 1980, noting a continuing decline in college applicants' mathematics skills, the party journal *Kommunist* carried a highly critical appraisal of the mathematics curriculum; textbooks were judged too abstract and complex not only for the average student but even for the college-trained engineer who tries to help his child puzzle out the assignments.[39]

Furthermore, the campaign to achieve high success rates gave rise to yet another problem—"percentomania," the practice of evaluating teachers as well as the principal and the entire school on the basis of how many students are promoted or earn high marks. To avoid sanctions from their superiors, teachers have been giving more As and Bs, but scarcely any Ds. Between 1975 and 1977 *Literaturnaia gazeta* received hundreds of letters from parents and teachers decrying the fact that the instructors' discretion was being undermined and professional standards lowered. Though the USSR Minister of Education M. A. Prokof'ev responded that "steps have been taken to eradicate this evil," the ministry's Chief Inspectorate, which is responsible for maintaining standards in the schools, asserted that the complaints were unfounded. Meanwhile, as the editors of *Literaturnaia gazeta* noted, tests administered by the ministry itself pointed up just how far the students' actual achievement lagged behind the official statistics that showed 99.9 percent mastering the material.[40]

Youth Problems and the School

Acting in concert with the official youth groups and the mass media, the schools pursue a conscious program of moral and political socialization designed to foster patriotism, "communist morality," devotion to the Soviet regime, and a Marxist-Leninist worldview. Students are not only exposed to fairly consistent values through the socializing agencies but are taught to orient themselves toward the student "collective," which reinforces official norms. The optimal result, as described by Urie Bronfenbrenner in *Two Worlds of Childhood*, is a young person who is responsible, disciplined, and conformist.[41]

Though Soviet upbringing *is* more purposeful and consistent than in the United States, some similar "youth problems" arise in the cities. The older students' social life revolves around an informal "peer group," whose values are not always consonant with those of the school. Especially in the major cities, young people enjoy more autonomy and have diverse options for leisure and self-expression. Some flaunt their independence outside of school by wearing conspicuously non-Soviet clothing, playing Western pop music on shortwave radios, and spicing their speech with foreign words. With evident dismay, one journalist describes the sight of young people on the street: "The words 'Free Love' are written in English on a girl's blouse. . . . The owner of a jersey urging people to vote for one of the candidates in an overseas presidential election acknowledges that he bought it secondhand in Odessa for 25 rubles. . . . One finds T-shirts emblazoned with the stars and stripes, portraits of rock-music idols, dollar bills, and inscriptions in English that the owners don't even attempt to translate before putting on."[42] Writing in the youth newspaper, another characterizes the slang of students, "mainly those from large cities," who sound like "strangers from the hinterlands of some sort of Michigan, Texas or California with their endless strings of distorted English words like *leibl* [label] and *batton* [button], *voch* [watch] and *beg* [bag]. . . ."[43]

Discipline has become increasingly problematic as the period of compulsory schooling has been lengthened, and educators frequently complain that young people are less respectful of their teachers and less serious in their study. Of the nearly 1,500 teachers who were polled in two major towns in the Bashkir Autonomous Republic, for instance, the great majority (65 percent) believed that students' attitudes toward school had "deteriorated."[44] As in other countries, children from low-income households, broken homes, and "problem families" characterized by alcoholism and child abuse repeat grades more often because of poor performance and are more likely to commit crimes.[45] Maintaining discipline, as Hedrick Smith learned, can be especially difficult in many "working-class" schools:

> "Practically all of my students are 'illiterate' but I
> closed my eyes to that," I was told by Medya, a middle-aged
> woman who taught literature to eighth- and ninth-grade
> classes in Moscow blue-collar schools for years. "Out of 40
> students, I always have five or six boys who fight all the
> time, smoke and drink. They are real hooligans. They get
> into gang robberies and some of the girls get pregnant. I
> had one 15-year-old girl last year who was in school for only
> half a year and was convicted of prostitution. But you
> can't give flunking grades because the principal wants to fill
> the quota for passing students. It has to get 98-99 per-
> cent. If the principals don't fill that norm, they get repri-
> manded. One teacher was fired a year ago for giving too
> many failing grades. The students know that. They will tell
> you right out, 'You cannot fail me.' "[46]

Juvenile delinquency has become a problem with which the urban schools must contend. According to studies conducted by the USSR Academy of Pedagogical Sciences, many teenagers think that ignorance of the law, or intoxication, mitigates guilt. One out of three secondary-school students reportedly felt that a student is not responsible for his misdemeanor; and one out of five believed that after committing a crime, it is possible to avoid punishment. To correct these misconceptions, in 1975 the school introduced a new course on "Fundamentals of the Soviet State and Law." All eighth-graders are now required to take it.[47]

The schools have also found it necessary to respond to teenagers' changing sexual mores. The "sexual revolution" that began in the West several decades ago has now reached the Soviet Union, where urban youth have adopted more liberal views toward sex.[48] When, in one study, upper-grade Moscow students (ages 14-16) were asked, "In your opinion, should boys and girls have intimate relations before marriage?" only 16 percent answered categorically, "Never." According to this same poll, one-third of the students valued their clique because it permitted "freer relations between boys and girls"—a fact that, in the words of a Soviet sociologist, "should cause alarm, particularly in light of what medical statistics show regarding abortions and illegitimate births among girl students."[49]

In the face of freer relations, an upsurge in teenage pregnancies, and an increased incidence of venereal disease, there has been growing sentiment that the school should break its long silence on matters of sex. A. G. Khripkova, vice-president of the Academy of Pedagogical Sciences, observed: "Nowadays many pupils in the upper grades have an understanding of sexual matters. . . . The youngsters find out everything from one another, and often what they learn is inaccurate, distorted and crude. I believe that the fundamentals of moral relations between the sexes should be studied when young people are still in school—as has been done in the Baltic republics for several years now, by the way." Beginning in 1981, she announced, some schools in Moscow and other cities would require students to take two new courses on an experimental basis: "Pupils' Hygienic and Sexual Upbringing" in the eighth grade, and "The Ethics and Psychology of Family Life" in the ninth and tenth grades.[50]

Preparing Young People for Work

The general-education school's effort in upbringing extends to preparing young people for work and the choice of an occupation. Children in the lower grades gain experience in "labor" by working in the school's garden, cleaning up the classroom, and doing crafts. In the upper grades the training is more explicit, often consisting of shop work for boys and "home economics" courses for girls. At some schools students are certified in occupational skill grades, and a growing number of schools successfully sell products that the students produce, thus helping to defray the costs of training.[51]

Labor study is expected not only to impart useful skills but also to contribute to the fostering of the "New Soviet Man"—one who respects labor and finds fulfillment through contributing to the general well-being. These combined objectives—the practical and the ideological—received particular attention during the years 1958–64. Arguing that the schools had become "divorced from life," Premier Khrushchev sponsored a reform that gave labor training a prominent place in education. After the eighth grade, students were encouraged to continue their schooling at night while holding down jobs, and those who continued in the upper grades of the day school were required to spend a year learning a trade.

(For this purpose an eleventh year was added to the upper grades.) Secondary-school graduates were expected to work for two years before matriculating at a university or institute, and the college curriculum was overhauled to give more time to on-the-job training.

Though designed to inculcate an appreciation for labor, the reform evoked opposition in many quarters—from parents who viewed manual work as an obstacle in their children's careers, from factory managers who often found the teenagers neither conscientious nor skilled, and from educators who deplored the fall in academic standards at both the secondary and college levels. Nor was there convincing evidence of its benefits to the young people themselves, who often learned specialized skills—for example, as lathe operators or barbers—that they never used after leaving school. Amid widespread criticism the reform was reversed between 1964 and 1966. The eleventh grade was dropped, and the amount of time given to labor training was drastically reduced.[52]

Yet the basic problems that Khrushchev publicized persist. Not only has the birth rate fallen so low that the population in the European part of the USSR is scarcely reproducing itself, but in Europe, at least, Soviet manpower resources can no longer be replenished by sizable reserves (rural residents, women, pensioners). To make matters worse, plants and other productive goods are aging, labor productivity has been increasing slowly, and young people's occupational preferences continue to run counter to the economy's needs. Though industrial enterprises and services in major urban areas need hundreds of thousands of new workers, many young people shun these jobs, instead setting their sights on positions requiring a college degree.[53] The least attractive jobs are often filled by immigrants from the villages.

The school, many argue, must make more of an effort to attract young people to the "mass" occupations where the labor shortage is acute. But as I. N. Nazimov, an economist at the Ukrainian Academy of Sciences' Institute of Economics, pointed out, many schools use the vocational-technical schools as a threat to pupils who do poorly—and do so against the backdrop of inspirational speeches about "the majesty of the working class." Furthermore, he contended, they often present an unrealistic picture of a "push-button civilization" in which the worker is seen as a person with a higher education, wearing a white smock and sitting at the control panel of a gigantic blast furnace.[54]

Inadequacies in the schools' labor upbringing are also blamed for the fact that so many young people choose an occupation haphazardly, become disillusioned, and change jobs, thus contributing to the excessively high rate of turnover in many branches of the economy. According to a survey of 1,000 youngsters enrolled in trade schools, half attributed their choice to "circumstances" and were already dreaming of changing their line of work. Such seemingly aimless career decisions, the economist A. V. Solov'ev observes, are by no means restricted to students in the unprestigious PTUs. One out of three students polled at the Pushkin Pedagogical Institute in Uralsk did not want to be a teacher; only half of the students interviewed at the Arkhangelsk Medical Institute expressed a calling for medicine; and three-fifths of the 3,000 young engineers surveyed in

Leningrad said that their principal motive in choosing a technical field was the desire to earn a college degree, regardless of the specialty.[55]

Addressing these problems, the CPSU Central Committee's 1977 resolution called on schools to improve labor upbringing and increased the amount of time devoted to labor training in the upper grades from two to four hours per week. Each district executive committee was instructed to determine, in view of projected manpower needs, which specialties students would master and make plans for the development of appropriate facilities. This resolution instructed all republics, provinces, districts, and cities to elaborate coordinated plans, down to the individual school, for the distribution of eighth-grade graduates and ordered that they be sent to school officials a year in advance. In addition, the resolution demanded that all secondary-school graduates who did not continue their education should be given work assignments in accordance with plans that conform to each district's manpower requirements.[56]

To implement the decision, the Ministry of Education has pressed for a rapid expansion of "production-training combines" (*uchebno-proizvodstvennye kombinaty*, abbreviated UPKs). Built and equipped by enterprises and usually shared by a number of schools, these workshops are designed to give young people real on-the-job training and to produce goods that can be sold at a profit. Between 1976–77 and 1979–80 the number of UPKs was increased dramatically from 483 to 1,675, and the number of students working in them rose from 578,000 to 1.5 million. In 1980, 2.67 million—or 95 out of every 100 ninth- and tenth-graders enrolled in urban day schools— were receiving labor training in shops, UPKs, or enterprises. Sixty-five percent of them were learning trades in industry, transportation, or communication, that is, specialties vital to the urban economy.[57]

But whether the schools provide effective labor upbringing is still much disputed. Qualified labor teachers are in short supply; appropriate texts are often unavailable; instruction tends to be dry; and much equipment provided by enterprises is obsolete. Furthermore, some maintain that the UPKs "ever more frequently forget about their main task and take upon themselves the responsibilities of the vocational-technical schools—they teach youngsters a particular occupation, the one as a rule most needed by the base enterprise. . . . Thus the task of broad labor orientation, for which the UPKs were created, gradually recedes to the background."[58] At the same time, it is far from clear that the UPKs are effective in performing this more limited function. In 1979 M. A. Prokof'ev stated that six out of ten young people who study at a UPK select an occupation for which they have been trained; yet results of studies published a year and a half later indicated that only one in six subsequently chose to work in the same specialty.[59]

Conclusion

There are distinctive features of urban educational policy in the USSR. Despite the country's extraordinary regional and ethnic diversity, educational objectives are laid down authoritatively by the central ministry as part of a national policy. Though strange for an American who is accustomed to local school governance, this practice is not in itself exceptional. Yet, as an official institution in a communist state, the school assumes specific ideological and economic functions that are far less prominent in Western societies where greater pluralism prevails in politics, the economy, and culture. The official ideology not only legitimates the party's monopoly of power but charts the road to the future by laying down guidelines for its policies, including collectivism, state ownership, central economic planning, and communist upbringing—all of which are reflected in the school's activities.

Indeed, many of the problems discussed in this chapter derive from the multiple, and sometimes conflicting, tasks that the school is expected to perform. For instance, the Soviet school encourages achievement and ambition while simultaneously attempting to attract young people to the "mass" occupations in industry and the services; it revamps the curriculum to stimulate independent thought but does its utmost to maintain ideological orthodoxy; it espouses equality as a social value, yet with the avowed aim of developing the country's scientific potential, it establishes special-profile schools for a select few. Though all modern educational systems have multiple objectives, the conflicts appear in sharp relief in the Soviet case because the tasks are so broadly defined, so explicit, and in many ways so ambitious.

Many problems will also strike a resonant chord in those familiar with urban education in other countries. In the USSR, as elsewhere, educational expansion has—as a by-product of its success—created concern that academic standards are falling and that discipline is too lax. There, as in other societies, not only does the towns' complex social-geographical structure leave its imprint on schools' composition, climate, academic quality, and prestige, but the families' social-economic status conditions students' scholastic performance and ambition, thus giving rise to marked disparities in educational attainment. Soviet schools, like those abroad, have also had to address problems characteristic of urban youth, who mature earlier, have higher expectations, and enjoy more autonomy than their parents did. This is not to say that the problems are identical in nature or in magnitude. Though alcoholism is a serious problem throughout Russian society, including among teenagers, drug abuse has certainly not reached the epidemic proportions that it has in many American schools since the mid-1960s. By all accounts, the level of violence in Soviet schools is far below that in many American urban schools. And regardless of how far labor upbringing falls short of official objectives, Soviet school-leavers face less uncertainty in finding employment than do young people in the United States today.

Notes

[1]Tsentral'noe statisticheskoe upravlenic (TsSU), *Narodnoe obrazovanie, nauka i kul'tura v SSSR* (hereafter *Nar. obraz.*) (Moscow, 1977), 26-27; TsSU, *Narodnoe khoziaistvo SSSR v 1980 g.* (hereafter *Narkhoz. 1980*) (Moscow, 1981), 458.

[2]V. Usanov, "Vstupaia v odinadtsatuiu piatiletku," *Nar. obraz.*, 2 (1981), 28.

[3]*Narkhoz. RSFSR 1978* (Moscow, 1979), 272-73, 278, 280, 288, 290.

[4]*Vestnik statistiki*, 6 (1980), 59-62.

[5]For details, see F. G. Panachin, "Educational Administration in the USSR," *Soviet Education*, *21*, 10-12 (August-October 1979), and K. I. Subbotina, "The Financing of Universal Secondary Education (Certain Theoretical and Practical Problems)," *Soviet Education*, *20*, 3 (January 1978).

[6]F. R. Filippov, *Vseobshchee srednee obrazovanie v SSSR* (Moscow, 1976), 102.

[7]*Izvestia* (July 23, 1971, and April 19, 1972); *Uchitel'skaia gazeta* (January 17, 1978, and December 18, 1980); *Zaria vostoka* (April 19, 1981).

[8]*Sovetskaia Rossiia* (January 12, 1980).

[9]To overcome these problems, it has been proposed that general plans for the construction of trade schools be elaborated and either that ministries be required by law to spend the money allocated for school construction or that funds and authority be transferred to the republic committees for vocational-technical education or local soviet executive committees. *Pravda* (June 20, 1978); *Sotsialisticheskaia industriia* (October 22, 1980); *Komsomol'skaia pravda* (January 30, 1981); *Pravda* (January 31, 1981).

[10]*Sovetskaia Rossiia* (January 11, 1981).

[11]*Komsomol'skaia pravda* (January 30, 1981).

[12]On family background's impact on academic success, see Murray Yanowitch, *Social and Economic Inequality in the Soviet Union: Six Studies* (White Plains, N.Y., 1977); Richard B. Dobson, "Education and Opportunity," in Jerry Pankhurst and Michael Paul Sacks, eds., *Contemporary Soviet Society: Sociological Perspectives* (New York, 1980), 115-37; and Richard B. Dobson and Michael Swafford, "The Educational Attainment Process in the Soviet Union: A Case Study," *Comparative Education Review*, *24*, 2, pt. 1 (June 1980), 252-69. Data on the status of college students' parents are reported in M. N. Rutkevich and F. R. Filippov, eds., *Vysshaia shkola kak faktor izmeneniia sotsial'noi struktury razvitogo sotsialisticheskogo obschestva* (Moscow, 1978), 190.

[13]*Lichnost' prestupnika* (Moscow, 1976), 273, cited in V. G. Alekseeva, "Neformal'-nye gruppy podrostkov v usloviiakh goroda," *Sotsiologicheskie issledovaniia*, 3 (1977), 69.

[14]John Dunstan, *Paths to Excellence and the Soviet School* (Windsor, Engl., 1978), 35; Usanov, "Vstupaia," 27; *Narkhoz. 1980*, 457. As of 1975, two out of three urban schools, but only one out of four rural schools, were "complete secondary" institutions. Being far larger than the elementary and eight-year schools, the "complete secondary" schools enrolled 86.5 percent of the urban and 64.5 percent of the rural students. *Nar. obraz.*, 28-31.

[15]Susan Jacoby, *Inside Soviet Schools* (New York, 1973), 78-79.

[16]Izaak Wirszup, "The Soviet Challenge," *Educational Leadership*, *38*, 5 (February 1981), 360.

[17]In the Tatar Autonomous Republic, for example, three times as many rural Tatar children were enrolled in Tatar-language schools as in Russian schools. In the cities the picture was dramatically different. In Almetevsk, eleven times as many Tatar children attended Russian school as against Tatar schools, while in the capital, Kazan, the ratio was 26 to 1 in favor of the Russian schools. Iu. V. Arutiunian, L. M. Drobizheva, and O. I. Shkaratan, eds., *Sotsial'noe i natsional'noe: Opyt etnosotsiologicheskikh issledovanii po materialam Tatarskoi ASSR* (Moscow, 1973), 235-40. This pattern appears to be characteristic of the Central Asian republics and other autonomous republics in the Russian Federation. In Georgia and the Baltic republics, in contrast, the great majority of urban children of the indigenous nationality attend native-language schools. See also Jaan Pennar,

Ivan I. Bakalo, and George Z. F. Bereday, *Modernization and Diversity in Soviet Education: With Special Reference to Nationality Groups* (New York, 1971).

[18]*Izvestia* (December 1, 1971). In some Estonian cities district departments of public education have established central funds for a portion of the resources given by the schools' patrons. Schools that are unable to gain sufficient support from their sponsoring enterprises can draw from the central fund. This policy levels some disparities in funding resulting from *sheftsvo*. See Subbotina, 74-77.

[19]On college entry rates, see Dunstan, 101, 164. Exact figures on the number of special-profile schools are not available. Dunstan (p. 172, n. 41) puts the number at about a thousand. In 1973, there were 542 such schools in the Russian Republic. Filippov, 59.

[20]*Izvestia* (March 23, 1972), and Dunstan, 96, 101.

[21]L. G. Zemtsov, "Sotsial'nye problemy obshcheobrazovatel'noi shkoly v SSSR na sovremennom etape" (Candidate of Science dissertation, Ufa Aviation Institute, 1971), 64. For further evidence, see Dunstan, 98-102, 164-65; Rutkevich and Filippov, 65; and A. Matulenis, "Orientatsiia uchashchikhsia spetsializirovannoi srednei shkoly na professional'noe obrazovanie," in F. R. Filippov, N. M. Blinov, and M. Kh. Titma, eds., *Sotsiial'no-professional'naia orientatsiia molodezhi v usloviiakh razvitogo sotsializma* (Moscow, 1977), 56-73. Special-profile schools vary in quality, prestige, and composition, however, just as regular schools do. Thus children of scientists and other professionals made up the overwhelming majority of students at an "English" school located in the Academic City on the outskirts of Novosibisk; only one student in twenty came from a blue-collar worker's home. On the other hand, workers' children reportedly accounted for nearly half the student body at a "French" school in one of Novosibirsk's industrial districts. Dunstan, 100.

[22]Zemtsov, 72. Certainly Zemtsov is not alone. V. Stoletov, President of the USSR Academy of Pedagogical Sciences, has at times been an outspoken critic of special-profile schools. See Dunstan, 74, 109, 168-69.

[23]*Narkhoz. 1980*, 458, and *Trud* (May 18, 1980).

[24]*Uchitel'skaia gazeta* (March 14, 1978), trans. in *Current Digest of the Soviet Press*, *30*, 12 (April 19, 1978), 22-23 (hereafter *CD*).

[25]*Uchitel'skaia gazeta* (February 12, 1981).

[26]*Sovetskaia Rossiia* (April 16, 1980); *Trud* (May 18, 1980).

[27]*Literaturnaia gazeta* (March 8, 1972), cited in Jacoby, 140.

[28]*Komsomol'skaia pravda* (January 17, 1975).

[29]*Sovetskaia Rossiia* (September 10, 1980).

[30]*Komsomol'skaia pravda* (January 17, 1975).

[31]I. I. Sheremet, "Sotsial'nyi sostav studenchestva," *Sotsiologicheskie issledovaniia*, 2 (1977), 77.

[32]*Literaturnaia gazeta* (December 12, 1971), 12.

[33]*Sovetskaia Rossiia* (September 10, 1980).

[34]*Izvestia* (August 18, 1980).

[35]*Pravda* (July 7, 1976) reported results of studies showing that most sixth- and seventh-graders had a strong interest in studying physics, but that only one out of five eighth-graders and one out of seven ninth-graders did. The abrupt decline was blamed on the fact that the students were expected to move too quickly from an introductory text to a more sophisticated treatment and that teachers were ill-prepared to deal with the new material.

[36]Wirszup, 360.

[37]CPSU Central Committee and USSR Council of Ministers, "O dal'neishem sover-

shenstvovanii obucheniia, vospitaniia uchashchikhsia obshcheobrazovatel'nykh shkol i podgotovki ikh k trudu,'' *Sobranie postanovlenii pravitel'stva Soiuza Sovetskikh Sotsialisticheskikh Respublik*, 1 (1978), 2-19. For an English summary, see *Soviet Education, 21*, 6 (April 1979), 8-20.

[38]As an illustration, Danilov pointed to the burden placed on students in the literature classes. In the eighth grade students were expected to read 2,730 pages in textbooks, 930 pages of literature included in the syllabus, plus 2,140 pages of outside reading. In the ninth grade the respective figures jumped to 3,570 pages of texts, 3,230 pages of required literature, and 6,850 pages of outside reading! Was there any doubt, he asked, why the dropout rate was five times higher in the ninth grade than in the eighth? *Uchitel'skaia gazeta* (June 28, 1979), *CD, 31*, 39 (October 24, 1979), 4.

[39]A. Pontriagin, "O matematike i kachestve eë prepodavaniia," *Kommunist*, 14 (1980), 99-112.

[40]For example, 25 percent of the sixth-graders could not identify parts of speech in Russian, 29 percent of the ninth-graders were unable to solve the math equations, 56 percent of the secondary-school students could not solve the geometry problems, and 19 percent of the tenth-graders did not know noun case endings. Officials of the Russian Republic's Ministry of Education insisted that the discrepancy between the low scores on the achievement tests and the high percentage with passing grades was meaningless because the tests measured retention of knowledge, whereas the success rate reflected students' daily school performance. The editors of *Literaturnaia gazeta* would not buy this argument (November 17, 1976), *CD, 28*, 51 (January 19, 1977), 14. See also *Izvestia* (September 28, 1979).

[41]Urie Bronfenbrenner, *Two Worlds of Childhood: U.S. and U.S.S.R.* (New York, 1972). See also Kitty Weaver, *Russia's Future: The Communist Education of Soviet Youth* (New York, 1981).

[42]*Izvestia* (October 2, 1981), *CD, 33*, 40 (November 4, 1981), 21.

[43]*Komsomol'skaia pravda* (November 26, 1981), *CD, 33*, 47 (December 23, 1981), 24.

[44]Zemtsov, 95.

[45]See V. D. Povov, "Papa, mama i syn-vtorogodnik," *Zhurnalist*, 5 (1973), 18-20.

[46]Hedrick Smith, *The Russians* (New York, 1976), 209.

[47]*Pravda* (December 24, 1976), *CD, 27*, 51 (January 19, 1977), 11-12. For a vivid social-psychological portrait of an eighth-grader who took the road to crime, see Valerii Agranovskii, "Down the Staircase," *Soviet Education, 20*, 2 (December 1977).

[48]See I. S. Kon, "O sotsiologicheskoi interpretatsii seksual'nogo povedeniia," *Sotsiologicheskie issledovaniia*, 2 (1982), 113-22.

[49]Alekseeva, 63-64.,

[50]*Komsomol'skaia pravda* (August 16, 1981), *CD, 33*, 33 (September 16, 1981), 7.

[51]See Jacoby, and Subbotina, 29-44.

[52]See Nicholas DeWitt, *Education and Professional Employment in the USSR* (Washington, D.C., 1961); Robert J. Osborn, *Soviet Social Policies: Welfare, Equality, and Community* (Homewood, Ill., 1970); and Philip D. Stuart, "Soviet Interest Groups and the Policy Process: The Repeal of Production Education," *World Politics*, 22 (1969-70), 29-50.

[53]See M. N. Rutkevich, ed., *The Career Plans of Youth* (White Plains, N.Y., 1969); V. V. Vodzinskaia, "Orientations toward Occupations," in Murray Yanowitch and Wesley A. Fisher, eds., *Social Stratification and Mobility in the USSR* (White Plains, N.Y., 1973), 153-86; and E. K. Vasil'eva, *The Young People of Leningrad: School and Work Options*

and Attitudes (White Plains, N.Y., 1976).

[54]*Ekonomika i organizatsiia promyshlennogo proizvodstva*, 3 (1977), *CD, 24*, 27 (August 3, 1977), 8.

[55]A. V. Solov'ev, *Professional'naia orientatsiia v sotsialisticheskom obshchestve* (Moscow, 1979), 58-59, 84.

[56]See Note 37, and *Pravda* (December 29, 1977), *CD, 29*, 52 (January 25, 1978), 7-8; *Izvestia* (January 10, 1978); and *Uchitel'skaia gazeta* (January 17, 1978).

[57]Usanov, 29, and *Narkhoz. 1980*, 457-58. See also L. A. Il'ina and V. V. Fat'ianov, "Interschool Production Training Combines," *Soviet Education, 19*, 11 (September 1977), 55-70.

[58]*Sovetskaia Rossiia* (January 20, 1980).

[59]*Izvestia* (September 28, 1979); *Pravda* (January 10, 1981, and February 9, 1981).

9

Urban Transport in the Soviet Union

If an American or Western European stops at a street corner in any sizable Soviet city, the first visual impression is one of comforting familiarity. The cars and buses look about the same, and they move, as anywhere else in the world, with scant regard for the sidewalk observer. If one lingers, however, and starts to take notes, more and more differences will become apparent.

The cars are smallish and not very colorful; a Rolls Royce would (and does) stop traffic. There is plenty of curb space for parking, and the traffic flow is not too heavy—at least not to the degree that could be expected in an industrialized country under similar circumstances. A very high percentage of the stream is made up of trucks and service vehicles. There is also a large proportion of buses, streetcars, and trolleybuses, which are mostly filled with passengers. If one could interview the automobile drivers, one would find that many of the cars are not privately owned. They frequently belong to government enterprises and operate in an official capacity.

A scenario of high efficiency and public purpose begins to suggest itself, as described and aspired to in anybody's statements of objectives regarding urban transportation. There is a reason to leave the street corner, however, to look into what actually occurs, how it is achieved, and to determine whether all is well.

The first such glimpse is offered by Table 1, which contrasts some basic transportation measures of two comparably sized cities: Rochester in the state of New York and Riga in the Latvian SSR.[1] Examples from Riga will be found throughout this chapter, but the initial observation would be the neat symmetry of a factor of 18 in both private car ownership and public transit use between the two places—in opposite directions.

Basic Planning Concepts

Urban transportation services are considered both theoretically and practically in the Soviet Union as vital to the existence of any city or settlement. There is also a continuous effort to minimize the need for such operations through efficient land use and activity arrangements. This is something that all urbanists strive for, but usually with much less dedication and fewer practical means of effectuation than Soviet planners. The fundamental difference is that Western societies have main-

Table 1
Comparative USA-USSR Statistics

	Rochester and Monroe County, New York	Riga, Latvian SSR	
Population in 1970	711,917	731,831	
Labor force	40%	60%	
Population in 1979-80	710,000		835,000
Passenger automobiles	385,557		21,000 (estimated)
Gasoline stations	498		11
Motor bus service	(in 1980)	(in 1975)	(in 1978)
Route kilometers	614	319	325
No. of vehicles	254	250	215+
Annual passengers	24.5 million	105 million	70 million
Trolleybus service			
Route kilometers	—	106	170
No. of vehicles	—	403	385
Annual passengers	—	174 million	185 million
Streetcar service			
Route kilometers	—	68	109
No. of vehicles	—	321	355
Annual passengers	—	145 million	192 million
Total transit passengers/year	24.5 million	424 million	447 million
Metro/subway	being studied		construction promised
Taxi vehicles	333		1,314

Sources: Personal communications.

tained that they can afford to absorb relatively high transportation costs and that personal satisfaction, entrepreneurship, and operational effectiveness are higher goals than productive efficiency, even if they result in sprawl, long commuting distances, and duplication of services.

The policy formulators and urban planners of the Soviet Union will not accept this in their theoretical statements and guidelines/norms, even if implementation of the idealized concepts on the ground is not always possible and is rarely achieved fully. There are market and human behavioral forces, as well as bureaucratic and financial constraints, that create a significant gap between planning aspirations and final urban reality. But formal objectives and targets are heavily weighted toward operational efficiency and tend to minimize other aspects of urban life. A brief description of Soviet approaches should give a basic perspective before the sectoral and specific aspects of transportation actions are discussed.

A strong concept of Soviet planning, for example, has always been the desire to locate residences and respective workplaces next to each other. The ultimate expression of this would be the building of dormitories around a specific factory, with age and social groups segregated by floor, when pure Communism is achieved. In the meantime, a checkerboard pattern of residential microraions[2] and industrial districts is advocated, which would allow the workers to walk across the street, in effect, requiring no mechanical (engine-supported) transport. Although it is very difficult to assess the degree of actual implementation of this concept, since no information is released on industrial activities or distribution (not even locational maps), it does not appear to have great practical consequences. Housing shortages, the exigency to build on readily available sites, and a reasonable degree of employment mobility militate against the desired reduction of the transportation service network for work trips. Quite the contrary, these commuting demands establish the principal parameters for service planning, as will be shown later. (On the other hand, there are informal indications that workers tend to select residences convenient to their workplaces if they have any choice—but largely with accompanying complaints of inadequate available transportation. None of this is quantifiable.)

Another instance of intentional minimization of urban travel needs is the hierarchical concept of residential space organization: the provision of microraions and progressively larger clusters with the appropriate level and amount of retail, educational, medical, cultural, service, and recreational facilities—most of them presumably reachable on foot. Again, this is a theory whose level of implementation generates a flood of complaints by municipal authorities and residents alike because the construction of these supporting installations lags by years behind the occupancy of the housing blocks.

In Riga, for example, which has massive new residential developments on the periphery, the basic schools, nurseries, and local shops appear to be in place, but other higher-level services can only be found in the core districts, and not a single social service building has been opened in the microraions, as promised. There are new residential groupings of approximately 100,000 population without adequate internal commercial, personal service, and entertainment centers.[3] Long and frequent trips by surface modes are necessary, and they constitute an irritating routine of contemporary urban life.

As Soviet cities grow, they become candidates for, and frequently receive, progressively heavier, high-volume public transit. Such development should carry with it a restructuring of the urban pattern—a pulling of high-density uses toward the access points—and an intensification of development along the lines, allowing more users to take advantage of these services by proximity. In the Western countries, under free real estate market conditions, such land use alterations often take place, even if they are not planned; in the Soviet Union they are in the guidelines but are not readily observable in the field.

The principal reason why this desirable transformation does not take place is the still prevailing housing shortage. It is not advisable to take down existing stock in the old core zones and replace it with higher-density blocks. Except for some isolated projects, the long talked-about redevelopment of central districts, which would, among other things, adapt them to modern traffic needs, has not yet really started. Housing development and transportation service planning has not been fully integrated in practice, although current standards clearly call for it. Residential complexes have been built primarily to get them up as quickly as possible, on sites that are immediately buildable. Under these conditions very little long-range planning and scheduling can be (or has been) done to achieve an operational balance and a symbiotic enhancement of urban amenities.

Riga again is an example where a new metro route is being added to a land use pattern that has been established under a previous set of conditions. Since the service is badly needed, there will undoubtedly be many riders; but this incremental approach is not likely to reap all the possible benefits from this major public resource investment.

The key Soviet planning document is the urban development plan, which is intended to outline comprehensively all elements for every significant community for the next twenty-five or thirty years.[4] The drafting of this document, its review, and final approval move primarily through the Gosstroi[5] chain of command. The overall plan is to be amplified by a ten- to fifteen-year urban passenger transportation plan which, in turn, is progressively elaborated by modes, districts, and special problems. Most of the critical work is done by nonlocal, specialized professional institutions.

All of this has to fit, of course, in the current overall five-year plan, which is the responsibility of Gosplan.[6] This plan attempts to balance national resources with local needs in an elaborate hierarchical, two-directional review process. The annual revisions are important particularly for implementation of specific urban features.

An idealized planning framework is in place, and it can be credited with significant accomplishments in several sectors. Specific urban demands, however, often conflict with industrial and defense priorities at the national level. There are also general problems, and they have been amply recorded: cumbersome and bureaucratic procedures, lack of understanding of true local needs, plain nonfulfillment of plans, and the unpredictable disruptions caused by actions from various ministries or industries that claim all-union precedence. Some components of the total urban transportation system are imbued with national interest; most of the others are regarded as local consumer endeavors.

The substantial amount of Russian transportation planning literature is largely trapped in the overall effort to establish norms and standards. These norms outline what can and should be done in a handbook format. They say little about what actually occurs in Soviet cities. There are no detailed case studies, and hard information is usually given only in an aggregated form. The standards are almost exclusively functional and physical, grouped by city sizes, and are concerned with such parameters as average number of trips per resident, passenger-kilometers, mean travel speed, trip length, passengers per square meter of vehicle floor, and kilometers of road per square kilometer (see Table 2). They are useful indicators; but such averages, even if they are carefully and reliably determined, do not necessarily indicate what corrective measures should be taken. And most importantly—in the Soviet Union as almost anywhere else—only those actions are implemented for which resources are available, after enough pressure has been generated through various means from different sources. The standards can remain unfulfilled or they can be changed, thereby doing no real harm except bruising a few egos.

Table 2
Basic Transport Service Norms in the Soviet Union

City classification	Population (in thousands)	Transportation mobility (trips per person per year)			Necessary transport services
		Actual 1976	Current range	Expected	
(Moscow/ Leningrad)		(620)			
Very large	1,000 to 2,000	380	350 to 400	580 to 800	Exclusive right-of-way rail with most other forms
Large	500 to 1,000	360	330 to 350	515 to 700	Streetcars, particularly in express service
Large	250 to 500	340	300 to 330	460 to 650	Bus and trolleybus, possibly streetcar
Big	100 to 250	280	200 to 300	305 to 550	Bus and trolleybus
Medium	50 to 100		100 to 250	300 to 450	Bus
Small	Less than 50		70 to 150	200 to 350	Bus

Sources: Moscow City Soviet Executive Committee, *Transportation in the City: Management Problems* (New York, 1979).

It has been observed by many outsiders that even if the Soviet system depends on elaborate planning schemes and procedures, their cities and urban services in the field show little evidence of long-range planning and purposeful preparation.[7] The overwhelming amount of real decisions appears to be made on an ad hoc basis within current resource constraints, to satisfy selective and narrow performance measures, in response to various political pressures; it is influenced heavily by blanket directives or constraints from the top.[8] These approaches seem to characterize at least the urban transportation sector and explain to a large extent the many existing problems and several accomplishments.

In addition, coordination problems exist at the operational and functional level. It can be observed, for example, upon leaving metro stations in cities that have this service, that these modes are not well connected to the housing blocks. There are frequently large open spaces around them, requiring long walks by everybody. It is difficult to explain why the Western European practice of placing a maximum amount of activities on top of a station is not being followed—except, most likely, because the implementation, management, and ownership responsibilities rest with separate agencies that do not always collaborate. It is not difficult to explain why metro stations are quite far apart in the outlying districts (2 or more kilometers): to provide fast service on the line even if access on foot becomes cumbersome.

Soviet urbanists and transportation planners take as one of their fundamental norms the allowable (desirable?) time distance for trips to work: thirty to forty minutes for medium-sized cities and one hour for large ones. Many studies have addressed this issue and have attempted to develop correlations between work-related travel and work-readiness, state of health, productivity, and fluctuations in labor tenure. Some have even calculated a 2.5 to 3 percent loss of productivity over the day if travel time exceeds by ten minutes the "standard" forty and the worker is crowded with seven other bodies in a square meter of space inside the vehicle.

Census figures for 1970 reveal that only 8.6 percent of commuters in very large cities and 53 percent in those with less than 50,000 population can arrive at work in forty minutes. In cities with over one million people, 25 percent of the workers have to spend an hour and a half in each direction, thereby, reportedly, losing 15 percent of their productivity.

In Riga (population 835,000) 68 percent of all workers use public transportation, while 32 percent can reach their places of employment by walking—at an average of fifteen minutes each way.[9] The time consumed by those who have to rely on overcrowded buses and streetcars averages fifty minutes (thirty-seven minutes in the vehicle and thirteen minutes of waiting). The average length of a commuting trip is only four kilometers, and 72 percent of all travelers do not have to transfer to another line. Complaints about service quality are most vocal in this city, and about a third of all workers who voluntarily terminate their employment at various establishments cite access difficulties as the principal reason.

Heavy Rail Systems

There is little doubt that the backbone of Soviet urban transportation systems in large cities is metro service. It is deservedly their greatest source of pride, and the one mode that offers lessons for transportation planners everywhere. High-volume, exclusive right-of-way rail operations are, of course, only feasible in high-density corridors with concentrated demands and focused activity centers. Many similar opportunities exist in Soviet cities because of the long-standing policy of building peripheral housing districts on a large scale. The dominance of core service zones and the existence of huge industrial complexes provide further support for rail service implementation.

At the present time seven cities are equipped with metro service: Moscow, Leningrad, Kiev, Tbilisi, Baku, Tashkent, and Kharkov (see Table 3). Many more lines are under construction or in an active planning stage for the next tier of metropolitan areas. The most important concept is the national policy that any city reaching the one-million population level should receive subway (metro or heavy rail) service. There are slightly more than a dozen cities in the Soviet Union that have achieved this range. Riga also is on the verge of having a line under construction, after a planning effort that extended over several years, although it has not reached the requisite population level (843,000 residents in 1980). In the United States only municipal governments of cities in the multimillion population class can think about comparable services, and recent policies from the White House place further constraints on the implementation of these very costly modes.

Table 3
Heavy Rail (Metro) Systems of the Soviet Union, 1978

	1980 population (millions)	Opening of first line	Length of routes (km)	Number of stations	Number of cars	Number of passengers per year (million)
Moscow	8.10	1935	164.5	103	2,392	2,083.4
Leningrad	4.64	1955	52.4	34	800	612.8
Kiev	2.19	1960	20.5	17	249	210.7
Tbilisi	1.08	1965	12.9	11	87	115.0
Baku	1.03	1967	18.7	11	72	109.7
Kharkov	1.46	1975	9.8	8	96	97.1
Tashkent	1.82	1977	11.3	9	75	7.6 (part of year)
Minsk	1.30	under construction	8.6	8	80	104.0 (projected)
Novosibirsk	1.33	under construction	9.2	7	125	
(New York subway— Transit Authority)	(7.07)	(1904)	(371.1)	(461)	(7,158)	(1,027.1)

Sources: For rail data: Union Internationale des Transports Publics, *UITP Handbook of Urban Transport* (Brussels, 1979). For population data: *The Statesman's Year-Book, 1981-82* (New York, 1982).

The metro services of the Soviet Union are first distinguished by the fact that each one is regarded as an all-union enterprise. The Moscow system (started in 1931) has always been a national showpiece, and there are reasons to conclude that the deep tunnel networks are regarded as defense components. The planning lead and implementation responsibilities therefore are taken by several national agencies: as major elements of the five-year plan (by Gosplan), as specialized and standardized designs (by central planning and engineering institutes), and as national construction and operating tasks (by the Ministry of Railroads).

This concern at the all-union level has several consequences. One of them is that the metro systems receive the proper attention and resource allocation. It is one of several instances in the Soviet Union where a concentrated, almost single-minded application of effort results in exemplary accomplishments. The work force associated with metros is an elite group, and the community takes great pride in the appearance and operation of the service.

In addition, centralization predetermines that all the physical details and elements are the same in each city. The vehicles are all identical, and operating procedures are standardized. This undoubtedly achieves considerable efficiencies, and all aspects of metro planning and construction in the Soviet Union are supposed to be cost-effective and of the highest practicality today.

There is another side of the coin, however, and that comes back to the issue of central authority weighed against response to local needs. City fathers are grateful for what they get and do not appear to have a major input in the layout of the system, in its implementation schedule, or the running of service. This leaves some obvious gaps that are a source for vocal discussion. Examples are the exact location of stations, the intervals between them, appropriate feeder services, timing of construction, and agreement with local development plans.

Nevertheless, the Soviet subways are fast, reliable, clean, and well used. Trains run with clockwork precision, stations are scrubbed down every night, and passenger behavior is much more orderly than on the surface. It would not be possible to imagine Moscow or Leningrad without their metros.[10] All of this is achieved by utilizing simple, tested, and reliable components and approaches, not sophisticated technology.

The vehicles are heavy and presumably not very energy efficient. But they are rugged, with simple and straightforward elements and layouts; and they are obviously well maintained. Although automated lines are under construction, the routinely utilized signal and control systems are quite basic. The complex and vulnerable electronics available today have to be contrasted with the practice of giving each motorman a good watch: since no surprises or breakdowns are likely to occur along the way on Soviet systems, trains are dispatched at regular intervals at one end, and they arrive with the same frequency at the other. All this does not prove anything about overall cost effectiveness or service quality, nor does it necessarily suggest transfer of technology between the Soviet Union and other places; but it does give food for thought, particularly in light of the current trends and attitudes toward automation in Western countries.

The spectacular and overdecorated stations of the Stalin era are still there, of course, and they are visited by everybody who goes to Moscow (or Leningrad). The ones being built today, however, follow a functional, sometimes stark style, and the result is almost indistinguishable from most similar facilities in the West, except that the Soviets seem to devote more effort to the appearance of the stations. In addition, the extremely deep placement of the early lines, requiring lengthy escalator rides, is no longer practiced.

The fare on every metro is five kopeks, dropped in a turnstile. A full analysis of the balance sheet of any public transit operation in the Soviet Union would be most interesting but, unfortunately, is impossible. Too much is integrated with and subsumed under other budget items so that a standard breakdown is not currently achievable. Perhaps such an investigation is not as important as recognition of the underlying principle: urban transit is a vital service without which cities cannot operate and should be available to everybody. Aside from capital costs, in previous years the authorities maintained that the metro generated "profits," but lately there are admissions that operational subsidies are involved. Nothing much is made of it; and as with many consumer-type services in the Soviet Union, a policy (not operational) matter is involved. Ultimately (it is said), when pure Communism is achieved, there will be no fares at all. In the meantime, the fare has remained the same for several decades while all costs have escalated.

Table 4
Urban Transportation Modes Available in Soviet Cities

Inventory of modes		Number of cities		
	1940	1954	1966	1971
Urban rail, streetcar, bus, and trolleybus	1	1	4	5
Streetcar, bus, and trolleybus	7	26	32	30
Bus and trolleybus	—	8	48	76
Streetcar alone	12	4	—	—
Bus alone	259	572	1,656	1,831
Cities with public services	337	671	1,819	2,017

Source: E. V. Ovechnikov and M. S. Fishel'son, *Gorodskoi transport* (Moscow, 1976).

Finally, under the heavy rail classification there is also commuter rail service. There are many railroad stations, and generally, Soviet rail passenger service is well run. Publications and official statements are largely silent on short-distance, metropolitan operations, although it is known that Moscow has nine local railroad lines with 73 stations within the city. Such service is found in a number of other cities, down to Kharkov (1.5 million population), Gorky (1.4 million), and Sverdlovsk (1.2 million).[11] Riga has an active line linking it to the seaside resort area. It appears that workers and shoppers have started to use rail service for commuting and other purposes simply because it is there, as has happened in many other countries, without awaiting "official" recognition of this activity as an urban/regional service.

There are more recent developments in planning thought that are concerned with suburbanization, i.e., residential expansion or full utilization of the surrounding greenbelts for recreational purposes. This undoubtedly will require a new or modified attitude toward rail service, distinguished from the regular operations by the metros and long-distance rails.

Bus, Trolleybus, and Streetcar Services

The standard surface modes of urban public transport are practically ubiquitous in Soviet cities. Almost everybody depends on them for mobility, and they crisscross the larger cities and are found in the smaller ones as well. Of the fifty billion passengers each year, fourteeen persons out of fifteen ride a bus, streetcar, or trolleybus.

The service, however, by their own admission is not as good as it should be. This issue generates one of the largest and most visible number of complaints from consumers and urban residents. Letters in the newspapers and other "approved" expressions of dissatisfaction are quite prevalent at the local level and occasionally swell to the national. The vehicles tend to be terribly overcrowded, in poor repair, and not properly heated or ventilated. Shelters for waiting are inadequate, stations are far from residential units, service personnel are seen as surly, and fellow passengers as rude and uncooperative. All of this is familiar to bus and streetcar riders almost everywhere in the world, except that in the Soviet Union there is a particular bitterness and urgency about these complaints.

As reported in *Pravda* (June 11, 1979), only 74 percent of all buses and trolley buses and 77 percent of streetcars were in operation at any given time. Schedules were achieved on only 92 percent of runs; a total of 15 million runs were delayed or missed entirely in a year, and eight persons per square meter (the norms call for three) are jammed regularly into public vehicles. This is a situation comparable to New York City's crisis, except that in the Soviet Union there are no real alternative means of mobility, and everybody suffers.

The immediate reasons for these deficiencies are easy to identify, and they have been recorded many times: spare parts are not available, repair tools are inadequate, manual maintenance efforts are ineffective, productivity is low, not enough new vehicles are produced, and vehicle designs are obsolete. The transport workers have little incentive for a more responsive attitude. Their productivity is measured by volume alone, such as passenger-kilometers generated, regardless of conditions along the way.

There are plenty of cries for reform, but the principal explanations have to be traced to the Soviet approach to consumer services and to dual subordination (local executive communities vs. national ministries). The party, as always, is a separate force. In many respects the provision of bus service is not much different from the supply and distribution of retail consumer goods.

The local authorities are responsible ultimately for providing adequate service to their citizens, while the agencies at the republic and all-union levels hold the strings and very rarely are in a position to allocate fully adequate resources. Things are complicated further by the existence of separate ministries for electrically powered and fuel-driven vehicles. The extension of a line to a new residential district becomes a significant bureaucratic procedure that often gets delayed well after people have moved into the apartments.

The organization of responsibilities and accounting in a strict vertical chain clearly works against horizontal integration and frequently places local officials in an adversary or negotiating posture. There are no central administrative bodies for all urban transport services at the municipal or regional level (except in Moscow), and there is no agency with comprehensive responsibilities at the national level. Gosplan is not able, nor is it a suitable means, to deal with short-term, practical, and operational plans at the direct service level.

The extreme crowding of vehicles during rush hours is an indication of a limited fleet in many instances. It also generates other problems, such as the physical difficulty of getting a ticket since no one can move around inside.[12] This latter condition apparently results in a rather high incidence of nonpayment of fares, although the official literature is silent on this issue.

The vehicles are of standard design and are on the plain side. They are manufactured at several specialized centers; Riga, for instance, is known for its streetcar production. Distribution of the units is not only national but encompasses most of Eastern Europe; Hungarian buses and East German light rail vehicles—in return—are often found in Soviet cities.

One of the most interesting elements of Soviet urban systems is the numerous and expanding trolleybus lines.[13] Their energy efficiency and nonpolluting and silent operation are deemed to be considerable advantages over their inflexibility in routing and unsightly catenary network.

Streetcar service in the Soviet Union has been in an ambivalent policy situation for some time. The trolleys (or *tramvais*) have always been in operation, but they have been regarded with scorn by some officials lately as not fitting the image of a modern city. The realities of life, however, and the superb service characteristics of streetcars have enabled them to survive. Their regained popularity in Western countries will also help their prestige in the Soviet Union. A number of significant streetcar/light-rail expansion projects are underway, in some cases involving the "light rapid rail" concept.[14] The most visible of these is in Kiev, with an exclusive channel, but there are notable efforts in Riga and in other cities.

The financial aspects of surface modes will also have to await further analysis before definite conclusions can be reached. The fares—five kopeks for

Table 5
Passenger Distribution among Public Transportation Modes

	USSR		Moscow			
	1970	1976	1940	1960	1967	1976
Metro	6.4%	6.8%	14.3%	28.4%	35.3%	39.0%
Streetcar	22.1	17.5	69.7	22.9	16.0	11.0
Trolleybus	17.0	17.5	7.6	21.6	18.0	17.0
Bus	54.5	58.2	8.2	27.1	30.7	33.0
Total number of passengers per year (in billions)	35.8	47.7	2.6	3.7	4.2	5.4

Sources: Provided to the author by several Moscow agencies.

buses, four for trolleybuses, and three for streetcars—are supposed to cover actual operating costs, but it is doubtful that any self-sufficiency is approached.

The Soviet Union has not moved beyond the provision of the standard surface services and has not augmented them with supporting elements and features. Their planners show considerable interest in the developments in Western Europe and North America encompassing such items as exclusive bus lanes or busways, preferential traffic signals, or even organized intermodal terminals. By their own admission they have to do much to provide, first, adequate basic capacity with satisfactory geographic coverage before further refinements toward passenger convenience can be considered.

In concluding this section, one should not be left with a completely bleak impression that may emerge from a recounting of the surface mode problems. Travel on buses and streetcars is one of the griefs, not joys, of the Soviet urban scene. Yet the massive scale of the operations—at least in comparison to American communities[15]—and the full dependence on these services should give some reasons for inspiration. Surface modes in the Soviet Union do not have the glamour or attraction of the metro, but they are the workhorses that do the best they can to serve literally every city resident every day.

Taxi and Paratransit Services

Taxi service in the Soviet Union is reasonably well developed, and vehicles are readily available, at least at the principal activity and tourist nodes. This service is essential to the overall operation of cities since it provides for individual mobility, which in other industrialized countries is satisfied by the almost universally available private car.

Taxi vehicles and their drivers operate, of course, through state-owned enterprises that provide central managerial and functional services. Vehicles are engaged at hack stands found at many locations or by telephone prearrangement. Empty cruising is frowned on.

An interesting aspect of the taxi industry is that private entrepreneurship is frequently in evidence. Thus a common sight in cities is to see urbanites flag down any moving vehicle. During peak hours and shortages, a few extra rubles will generate service that otherwise might not be available. Taxis around the world are the one type of transportation where the forces of supply and demand operate at the most intimate personal level and where regulations can be bent easily by mutual consent.

Since Soviet cities are compact, supplied with regular transit lines, and the overall administrative system is not geared toward the operation of individual and nonroutine services, paratransit generally is not known. There are exceptions, however, and there might be a trend toward a varied, flexible response.

It is known that some economic enterprises provide, or are compelled to provide, access services for their own workers. Little is known, however, about such operations because, in effect, they represent evidence that regular transit services are not always adequate, and they move outside the official, orthodox framework.

In addition, one occasionally encounters "marshrut taxis" that are minibus services established along fixed routes interconnecting special origin and destination points, where full bus operations are not suitable, feasible, or desirable. Such linkage may be provided, for example, between the end of a subway line and a seasonal recreation place, or even on principal corridors in cities where a premium service is supportable.

In standard terminology these are jitney services, which are becoming quite popular in many cities around the world and are becoming legitimized again as true urban transport operations. It is not just a political footnote to observe that even in a "classless society" there is room for premium, flexible service; there is a functional justification for responsive and adjustable services beyond the standard modes to satisfy the diverse urban needs of any society.

Pedestrians

Most urban dwellers in the Soviet Union walk long distances frequently each day either to or from line transit stations, within the large residential or central activity districts, or to reach various retail and personal service establishments. There are practically no short-distance and very few feeder services that would offer a higher convenience level to the residents. They are supposed to walk, which is good for the overall efficiency of the total system and shields the government from the headaches of operating small-scale, localized transport services at numerous locations. But the climate is harsh, packages have to be carried, and both the young and old get tired. Better transportation responses presumably will be made as the general standard of living moves upward and specific requests are articulated by consumers.

The other side of the pedestrian coin is the availability of proper channels and spaces. Beyond regular sidewalks and extensive parks with paths for strolling, there is nothing much to report. Pedestrian enclaves, auto-free zones, and significant malls do not exist, at least not beyond the usual scattered elements that are found in every city. There is, however, considerable discussion about implementing such schemes and catching up to the cities of Western Europe particularly, where practically every sizable community has implemented some sort of automobile-free pedestrian environment. There have been suggestions for many years in Riga, for example, to close the entire medieval part of town to cars as the restoration work proceeds. The principal pedestrian improvement today is an underpass near the central rail and bus stations, and many more recommendations have been advanced.

The pedestrian in the Soviet Union is controlled, not catered to. There are relatively few pedestrian amenities along regular paths and sidewalks (such as trees and benches), although practically every city has exceptions in the form of formal boulevards and allees. An exemplary level of cleanliness is maintained on most streets, and ice cream or kvass can be bought at the busiest places. Militiamen frequently insist that streets are to be crossed at only officially designated points, and there is quite a bit of mutual policing as well. Even the pedestrian underpasses below the extremely wide avenues of Moscow appear to be designed more for the convenience of the relatively few vehicles than the numerous walkers. The elderly and handicapped are particularly sensitive to these constraints.

Suburban Links

The concept of suburbs is a new element in the theory and practice of Soviet urban planning. While the large peripheral housing developments remain contiguous to the existing districts, it is recognized currently that there are plenty of reasons to travel beyond the traditional compact city. They include recreational activities, which are deliberately placed in the adjoining greenbelts, dachas for a growing number of families, allotment gardens, airports, and even some factories and housing groups which, regrettable as it is, break out of the controlled metropolitan space. In addition, residents of nearby rural settlements are increasingly drawn into the metropolitan labor market.

Since this situation is becoming accepted, access becomes a problem, and different solutions have to be explored. The earlier body of theoretical work tried to define the difference between migration and commuting and to decide on the proper terminology, such as pendulum movement or shuttle travel. Whatever it is called, it has arrived; and recent discussions have focused on the practicalities of various modes to satisfy this mobility need, although it is not the most efficient way to structure urban areas and allocate resources for services. There is a pragmatic recognition, however, that good commuting services expand the tributary area for labor, give more flexibility, relieve pressures on housing in the core, and make social and cultural facilities more usable.

Looking from the perspective of any metropolitan area, which encompasses satellite towns and old rural settlements, the surburban population may amount to 25 to 40 percent of the corresponding central city. Where there are major resorts nearby, as in the Riga region, the figures can be particularly high, with wide seasonal fluctuations. Not surprisingly, the statistical base for this emerging and unusual demand is not particularly strong. Reverse commuting to peripheral industrial centers also exists.

The available railroad lines are usually not well placed for suburban travel, nor are they equipped for this type of service. The private automobile is still relatively rare and is not acceptable, functionally or conceptually, as a means of mass mobility.

Planning work is underway to develop appropriate services that will most likely choose from regular or special bus routes, extensions of the metros, or conversions of rail lines. There is even extensive discussion on the applicability of high technology modes (automated guideways, air or magnetic levitation, monorails, and people movers), but they are most likely to remain at the review stage since such attempts have proven not to be productive in similar situations elsewhere, and the Soviet urban environment does not appear to be conducive to such approaches—unless, of course, it is decided to do something in a few isolated instances for propaganda purposes.

This sector, then, remains an area that is likely to see considerable development in the near future, but it is equally likely that the ideas, concepts, and methods will flow from the West to the East. Perhaps some new and interesting applications will be found within the Soviet Union's urban context.

Automobiles and Their Use

The private car is the dream of every family anywhere in the world, and Soviet citizens are no exception. People will break their backs to gain the mobility, privacy, and status that the automobile embodies. Before discussing the practices and problems of this mode in Soviet cities, a few statistics are in order.[16]

There were 40 persons per passenger vehicle in the Soviet Union in 1978, while there were 1.9 in the United States, 3 in France, and 14 in Hungary. The Soviet Union in this respect is comparable to Guatemala, Chile, Iran, Jordan, the Ivory Coast, and Cook Island. Since the base is very low, the automobile growth rate is high; the impact on cities is sudden and drastic. Personal mobility (the number of kilometers traveled each year) is steadily moving upward, and private automobiles make a major contribution to this trend.[17]

The growth in annual production of vehicles is shown in Table 6. The total USSR fleet of motor vehicles in 1978 is 12.8 million units, of which 6.6 million are cars and 6.2 million are trucks and buses. The corresponding figures for the United States are 148.8, 116.6, and 32.2 million, respectively.

The distribution of cars is not even, and the highest concentrations are found in the cities of the western republics. In 1977 there were 16 residents for each automobile in Estonia and 22 in Latvia. The impact of automobiles is perhaps stronger in Tallinn and Riga than in all other cities, except Moscow and Leningrad.

Table 6
USSR Motor Vehicle Production

	Passenger cars	Trucks	Buses	Total
1946	6,289	94,582	1,300	102,171
1950	64,554	299,441	3,900	362,895
1955	107,806	328,962	8,500	445,268
1960	138,822	384,769		523,591
1965	201,000	415,000		616,000
1970	352,000	570,000		922,000
1975	1,201,000	696,000	67,000	1,964,000
1979	1,314,000	781,000	78,000	2,173,000
(USA in 1979)	(8,433,662)	(3,046,331)		(1,479,993)

Source: Motor Vehicle Manufacturers Association, *World Motor Vehicle Data* (Detroit, 1980).

A standard vehicle costs about 9,000 rubles,[18] which is only meaningful when translated into the observation that a Soviet citizen has to work five to eight years to earn enough money for an automobile. It should be kept in mind, however, that while an American can earn enough money in a matter of months equivalent to the purchase price of a car, his tax situation is different, and his Soviet counterpart has only marginal expenditures on housing and medical bills.

Everybody in the Soviet Union knows about the waiting periods for a new car that can extend into several years. It is equally well known that this period can be considerably reduced by having a friend or relative pay hard currency from the outside or by being bumped up the list through official action. A good used car can carry a premium price if it is available immediately to the buyer. The explanations for this supposedly irrational behavior by the Soviet citizen are the tremendous pent-up demand and the shortage of any other consumer goods on which money could be spent.

There is an obvious conflict among socialist policies of equality, public efficiency, and individual (selfish) aspirations toward a more comfortable life. The latter concept is officially acceptable today since "strains on the human nervous system" are lessened by personal travel. In addition, nonworking time is saved that presumably is utilized in beneficial cultural and political activities, rural and urban living conditions are equalized, and social contacts are broadened by the automobile. The overall target is to reach about 6 persons per car in twenty to twenty-five years. It is not clear what this objective is based on.

Automobiles are frequently bought only for recreational purposes. In Estonia 80 percent of the kilometers traveled by cars went for nonwork trips, while 40 percent of car owners used their vehicles for commuting to work in the summer and 20 percent in the winter.

It is also important to note the special classifications of vehicles in the Soviet Union. There are the completely private automobiles (the preferred label is personal) in full ownership and use of individuals and families, but there is also a very large fleet of government-owned passenger vehicles (approximately one-fifth of all automobiles) which are owned by various enterprises and agencies and are assigned to top functionaries or are utilized for official purposes. It is a well-known fact that increasing rank within the privileged class carries with it increasing access to these vehicles. The number of automobiles in operation in any given city is somewhat of a moot point and an undeterminable figure by regular channels.

Future automobile use in Soviet cities is largely a question of how many vehicles the government will choose to manufacture and distribute among the population. There are indications, however, that the trickle is turning into a respectable stream—although it is not yet a flood—and that it will most likely be politically impossible to reverse the trend under normal circumstances. Soviet planning literature frequently mentions congestion and environmental impacts, but it is also admitted that these are not topics for "spontaneous discussion at workers' meetings."

To be an automobile owner in the Soviet Union is not an unmixed blessing—as any one of them will explain at great length under the proper circumstances and as letters to the editor amply indicate. The basic problem is that a service infrastructure to support this consumer sector has not yet been established.

After receiving his vehicle, having paid cash for it, the proud possessor has to start worrying about a regular source of fuel. Service stations are few and far between, and localized gasoline shortages occur. There are plenty of indications, but no official confirmation, that those who have direct access to government fuel pumps are not only in an enviable position, but that many of them also find ways to channel a part of this resource into private tanks. Similarly, there is an extensive black (or gray) market for spare parts and accessories. Tires are a particularly scarce item, but there are constant dislocations in supply within any given geographic area—car radios or sparkplugs may be the items of demand at any given time.

To maintain an automobile in operating order is a continuous challenge. The scarcity and unreliability of repair establishments force practically everybody to become an amateur mechanic. Other protective actions have to be taken as well. There is widespread pilferage, rarely admitted by official sources, which requires, for example, that windshield wipers be removed and locked away every time the car is parked for a long period in an unsupervised place. Due to the harsh winters, common practice is to place the vehicle on blocks for two to four months each year depending on geographic location.

Parking places are somewhat of a problem, although there is still plenty of space along most curbs. In the new housing developments, designated and improved lots are frequently located a considerable distance away from the apartments. One kilometer is not unusual, if an equipped lot is available at all; garages are rare.[19] For central city districts there is extensive discussion today about organizing proper storage facilities and possibly requiring new buildings to provide an adequate number of spaces as a part of the structure. Park-and-ride lots at transit stations are a new idea still being discussed.

One more dimension of automobile use in the Soviet Union should be mentioned. This is the very strict group of laws regarding drunken driving and their very strict enforcement, including spot checks on the street at night.[20] The doleful people holding on to a glass of lemonade at even the most lively parties are automobile owners who will have to drive home later.

Obviously, a street traffic crisis does not exist in Soviet cities, although local guides point with poorly concealed pride to occasional traffic jams. Yet there are threats. Now is the time to prepare the infrastructure for the foreseeable impacts. Soviet planners are aware of this, and it remains to be seen whether they will learn from the mistakes that have been made in the Western countries, or whether they will be trapped in schemes and policies of their own design. They certainly have studied cases in Western Europe and North America, and they talk about pollution loads, wasted energy, safety issues, and service efficiency. There is always a difference, however, between what the more thoughtful observers suggest and what the real decision-makers choose to implement. This problem is perhaps a little bit more serious in the Soviet Union than elsewhere.

There have been questionable efforts in the past. Stalin, for example, through a personal decision, caused extremely broad avenues to be cut through Moscow. Even today they have excess capacity, and they constitute barriers to pedestrians. It is hinted that the reasons for their construction were to create an image of grandeur (there are no wider city streets anywhere) and concern with personal safety (they allow fast and free movement of official motorcades).

A limited access ring-road was opened in the 1960s, with considerable fanfare, completely around Moscow. It is still heavily underutilized, but it serves admirably to delineate precisely the urban area of the principal city. It stands also in stark contrast to the generally deplorable national road network for long-distance driving. Cloverleaf interchanges and highway service areas are still admired and are tourist attractions.

In recent years, however, a number of praiseworthy urban highway projects have been undertaken at many locations, albeit they remain isolated elements in the overall metropolitan networks. In Riga, for example, a very decent grade-separated expressway has been built to the seashore resort area from the city core, and several major bridges have been completed, while others are in planning stages. This construction effectively ties together the two halves of the urban area bisected by a large river. It is suggested, however, that the large, advanced-design bridge opened recently with a high pylon for suspension cables features several elements of an engineering spectacle rather than a response to true necessity. The approach arrangements are also of questionable adequacy where linkages are made to regular surface streets.

Urban Goods Handling

While it is not particularly obvious to every city resident in North America, the internal freight distribution systems here are inefficient and disjointed. Shippers and receivers act largely independently, utilizing their own vehicles to satisfy their individual needs. There is no effective coordination or integration of services. There is much duplication, empty movements, storage problems, etc. But the goods and their handling remain under the direct control of the owners, and consumer needs can be satisfied regardless of the cost.

In the Soviet Union, on the other hand, goods movement is a government (municipal) responsibility.[21] Special enterprises provide this service, and in larger places they might be oriented toward different purposes, such as household movements or supply of construction sites. In the first case families call in and request service (and pay for it); in the second a long-term contract may be executed. This is the equivalent of giving monopoly powers within a metropolitan area to, let us say, United Parcel Service and a few other specialized trucking outfits, with all private vans and trucks expropriated. These organizations would be in a position to consolidate shipments, establish rational schedules and chains of deliveries, acquire suitable vehicles, train personnel, provide centralized warehouse facilities, etc. This is a theoretical dream in North America and only a partially achieved fact in Western Europe.

Monopoly has its problems, and bureaucracy, particularly in the Soviet Union, creates its own constraints. This clearly is a field, however, where actual experience in the Soviet Union should provide good indicators as to what is possible and productive in other situations.[22] It is ironic to note that reprimands appear occasionally in the official press complaining about managers of economic enterprises who try to use their own freight vehicles and do not take advantage of the large-scale trucking organizations.

Most American transportation specialists who have visited Moscow have probably been taken to Avtokombinat I of Glavmosavtotrans, which appears to be a showcase urban freight operation. With 2,100 trucks and 5,000 employees at sixteen branches, this enterprise, which specializes in the movement of prefabricated building elements, is only one of forty-five such units of the Moscow motor transport agency, i.e., the general usage service in contrast to proprietary operations by different production units (what would be called private trucking in the capitalist countries). It is not necessarily typical of organizations with the same purpose in other Soviet cities.

Glavmosavtotrans is subdivided into eight transport administrations that are responsible for movements ranging from construction materials (Mosstroitrans) to bakery products (Moskhlebtrans). The total of 37,000 vehicles and 90,000 employees move about 600,000 tons of goods per day. This is only one-half of the total volume in Moscow, but it accommodates 75 percent of construction freight, 50 percent of industrial freight, and 100 percent of service to retail establishments.

Conclusion

The urban transportation situation in Soviet cities is quite uneven. Some splendid achievements, such as the metro, have to be contrasted with chronic problems in providing routine services. Much is colored by whether an activity has "all-union" significance or whether the responsibility is placed on local consumer service agencies. In addition, semi-independent and economically powerful enterprises can enter into the urban development picture and considerably modify the local service patterns.

It is dangerous to attempt global comparisons of transport systems because they reflect more than anything else the importance assigned to this service by the respective societies within a fixed overall resource capability. No city anywhere in the world really has flawless networks and operations. The differences are immense among urban areas as to the extent and quality of mobility. One does not have to look for such extreme cases as, for example, Hamburg and Bangkok; the point can also be made by contrasting New York and Los Angeles. With these cautionary notes in mind, it can be suggested, nevertheless, that the urban transport situation in Soviet cities is not satisfactory, that it is not even up to the level that could be expected, recognizing all existing constraints, and that it does not respond adequately to the fundamental socialist concepts of equity, unconstrained accessibility, and efficient communal operations. Yet the public transport systems are massive, they are vital to the cities and their residents, and they contain many interesting features.

Urbanists in the Western industrialized countries have been fascinated for decades by the organization and development of Soviet cities. Much of this interest has been superficial speculation on what the "other side" is doing, as seen on quick tourist-type trips; but lately these contacts and curiosity about professional aspects have become quite serious. There is an increasing demand for reliable and integrated information that explains and documents their methods and achievements. A respectable body of data and evaluations has started to accumulate.

It could be postulated that the socialist system as applied to urban management is so different from the free-market approach that there can be very little productive transfer of knowledge from one to the other. If one looks, however, at various urban sectors and specific services, it becomes apparent that the problems at an operational and functional level—not surprisingly—are quite similar, and that the attempted solutions within the contemporary framework of technology are going in the same direction. This is particularly true in transportation.

There are good reasons to ask such questions. It is possible, but by no means proven, that some or many of the Soviet approaches may be practically useful for urban managers and planners in the West. They too, after all, have an industrialized society, their residents demand largely the same urban services, but their planning and managerial activities take place in an economic/political framework that in several dimensions could be regarded as a laboratory situation for nonsocialist societies. This includes a centralized hierarchy of decision-making, public ownership and operation of facilities, strict control of activity location, and a search for reliable standards.

There are promising areas of inquiry. The two topics where immediate returns could be expected are the robust design and reliable operation of heavy rail rapid transit and the organization of urban freight distribution centers with accompanying service activities.

Learning from others is not always easy or simple. In this case particularly there are fundamental differences in concepts and attitudes. Even at the detailed level, for example, it is quite noticeable that the Soviets concentrate on work trips, and that there is a major concern about losses in productivity caused by tiring daily travel. Another observation might be that their approach toward solution appears to stress operational speed, while Westerners are preoccupied with convenience. The attempt there is to express everything in overall numbers and ratios—even for situations such as access to recreational areas where planners here would rely almost entirely on empirical surveys.

Notes

[1] Riga is the largest city of the western Soviet republics and the capital of the Latvian SSR (a formerly independent country annexed by the USSR in 1940). The city is an institutional and cultural center and has undergone much technological and industrial development in the last several decades. It is perceived by Soviet citizens to have a considerably higher than average standard of living.

[2] The Soviet "microraion" corresponds to the "neighborhood" of Western planning practice, i.e., a self-centered apartment district housing from 4,000 to 20,000 residents with its own local commercial services, schools, and recreation facilities, not crossed or penetrated by major traffic arteries.

[3] These criticisms and complaints appear regularly in the local press, articulated by residents as well as responsible officials.

[4] See, for example, the introductory section of part 2 of *Transportation and the Urban Environment* (Washington, D.C., 1978); contributions by H. W. Morton and T. M. Poulsen in *Soviet Housing and Urban Design* (Washington, D.C., 1980); the initial sections of *Transportation in the City: Management Problems* (New York, 1979); and works on Soviet city government such as B. M. Frolic, "Soviet Urban Politics," unpublished doctoral dissertation (Ithaca, 1972), W. Taubman, *Governing Soviet Cities* (New York, 1973); F. E. Ian Hamilton, *The Moscow City Region* (London, 1976); and D. Cattell, *Leningrad: A Case Study of Soviet Urban Government* (New York, 1968).

[5] Gosstroi is the State Committee for Construction which defines functional policies, sets standards, and operates technical institutes.

[6] Gosplan is the State Committee for Planning which coordinates all resource allocations and drafts a comprehensive program for capital expenditures. The five-year national plan is its principal tool.

[7] The exceptions would appear to be the massive peripheral housing developments that are found in and around every sizable city, but upon closer examination, their location and

implementation process are largely opportunistic as well.

[8]Martin Crouch provides more details on the process in the first few pages of "Problems of Soviet Urban Transport," *Soviet Studies*, *31*, 2 (1979), 231-56.

[9]Nothing is said about commuters by private car.

[10]The regular daily volume of passengers carried by the Moscow metro is about 5.2 million, and it goes up to 7 million on special holidays. In New York City the daily subway volume has dropped to about 3 million, and much less on weekends.

[11]See Martin Crouch, 237-39, for additional information.

[12]On all surface modes fares are paid through the self-service honor system. The correct amount of coins (change is obtainable only from other passengers) is dropped in a box near the entrance, and a ticket is torn off from a roll. The usual practice in a full vehicle is to pass the money and the tickets from hand to hand over the heads of other passengers. Tickets can also be bought at retail outlets near a stop.

[13]Electrically powered bus-type vehicles with rubber tires, but catenary power pick-up.

[14]Exclusive right-of-way, some tunnelling, automated controls, etc.—sometimes also called "premetro."

[15]See Table 1 with statistics on Riga and Rochester.

[16]See also the comparative Riga-Rochester Table 1.

[17]The prospects of the Soviet automobile industry have been analyzed by various Western public and private agencies, including Toli Welihozky, "Automobiles and the Soviet Consumer," *Soviet Economy in a Time of Change* (Washington, D.C., 1979), 811-33.

[18]This is the ever-popular Zhiguli, a close copy of Fiat. It is retailed in the West as a Lada for about $4,600, which is over $1,000 less than the comparable Italian prototype.

[19]Standards have been formulated for future buildings, but it is not known how well they are achieved or how realistic they are. These norms include, for example, one parking space for each fifteen to thirty workers in a factory, one space for each four to seven sales positions in a department store, one space for each twenty to thirty visitors to parks and beaches, twenty to thirty spaces for each 1,000 inhabitants in microraions, and fifty to seventy for each 1,000 residents in central city districts.

[20]The accident statistics in the Soviet Union are appalling. In 1976 in the Latvian SSR, 671 people were killed in traffic accidents, or about 27 for each 100,000 residents. In the United States during the same year this average was 22, with about a dozen times the number of automobiles on a per capita basis. The large number of motorcycles in operation in the Soviet Union does not explain it all.

[21]This discussion will not be concerned with the long-distance, interregional freight transportation questions, which remain among the most serious problems of the Soviet Union.

[22]Such a study by Professor James Robeson of Ohio State University, involving extended visits to the Soviet Union and joint research with their specialists, has taken place.

Gertrude E. Schroeder

10

Retail Trade and Personal Services in Soviet Cities

Introduction

In market economies the secular increase in urban living standards (real per capita consumption of goods and services) has been accompanied by concomitant development of an efficient retail distribution system supporting the enhanced flow of goods and services and catering to the needs of consumers. Real per capita consumption in urban areas in the USSR has more than doubled since 1950, but however measured, the flow of utilities from a modernized infrastructure supporting consumption has lagged behind. At present, the real per capita consumption of the Soviet urban populace is probably little more than one-third of that in the United States and one-half to three-fourths of that in major countries of Western Europe.[1] Although lags behind the United States and the United Kingdom have been somewhat reduced in the postwar period, the gaps relative to other major countries have increased, notably so in the case of Japan. If we take into account the quantitative and qualitative lags in provision of an efficient retail distribution system, the relative gains of Soviet consumers have been smaller in terms of welfare.

Relative to other countries at similar levels of development, the Soviet Union devotes much less labor to retail trade and to provision of personal and repair services for its population. Using census data on labor allocations, Gur Ofer found a large "trade gap" circa 1960 between the USSR and other countries at comparable levels of development.[2] Although an urban/rural disaggregation was not made, the gap clearly was relevant to urban areas. Ofer concluded that the USSR was making progress and by the 1980s would have gone a good part of the way toward a more normal pattern of labor allocation. In fact, however, Soviet underallocation of labor to the trade sector relative to other countries remains great. Lacking 1979 census data, we refer to statistics on employment in "trade, restaurants, and hotels" in 1977 as reported to the International Labor Office by both Western and Communist countries.[3] In 1977 the Soviet Union employed 9.2 million workers in those activities, 9.7 percent of the total nonagricultural labor force. The share was the same as in Romania, and lower by far than the twelve Western countries compared, where the shares ranged from 15.5 percent to 25.3 percent. In Italy and Japan, countries roughly at the same level of development as

202

the USSR as measured by per capita GNPs, the shares were 21 percent and 25 percent, respectively. The share in the United States was 23 percent. In 1977 the USSR employed 2.45 million workers in personal and repair services, 2.6 percent of the nonagricultural labor force; a comparable U.S. figure cannot be obtained but would likely be about three times as large. The shares of employment in commercial services (including wholesale trade) in total nonagricultural employment has risen very slowly in the USSR: it was 8.9 percent in 1950, 8.4 percent in 1960, 9.2 percent in 1970, and 9.7 percent in 1980. But the shares have been rising as fast or faster in other countries.

Moreover, because of the Soviet government's proclivity for skimping on investment in urban, consumer-oriented infrastructure, retail and services facilities are sparse and poorly equipped by Western standards. Methods of distribution are generally backward, and the system functions poorly. Evidence of the unsatisfactory state of affairs in urban retail markets is provided both by observations of foreign visitors and by a mass of reporting in the Soviet press.

Soviet retail marketing has been investigated by Ofer, as well as by Goldman,[4] Hanson,[5] and Skurski[6] in different contexts. The backward state of provision of personal and repair services has been noted,[7] but the sector has yet to be studied in depth. This chapter aims to further these investigations by focusing on the availability of trade and personal service facilities in urban areas. The next part of the chapter first considers trends in supplies of goods and services available to urban consumers. Then it looks at the provision of retail facilities in cities, considering their planning and organization, as well as levels and trends in availabilities in the USSR as a whole and in union republics and large cities. A concluding section assesses the prospects for reducing the large "trade and services gap," by international comparison, that is the legacy of long-continued past neglect.

Supplies of Goods and
Personal Services

Since 1955 the Soviet urban population has nearly doubled, and total sales in state and cooperative retail trade have increased sixfold in current prices and 4.4 or 5.9 times in real terms, depending on whether Western-constructed price indexes or official retail price indexes are used as deflators (see Table 1). The official index, which shows virtually no price change during the period, is widely believed to be unreliable. Retail sales per capita tripled in current prices and more than doubled in real terms, using the Western-constructed deflator. Real per capita sales in restaurants rose 1.6 times. Besides sales of goods, published retail sales data include receipts of establishments providing so-called "productive" services, such as tailoring, laundry, dry cleaning, photography, and repair of cars, household appliances, furniture, and housing. It is not possible to separate the data.

As would be expected, per capita sales of food and beverages have risen less rapidly than sales of other goods—1.8 times compared with 2.8 times in real terms. Although data for urban areas are not published separately, it is clear that

Table 1
Indicators of the Growth of Urban Retail Trade and Personal Services, 1955-1980

| | | Retail sales | | | |
	Total (1)	food and beverages (2)	other goods (3)	Restaurant sales (4)	Sales of personal and repair services (5)
		values in billion current rubles			
1955	32.1	16.9	15.2	4.8	0.4
1960	53.7	28.1	75.6	6.0	0.7
1970	106.8	54.2	52.6	13.2	2.6
1980	193.8	88.2	105.6	21.1	5.7
		values in billion constant rubles			
1955	32.1	16.9	15.2	4.8	0.4
1960	53.0	26.9	23.7	5.8	0.7
1970	93.1	44.9	45.9	10.9	2.6
1980	141.8	60.5	82.1	14.5	5.7
		values per capita in constant rubles			
1955	363	192	172	54	4.5
1960	469	249	220	56	6.5
1970	653	323	330	78	18.7
1980	844	358	486	86	33.7

Sources: Values in current prices were obtained or derived from data in *Narodnoe khoziaistvo SSSR* (hereafter referred to as *Narkhoz*), 1965, 631-32, and 1980, were estimated from a variety of evidence.

Values of retail and restaurant sales in constant rubles were obtained by deflating the current values with price indexes for food and other goods devised by the author. Their derivation and limitations are discussed in Gertrude E. Schroeder and Barbara Severin, "Soviet Income and Consumption Policies in Perspective," in *Soviet Economy in a New Perspective* (Washington, D.C., 1976), 631. These indexes were developed to provide an alternative use of the indexes of state retail prices published by the Soviet government. The Soviet indexes, which show virtually no price change during 1955-80, are believed to be seriously unreliable.

Notes:

Col. (1) Total retail sales minus sales in restaurants.

Col. (2) Retail sales of food minus sales in restaurants.

Col. (3) Total retail sales minus sales of food and beverages (Col. 1 less Col. 2).

Col. (4) Sales in restaurants (public catering sales), considered to consist almost entirely of food and beverages.

Col. (5) Reported or estimated sales of "everyday" services (*bytovye uslugi*). A substantial share of these sales is included in the data on sales of nonfood goods, but there is no way to deduct them with accuracy. Although the data are reported to be in constant prices, they are thought to actually reflect current values.

sales of durables increased much faster than sales of clothing and related goods, reflecting rapid development of consumer durables production capacities from very low levels. As a result, by 1980 nearly all urban families had refrigerators, and 91 percent had television sets, compared with 17 percent and 32 percent, respectively, in 1965.[8] Car ownership, although very low by comparison with Western countries and even Eastern Europe, has risen dramatically—from about 2 per 100 families in 1970 to 9 in 1980 for the USSR as a whole. The shares in urban areas undoubtedly were substantially higher.

Some data on state-provided personal and repair services are also shown in Table 1; the data include the services that are also counted in retail sales, as well as so-called "nonproductive" services like barber and beauty shops and public baths. Sales were minuscule before the mid-1960s, when the government launched a long-overdue drive to expand these services. Even with rapid growth, sales amounted to a mere 34 rubles per capita in 1980. Even that figure is too high, since the data include a sizable amount of purchases by enterprises and government institutions and also goods manufactured in service facilities; both have been rising faster than the total. Because of the low volume and poor quality of state-provided services, consumers have turned to private persons to help fill the gap. According to one Soviet survey, private persons supplied nearly half of all personal and repair services in urban areas in the 1960s, but only 15 percent in 1971.[9] A Western study, based on a sample of Jewish émigré families, suggests a larger share for the early 1970s.[10] No doubt the situation differs by kind of service. A recent Soviet source states, for example, that six out of every ten car repairs are done by private mechanics.[11]

Although the flow of goods and services in the urban retail network has expanded greatly in the postwar period, along with money incomes, daily shopping has always been a frustrating experience for consumers, mainly women, who do most of it. The situation has gotten worse since the mid-1970s as a result of slowing economic growth and poor harvests in 1979–81. Because of multiple shortcomings throughout the entire production-distribution system, supplies are irregular, product assortment frequently does not match consumer demand, and quality is often poor. Hence random shortages are a perennial feature of the Soviet scene—toothpaste and eyeglasses today, cotton cloth and meat tomorrow. Providing matched flows of complementary goods seems to be particularly difficult; there may be cameras but no film, and spare parts for almost anything are always scarce. So queues are common, shoppers are forced to go from store to store in search of desired items, and people must spend an inordinate amount of time in shopping and obtaining needed services. According to one source, the average family spends 1.9 hours per day in such activity.[12] Shortages have also produced hoarding, covert price increases, black markets, and corruption. The practice of sales clerks' "reserving" scarce items for customers in return for bribes is evidently widespread.

The causes of these chronic problems of unreliability of supplies and poor quality and mix of goods and services in urban consumer markets are deeply rooted in the government's strategy of economic development and in the nature of

the economic system. That strategy has long given overriding priority to investment and defense over consumption, skimping on investment in consumer goods
production and development of distribution infrastructure. Centrally planned
socialism has proved to be particularly unsuited for managing the production and
distribution of goods and services for an increasingly affluent population. The
malaise in urban consumer markets comes about because producers respond to
planners rather than to consumers, prices are arbitrary and inflexible, and the
links between suppliers, producers, shippers, and distributors are administrative
(bureaucratic) rather than economic in nature. Discussion of these large matters
is beyond the scope of this essay.[13] In the sections to follow, we focus on a
relatively neglected aspect of the whole picture—the availability and quality of
retail marketing and service facilities.

Urban Retail Trade and Service Facilities

Organization and Planning

Management of the urban retail network is fragmented. The principal
agency is the Ministry of Trade, a union-republic body, with units in the cities
(called *torgs*) being dually subordinate to the ministry and to local government
bodies (city soviets). In the larger cities retail administrative units are organized
by product and supervise individual stores. It appears that Ministry of Trade
facilities account for well over half of total urban turnover in state and cooperative trade. About 10 percent of that turnover is accounted for by the network of
stores under the jurisdiction of consumer cooperatives, which while primarily
serving rural areas, also supply fresh produce in large cities and a general line of
goods in small cities.[14] Pharmacies are managed by the Ministry of Health, sales
of newspapers and magazines by the Ministry of Communications, bookstores by
the State Committee for Publishing, and military stores by the Ministry of
Defense. In addition, a substantial share of trade turnover reflects sales of goods
and public catering services by departments of worker supply subordinate to
industrial and other ministries. In recent years, also, several hundred so-called
"firm stores" (manufacturers' direct outlets) have been opened in cities. Finally,
there is a network of urban farmers' markets (collective farm markets), which is
monitored by special administrations subordinate to local soviets. Despite this
organizational diversity, policies and practices of all organizations generally
must follow those laid down by the Ministry of Trade.[15]

Administrative fragmentation also characterizes the provision of personal
and repair services. There is no overall ministry for the sector at the national
level, and republic ministries were not established until 1965. In Belorussia, for
example, some four-fifths of such services are produced in facilities under the
jurisdiction of the republic Ministry of Everyday Services, and the rest are
scattered among thirty other ministries.[16]

Until the mid-1960s the planning for retail trade and services facilities in cities seems to have produced networks that "grew like Topsy," with little systematic attempt to coordinate the provision of such facilities with plans for developing the city as a whole. Moreover, the low investment priority given these sectors meant inadequate funding, delayed fulfillment of construction plans, and lax supervision over quality. The fact that a multiplicity of administrative agencies was involved compounded the problems. Related matters, such as supplying the stores with modern equipment, providing more goods in packaged form, and giving them access to convenient wholesale warehouses, also were neglected.

The sorry state of these networks in the cities was clearly visible, and the need to do something about it became acute as government policies upgrading the priority for consumption resulted in both a rapid increase in the flow of goods through the trade network and relatively more affluent and demanding consumers. The government's dissatisfaction with the state of affairs was reflected in periodic major decrees, especially after 1965, calling on one and all to put matters right. These decrees were not accompanied by a major shift in investment priorities for the sectors, however; thus the share of investment in trade, material-technical supply, and procurement in total investment was 3.1 percent in 1960, 2.7 percent in 1970, and 2.6 percent in 1980.[17] Although data are sparse, investment in retail trade probably accounted for no more than two-thirds of such investment.[18] Statistics on investment in personal service facilities are not systematically published; but according to various sources, investment in the sector totaled 5.4 billion rubles during 1965–80, 0.4 percent of total investment during the period.[19]

At present, planning for retail trade and service facilities is carried out in accordance with general guidelines, standards, and procedures laid down by the State Planning Committee (Gosplan). Long-term desired targets, referred to as "rational norms," play a large role in guiding plans for additional facilities in both sectors. In the latest compilation of planning methodology, for example, Gosplan has set "near-term" norms (time period not specified) or goals for planning the addition of retail outlets. The norm, expressed in floor space per 1,000 population, is 185 m^2 in urban areas for the country as a whole, with differentiation by type of store (food and nonfood) and by region.[20] The overall norm is to rise to 210 m^2 in 1990.[21] Factors for planning addition of new restaurants are expressed in restaurant seats per 1,000 inhabitants or members of the groups being served. The norm for restaurant seats in urban restaurants open to the general public, for example, is 28 seats per 1,000 population. An intricate set of norms also underlies planning for expansion of the numerous kinds of personal and repair services.

Detailed planning for number, size, kind, and location of all of these facilities is carried out by local agencies of the diverse organizations responsible for managing the sectors—under Gosplan's guidelines and within the limits of investment allocation. The largest role, evidently, is played by departments for trade and for personal services under the city soviets. These units also operate under policy directives handed down by the Ministry of Trade and the State

Committee for Civil Construction and Architecture. In line with a large-scale effort to foster "complex" or comprehensive planning for a city as a whole, these bodies have issued general guidelines concerning size, location, and architectural style for retail trade facilities.[22] Following many years of increasing specialization of facilities, the current thrust is toward construction of large, general purpose stores and trade centers and larger specialized stores. In the area of personal and repair services, the proclaimed policy is to foster large establishments and centralized repair facilities and combines.

At the city level annual plans for expansion of retail trade and service outlets now encompass all planned new or reconstructed facilities, irrespective of what entity actually is to supply the funds or manage the facilities. These plans are gradually being incorporated into comprehensive long-range plans for development of individual cities as a whole. At the beginning of 1979, long-term plans for development of retail trade facilities had been drawn up for 230 cities.[23] The ongoing efforts to do a better job of providing infrastructure in Soviet cities, part of a larger program for comprehensive consumer welfare planning,[24] have been given impetus by the omnibus economic reform decree of July 1979,[25] directing that plans for development of cities be specifically included in the long-term state plans, and by a party-government decree of March 1981 that increased the authority of local soviets in decisions about social amenities for their cities.[26]

Finally, both planning and the actual construction of trade and service facilities are hampered by the existence of multiple sources of financing investment. The bulk of such investment is financed by the state budget as part of the budgets of the Ministry of Trade and the republic ministries of everyday services. Another major source of funds comes from a provision that 5 percent of sums allocated to investment in housing is to be used for retail trade facilities, but housing investment is managed by ministries of housing-communal economy and by numerous other ministries that provide housing for employees in subordinate enterprises. Other funds are under the control of the numerous ministries that operate their own trade and service facilities. Fragmentation of responsibility for investment funding is often blamed for the chronic underfulfillment of plans for commissioning new facilities in the sectors. In an attempt to remedy this situation, a party-government decree on retail trade, issued in July 1977, stated that beginning in 1979, local soviets are to serve as sole clients for construction of trade and public catering facilities in their cities, with the 5 percent deductions from housing funds to be under their control.[27] However, this measure has not been implemented on schedule.[28]

Availability of Facilities

General

a. *Retail outlets.* In 1980 there were 363,000 retail outlets in Soviet urban areas, an unknown but possibly substantial number of which were accessible only to elite groups or persons with hard currency. The network has expanded greatly in the postwar period (Table 2). The number of state and cooperative retail outlets rose by two-thirds during 1955–80, and their composition and quality improved markedly. In 1980, 31 percent of the total consisted of *palatki* (stands, stalls, kiosks of primitive construction and often seasonal); their share was 39 percent in 1955. The number of stores (*magaziny*) kept up with the growth of the urban population, but total floorspace grew somewhat less rapidly than retail sales in real terms. Although data for total urban stores are not published, the average size of all state stores, most of which are urban, increased from 54 m² in 1955 to 110 m² in 1980. Retail turnover per establishment rose from 14,000 rubles in 1950 to 53,000 in 1980. According to a Soviet source, the average area of newly built urban stores increased from 146 m² in 1965 to 230 m² in 1978.[29] Nonetheless, the availability of retail floorspace per 10,000 persons in cities is still well below the official norm—1,675 m² in 1977, compared with a norm of 1,850 m².

Table 2
USSR: Urban Retail Trade and Service Facilities Selected Years 1955–1980

	Retail trade outlets		Restaurants		Service facilities	
	total (000)	per 10,000 population	total (000)	per 10,000 population	total (000)	per 10,000 population
1955	220.9	25.0	83.1	9.4	n.a.	
1960	278.3	27.3	108.8	10.7	n.a.	
1970	345.7	25.2	166.5	12.1	136.5	9.9
1977	360.6	22.6	196.9	12.3	154.4	9.7
1980	363.3	21.7	207.8	12.4	157.0	9.4

Sources: *SSSR v tsifrakh* (1980), 195; *Narkhoz* (1979), 470, 480; *Vestnik statistiki*, 6 (1981), 74–75.

Although most urban retail stores are small, specialized, poorly lighted, and with little or no modern equipment, the trend in recent years has been toward construction of large department stores and shopping centers and conversion of stores to self-service. Nonetheless, the USSR in 1979 had only 670 department stores, many of which would hardly be called that in the West, and only a handful of shopping centers. In the 1970s the shift to self-servicing took on the status of a campaign, following a Council of Ministers' decree ordering a speed up. Although data are not available for urban areas, a Soviet source states that during 1966–78, 235,000 stores had been converted to this "progressive" method and that the share of self-service stores in total trade turnover rose from 7 percent to 59.8 percent.[30] The first self-service department store was opened in Leningrad in 1970, and more than 150 such stores with an average floorspace of 1,000 m² were built during 1971–75 in various large cities.[31] Judging from the numerous press complaints, however, a large measure of skepticism about those figures seems in order; in many cases what is called a self-service store would hardly seem to deserve that designation. In most stores shoppers still must wait in three lines to make a purchase—one to select the item and learn its price, a second to pay for the item, and a third to obtain it.

The attempt to modernize the Soviet retail trade network is hampered by inadequate amounts and poor quality of equipment provided to the sector: one source declares the trade branch to be the worst equipped of any branch of the economy.[32] A perennial problem is the small share of products delivered to the trade network in packaged form—only 28.6 percent of all food products (not counting fruits and vegetables) in 1978, little different from 1975.[33] As a result, a sizable part of retail floorspace is devoted to packaging and preparing goods for sale. Although nearly all stores now have refrigeration equipment, complaints about its technical obsolescence and poor quality are common, as are laments about lack of cash registers, storage facilities, and materials-handling equipment. Deliveries of equipment to the network were scheduled to rise by 40 percent in the plan for 1975–80, but those plans were not met. Actual deliveries were lower relative to planned demand by larger margins in 1980 than in 1975.[34]

b. *Restaurants*. The number of public dining facilities has more than kept up with urban population growth, rising from 9 per 10,000 population in 1955 to over 12 in 1980. The average size of these facilities, measured by number of seats, doubled between 1965 and 1980, when the average urban dining facility had 65.8 places.[35] The bulk of these dining facilities are not open to the general public but are attached directly to factories, clubs, institutions, and organizations. For the country as a whole (urban data are not available), only 27 percent of the restaurants and cafeterias with 21 percent of the seats were open to the general public in 1980. Moreover, their share is declining; in 1965 the corresponding percentages were 32 and 29.[36] Despite considerable progress, present public dining availabilities are far below established norms. Thus, as of January 1, 1979, the norm for canteens in industrial enterprises was met by only 52.4 percent, by 51.7 percent in general education schools, and by 68.6 percent in tekhnikums and colleges.[37] Complaints about restaurants similar to those concerning retail trades are perennial themes in the press—poor quality of food and service, obsolescent and inadequate equipment, and low level of mechanization of labor.

c. *Personal and repair services*. Provision of personal and repair services for urban residents is grossly inadequate. In 1965, the first year for which national data were published, there were only 113,000 such establishments to serve an urban population of some 122 million. By 1980 their number had risen to 158,000, serving an urban population of 167 million, along with many rural residents who come to cities to obtain these services. Facilities have been increasing rapidly in size; sales per establishment rose from 14,000 rubles in 1965 to 36,000 rubles in 1980. Like retail trade, the personal services sector has been the subject of several government decrees demanding better performance in this long-neglected area. Judging by press reporting, however, the sector continues to suffer the same woes as in retail trade and public dining—low priority (despite much rhetoric to the contrary), poor quality of service, primitive technology, and

Table 3
USSR and Republics: Number of Urban Retail Trade and Service Facilities in 1977

	Retail trade outlets		*Restaurants*		*Service facilities*	
	total (000)	per 10,000 population	total (000)	per 10,000 population	total (000)	per 10,000 population
USSR	360.6	22.6	196.6	12.3	154.4	9.7
RSFSR	186.8	20.0	110.9	11.9	749.9	8.0
Ukraine	79.2	26.6	37.1	12.5	37.1	12.5
Belorussia	10.3	20.5	6.2	12.3	5.7	11.3
Moldavia	4.0	27.0	2.0	13.5	2.0	13.5
Kazakhstan	17.4	22.0	9.0	11.4	6.4	8.1
Georgia	9.2	36.4	4.5	17.8	5.8	22.9
Azerbaidzhan	10.3	34.3	5.1	17.0	5.4	18.0
Armenia	4.9	26.3	2.4	12.9	2.7	14.5
Uzbekistan	15.5	27.0	7.4	12.9	6.3	11.0
Kirghizistan	3.2	23.9	1.7	12.7	1.5	11.2
Tadzhikistan	3.6	28.0	2.2	17.1	2.1	16.3
Turkmenistan	3.8	29.5	1.6	12.4	1.8	14.0
Estonia	2.4	24.2	1.4	14.1	0.7	7.1
Latvia	4.7	28.2	2.2	13.2	1.1	6.6
Lithuania	4.5	23.0	2.3	11.8	0.9	4.6

Sources: *Narkhoz* (1979), 480; *Narkhoz* (1977), 11; *Narkhoz za 60 let* (1976), 43; *Vestnik statistiki*, (1979), 73-74.

chronic failure to meet plans for opening new facilities.

Regional differences

Availability of retail and service facilities differs widely among the fifteen Soviet republics, and probably even more so among their administrative subdivisions. Relevant data for the republics for 1977 are assembled in Table 3, and indicators of the relative size of establishments are given in Table 4. In terms of numbers of establishments relative to population, the Transcaucasian republics are best endowed, generally by a sizable margin, but the average size of facilities tends to be relatively small. The Central Asian republics also have relatively more small establishments. Poorest endowed as measured by number of facilities are the RSFSR and Kazakhstan. These republics also are below the national average on our indicators of size of facility. Incomplete data for the RSFSR reveal great variation within that large republic, which in 1980 had 58 percent of the total urban population in the USSR. The Baltic republics, the most affluent by overall measures of levels of living, have more facilities of all kinds relative to population, and they also tend to be larger, notably so for personal and repair services.

Besides state and cooperative retail trade facilities considered in Tables 3 and 4, urban areas in all republics are served by a network of collective farm markets (CFMs), most of them in small cities. These facilities are distributed quite unevenly among republics, and the pattern tends to follow that already noted for state and cooperative retail trade. The RSFSR and Kazakhstan, with 64 percent of the urban population, had in 1978 only 46 percent of urban CFMs; the Western republics, with 23 percent of the population, had 33 percent of the markets; and the Transcaucasian-Central Asian group, with 11 percent of the population, had 17 percent of the markets.[38] Corresponding figures for the Baltic are 3 and 3.5.

All republics have made substantial improvement in provision of retail trade and service facilities in recent years, but the pattern is quite diverse. We can compare the situation at the end of 1980 with that in 1953, the earliest year for which systematic data are available. Over that period the number of retail establishments (expressed per 10,000 population) declined by percentages ranging from a mere 5 percent in Georgia to 34 percent in Belorussia and Lithuania; the latter two republics were experiencing especially rapid urbanization and building many new, large stores. No doubt the average size of stores increased everywhere, but comparable series are not available to determine if this is so. The number of restaurants per 10,000 population rose in all republics except Uzbekistan—by 13 to 37 percent—while the number of seats in dining facilities per 10,000 population nearly doubled everywhere except in Uzbekistan, where it rose by 69 percent.

The patterns are even more diverse with respect to development of the primitive personal and repair services sector. Data for urban areas are available only since 1965, and their comparability over time is open to question. They indicate that in 1965 all republics had small numbers of service facilities relative

213

Table 4
USSR and Republics: Indicators of Relative Size of Urban Retail Trade and Service Facilities in 1977

| | Floorspace in stores (m²) | | Seats in restaurants | | Sales of personal and repair services | |
	per* enterprise	per 10,000 population	per restaurant	per 10,000 population	per facility (00 rubles)	per capita (rubles)
USSR	75 (111)	1,675	62	756	30.2	29.3
RSFSR	82 (123)	1,630	63	747	36.1	28.9
Ukraine	70 (100)	1,833	65	800	25.4	31.6
Belorussia	95 (131)	1,914	66	799	30.8	34.9
Moldavia	68 (101)	1,793	64	843	23.7	32.0
Kazakhstan	69	1,550	50	579	29.9	24.2
Georgia	56	2,034	49	858	15.1	34.6
Azerbaidzhan	47 (78)	1,550	46	745	12.5	22.5
Armenia	60	1,524	60	741	16.9	24.5
Uzbekistan	53	1,370	53	652	20.0	21.9
Kirghizistan	58 (92)	1,392	52	655	27.3	30.5
Tadzhikistan	62	1,717	47	801	17.1	27.9
Turkmenistan	51	1,512	48	589	14.9	20.9
Estonia	75	1,794	69	961	50.4	35.6
Latvia	69	1,897	78	1,004	58.4	39.9
Lithuania	80 (110)	1,802	75	861	69.3	32.0

Sources: *Vestnik statistiki*, 7 (1979), 73–75; *Narkhoz SSSR* (1977), 482, 484.
*Calculated as the total floor space in stores (*magaziny*) divided by the total number of outlets. Numbers in parentheses represent floorspace per store (excluding stalls, stands, and kiosks).

to population and that they were tiny in size. Between 1965 and 1980 the number of service enterprises per 10,000 population in most republics either decreased or increased negligibly. Sales per enterprise, however, rose rapidly and at widely varying rates among the republics—from 80 percent in Turkmenistan to 442 percent in Estonia. Sales per enterprise at least doubled in all republics but two. If these data are reasonably trustworthy, it is evident that a variety of approaches to developing this sector were taken. The Central Asian republics, the Ukraine, and Georgia substantially raised the number of enterprises relative to population, adding both large and relatively small firms. The Baltic republics and Moldavia evidently went in for building large units. This diversity in development rates and patterns and in the levels and configurations now existing suggests that regional authorities have had considerable latitude to exercise local preferences and experiment with different approaches. Some local governments evidently have been more activist than others. One gets similar impressions from reading the regional press on the problems, policies, approaches, successes, and failures in developing and managing the complex retail trade and personal services sectors, which must cater to the preferences of millions of individuals on a daily basis.

Differences among cities

Given the Soviet government's penchant for attempting to enforce uniformities and standardization via its ubiquitous system of norms, one might expect to find much uniformity in provision of trade and service facilities among cities. In fact there is great diversity. Data for 1977 are given in Table 5 for all Soviet cities over one million in population and for the capitals of the smaller republics; data for other cities are hard to come by. When expressed per 10,000 persons, the number of retail trade outlets ranges from 11 to 25 among the twenty-five cities; the range for number of restaurants is narrower—from 8 to 14; the number of service facilities ranges from 4.4 to 8.1. No clear pattern seems to prevail, either by size of city or by region. The fragmentary data available on the size of establishment by city show what one might expect—that the average size of establishment tends to be larger in the big cities than in smaller ones—but that the pattern is not uniform. Thus the average store in Moscow had an area of 275 m², while the average store in Minsk had 241 m²; but corresponding figures for the number of seats per restaurant are 85 and 93, and for sales of services per establishment 74,000 rubles and 93,000 rubles. In Alma-Ata there were 67 seats per restaurant and services sales of 69,000 rubles per facility. In Baku there were 63 seats in the average restaurant, compared with 89 in Kiev.

The fragmentary evidence indicates that provision of trade and service facilities has been improving steadily in these major cities, with the average establishment getting larger and more specialized. The drive for bigness and specialization in Minsk, for example, has resulted in the concentration of all sales of television sets in this city of over a million in only two stores.[39] Even the largest cities display the pattern of trade and restaurant facilities that characterizes the country as a whole. Thus in Moscow in 1977 half the total number of retail outlets consisted of *palatki*, and only 31 percent of the dining facilities with 25 percent of the total seating capacity were open to the general public.[40] To the extent that the data permit a calculation, the planning norms for availability of facilities relative to population have not been met anywhere.

To provide a comparative perspective, we obtained data for cities of comparable size in the United States and for three large cities in Eastern Europe, the only ones for which data were readily available. Even though comparison with the United States may seem inappropriate, and comparison of number of units is certainly crude, the figures do provide a rough idea of the gap between the two countries. Even for the largest cities, the gaps between the USSR and the United States are enormous and are large even when compared with the three cities in Eastern Europe. Thus New York, Chicago, and Los Angeles had three to four times as many retail outlets as Moscow, nearly twice as many restaurants, and over three times as many service establishments (counting only those with payrolls in the United States; if totals are used, U.S. cities had six to eight times as many).[41] Or we might compare the situation in Minsk with that prevailing in such U.S. cities of comparable size as Cincinnati, Milwaukee, and Seattle; the results are similar to those given by a comparison of the largest cities in both countries. Although data on size of establishment in the United States are not at hand, America surely does not suffer by comparison with the USSR on this count.

The gaps in provision of all three types of services between the United States and the USSR tend to be similar irrespective of the size of city. Also, the variability in provision of these facilities relative to population tends to be smaller in the United States than in the USSR. If data would permit the comparison, one would also probably find, however, that the United States provides a much wider range of sizes of establishment. In New York City, for example, nearly one-fourth of the retail trade establishments were small individual proprietorships without formal payrolls; in the services the share was even larger. There were nearly twice as many of these small outlets as in all of Moscow. These establishments are scattered all over New York and provide great convenience utilities for local residents. As an illustration of the gaps in personal services, we can compare similarly populated Tallin, Estonia (with high per capita incomes by Soviet standards), and Harrisburg, Pennsylvania. The former had 20 laundry and dry cleaning establishments, compared with the latter's 123; comparisons for beauty and barbershops are 120 and 773. In contrast, Tallin had 30 shoemaking and repair shops, compared with 19 in Harrisburg.

Conclusions

Despite much progress since the days of Stalin, supplies of goods and personal services available to Soviet urban residents compare unfavorably with availabilities in countries with similar per capita GNPs in both Western and Eastern Europe. In terms of dependability of supply and quality, the comparison is even more unfavorable to the USSR. In addition, retail distribution facilities are inadequate and poorly equipped, and customers are poorly served by international standards. Moreover, prospects for reducing these gaps are dim.

Table 5

USSR Cities: Retail Trade and Service Facilities in 1977

City	Population (000)	Retail trade outlets		Restaurants		Service facilities	
		total number	per 10,000 population	total number	per 10,000 population	total number	per 10,000 population
Moscow	7,909	10,180	13	7,902	10	4,010	5.1
Leningrad	4,480	6,699	15	4,497	10	2,084	4.7
Kiev	2,131	3,273	15	1,978	9	1,449	6.8
Tashkent	1,732	3,200	18	1,629	9	1,004	5.8
Baku	1,460	3,692	25	1,665	11		
Kharkov	1,428	1,561	11	1,622	12		
Gorky	1,332	2,095	16	1,295	10		
Novosibirsk	1,324	1,431	11	1,159	9		
Minsk	1,273	1,373	11	1,071	8	555	4.4
Kuibyshev	1,221	1,614	13	1,182	10		
Sverdlovsk	1,204	1,595	13	1,276	11		

Dnepopetrovsk	1,060	1,620	16	1,000	10		
Tbilisi	1,052	1,957	19	1,222	12		
Odessa	1,051	2,197	21	1,079	10		
Omsk	1,042	1,363	13	1,191	11		
Cheliabinsk	1,019	1,420	14	1,150	11		
Yerevan	982	1,782	18	986	10		
Alma-Ata	895	1,872	21	991	11	571	6.4
Riga	827	1,814	22	937	11		
Frunze	522	741	14	524	10		
Kishinev	494	934	19	568	11		
Dushanbe	474	985	21	531	11		
Vilnius	470	654	14	534	11		
Tallin	422	787	19	583	14	342	8.1
Ashkhabad	311	594	19	282	9		

Sources: *Vestnik statistiki*, 11 (1978), 86,90; annual statistical handbooks of the republics.

The 1980s will almost certainly be a decade of stringency for Soviet consumers. Unless productivity can be raised substantially, economic growth is bound to be slow because of demographically determined reduction in the growth of the labor force—to half the rate of the 1970s. Investment growth has slowed markedly, and the Eleventh Five-Year Plan (1981–85) projects a further slowdown. Large funds will be required to develop energy and raw materials resources in Siberia, and competition for scarce investment funds will be intense. In such an economic climate, it seems unlikely that investment allocations to consumer-oriented sectors could be sufficient to appreciably reduce the legacies of past parsimony.

The plan for 1981–85 schedules a sharp increase in the availability of food compared with the preceding five years; production of soft goods and consumer durables is supposed to rise at about the rates achieved in 1976–80. Total retail trade is scheduled to grow by 23 percent, compared with 24 percent in 1976–80 and 36 percent in 1971–75. Personal and repair services are to rise by 40 percent, compared with 43 percent and 64 percent in the two previous five-year periods. Plans call for urban retail trade and services to grow more slowly than in rural areas. However, investment in trade facilities is to be reduced, and employment is to increase only slightly.[42] Although total retail floorspace is to increase about as much as in the previous five years, restaurant seats are to be added at a slower rate.

Since the problems of irregularity of supply and poor quality and mix of goods and services are rooted in the nature of the economic system itself, their solution requires a radical reform to permit consumer guidance of production, flexibility of prices, and incentives geared to satisfying customers rather than meeting plan targets. Whether the political leadership of the 1980s will be bolder than their predecessors in launching systematic reform remains to be seen.

With or without massive infusions of investment funds to modernize physical facilities, the management of the urban retail trade and personal services sectors probably could be improved substantially if the Soviet government would transfer authority over the sectors to local authorities. Greater decentralization in these areas has been advocated for decades, and many party-government decrees have sought to increase the powers of local governing bodies. Heretofore these efforts have met with little success, as Moscow central planners have continued to dictate to the sectors, and central ministries have dragged their feet on transferring in-house facilities to the control of local soviets. With the increased emphasis on "comprehensive" or program-goals approaches to planning and with the acute labor shortages in prospect, local authorities now seem to be taking a more active part in planning and managing development of local infrastructure in the cities. The latest major decree on this subject, published in March 1981, goes farther than before in creating the potential for even greater control by local soviets over development of trade and service facilities in their cities. Local budgets are given additional sources of revenue, and central ministries are urged to transfer their trade and service facilities to local control. The time is ripe for just such steps. Whether they will be carried out or will meet the fate of past efforts in that direction remains to be seen. Perhaps the exigencies of the 1980s will provide the catalyst.

Although there are no signs as yet, the stringencies of the 1980s also might induce the government to emulate Eastern Europe in allowing more legal private activity, especially in the provision of personal and repair services. Permissive legislation and removal of discriminatory taxation of private incomes not only would coopt one sector of the so-called "second economy" but might unleash pent-up energies and provide outlets for the savings of the populace. Everybody would benefit, except hard-core ideologists opposed to expansion of private activity no matter what the cost. If sanctions against private activity are relaxed, Soviet cities will be somewhat less frustrating places in which to live and work.

Notes

[1]Gertrude E. Schroeder and Imogene Edwards, *Consumption in the USSR: An International Comparison* (Washington, D.C., 1981).

[2]Gur Ofer, *The Service Sector in Soviet Economic Growth* (Cambridge, 1973), 154-65.

[3]International Labour Office, *Yearbook of Labour Statistics* (Geneva, 1980).

[4]Marshall Goldman, *Soviet Marketing* (New York, 1963).

[5]Philip Hanson, *The Consumer in the Soviet Economy* (London, 1968).

[6]Roger Skurski, "Productivity, Growth and Efficiency in Soviet Consumer Goods Distribution," *The ACES Bulletin*, 18, 3 (1976), 79-109.

[7]Gertrude E. Schroeder and Barbara S. Severin, "Soviet Consumption and Income Policies in Perspective," *Soviet Economy in a New Perspective* (Washington, D.C., 1976), 626.

[8]*Narodnoe khoziaistvo SSSR v 1980 g.* (hereafter *Narkhoz SSSR*) (Moscow, 1980), 407.

[9]V. I. Dmitriev, *Metodicheskie osnovy prognozirovaniia sprosa na bytovye uslugi* (Moscow, 1975), 46.

[10]Gur Ofer and Aaron Vinokur, *Private Sources of Income of the Soviet Urban Household* (Santa Monica, August 1980), 10-32.

[11]*Sovetskaia Rossiia* (October 17, 1981).

[12]*Ekonomika i organizatsiia promyshlennogo proizvodstva*, 3 (1978), 91.

[13]For elaboration on these points, see Schroeder and Severin and Gertrude E. Schroeder, "Consumption," in Abram Bergson and Herbert S. Levine (eds.), *The Soviet Economy toward the Year 2000* (New York, 1983).

[14]The shares of the various organizations were estimated from data in *Narkhoz* (1979), 453, and the statements that the Ministry of Trade accounts for about half of total trade turnover, in V. G. Tikhonovskii (ed.), *Organizatsiia torgovli* (Moscow, 1978), 6, and that 30 percent of the trade turnover of cooperatives is urban sales, in *Planovoe khoziaistvo*, 7 (1978), 7.

[15]A recent general description of the organization of retail trade is given in Iu. A. Gusev, *Skol'ko, chto i gde my pokupaem* (Moscow, 1979),60-80.

[16]V. I. Drits (ed.), *Sotsial'naia infrastruktura—resul'tat i faktor effektivnosti proizvodstva* (Minsk, 1980), 165.

[17]Sovet Ekonomicheskoi Vzaimopomoshchi, *Statisticheskii ezhegodnik stranchlenov Soveta Ekonomicheskoi Vzaimopomoshchi* (Moscow, 1981), 141, 146.

[18]This estimate is based on data given in ibid. and a figure for planned investment in 1971–75 given in A. I. Struev, *Torgovlia v desiatoi piatiletke* (Moscow, 1977), 9.

[19]V. M. Rutgaizer (ed.), *Kompleksnii plan razvitiia sfery obsluzhivaniia naseleniia* (Moscow, 1977), 153; *Narkhoz SSSR* (1975), 507; *Ekonomicheskaia gazeta*, 21 (1982), 2.

[20]USSR Gosplan, *Metodicheskie ukazaniia k razrabotke gosudarstvennykh planov ekonomicheskogo i sotsial'nogo razvitiia SSSR* (Moscow, 1980), 669.

[21]Tikhonovskii, 30.

[22]I. P. Kardashidi, *Razvitiia material'no-tekhnicheskoi bazy torgovli* (Moscow, 1980), 34-35.

[23]*Voprosy ekonomiki*, 6 (1980), 112.

[24]For a description of this approach, see David Cattell in Henry W. Morton and Rudolf T. Tokes (eds.), *Soviet Politics and Society in the 1970s* (New York, 1974), 219-60.

[25]*Sobranie postanovlennii pravitel'stva SSSR*, 18 (1979), 390-431.

[26]*Izvestia* (March 29, 1981).

[27]*Pravda* (July 19, 1977).

[28]V. Shimanskii and Ia. Orlov, *Torgovlia i blago naroda* (Moscow, 1980), 156-57.

[29]Shimanskii and Orlov, 158.

[30]Ibid., 181.

[31]Gusev, 68-69.

[32]Ibid., 72.

[33]Shimanskii and Orlov, 188.

[34]*Sovetskaia torgovlia*, 7 (1981), 8.

[35]*Narkhoz SSSR* (1979), 475, and *Vestnik statistiki*, 6 (1981), 75.

[36]*Narkhoz SSSR* (1980), 444.

[37]Shimanskii and Orlov, 215, 217.

[38]*Vestnik statistiki*, 5 (1979), 78-79.

[39]*Voprosy ekonomiki*, 6 (1980), 112.

[40]*Moskva v tsifrakh* (1978), 90, 94.

[41]Data for this comparison are from *1977 Census of Retail Trade* (Washington, D.C., 1977) and *1977 Census of Service Industries* (Washington, D.C., 1980). U.S. data are available for "all establishments" and "establishments with payrolls," the latter being the more conservative estimate.

[42]*Sovetskaia torgovlia*, 3 (1982), 7.

Zvi Gitelman

11

Working the Soviet System: Citizens and Urban Bureaucracies

*"Even with the best of intentions, devout human-
ism and the utmost intelligence, the administrative authorities were unable to do more than solve instantaneous
and transitory conflicts and were incapable of eliminating
the permanent conflicts between reality and the principles of administration. . . . Even the best intentions were
bound to fail in breaking through the bureaucratic
relation."*

Karl Marx, quoted in Andras Hegedüs,
Socialism and Bureaucracy, p. 12

*"When you examine . . . such things as collectivization, in-
dustrialization and cultural revolution, or the struggle
against political deviation . . . Trotskyism, cubism, cosmo-
politanism, Weismannism, Morganism, modernism, and
contemporary revisionism—do not overlook the humble
drudge with the simple unmemorable, greedy face. . . .
And while you plan great reform programs, build castles in
the air, search for mistakes in Hegel, create a line of poetry, or
try to see an X chromosome through a microscope, our humble
drudge, with his sharp little eyes, watches carefully to see if,
under the guise of struggling against an alien ideology, he can
get something from you: an apartment, a wife, a cow, an invention, a position, an academic title."*

Vladimir Voinovich,
The Ivankiad, p. 118

Research for this essay was supported by the Ford Foundation, the National Council for Soviet
and East European Research, and the Sapir Development Fund (Israel). Amy Saldinger, Konstantin
Miroshnik, and Wayne DiFranceisco provided invaluable research assistance. To all these people and
institutions, my profound gratitude.

In the Soviet political system the physical and psychological distances between the top elite and the mass of citizens are greater than in most democratic, and perhaps other "socialist," states. This is due to the sheer physical size of the country, to Russian traditions of physical, cultural, and political separation between rulers and masses, to a pervasive distrust of the masses and insecurity about them that grows out of Leninist fears of "spontaneity," and to the multilayered hierarchical organization of every aspect of public life. Since the Soviet politician's career does not depend on electoral success, but rather on bureaucratic politics, he is not compelled to "go to the people" or "press the flesh" except on a few carefully orchestrated occasions. On the other hand, in the absence of a significant private sector outside agriculture, it is the government which controls many of the basic desiderata of life—jobs, housing, higher education, for example—which in other systems are only marginally or indirectly affected by the state. Therefore government-citizen contacts are much more frequent than they are in, say, the American system. But these contacts are most often at the local level, between citizens and lower-level employees of the various branches of the state administration. This makes the local officials "the target for citizen demands which in another regime might be handled by non-political subsystems."[1] Not only does this place a very heavy work load on local officials, but it also means that the Soviet citizens' most frequent and most meaningful contact with the political system is as a client, indeed a supplicant, making demands and requests of lower-level officials who are empowered to speak in the name of the state. Soviet legal sources assert that civil servants "always act by commission of the state and in its name,"[2] but they insist that since there is an identity of interests between the state and its citizens, civil servants simultaneously represent the interests of the citizenry. This contrasts with "bourgeois" civil servants who are divorced from the masses, serve the interests of the ruling bourgeoisie, and constitute a "privileged caste."[3]

In contrast to such legalistic assertions, some social scientists in the USSR admit that there might be an adversary relationship between government officials and the citizens they are supposed to serve. As one Soviet student of administration puts it delicately, "Administrative relations are perhaps the most flexible of social relationships. . . . Administrative relations . . . lie in the sphere of subjective relations and are much more liable to be influenced by people than other social relationships."[4] Thus there is room for maneuver, for kindness or abuse, for flexibility or rigidity, for satisfaction or frustration, in the myriad contacts between Soviet officials and Soviet citizens. Most Western studies of Soviet officialdom have concentrated on such important questions as the activities of bureaucracies as interest groups; politics within and between the elites of various bureaucracies; the relationship of state bureaucracies to the party; the demographic and attitudinal characteristics of various hierarchies; and most broadly, whether or not those hierarchies are "functional" and "dysfunctional."[5] This essay, however, deals with the relationship between some state hierarchies and Soviet citizens, largely from the perspective of the citizens. The aim is to gain insights, not only into Soviet people's evaluation of specific bureaucracies, but also into their relationship with the Soviet state on the mundane, but vitally important, level of "daily life."

The Citizen and the Bureaucrat

The ability of an organization, private or public, to satisfy the desires of its clients, would seem to depend on three things: (1) the material resources available to the organization and decisions about their allocation; (2) the structure of the organization, which may speed or impede effective delivery of its goods or services; (3) the quality and attitudes of the organization's personnel. Most clients are in no position to distinguish between the latter two; harrassed clerks who treat clients brusquely and cannot meet their demands may be well intentioned and even highly competent, but a lack of funds or an inefficient structure may frustrate their attempts to serve their public. On the other hand, employees may effectively sabotage an organization whose resources and structure are satisfactory. One can also conceive of the opposite situation—a client who does not achieve his goal may still be positive toward the organization if he comes away with the feeling that its employees did their best for him but that only objective limitations prevented them from delivering the goods. This leads to a consideration of bureaucratic *style*, the way in which employees deal with clients. In market economies employees of private organizations, and, to a lesser extent, of public bureaucracies, are taught to be friendly, courteous, understanding, and at least to pretend that "the customer is always right." This is clearly not the norm in the USSR. A former prime minister of socialist Hungary, Andras Hegedüs, puts it this way:

> The "client" is conceived as some kind of strange out-
> sider, or even some downright malevolent person, over
> whom the administration, as the representative of the
> whole society, holds power. . . . This mystified social inter-
> est represents a much greater power for the individual
> official than it did for a king ruling by divine right or any
> capitalist company. And to make the situation more gro-
> tesque and complicated, this tendency to make a derived
> power absolute often penetrates much more deeply into
> the lower ranks of the hierarchy than into the upper ones.
> The lower ranks are inclined to take out on the client
> their lack of a substantial deciding voice in the administra-
> tive system.[6]

This behavior is explained by structural factors, such as the lack of a market incentive to attract customers, and by historical and cultural ones. Soviet officials display the syndrome of the "slave who became king." Themselves only a generation or two removed from the peasantry or the proletariat, subservient classes under both the tsars and Stalin, Soviet employees are acutely conscious of their powerlessness vis-à-vis their bureaucratic superiors, on the one hand, and their power over hapless citizens, on the other. In many instances their authority is so limited that they cannot satisfy the desires of the citizens even if they want to, but the citizen sees them as the representatives of the all-powerful state who should be meeting their needs. Realizing the limited jurisdiction of lower-level employees, more sophisticated Soviet citizens almost automatically demand to "see your supervisor," a demand often made of employees dealing with Soviet immigrants in Western countries. The combination of very narrow jurisdiction and insistent demands for service frustrate the official, who takes it out on the citizen. After all, the citizen by his very request reminds the employee of the latter's powerlessness, as Hegedüs points out.

This pattern was well established in tsarist times and was reinforced in the Stalinist period. Both Russian and Soviet political culture are suffused with the idea that "high politics" and policymaking are not the proper concern of the individual citizen but should be left to the ruling group. The executor of policy, the bureaucrat, is thus the proper point of contact between citizen and state; but the bureaucrat, too, does not make policy. He can only refer matters requiring policy decisions, even of the most trivial sort, to his hierarchical superiors. Isaac Deutscher observed that overcentralization in the 1930s "instilled a grotesque fear of initiative and responsibility in all grades of the administration; it reduced every official to a cog; it often brought the whole machinery to a standstill. . . . The whole administrative machinery was clogged by such red tape and bureaucratic hypocrisy as would have given material to a great pleiad of satirical writers, if the satirical writers, too, had not been paralyzed by the fear of responsibility."[7] Fear and bureaucratic paralysis have dissipated in the past thirty years, but overcentralization and the tendency to avoid decisions by referring matters higher up the bureaucratic ladder still characterize the system.

Since official agencies provide the basic necessities of life in the USSR, contacts with them are vitally important to Soviet people. How these contacts are evaluated may tell us not only about people's attitudes toward particular agencies but also about their overall affect toward the entire system. Moreover, the ways in which Soviet people go about obtaining what they want from these agencies may differ from the formal patterns which are prescribed. A description of the actual strategies employed by citizens provides insights into the informal workings of the system, of how citizens "work the system." Therefore we shall deal here with three questions: (1) How do former Soviet citizens evaluate some Soviet urban service agencies and their personnel? (2) How did they "work the system"—what strategies and tactics did they employ to extract what they wanted from the system? (3) Do different groups of people deal with the bureaucracies in different ways? In other words, do views of the bureaucracies vary significantly and consistently by republic, sex, age, education, occupation, or other variables? Perhaps the bureaucracies themselves operate differently in different republics, indicating that the Soviet system is less monolithic and its administrative practices less uniform than often assumed in the West.

Two problems of method should be addressed. First, "Bureaucracy is a word with a bad reputation. If you ask people to supply an adjective to go along with the noun, their choices will almost inevitably be pejorative. . . . Complaints about government bureaucracies have probably been commonplace at every period of history and in every country.''[8] But people do not inevitably give a negative assessment when asked to evaluate a public bureaucracy in the light of their own experience. In fact, a major study of interactions between citizens and American public bureaucracies found that two-thirds of the respondents were satisfied with the ''bureaucratic encounter'' they judged their most important one. True, private agencies were seen more favorably, and people had a more positive picture of the way a *personal* experience was handled and a more negative *generalized* attitude toward government agencies.[9] Soviet émigrés, too, have differentiated attitudes toward bureaucracies and, despite a generalized hostility, are prepared to speak favorably about individual experiences. One woman recalls several instances of kindness and extending themselves on the part of Soviet officials even after she had been identified as an intended émigré and, hence, a traitor to the motherland. ''. . . It became beautifully clear to me that in every bureaucrat somewhere there sits a human being, and you have to be able to find him. . . . There's only a very small group of people who have become petrified, become completely hard and unreachable in the process of serving the Soviet Union. . . . But . . . there aren't many such people. In most others a soul still shines through.''

In addition to the fact that views of bureaucracy are not uniformly negative, a differentiation of outlook is made more likely if people are asked to *compare* bureaucracies with each other. Even in cases where there is a generalized hostility to bureaucracy, people will be induced to differentiate among degrees of hostility. Parenthetically, it should be noted that the public's skeptical views of bureaucrats are reciprocated in both American and Soviet societies, as well as others.[10] In a Soviet survey involving 1,500 citizens and 1,000 local administrators, significant differences emerged in the views of the two groups on the proper and actual roles of citizens and administrators.[11] The tendency in Soviet literature, as in American, is to assume initially that citizens' grievances against the bureaucracy are justified, though many Soviet scholars do point to shortcomings not only of Soviet officials but of the administrative system in which they operate. One author bemoans the lack of competitive examination for entry to government service (he even cites ''bourgeois'' Britain, Japan, France, and the United States as examples for the USSR to follow) and asserts that Soviet officials often lack any knowledge of administrative techniques and of Soviet legislation.[12] A critical analysis of the pension administration points out that in the RSFSR in 1976, more than two-thirds of the regional and local social security inspectors lacked secondary-specialized or higher education.[13]

The second problem of method is the use of émigré informants as substitutes for Soviet citizens who, of course, cannot be systematically interviewed by Western scholars. The problem of using émigrés as sources of information about the Soviet system has been dealt with extensively[14] and, in my opinion, successfully. Whether or not one can use an émigré sample to generalize to the Soviet population as a whole, in this study we shall be comparing *within* an émigré group and will observe *relative* differences that are more significant than the absolute answers to questions about the bureaucracies. Furthermore, as Inkeles and Bauer pointed out twenty years ago, it is likely that "comparable groups in the Soviet population will stand in the same relationship to each other as do members of our sample."[15]

It is often mentioned that aside from its statistical unrepresentativeness, the emigration is likely to be more biased against the Soviet system than the population it left behind. The assumption of bias is not necessarily correct because many people left the Soviet Union for personal, economic, and family reasons rather than because of political, cultural, or ethnic disaffection. Some unknown, but considerable, proportion are "secondary migrants" who made no independent decision to leave but did so as dependents of all generations. Moreover, there are areas where problems of bias can be minimized. For example, concrete, detailed questions about personal experiences could elicit factual information with less evaluative coloring than attitudinal questions and with more reliable information than that obtained by asking people about matters where they had no direct experience (e.g., experiences as consumers compared to how foreign policy decisions are made). Even without a representative sample, if large numbers of people with a particular characteristic, say, republic of residence, exhibit patterns of behavior or outlook that are strikingly and consistently different from those displayed by parallel groups, it seems reasonable to conclude that there are real differences between the two groups. Finally, the ethnic imbalance of the present emigration need not color certain kinds of research. First, it is sufficiently large that members of many nationalities can be found in it. Second, the dominant émigré ethnic group, Jews, is quite diverse, speaking different languages, coming from vastly different geocultural areas, and representing several levels of education and many occupations. Third, for many purposes ethnicity will be less important than, say, level of education or republic of residence. For example, the way Georgian Jews interact with a local bureaucracy more likely resembles the way non-Jewish Georgians do so than the way Ukrainian or Lithuanian Jews do.

The Sample

A total of 1,161 ex-Soviet citizens, almost all of whom had left the USSR in 1977–80, was interviewed between April 1980 and March 1981. The interviews were conducted in Israel (n = 590), the Federal Republic of Germany (n = 100), and the United States (n = 471). The sample was purposely drawn in line with some preliminary hypotheses so that a certain distribution by age, sex, education, nationality, and republic of residence could be achieved. Six hundred women and 561 men were interviewed, the youngest being 22 (to insure that respondents would have had at least some personal dealings with Soviet bureaucracies). Most reached maturity in the Stalinist and post-Stalinist eras.

About 40 percent of the Soviet immigrants to Israel and the United States have claimed some form of Soviet higher education, and this is reflected in the educational profile of our respondents, 47 percent of whom had higher education,

Table 1
Period of Birth of Respondents

1893-1917	1918-29	1930s	1940s	1950s
173	195	259	320	214

with 38 percent having secondary and only 15 percent elementary schooling. In regard to nationality, 77 percent (n = 889) had been registered as Jews on their internal Soviet passports. (All Soviet citizens are classified officially by their ethnic group or "nationality.") There were 129 registered as Russians, 98 as Germans, 18 as Ukrainians, and 27 of other nationalities. The areas in which the respondents lived most of their lives are shown in Table 2.

Table 2
Respondents' Area of Residence in USSR[16]

RSFSR	Ukraine	Moldavia	Baltic	Georgia	Central Asia
330	247	120	174	120	165

The men and women are quite evenly distributed by age and region, but males dominate the blue-collar professions and females the white-collar ones, despite very similar educational levels (48 percent of the men and 46 percent of the women have higher education). As might be expected, there are more young people from Georgia and Central Asia, where birth rates are higher, than from the other regions. Educational levels are highest among those from the RSFSR (69 percent have higher education, as do 72 percent of the ethnic Russians, followed by people from the Baltic, Ukraine, and Georgia). Those from Moldavia, where Jews are less urbanized than in any other European area, and from Central Asia have the lowest educational levels (23 percent of the Moldavian Jews and 18 percent of the Central Asians have higher education). They also have the lowest proportion of Communist Party members, though among ethnic Germans, where only 16 percent have higher education, there is only one ex-party-member. Those from the Baltic report having had the highest incomes, whether by family unit or per capita, followed by the RSFSR and the Ukraine. The Moldavians had the lowest incomes of the European groups and on a per capita basis were outranked by the Georgians. The Central Asians had the lowest incomes of any group.

These people were interviewed in Russian or Georgian by native speakers. There were remarkably few refusals to be interviewed, and the average interview lasted between two and three hours. In addition to the standard questionnaire administered to the entire group, over forty "in-depth" interviews were conducted with people who themselves had been officials of the Soviet government agencies we investigated, or who seemed to have unusual savoir-faire and knowledge of how things were done in their respective republics.

General Evaluations of
the Soviet Bureaucracy

Not surprisingly, the émigrés interviewed have a somewhat negative view of Soviet bureaucracy in general. Two-thirds do not think that most Soviet government offices "work as they should." They take a somewhat more charitable view of the workings of government offices in the countries to which they have immigrated.[17] Their most frequent complaints about bureaucracy in general focus on both structure and personnel; the main problems are said to be waste of time caused by the procedures, being shuffled back and forth among offices, and officials who do not want to understand them.[18] But it is not a strictly rational bureaucracy that they prefer. When asked whether they prefer the government official who treats everyone equally or the one who "treats each case individually, taking account of its special characteristics," over 60 percent preferred the latter in all circumstances, and the proportion among young people was even higher. It is the Europeans who are most in favor of individualized treatment, while only slightly more than a third of the Central Asians prefer this option. This is explained when we control for education, because we find that this preference is highly correlated with higher education. The more highly educated are apparently confident of their ability to deal with bureaucrats and to manipulate the system, so they prefer a more flexible one, whereas the less educated are insecure and want equal treatment guaranteed to all, probably correctly assuming that they are likely to be treated worse by a bureaucracy with room for maneuver than their more educated counterparts.

Nine sets of adjectives, each ranging from a positive to a negative quality and describing "the majority of government officials in the USSR," were presented to respondents who were asked to indicate where along a seven-point scale they would place these officials. On every set but one the modal response was in the middle; but on every set of adjectives more people, though not a majority in all cases, favored the negative end of the scale. The Israeli sample, which included all the Georgians and most of the Central Asians, rated the officials higher than the American sample did, and the German group rated them lowest of all, with most of their modal responses distinctly on the negative side of the scale. This is consistent with the finding that despite their relatively low level of education, which is correlated with more positive assessments among the other nationalities, 92 percent of the Germans do not think that most Soviet government offices run as they should.

In a further probe of generalized attitudes toward officaldom, eleven occupations were given to respondents to evaluate. These included physician, worker, teacher, scientist, military officer, "brigadier" in a factory, and four kinds of officials. Employees of the Communist Party ranked lowest of all the occupations, and officials of offices that assign housing were next lowest. Pension officials were seen more favorably, ranking ahead of military officers, for example, and those in charge of admissions to higher education were evaluated even more positively, outranking brigadiers and ordinary workers. When asked how the Soviet population as a whole might rank these occupations, the evaluations emerged in the same order. Older, less educated people and Central Asians evaluate the officials more positively, and again, it is the Germans who take the dimmest view by far of Soviet officials.[19] As we shall see, from among the agencies we have focused on (they do not include the party), those dealing with housing are seen most negatively, and this is reflected in the rankings of various occupations.

Thus, while the overall disposition of the ex-Soviet citizens toward Soviet local officials is generally negative, it is not undifferentiatedly so. People do distinguish among bureaucracies, and different groups of émigrés evaluate the bureaucracies differently. We shall explore this further by examining evaluations of particular bureaucracies and the methods Soviet citizens use to deal with them.

Remembrance of Bureaucratic Encounters Past

The émigrés were asked to recall their experiences with certain Soviet bureaucracies, about which they were questioned in some detail. Those bureaucracies include agencies dealing with housing and employment, basic necessities of life; agencies distributing pensions and admitting students to institutions of higher learning, matters affecting only certain segments of the population; and the militia (police), which is a "constraint" or "control," rather than a "service," agency.

Those agencies which provide housing, most frequently the *zhilotdel* (housing department) of the local soviet, are evaluated most negatively, and those providing pensions, in almost all cases the *gorsobes* or *raisobes* (local or district social security administrations), are evaluated most positively. Understandably, a poor evaluation of an agency goes hand in hand with resort to informal and even illegal methods of obtaining the services the agency is supposed to provide. Why does the housing sector get the worst marks and the pension agencies the best? In the absence of any evidence that employees in the housing fields are any less educated or trained than those in the pension area—in fact, what little information there is on them points in the opposite direction—or that the housing agencies are more poorly organized and structured than the pension agencies—again, the evidence is in the opposite direction—we assume that it is the chronic housing shortage that makes for fewer satisfactory outcomes in the encounters between citizens and housing officials. As Henry Morton points out in his excellent analysis of the politics of Soviet housing, despite the fact that since 1957 the USSR has been building 2.2 million housing units annually, in the mid-1970s the average per capita living space in urban areas was only 8 square meters (10 in Moscow). An estimated 30 percent of urban households still shared apartments, and it is not uncommon for people to wait as long as ten years to get an apartment.[20] Even getting on the list is a problem, as only those with less than a certain minimum living space (this varies from city to city) are eligible. Twenty percent of our respondents had been on a waiting list for an apartment. The majority (59 percent) lived in an apartment owned by the state, 19 percent in privately owned dwellings (mostly in Central Asia and Georgia), 16 percent in cooperatives, 3 percent in communal apartments, and a similar proportion in rented quarters. There are significant disparities in housing space across the republics, especially if measured on a per capita basis. In 1976, for example, housing space per capita was 15.1 square meters in Estonia but 9.0 in Uzbekistan, and in the RSFSR the larger cities have been benefiting more than the smaller ones from new construction.[21] This does not necessarily mean that housing conditions are better in, say, Estonia than in Uzbekistan. In the southern areas, particularly Central Asia, housing is a less critical problem, partially for climatic reasons. Moreover, Central Asian houses, often privately owned, are built around courtyards which increase the amount of space actually used by a household. And, as Michael Rywkin points out, per *family* space is much higher in Uzbekistan than in the RSFSR, though per *capita* space is lower, and "a six-person family does not need exactly double the space of a three-person one."[22] Among our own respondents we find that 86 percent of the Europeans had *less* than 60 meters of living space per household, whereas 64 percent of the Asians had *more* than 60 meters, and 36 percent had more than 100 meters. In Georgia, 74 percent had more than 60 meters! These differences are the likely explanation for the fact that the Asians and Georgians are more kindly disposed toward housing officials than the Europeans, rating them higher on efficiency, fairness of treatment, and the efforts they make on behalf of clients.

Whereas to obtain housing is probably the greatest struggle the citizen would normally wage against the state, getting a pension seems to be one of the most routine procedures. Soviet pensions are not very generous, though people can retire earlier than they do in many Western countries, and some privileged groups—military officers, members of the Academy of Sciences, high party officials—receive handsome pensions.[23] A Soviet author points out that the clientele of social security organs—the aged, sick, and disabled—are less able to defend themselves and frequently are more ignorant of their rights than younger and healthier citizens. This demands particular sensitivity, conscientiousness, tact, and knowledge of legal intricacies on the part of social security employees, and he implies that these qualities are often lacking.[24] Nevertheless, we find our respondents taking a much more benign view of the social security organs (70 percent of those who had dealings with these organs received old age pensions, 21 percent disability pensions, and the rest other types of pensions). It is possible that old age, lower education, and the realization of dependence induce docility and a willingness to settle for whatever the state will provide, whereas the struggle for housing is carried on by younger people who are still trying to ''make it'' in society. However, given the earlier retirement ages in the USSR, and the later age at which people obtain their own living quarters (often when they are in their late 30s or 40s), the difference in age between the two clienteles may not be very great. Moreover, the contrasts in evaluation of the two hierarchies are too great to be strictly a function of different groups' stage in life. Pensions are simply granted more routinely than housing, and less informal manipulation is required to obtain the pension.

The contrast in evaluations of housing and pension agencies becomes readily visible in the following tables which show overall evaluations of the agencies, followed by evaluations of specific attributes. From Table 3 we can also see that housing agencies rank the lowest of five on which we have data.

Table 3
Overall Evaluation of How Housing and Pension Agencies Handled Respondent's Case (in %)

	Housing (n = 196)	Pension (n = 231	Raspre-delenie* (n = 314)	Jobs** (n = 832)	Admissions committees in higher education (n = 597)
Very well	4.1	8.2	11.1	9.4	9.3
Well	30.1	74.0	61.5	78.4	75.0
Poorly	48.5	14.7	18.2	8.4	12.0
Very poorly	17.3	3.0	9.2	3.8	3.7

*Job assignment to graduates of higher educational institutions.
**Jobs which were obtained other than through *raspredelenie*.

Respondents were asked specific questions about their treatment by the agencies and what their impressions were about their operations and personnel. Had they been treated with respect? Did they think that the agency operated efficiently and fairly? Was everyone treated equally by the agency? In Table 4 the responses to these questions are combined and compared. (The percentage displayed is that of the affirmative answers given, and the figures in parentheses are the number of respondents.)

On nearly every dimension housing ranks lowest and the pension agency the highest, with a very wide gap between the two. Perhaps it is inevitable that when an agency cannot satisfy the demands of most clients, it will be thought of as inefficient, unfair, and biased in favor of some groups. Whether or not the harsh

Table 4
Characteristics of Three Agencies* as Seen by Respondents

	Housing	Raspredelenie	Pensions
Respectful	51%	80%	78%
	(309)	(299)	(241)
Efficient	17%	53%	75%
	(304)	(277)	(236)
Fair treatment given	10%	34%	NA
	(296)	(282)	NA
All are treated equally	9%	NA	74%
	(257)	NA	(171)

*Not all the same questions were asked in regard to the other agencies in Table 3.

judgment of the housing agencies is "objectively" justified is of little importance for our purposes because we are dealing with the perceptions and evaluations of the clientele. Unsatisfactory outcomes breed negative images of the operation of the agency; and it is likely that even if the operation and the personnel could be objectively assessed positively, as long as the outcome did not yield the hoped for results, clients would tend to blame the agency rather than the objective material constraints or high-level policy decisions (or the combination of both) that are responsible for the paucity of satisfactory outcomes.

In a probably unsuccessful attempt to force the interviewees to distinguish between the bureaucracy and its personnel, they were asked in an open-ended way to characterize those employed by the respective agencies. Only 5 percent spoke of the housing personnel in explicitly positive terms, another 10 percent admitted that there were "all kinds of people" in the housing offices, but 23 percent spoke of them in strongly pejorative terms. The majority (54 percent), however, used expressions such as "ordinary bureaucrats," the "usual Soviet employee," and other terms with mildly negative connotations. The pension officials were seen more positively, 38 percent using explicitly positive adjectives to describe them and only 11 percent explicitly negative ones. But one-third did use the mildly negative characterizations. Pressed to recall their own personal experience with these officials, over 60 percent insisted that housing officials had done either nothing at all for them or less than they were required to, whereas only 17 percent said so of pension officials (78 percent said the pension people had done just what they needed to for them). Not surprisingly, 86 percent thought the pension officials had been fair, but only 45 percent said so of housing officials. The great majority believe that *blat* (influence and favoritism), personal connections, and even bribery are the means by which the housing officials operate.

The characterization of the militia is different from that of the other employees, and a remarkable consensus was elicited by this open question. Asked what type of people joined the militia in the localities of their residence, nearly a third answered "peasants, people from the countryside" who were using militia work to gain urban residence permits, and 23 percent mentioned "uneducated, uncultured people." Another 20 percent described them as people with little education who sought to avoid factory work. But only a third said the militia had been unfair in their personal contacts with them, and the great majority assert that police would treat them like anyone else if they were, say, stopped for a traffic violation. Thus the attitude toward the militia seems to be one of condescension and even contempt, but not hatred or fear.

Contrary to the popular Western image of a rigid, monolithic system that tolerates no deviations from prescribed norms is the finding that in the personal experience of the émigrés, most officials were willing to "bend the rules" and not work "strictly according to regulations." Not only is this true of the militia as well, but they are seen as willing to bend the rules more than the other agencies. In fact, only the pension officials are described as working by the book, and this is undoubtedly because the transactions were so routine that there was no need to go outside prescribed procedures.

Finally, there is widespread agreement that ethnic biases enter into decision-making, especially in connection with entering higher educational institutions and being assigned to jobs after graduating from them. An even stronger consensus exists that Communist Party members are definitely favored in higher education and job assignments and, to a lesser extent, in the distribution of housing. Once again, the pension officials are an exception, as few of the respondents felt that pension officials favor party members or discriminate against members of certain nationalities. The police do discriminate, according to nearly 90 percent, but in favor of party members and others with important positions or "good connections" and against the poor, drunkards, and Jews. No doubt Americans are familiar with parallel images of the police in some American communities.

Some Correlates of Evaluations and Behavior

We cannot enter into a detailed analysis here on the ways in which particular groups relate to the various bureaucracies. But some generalizations can be made. First, less educated people are more inclined to resort to bribery, and more educated ones will "pull strings" and use personal connections to extract what they want from a bureaucracy or in regard to the militia. Better educated people are more likely to know people in positions of authority, to know how to get to them, and to be confident of their abilities in confrontations with the authorities. The less educated are more inclined to the more direct and less complicated tactic of bribery, and this has probably been the pattern in Russia and elsewhere for centuries. Second, younger people are generally less persuaded of the fairness of the institutions, are less respectful of them, and see more ethnic discrimination against Jews, especially in regard to admissions to higher education (in fact, admissions of Jews have declined more than 40 percent over the last decade) and *raspredelenie* (job assignments to graduates of higher educational institutions) decisions. The exception is in regard to pensions, where the younger pensioners have a more positive view of the pension-dispensing bureaucracies, perhaps because pensions have improved considerably in recent decades.

Third, party members agree with nonparty people that they are in a privileged position, and that especially in regard to employment and admission to higher education, they will get preference. Interestingly, however, party members deny that they are favored in housing decisions, though nonparty people are convinced of it.

Fourth, while there are no significant differences in the attitudes and reported behavior of men and women, except that women take a more positive view of the militia (perhaps because they are less often its targets and see themselves as protected by the police), there are significant differences among the nationalities. Germans, for example, are the most alienated from the militia, perhaps because of their tragic experiences in the 1940s and 1950s and continued popular discrimination against them.[25] Germans see the militia as arbitrary, and they see little sense in appealing a policeman's action. If stopped for a traffic violation, to a greater extent than Jews or Russians they will simply pay the fine or try to bribe, but they will not argue or appeal. Every German respondent with elementary education feels the militia do not treat people equally, though the more highly educated are more differentiated in their views. Among Jews, on the other hand, the relationship between education and feelings about the militia is reversed: it is the highly educated Jews who perceive the militia as treating people unequally, while the less educated are more mixed in their views.

The difference between European and Georgian-Central Asian perceptions can be seen in Tables 5 and 6.

Of course, for the less educated Asians-Georgians, especially Asians, ser-

Table 5
Respondents' Willingness to Have Their Children
Be Militia Men (in %)
(n = 1,053)

	Europeans	Asians-Georgians
Unwilling	93.4	77.3
Willing	6.6	22.7

Gamma = .61

vice in the militia is a channel for upward mobility, as it has been for immigrant and underprivileged groups in other countries. But the differences we observe may also reflect different affects toward the militia. The question of social status enters into Table 6 as well. Here respondents indicate whether they feel employment decisions are influenced by ethnic considerations. The lower Asian-Georgian perception of ethnic prejudices entering the process may result from their experience with lower-level occupations where, all reports suggest, ethnicity is far less important than in the employment of people with higher education who are seeking a professional position. In fact, the higher the education of the respondent, the more likely he or she is to perceive ethnic discrimination in employment (gamma = .49).

Table 6
Ethnic Discrimination in Employment Decisions, in %
(n = 731)

	Europeans	Asians-Georgians
There is discrimination	57.6	36.1
There is no discrimination	42.4	63.9

Gamma = .41

The alternative explanation is that there is simply less discrimination in employment decisions in Georgia and Central Asia than in the European republics. Georgians and Central Asians, as well as Moldavians, do feel that the titular nationalities of their respective republics are given preferential treatment in admission to higher education, and this matches other sources which suggest that in an effort to raise the educational levels of Asian and the largely rural Moldavians, Soviet authorities do favor these nationalities in admissions decisions. Moreover, local officials in these republics, especially in Georgia where educational levels are already quite high, are given freer rein than elsewhere to follow their natural inclination to favor people of their own nationality.

A last observation is that those who themselves worked as employees (*sluzhashchie*) in the USSR are more inclined than any other occupational group to see the operations of the bureaucracies as quite fair and relatively efficient. They are also inclined to play by the formal rules of the game and to choose prescribed behavior in bureaucratic encounters. It is this group which has the highest proportion (two-thirds) of people with secondary and secondary-specialized education. They appear to be loyal to their class and to the system which employed them, though it may be that they are simply more conversant with the proper rules of the game and therefore more inclined to respond in those terms. But the latter would not explain their more positive evaluations of Soviet officials, so their reported responses are probably a true indicator of their behavior in the Soviet context.

Clearly, not only do the émigrés differentiate among Soviet bureaucracies, but there are meaningful differences among groups of émigrés in their approaches to Soviet bureaucracies. The greatest differences seem to be among age groups, nationalities, educational groups, and the different republics. As regards the latter, the differences between Asia-Georgia and Europe are greater than those within the European USSR. Education and occupation are very highly correlated in our sample (.75), as are occupation and income (.54). The correlation between education and income is lower (.27), but high enough so that analysis by occupation and income turns up results very similar to analysis by education. There are very few differences between men and women in their approaches to the bureaucracies.

Battling the Bureaucracies

Varied evaluations of agencies are matched by different tactics employed toward them. As we have seen in the use of connections by the better educated and bribery by the less educated, different groups are inclined to different tactics. At one end of the spectrum are the housing agencies, where nearly two-thirds of the respondents report that they tried to advance their position on the waiting list either through appealing to a higher Soviet organ or, less frequently, using illegal tactics. The intervention of one's supervisor at work is often sought. Of those who went through the appeal process (n = 129), just over half report that the appeal was successful and they obtained the apartment. Those who do not appeal successfully will use other tactics and enter what Morton calls the "subsidiary housing market" (private rentals, cooperatives, exchanges of apartments and private houses).[26] Exchanging apartments is the remedy most often prescribed by our respondents for those who have been unsuccessful in getting one from the official lists, but bribery is the second best. When a respondent reports that he was 247th on the housing list and that in fifteen years he had advanced only twenty places, one can understand the resort to other means. The list is quite "flexible," as Soviet sources explain. "Too often the decisive factor is not the waiting list," *Pravda* commented, "but a sudden telephone call . . . [after which] they give the flats to the families of football players and the whole queue is pushed back."[27] Even to purchase a cooperative apartment involves waiting lists. A young Muscovite woman reports that the *raiispolkom* turned down her request to purchase a coop though they were living four in a one-room communal apartment and the factory building the coop had already agreed to sell to them. "When I had exhausted all our legal arguments . . . I raised an extraneous one, complaining that it was very awkward to entertain foreigners in such crowded conditions and we were embarrassed. The *raiispolkom* responded that we had no business entertaining foreigners anyway—why did we invite them to our homes? I explained that we didn't invite them but that they showed up at our place and that it would be rude to turn them away. It is my impression that the foreigner argument was crucial in eventually obtaining permission to purchase the coop." Another woman from Moscow, who had been living with her husband and baby boy in seven square meters, was even trickier. Her husband's factory had built a cooperative building, but several months went by and the apartments had not been assigned. She called the factory from a public phone, identified herself as a reporter from *Izvestia* who had received many complaints from workers about the failure to assign apartments, and requested an interview so that she could write an investigative article. She was assured by a nervous official that the apartments were being assigned, and indeed, within the week she and many others got their assignments.

Another illustration is the case of S. K., a secretary from Kishinev. From 1946 to 1951 she lived with nine people in one room, then in a 2 × 2 meter room with her husband, and finally in a seven-square-meter apartment when her son was born. She changed jobs only because her new boss promised her better living conditions. Later, by going to the minister of transportation of the Moldavian Republic, she was able to wind up with a three-room apartment for her four-person family.

Finally, we have the case of a "Bukharan" Jewish woman (of the Sephardic, Persian tradition) from Tashkent who grew up in an eight-room private house with her own room. After marriage she applied for a coop because all her mother's children and grandchildren were registered as living in the big house, making it look like crowded conditions. The Uzbek clerk could not read Russian well and asked her to fill out the application for the coop and then asked her to have it typed. "When I brought the typed version I put a bottle of vodka on the desk. He didn't take money, only vodka. Uzbeks don't take money. They are very humane people. He took vodka because, as an Uzbek, he is not allowed to drink. He can't go to a store to buy vodka because the clerks are Uzbeks and it would be embarrassing. So they get vodka from us, the 'foreigners.' "

By contrast, no unusual measures seem necessary in regard to pensions, and appeals within the system are the most frequent tactic. Though these can sometimes be drawn out, the émigrés are sanguine about their efficacy, and 86 percent are sure that if necessary, one can initiate an appeals process within the *sobes* structure.

Getting into higher education is another matter, especially for Jews in the periods 1945–58 and from 1971 to the present. Though respondents indicate that *blat* rather than bribery is used to gain entrance to higher education, a former member of an admissions committee recalls the widespread use of bribery. Another person who held a similar post in a polytechnic in Leningrad reports that in his institute the bribes ran about 500 rubles, but into the thousands for the pediatric faculty and the First Medical Institute in Leningrad. But other forms of chicanery are more prevalent. A Georgian Jew tells how he paid 100 rubles in Kulashi to have his nationality changed from Jew to Georgian so that he would be admitted to the pediatric institute in Leningrad. (This trick having worked, he returned as a pediatrician to Kulashi. But when he went to change his nationality back to Jew—"everyone knew me there and it was silly to be registered as a

Georgian''—''the boys'' demanded 200 rubles, for, they explained, since the Jews were getting out of the country, it was now worth more to be a Jew!) Our Leningrad informant, who was himself helped in getting into the school of his choice because he was a basketball player, tells us that athletes and residents of Leningrad were favored for admission, as were children of faculty. But certain departments were known to be closed to certain people, and others were heavily populated by certain groups. For example, two informants note that the Oriental faculty in Leningrad State University is full of the children of Central Asian Party big shots, and ''everyone knows you can't get in there because it is a school for spies and 'reliable cadres.' '' Leningrad State and Moscow State Universities, the two most prestegious universities in the country, are now practically closed to Jews, as are shipbuilding and aviation institutes. Admissions committee members in Leningrad got written instructions not to admit anyone to the journalism faculty without recommendations from the party *raikom* (district committee). Even certain specialties in the philological faculty were explicitly closed to Jews. In such cases bribery, connections, and other tactics will not work, except in very rare cases, and people learn quickly to give up on these institutions.

For those departments and schools that are realistic possibilities, the way in is not always a direct one. A very common practice is to hire a tutor for the applicant, not so much to prepare him or her as to prepare the way with the admissions committee. Often the tutor is a member of the faculty, and he will see to it that his student gets in, sometimes by turning over some of his fees to his colleagues (reported in Moscow, Kharkov, Leningrad). One operator told parents: ''I'll get your child into the institute for 1,000 rubles. Give me 300 now and the rest only if he gets in.'' The advance would be used to bribe clerks to put the child's name on the list of those admitted, bypassing the admissions committee, and then the rest was pocketed by the ''fixer.'' One admissions committee member admitted frankly that he gave higher admission grades to students who had been tutored by his friends. A Jew himself, he admitted to favoring Jews on the examinations and giving Ukrainians, whom he doesn't like ''because they are all anti-Semites,'' an especially rough time. ''Of course, when a pretty, pleasant girl showed up, I would try a little harder to get her into the institute.''[28]

If citizens and members of admissions committees monkey with the system, so, of course, does the party. A woman who taught in several pedagogical institutes reports that at the final meeting of the admissions committee, a representative of the party district committee and another of the ''public'' (usually someone working with the party) would come and express their opinions freely. They would insure that certain ethnic distributions were achieved and that certain individuals were admitted or turned down. In Kharkov, it is claimed, there are three lists of applicants: those who must be admitted, those who must not, and the rest. In the Kharkovite's experience, the party did not directly participate in the admissions process but did so indirectly by approving members of admissions committees, making up the above-mentioned lists, and providing written guidelines for admission policies.

If one gets into the institute or university and then graduates, a *rasprede-*

lenie commission will normally assign the graduate his or her first job. Very often this is an undesirable position in an even less desirable location. For example, it is common practice to assign teachers or physicians, many of whom are single women, to rural areas in Siberia and Central Asia. To avoid such assignments, some will simply take a job outside their field, others arrange fictitious marriages with spouses who have residence permits in desirable locations, and many will simply appeal the decision and try to get a "free diploma," that is, a diploma without a specific job assignment, which leaves them to their own devices. Several informants report being assigned to jobs in Central Asia, only to find upon arrival that there was no need for them, that the local institutions had not requested them, and the local authorities were not overly eager to have nonnatives take jobs there.[29] Despite the inconvenience, such contretemps were welcomed because they freed the person from the assignment. Of course, there is always the tendency to use *blat*, to try and pull strings with the job assignment commission, and this is reported to work fairly well. The other use of *blat* is to get some "big boss" to specifically request the graduate as an employee of his institution. As I have been told in the USSR on several occasions, "in a socialist country you must have connections."

Getting nonprofessional jobs is less complicated. The most frequent way of finding a job is through a friend or relative; and as in the United States, we have instances of three generations employed in the same factory. However, payoffs are sometimes involved. A former teacher from the Transcarpathian Ukraine, who later worked in construction, found a teaching job in a small Ukrainian city; but the principal made it clear that a "tax" would have to be paid, and not for him alone. (The "tax" was paid but returned within days because the "higher-ups" would not accept it as they did not want the teacher employed under any circumstances.) For a construction job that paid 190 rubles a month, the man had to pay 260 in advance, and this was shared by the director, chief engineer, supplies chief, and other bosses in the enterprise. Later the cashier automatically deducted a small sum from his monthly pay, and everyone understood that it was going to "the enterprise." This particular enterprise also had "dead souls" on the payroll whose salaries went to people very much alive. When our informant moved to Siberia, he found that practices were quite different. Money bribes were not given in labor-hungry Siberia, but appreciation was expressed, at most, with a bottle of vodka.

Ethnicity does enter into employment. A former polytechnic instructor in Kharkov reports that in the personnel department, he once saw each employee's nationality listed after the surname, with the nationalities color-coded for faster recognition: red for Russians, green for Ukrainians, blue for Jews. In Transcarpathia the Ukrainians tried not to hire Russians or other non-Ukrainians, it is claimed; but most ideologically sensitive posts were held by Russians, many of whom came to the area in the late 1940s, when Soviet rule was established. In Siberian cities the European workers stuck together, and there was no social contact with native peoples (reported for Omsk, Kemerovo, Krasnoiarsk). It seems that in many regions people will try to hire others of their own ethnic group. A man from Kokand (Uzbekistan) relates that the dental polyclinics there were heavily staffed by Armenians and Jews, so the pressure was on to hire Uzbeks. Only by pulling strings did this Jew get hired, and then only for a half-time job. But he did not mind very much because under the accounting system he was paid for full time. Moreover, he could make substantial sums in private practice. As he puts it, "Over there when you find a job you don't ask 'what will my salary be' but 'how much will I have on the side?' " In fact, the likelihood of substantial illegal income made him avoid party membership, for which he was recommended when in the army. A party member would have to be on his good behavior, and so he claimed that his grandfather was fanatically religious and would not allow him to join the party. Significantly, this excuse was immediately accepted in Central Asia, where the patriarchal family and religious traditions are more familiar than in the European areas.

Party membership enters the picture in another, more important way. A former employee of the "first (cadres) department" of several enterprises confirms that party members are favored for employment. Party members were considered "more reliable, unable to harm Soviet power, more suitable." The first department of an enterprise works closely with the secret police and is staffed largely by party members.

Finally, we have some observations on the militia, including some by a former militia man. As we have seen, the police are seen as people one can deal with. Nearly 90 percent feel it would be possible to bribe a traffic policeman who stopped them for a violation. The police in Uzbekistan, said one young woman, "are very nice people. If you break the law, they take only five rubles and you can go on. I know because my father was a taxi driver. As long as he had five rubles there were no problems. . . . I know from my own experience that they are humane. Even when you go against the law. . . . They let me cross a closed street on May Day." The former militia man deals with more serious matters. A Russian of working-class origins, he served in the Ministry of Internal Affairs in lieu of military service. He became a highway patrolman, rising to sergeant and later junior lieutenant. He tells how in cases of accident it was important to find out who was involved because if one person was KGB, military, or party, he could not be blamed. Reports were rigged to insure this. He admits that for him "There was a big difference among drivers. There were actually two kinds—those who could be useful in the future and those who could not. For the first group many changes could be made to help them. . . . Witnesses could always be found to sign what you wanted them to." He gives a further example of corruption: "Once I found out about a man who was using his car to drive parents to their children's summer camps. I knew he had done it four times, calculated that he must have made 400 rubles, so I stopped him on the road and suggested that he give me half. I and all of the rest of my friends were doing this kind of thing, but they were worse. I was practically the most honest inspector in our area." To compensate the boss who did not go out on the road himself, and was therefore deprived of extra income, each highway patrolman contributed 20 rubles a month to the unfortunate *nachal'nik* (boss).

A Concluding Word

These have been some preliminary findings from a project on bureaucratic encounters in the USSR, and this is not the place for grand generalizations about the system in which they took place. But it should be obvious already that on the output side the Soviet system is not as rigid nor as monolithic as it is sometimes assumed. Its resources are limited, its procedures often clumsy, and its personnel not necessarily more qualified than their counterparts in other countries; but it is a permeable, even flexible system. Obviously, some of its bureaucracies are more flexible than others. In those sectors where the bureaucracy cannot be responsive to the demands of its clients, the latter prove to be inventive, imaginative, and hard fighters for what they need from the system. Scarcity promotes corruption; but even where the question of scarcity does not arise, as with the militia, Soviet people seem to have evolved understandings and practices that make life more livable for clients and authorities alike. The former get more or less what they want, and the latter make an extra ruble and perhaps have the satisfaction of doing a kindness to a fellow human being.

There seems to be a ''second polity'' that parallels the ''second economy.'' Just as the latter makes the economy work in ways not described by the textbooks—whether or not this is a ''good thing'' is a matter of contention—so too do the informal practices of bureaucrats and citizens operate the political-administrative system.

The nature of the bureaucratic encounter varies both by the bureaucracy as well as by the clientele. This means that the most common interactions between the citizen and the state do not follow a uniform pattern. It is likely, therefore, that we might be able to speak of differentiated *sub*systems within the USSR, that different groups of people relate to the state in significantly different ways, and that bureaucracies opeate differently in the many and varied regions of the country. If that is the case, a logical question is whether there is systematic differentiation in the overall relationship of different groups of people to the system. If different groups have had divergent experiences in their contacts with the state, are their feelings toward it similarly varied? More basically, is there a cumulative process at work whereby the outcomes of bureaucratic encounters shape one's overall relationship to the Soviet system? Or do people separate their diffuse support, or lack of it, from their support or nonsupport of specific workings of the system? This issue is an item on the agenda of further explorations.

Notes

[1]Theodore H. Friedgut, ''Citizens and Soviets: Can Ivan Ivanovich Fight City Hall?'' *Comparative Politics, 10*, 4 (July 1978), 462. See also the pioneering article by James H. Oliver, ''Citizen Demands and the Soviet Political System,'' *American Political Science Review, 63*, 2 (June 1969).

[2]See, for example, V. M. Manokhin (ed.), *Sovetskoe administrativnoe pravo* (Mos-

cow, 1977), 121-22; Manokhin, *Sovetskaia gosudarstvennaia sluzhba* (Moscow, 1966), 83; A. M. Lunev, *Administrativnoe pravo* (Moscow, 1966), 136.

[3]G. I. Petrov, *Sovetskoe administrativnoe pravo: Chast' obshchaia* (Leningrad, 1960), 199-200.

[4]V. G. Afanasev, *Nauchnoe upravlenie obshchestvom* (Moscow, 1971), 121.

[5]The literature on these subjects is considerable and familiar to students of Soviet politics. Much of it is cited in Karl W. Ryavec, "The Soviet Ministerial Elite: 1964-1979, A Representative Sample," Program in Soviet Series, 6 (1981). Among the most important works are Jerry Hough, *The Soviet Prefects* (Cambridge, Mass., 1969); H. Gordon Skilling and Franklyn Griffiths, *Interest Groups in Soviet Politics* (Princeton, 1971); John Armstrong, *The Soviet Bureaucratic Elite* (New York, 1959) and his "Sources of Administrative Behavior: Some Soviet and West European Comparisons," *American Political Science Review*, 59, 3 (September 1965); Zbigniew K. Brzezinski, "The Soviet Political System: Transformation or Degeneration," *Problems of Communism*, 15, 1 (January-February 1966).

[6]Andras Hegedüs, *Socialism and Bureaucracy* (New York, 1976), 25.

[7]Isaac Deutscher, *Stalin: A Political Biography* (New York, 1960), 364. On the historical development of the bureaucracy, see Walter M. Pintner and Don Karl Rowney, *Russian Officialdom* (Chapel Hill, 1980).

[8]Carol H. Weiss, "Efforts at Bureaucratic Reform," in Weiss and Allen H. Barton (eds.), *Making Bureaucracies Work* (Beverly Hills, Calif., 1979), 7-8.

[9]Daniel Katz, Barbara Gutek, Robert Kahn, and Eugenia Barton, *Bureaucratic Encounters* (Ann Arbor, 1975), 114-15, 120.

[10]On the United States, see, for example, Joel Aberbach and Bert Rockman, "Administrators' Beliefs About the Role of the Public: The Case of American Federal Executives," *Western Political Quarterly*, 31, 4 (December 1978).

[11]R. A. Safarov, *Obshchestvennoe mnenie i gosudarstvennoe upravlenie* (Moscow, 1975).

[12]Iu. A.Tikhomirov (ed.), *Sluzhashchii sovetskogo gosudarstvennogo apparata* (Moscow, 1970), 64, 75.

[13]E. G. Azarova, "O zashchite pensionnykh prav grazhdan," *Sovetskoe gosudarstvo i pravo*, 2 (February 1979), 48-49. See also the detailed study of citizens' complaints and petitions to the state apparatus, V. V. Mal'kov, *Sovetskoe zakonodatel'stvo o zhalobakh i zaiavleniiakh* (Moscow, 1967).

[14]Alex Inkeles and Raymond Bauer, *The Soviet Citizen* (New York, 1968).

[15]Ibid., 27.

[16]Of those from the Baltic, 99 lived in Latvia, 49 in Lithuania, and 26 in Estonia. The Central Asians include 87 from Uzbekistan, 39 from Kazakhstan, 25 from Kirghizia and Turkmenistan, and 14 from Tadzhikstan.

[17]Of those in Israel, 60 percent think the government offices do not work as they should; of those in the Federal Republic of Germany, 38 percent; and of those in the United States, 25 percent (though 47 percent of the Americans expressed no opinion). In all cases the more educated the immigrant, the more critical he is of the immigrant country's government offices. This is also true regarding the Soviet bureaucracy, except that those who were themselves its employees are more sympathetic to it than the (less educated) manual workers.

[18]Understandably, the less educated are most bothered by the necessity of filling out forms, while the most educated are most disturbed by the waste of time and failure of officials to understand them.

[19]Thus 67 percent of the Germans rate housing officials negatively, compared to 43 percent of the Jews; 87 percent of the Germans are negative on party officials, compared to 45 percent of the Jews. Even pension officials are rated negatively by 61 percent of the Germans, but by only 34 percent of the Jews.

[20]Henry W. Morton, "Who Gets What, When and How? Housing in the Soviet Union," *Soviet Studies*, *32*, 2 (April 1980), 235-36.

[21]See Carol R. Nechemias, "Welfare in the USSR: Health Care, Housing and Personal Consumption," unpublished paper, 30-31.

[22]Michael Rywkin, "Housing in Central Asia: Demography, Ownership, Tradition. The Uzbek Example," Kennan Institute for Advanced Russian Studies, Occasional Paper Number 82 (December 1979), 5.

[23]See Bernice Madison, *Social Welfare in the Soviet Union* (Stanford, 1968); Klaus Von Beyme, "Soviet Social Policy in Comparative Perspective," *International Political Science Review*, 2, 1 (1981), 90; Mervyn Matthews, *Privilege in the Soviet Union* (London, 1978).

[24]V. I. Maksimovskii, *Upravlenie sotsial'nym obespecheniem* (Moscow, 1974), 35.

[25]See Sidney Heitman, *The Soviet Germans in the USSR Today* (Cologne, 1980), and Rasma Karklins, *Interviews mit deutschen Spätaussiedlern aus der Sowjetunion*, Berichte des Bundesinstituts für ostwissenschaftliche und internationale Studien, 42 (1978).

[26]See Morton, 242 ff., for colorful descriptions of how these operate.

[27]*Pravda* (February 16, 1973), quoted in Morton, 250.

[28]Corruption is involved in admissions even to military schools. *Krasnaia zvezda* reports a case in which a general got his relatives admitted despite their poor grades and admits this is not an isolated case. "When applications to the military school are being considered, the admissions committee is besieged with phone calls. . . . There are really two competitions for admission: the regular competition and the competition of relatives." V. Filatov, "Plemianniki: K chemu privodit protektsiia pri priëme v voennoe uchilishche," *Krasnaia zvezda* (November 12, 1980).

[29]An article in *Izvestia* discusses the problem of institute graduates assigned to jobs failing to show up for them or signing up and then "deserting." In 1979 only 187 of 323 graduates of three agricultural higher schools showed up at their assigned places of work. It is also admitted that "not all farm managers create proper conditions under which young specialists can work." Housing is not provided, the jobs are ill suited to the graduates, and so on. See S. Troyan, "They Never Arrived for Their Assigned Jobs," *Izvestia*, June 11, 1980, translated in *Current Digest of the Soviet Press*, *32*, 23 (July 9, 1980), 16.

Conclusion

Urbanization is a major component of economic development and modernization. The contributors to this volume have attempted to analyze the Soviet urban experience in both an historical and contemporary perspective and to provide, where applicable, appropriate comparisons with other countries, as well as to ask what we have learned from the Soviet urbanization process.

Before we summarize our findings, we would like to analyze the Soviet urban experience in terms of *systemic features*, *historical trends*, and *comparative analysis* to help us understand the various forces underlying Soviet urbanization and to isolate those factors peculiar to the Soviet case (as opposed to others generally associated with urban development).

Our analytic framework requires some elaboration. Although there is considerable debate over the exact definition of features described as systemic, we focus on five basic *system* components.

First, *property rights* or *ownership* arrangements strongly influence the uses to which resources are put in a particular system. As we have seen, in the Soviet case the means of production are primarily owned by the state, while in the West we are most accustomed to private ownership or a combination of private and state ownership.

Second, the *coordination mechanism* greatly affects the manner in which decisions about the use of resources are made and implemented. In the Soviet case the national economic *plan* and its various components dominate; in the West the market is generally dominant, although it is affected by varying forms and degrees of state intervention.

Third, the *locus of decision-making*, while difficult to characterize precisely, is nevertheless influential. The Soviet system can be described as highly centralized, meaning that important decisions are made at the top levels in the hierarchy. Conversely, market systems are generally identified as being relatively decentralized since many decisions are made by firms and individuals at the local level working through the market mechanism.

Fourth, any system needs to provide *incentives* in order for participants to work effectively. Incentives have been characterized as *moral* and/or *material* by nature. Although the Soviet system probably places more emphasis on moral suasion than is the case in Western countries, many would argue that material incentives are dominant in both East and West.

Fifth, *policy* is a crucial element in understanding the directions in which any system develops through time. In part, the Soviet urbanization experience can be directly related to specific Soviet urbanization policies.

244

Turning to our second analytic category, we attempt to place Soviet urbanization in a *historical* context to explain both prerevolutionary development and, particularly, Stalin's impact on the nature and shape of Soviet urban growth. His policy, which greatly favored the rapid buildup of heavy industry and the military at the expense of the consumer, is still felt to this day.

Finally, the Soviet urban experience needs to be placed in *comparative* perspective to help us see contrasts and similarities to our own. The reader should be aware that when we make comparisons, such factors as physical size, historical, ethnic, and cultural differences (including our own ethnocentric values), level of economic development (e.g., comparing gross national products), natural conditions, resource endowment, and many others are important in understanding and explaining observed differences in Soviet and Western urbanization patterns.

The Soviet pattern of urbanization, we have found in this book, does differ *systemically* from ours. Let us examine some areas of difference.

Under Soviet conditions of socialism the state owns and manages the means of production. There are over sixty ministries in charge of producing steel, coal, electricity, agricultural products, machinery, commercial fishing, construction, and so forth. (Imagine similar departments existing in Washington, D.C., directly managing the American economy!) The State Planning Committee, and not the market, coordinates economic activity. Yearly and five-yearly production targets are set in terms of tons of steel or the number of housing units to be produced. In reality, however, the planning task is so large and complex that planners cannot oversee all economic activity, nor can they guarantee that their directives will be enforced. Other, less controlled (and therefore less visible) forces thus enter the management vacuum.

Soviet cities are also guided in their day-to-day operation and in their short- and long-term projections by planned targets that need approval by republic and all-union authorities. However, implementation of comprehensive urban planning is not possible because city governments are still greatly dependent on factories located in cities (but belonging to central, national ministries) for the financing and, in numerous instances, also the construction of housing, schools, shopping facilities, utilities, and other urban services owned by the factories and not by the municipalities. Thus, although urban planning is supposedly centralized, in effect it is often haphazard and decentralized because city fathers—local communist party and government leaders—do not control all the purse strings. Therefore comprehensive urban planning remains a goal and not a reality.

As in the West, the demand for services in Soviet cities is much greater than the cities' capacity to deliver them. This is aggravated not only by a lack of funding and poor execution of plans but also by a *policy* of providing services without direct, or at best partial, payment by the user. Thus the urban consumer is led to believe that housing rent, water, gas, heat, electricity, and the telephone are very cheap, and this encourages him to increase his consumption of them. In fact, however, these services are very costly to the state and the city, which consequently must repeatedly bargain with higher authorities to obtain additional funding for them.

Historically, as industry developed in the latter half of the nineteenth century under the tsars, cities and towns did grow; but they did so slowly, since most of the population was still engaged in agriculture and remained on the land. In 1913 only 13.2 percent of the people lived in urban areas, and they were concentrated primarily in a few industrial centers and ports.

Soviet Russia inherited poorly developed cities and towns. Before 1917 most of the housing in urban and rural areas consisted of small wooden family homes almost completely lacking in utilities. Under Soviet rule conditions worsened. During the 1918–21 Civil War, which followed the Revolution, cities fell into ruinous neglect. After the war municipalities lacked the means to make adequate repairs; and even when they tried, supplies were often not available.

The Stalinist policy of rapid industrialization combined with forced collectivization of private farms, begun in 1929, brought millions of peasants from the countryside to new industrial sites. Small towns rapidly became large cities as the urban population more than doubled between 1929 and 1939.

But because Stalin purposely underinvested in urban services in favor of developing heavy industry, the quality of city life again declined precipitously. Housing conditions that were already overcrowded in the 1920s, with the majority of families living in communal apartments, worsened in the 1930s as many new arrivals were forced to live in primitive dormitories and barracks.

Only after Stalin died in 1953 did his successors embark on an ambitious program to improve the quality of urban life—which in the 1980s still falls short of providing the amenities promised. For instance, the Communist Party Program of 1962 pledged that within eighteen years every Soviet family would live in separate quarters; but by 1980, 20 percent of the urban population still lived in shared apartments (a vast improvement, of course, over preceding decades). Progress, despite chronic shortages, is also noticeable in other sectors of the urban economy; but a continuing problem for Soviet leaders is that consumer expectations continue to greatly exceed the system's capacity to produce goods and services that are in demand. This has led to the growth of a thriving black market where private entrepreneurs sell these goods and services illegally to an eager public.

Soviet and Western urban development invite *comparison*. But one fallacious Western tendency is to judge the contemporary Soviet city by current Western standards. (Soviet leaders share responsibility in this by insisting on an across-the-board comparison with the West, particularly with the United States.) Such comparisons fail to properly position the USSR in a comparative context, and therefore they draw overly negative conclusions. Were the USSR viewed as a developing nation, then its industrial and urban achievements would be seen more accurately and would receive higher praise. We can see, for instance, that during the early period of Western industrialization, towns and cities expanded rapidly, mostly without planning, and working and living conditions in them were abominable. Workers lived in unsanitary, crowded tenements, often in company towns where factory owners dominated their lives. Similar conditions of early industrialization and urbanization prevailed under tsarism in the late nineteenth and early twentieth centuries and under Stalin.

Another, frequently difficult task of comparative analysis is to find equivalencies. For example, although the Soviet Union and the United States are roughly comparable in size and population, they are not so in climatic conditions or in economic development—the USSR's GNP (Gross National Product) is approximately half of ours. In this respect Italy could perhaps provide a better comparison because its GNP is at a similar level as the Soviet Union's, although it is smaller in size and population. Therefore we can see that although comparisons can be intellectually challenging, can provide valuable insights, and are often inevitable, they need to be judiciously applied.

We now turn to comparisons based on a summary of the observation made in this book about the Soviet city. Soviet objectives in town planning, as in most countries, are to minimize cost, establish viable neighborhoods with schools, shopping facilities, and medical and other vital services, maximize the production efficiency of workers, shorten their commute to work, and protect the environment. Where they differ is in the use of standardized planning of urban centers that produces compact, high-density cities without suburbs but with layouts of similar design and similar looking multidwelling apartment buildings of 5, 9, 12, 16, or 22 stories made from precast concrete. In cities with a population of over 100,000 (of which there were 272 in 1980), the building of single-family homes is prohibited. Consequently, practically all Soviet residential areas look alike. The contemporary Soviet city is thus functional, but it lacks individuality and personality.

In contrast to the West, Soviet cities suffer from labor shortages because rural-to-urban migration has declined significantly along with the urban birth rate. Although since the introduction of rapid industrialization in 1929 the Soviet urban sector has grown rapidly, and thus brought profound changes to Soviet society, much of that urban growth resulted from population moving from rural to urban areas and, within the urban sector, from smaller cities to larger ones. In recent years, however, population growth in cities has been more the result of births over deaths and less of migration. Nevertheless there would still probably be a sufficient supply of labor, and perhaps even a surplus, if more work operation were mechanized, if plant managers did not have to hoard workers to storm the plan at the end of the month or send them to farms to collect the harvest, and most significantly, if workers were offered higher wages and promotional opportunities as incentives to work more productively. Increased productivity, however, might lead to a lower demand for labor and hence unemployment, which the regime and the populace would not accept.

The Soviet government has instead a policy of full employment that is based on low wages, the prohibition of strikes, and no firings (until Andropov's August 1983 decree that workers can be dismissed for drunkenness and persistent shirking. However, with more than two million jobs in Soviet industry unfilled, workers have little difficulty in finding new positions). A relatively free labor market does exist in the USSR, and workers can and do move from city to city, except to those that are restricted, like Moscow and other large urban centers.

Soviet authorities have given urban education priority over rural schooling. Soviet schools are charged with instilling communist morality, patriotism, and loyalty to the Soviet regime and with providing a curriculum that heavily emphasizes mathematics and the sciences. Career aspirations are largely determined by social status and income. Children of middle-class parents are more likely to get higher academic grades and to aspire to a university education than do the offspring of blue-collar workers, who are inclined to enroll in trade and technical schools. Admission to prestigious universities is highly competitive, produces emotional stress, and can be costly. A high school graduate can normally only apply to a single institution of higher education because entrance examinations are given once a year, usually in August. The *fakultet* (department of school) to which a candidate applies, if it is prestigious, may have one place for thirty or more applicants. Although tuition for higher education is free, private tutoring costs to prepare a student in several subjects for the entrance examination may amount to several thousand rubles. In addition, a bribe to the admission committee may also be necessary to assure acceptance.

The various forms of public transportation—bus, trolley, trolley car, and subway—though chronically overcrowded, are fuel and cost efficient because of the compact size of cities. Their operation is crucial since relatively few people (compared to the West) own cars. However, the number of cars has been increasing, to 8.5 million in the early 1980s, and with them have come problems in parking and servicing (there are relatively few mechanics available, and spare parts are hard to get) and a steep increase in deaths attributed to traffic accidents. The death toll from accidents was reported to be about 50,000—higher than in the United States.

Soviet medical care is comprehensive and free—except for gratuities that doctors and nurses expect for services rendered. The quality of care often depends on one's social status or contacts, which determines admittance to superior or ordinary medical institutions. Western medical care has been criticized for overemphasizing and overspending on technologically advanced diagnostic tools while neglecting the personal and psychological needs of patients. Soviet investment in medical care is much lower than ours and is labor intensive. The USSR has more doctors than any other country, but it lags behind the West in diagnostic equipment and the development of new drugs, and it suffers from chronic shortages of ordinary medicines.

Because the USSR does not publish national crime statistics, it is not possible to compare accurately the Soviet crime rate with that of other countries. But people are generally not afraid to walk in cities at night, even though streets and courtyards are often dimly lit. Although theft and burglary seem to be on the rise, they are still significantly lower than in the West, as far as one can judge. An apparent paradox is that criminality is lower in large cities than in medium-sized and smaller ones. This can be explained by the fact that Soviet authorities do not permit those convicted of violent crimes and recidivists to settle in large population centers. Through this policy criminal activity has been geographically redistributed away from large cities, and thus urban crime patterns in the USSR differ from those found elsewhere.

Factors that detrimentally affect the quality of urban life include the problem of daily shopping, coping with chronic shortages that hit everything from food to everyday items, and long lines. Even in big cities the number and variety of stores are limited, and their selections of quality and fashionable goods leave much to be desired by Western standards. A great burden for the urban woman after a long day of work, travel, and shopping is coming home to prepare dinner and attend to household chores (her husband usually does not help) without the assistance of labor-saving devices like dishwashers, washing machines, and dryers. The people who still live in communal apartments (20 percent of the urban population) and the 5 percent who are domiciled in workers' dormitories frequently live in substandard or squalid conditions. Older and even new housing developments look unkempt and neglected. The outer facades of buildings are poorly finished, landscaping is unattended, and sidewalks and pathways in courtyards are often poorly paved, frequently muddy, and therefore difficult to walk on.

The Soviet citizen's opinion of urban bureaucracy varies with the agency in question, the geographic location of the city, and a person's income and social position. In a poll of émigrés, officials dispensing pensions were generally viewed positively, while those in charge of housing allocation were evaluated negatively, perhaps because the former had the money to hand out whereas the latter were swamped with housing applications far too numerous to satisfy. The Western image of the Soviet bureaucrat as unyielding is not accurate because an official, if entreated, pressured, or bribed, can be persuaded to bend the rules.

A unique experiment in urbanization has been the building of factories and cities in the inhospitable climate of Siberia. The cost of both is extremely high and one that only a state, and not private enterprise, could assume. A cheaper option—chosen by the Canadians for similar climatic conditions—would have been to send teams of workers to extract Siberia's rich mineral and fossil resources and ship them to developed areas of the country for processing, but not to settle people there.

Any summary of the Soviet urban experience is difficult because the city is not an island unto itself but a dependent part of the larger political-economic system. Its positive features are that it offers full employment, relatively efficient (if overcrowded) public transportation, a lower urban crime rate than in the United States, and an absence of gross blight. Streets and parks are clean, cared for, and unlittered. The city also provides the possibility of upward mobility through educational opportunity. These positive results have in part been achieved by a means unacceptable in Western societies: the strict control of movement of people into large urban centers. If migration were left unchecked, large cities, because they offer a much better quality of life, would be flooded with migrants who would transform them into Soviet-style Bombays.

A major problem of cities, particularly in the European part of the USSR, is that they have an immobile labor force that is aging and an increasing number of pensioners who do not move south or to the provinces. This prevents industry, commerce, and other sectors from importing badly needed personnel. A severe housing shortage compounds this problem, as do the scarcity and inferior quality of consumer goods and services, which adversely affect the quality of urban life.

There are similarities between the Soviet and Western urbanization process. Those living in cities in both societies are now better educated and technically trained than previous urban generations. The birth rate has declined, the stability of the urban family has been undermined by the high divorce rate, and the number of abortions is on the rise. And American and Soviet cities are both underfinanced and therefore cannot provide the kind and quality of services that they would like and that citizens expect.

There are also differences. In the West primarily private enterprise and the market spurred urban development. In the USSR urban growth was planned and implemented by state agencies within the context of public ownership of the means of production. But comprehensive urban planning has not been achieved because cities are still not fully in control of the financing, constructing, and administering of many urban services. A second difference is that the Soviet government has tried to limit the size of cities: a residence permit is required to live legally in a city, and many large urban centers are closed to newcomers.

Although Soviet urban development has many similarities to other countries undergoing a similar process, it also manifests unique characteristics that are the result of continuities of Russia's historical tradition and systemic changes introduced under Lenin's and Stalin's rule.

Bibliography

1. The Contemporary Soviet City

James H. Bater, *The Soviet City* (Beverly Hills, 1980).

David T. Cattel, *Leningrad: A Case Study of Soviet Urban Government* (New York, 1973).

B. M. Frolic, "Moscow,the Socialist Alternative," in H. Wentworth Eldredge, *World Capitals* (Garden City, N.Y., 1975).

Henry W. Morton, "Who Gets What, When and How? Housing in the Soviet Union," *Soviet Studies*, *31*, 2 (April 1980).

————, "The Soviet Quest for Better Housing—an Impossible Dream?" in *Soviet Economy in a Time of Change* (Washington, D.C., 1979).

Robert J. Osborn, *Soviet Social Policies* (Homewood, Ill., 1970).

William Taubman, *Governing Soviet Cities* (New York, 1973).

2. The Sources of Soviet Urban Growth

Jeff Chinn, *Manipulating Soviet Population Resources* (New York, 1977).

Peter J. Grandstaff, *Interregional Migration in the USSR: Economic Aspects, 1959–1970* (Durham, N.C., 1980).

Paul R. Gregory, "Fertility and Labor Force Participation in the Soviet Union and Eastern Europe," *Review of Economics and Statistics*, *64* (February 1982), 18-31.

Robert A. Lewis, "The Postwar Study of Internal Migration in the USSR," *Soviet Geography: Review and Translation*, *10* (April 1969), 157-66.

Robert A. Lewis and William J. Leasure, "Urbanization in Russia and the USSR: 1897–1966," *Annals of the American Association of Geographers*, *59* (December 1969), 776-96.

Gur Ofer, "Industrial Structure, Urbanization and the Growth Strategy of Socialist Countries," *Quarterly Journal of Economics*, *90* (May 1976), 219-44.

David E. Powell, *Rural Youth Migration in the Soviet Union* (Washington, D.C., 1975).

Robert C. Stuart, "Migration and the Growth of Soviet Cities," *Yearbook of East-European Economics* (Munich, 1982), 253-71.

Robert C. Stuart and Paul R. Gregory, "A Model of Soviet Rural-Urban Migration," *Economic Development and Cultural Change*, *26* (October 1977), 81-92.

3. Financing Soviet Cities

Franklyn D. Holzman, *Soviet Taxation* (Cambridge, 1955).

Paul R. Gregory and Robert C. Stuart, *Soviet Economic Structure and Performance*, 2nd ed. (New York, 1981).

Carol Weiss Lewis, *The Budgetary Process in Soviet Cities* (New York, 1976).
Carol W. Lewis and Stephen Sternheimer, *Soviet Urban Management: with Comparisons to the United States* (New York, 1979).
Frederic L. Pryor, *Public Expenditures in Communist and Capitalist Nations* (London, 1968).

4. The Soviet Urban Labor Supply

Abram Bergson, "Soviet Economic Slowdown and the 1981–1985 Plan," *Problems of Communism* (May-June 1981), 24-36.
Jeff Chinn, *Manipulating Soviet Population Resources* (New York, 1977).
Murray Feshbach, "The Structure and Composition of the Industrial Labor Force," in Arcadius Kahan and Blair A. Ruble (eds.), *Industrial Labor in the USSR* (New York, 1979), 3-18.
Murray Feshbach and Steven Rapawy, "Soviet Population and Manpower Trends and Policies," *Estimates and Projections of the Labor Force and Civilian Employment in the U.S.S.R. 1950 to 1990* (Washington, D.C., 1976).
Gail Warshofsky Lapidus, "Occupational Segregation and Public Policy: A Comparative Analysis of Soviet and American Patterns," *Signs*, *1*, 3 (Spring 1976), 119-36.
William Moskoff, "Part-Time Employment in the Soviet Union," *Soviet Studies*, *34*, 2 (April 1982), 270-85.
David E. Powell, "Labor Turnover in the Soviet Union," *Slavic Review* (June 1977), 268-85.

5. The Urban Family and the Soviet State

James H. Bater, *The Soviet City: Ideal and Reality* (Beverly Hills, 1980).
S. Bogatko and M. Kryukov, "Behind the Discussion of the 26th Congress: Atommash," *Pravda* (July 11, 1981), 2, in *Current Digest of the Soviet Press*, *33*, 28 (August 12, 1981), 6-7.
Jenny Brine, Maureen Perrie, and Andrew Sutton (eds.), *Home, School and Leisure in the Soviet Union* (London, 1980).
Jeff Chinn, *Manipulating Soviet Population Resources* (New York, 1977).
Christopher Davis and Murray Feshbach, *Rising Infant Mortality in the U.S.S.R. in the 1970's* (Washington, D.C., 1980).
Helen Desfosses (ed.), *Soviet Population Policy: Conflicts and Constraints* (New York, 1981).
Peter H. Juviler, "The Soviet Family in Post-Stalin Perspective," in Stephen F. Cohen, Alexander Rabinowitch, and Robert Sharlet (eds.), *The Soviet Union since Stalin* (Bloomington, Ind., 1980), 227-51.
Gail Warshofsky Lapidus (ed.), *Women, Work, and Family in the Soviet Union* (Armonk, N.Y., 1982).
Robert J. Osborn, *Soviet Social Policies: Welfare, Equality, Community* (Homewood, Ill., 1970).
S. Frederick Starr, "Visionary Town Planning During the Cultural Revolution," in *Cultural Revolution in Russia, 1928–1931* (Bloomington, Ind., 1978).

6. Urbanization and Crime

Valery Chalidze, *Criminal Russia* (New York, 1977).

Walter D. Connor, *Deviance in Soviet Society: Crime, Delinquency and Alcoholism* (New York, 1972).

Walter D. Connor, "Criminal Homicide, USSR/USA: Reflections on Soviet Data in a Comparative Framework," *Journal of Criminal Law and Criminology*, *64*, 1 (1973), 111-17.

Peter H. Juviler, *Revolutionary Law and Order: Politics and Social Change in the USSR* (New York, 1976).

Louise I. Shelley, "Crime and Delinquency in the Soviet Union," in Jerry G. Pankhurst and Michael Paul Sacks (eds.), *Contemporary Soviet Society* (New York, 1980), 208-26.

Louise I. Shelley, "The Geography of Soviet Criminality," *American Sociological Review*, *45*, 1 (1980), 111-22.

A. Shtromas, "Crime, Law and Penal Practice in the U.S.S.R.," *Review of Socialist Law*, 3 (1977), 297-324.

Peter H. Solomon, Jr., *Soviet Criminologists and Criminal Policy* (New York, 1978).

Ilya Zeldes, *The Problems of Crime in the U.S.S.R.* (Springfield, Ill., 1981).

7. Soviet Urban Health Services

Mark G. Field, *Soviet Socialized Medicine* (New York, 1967).

Walter D. Connor, *Socialism, Politics and Equality* (New York, 1979).

Richard Cooper, "Rising Death Rates in the Soviet Union," *New England Journal of Medicine*, *304* (May 21, 1981), 1259-65.

William A. Knaus, *Inside Russian Medicine* (New York, 1981).

Alastair McAuley, *Economic Welfare in the Soviet Union: Poverty, Living Standards and Inequality* (Madison, Wis., 1979).

Mervyn Matthews, *Class and Society in Soviet Russia* (New York, 1972).

Frank Parkin, *Class Inequality and Political Order* (New York, 1971).

8. Soviet Education: Problems and Policies in the Urban Context

Urie Bronfenbrenner, *Two Worlds of Childhood: U.S. and U.S.S.R.* (New York, 1972).

Richard B. Dobson, "Education and Opportunity," in Jerry Pankhurst and Michael Paul Sacks (eds.), *Contemporary Soviet Society: Sociological Perspectives* (New York, 1980).

John Dunstan, *Paths to Excellence and the Soviet School* (Windsor, England, 1978).

Susan Jacoby, *Inside Soviet Schools* (New York, 1973).

Mervyn Matthews, *Education in the Soviet Union: Policies and Institutions since Stalin* (Winchester, Mass., 1982).

Felicity Ann O'Dell, *Socialization through Children's Literature: the Soviet Example* (London, 1978).

Jaan Pennar, Ivan I. Bakalo, and George Z. F. Bereday, *Modernization and Diversity in*

Soviet Education: with Special Reference to Nationality Groups (New York, 1971).
Soviet Education. (This journal, published by M. E. Sharpe, Inc., consists wholly of translations of recent Soviet publications on various aspects of education.)
Robert B. Tabachnik, Thomas S. Popkewitz, and Beatrice Szekely (eds.), *Studying Teaching and Learning: Trends in Soviet and American Research* (New York, 1981).
E. K. Vasil'eva, *The Young People of Leningrad: School and Work Options and Attitudes*, translated by Arlo Schultz and Andrew J. Smith, with an introduction by Richard B. Dobson (White Plains, N.Y., 1976).

9. Urban Transport in the Soviet Union

L. A. Bronstein and A. S. Shul'man, *The Economics of Auto Transport* (Moscow, 1976).
Martin Crouch, "Problems of Soviet Urban Transport," *Soviet Studies*, *31*, 2 (April 1979), 231-56.
Imogene U. Edwards, "Automotive Trends in the USSR," *Soviet Economic Prospects for the Seventies* (Washington, D.C., 1973), 291-314.
Roland J. Fuchs and George J. Demko, "Commuting in the Soviet Union and Eastern Europe," *East European Quarterly*, *11*, 4 (Winter 1977), 463-75.
Sigurd Grava, "Politics and Design of the Moscow Metro," *Existics*, *43*, 256 (March 1977), 174-78.
————, "The Metro of Moscow," *Traffic Quarterly*, *30*, 3 (April 1976), 241-67.
————, "Provision of Transport Services in New Microraions of Soviet Cities," unpublished memorandum (January 1977).
————, "The Heavy Urban Transport Modes of Kiev," unpublished memorandum (January 1977).
————, "Current State of Planning in Riga," unpublished memorandum (January 1977).
G. P. Kiselev, "Commuting: An Analysis of Works by Soviet Scholars," *Research Memorandum 76-64*, International Institute for Applied Systems (Laxenburg, Austria, 1976).
John M. Kramer, "Soviet Policy towards the Automobile," *Survey*, *22*, 2 (Spring 1976), 16-35.
I. A. Molodykh (ed.), *A Cost-Benefit Analysis of Urban Public Transit Systems* (Moscow, 1977).
————. *Passenger Transportation in the Suburban Areas of Large Cities* (Moscow, 1976).
The Moscow City Soviet Executive Committee et al., *Transportation in the City: Management Problems* (New York, 1979).
E. V. Ovechnikov and M. S. Fishel'son, *Urban Transportation* (Moscow, 1976).
G. B. Poliak and E. V. Sofronov, *The General Plan and Budget of Moscow* (New York, 1976).
U.S. Department of Transportation, *Transportation in the Urban Environment* (Washington, D.C., 1978).
Toli Welihozkiy, "Automobiles and the Soviet Consumer," *Soviet Economy in a Time of Change* (Washington, D.C., 1979), 811-33.
Paul M. White, "Planning of Urban Transport Systems in the Soviet Union: A Policy Analysis," *Transportation Research*, *13a*, 4 (August 1979), 231-40.

10. Retail Trade and Personal Services in Soviet Cities

Marshall Goldman, *Soviet Marketing* (New York, 1963).

Philip Hanson, *The Consumer in the Soviet Economy* (London, 1968).

Gur Ofer, *The Service Sector in Soviet Economic Growth* (Cambridge, 1973).

Gertrude E. Schroeder and Barbara S. Severin, "Soviet Consumption and Income Policies in Perspective," *Soviet Economy in a New Perspective* (Washington, D.C., 1976), 620-60.

Roger Skurski, "Productivity, Growth and Efficiency in Soviet Consumer Goods Distribution," *The ACES Bulletin*, *18*, 3 (1976), 79-109.

11. Working the Soviet System: Citizens and Urban Bureaucracies

John Armstrong, *The Soviet Bureaucratic Elite* (New York, 1959).

————, "Sources of Administrative Behavior: Some Soviet and West European Comparisons," *American Political Science Review*, *59*, 3 (September 1965).

Klaus Von Beyme, "Soviet Social Policy in Comparative Perspective," *International Political Science Review*, *2*, 1 (1981).

Zbigniew K. Brzezinski, "The Soviet Political System: Transformation or Degeneration," *Problems of Communism*, *15*, 1 (January-February 1966).

Theodore H. Friedgut, "Citizens and Soviets: Can Ivan Ivanovich Fight City Hall?" *Comparative Politics*, *10*, 4 (July 1978).

Jerry Hough, *The Soviet Prefects* (Cambridge, Mass., 1969).

Alex Inkeles and Raymond Bauer, *The Soviet Citizen* (New York, 1968).

Bernice Madison, *Social Welfare in the Soviet Union* (Stanford, 1968).

Mervyn Matthews, *Privilege in the Soviet Union* (London, 1978).

Henry W. Morton, "Who Gets What, When and How? Housing in the Soviet Union," *Soviet Studies*, *32*, 2 (April 1980).

Carol R. Nechemias, "Welfare in the USSR: Health Care, Housing and Personal Consumption," unpublished paper.

James H. Oliver, "Citizen Demands and the Soviet Political System," *American Political Science Review*, *63*, 2 (June 1969).

Walter M. Pintner and Don Karl Rowney, *Russian Officialdom* (Chapel Hill, N.C., 1980).

Karl W. Ryavec, "The Soviet Ministerial Elite: 1964–1979, a Representative Sample," *Program in Soviet Series*, 6 (1981).

Michael Rywkin, "Housing in Central Asia: Demography, Ownership, Tradition: the Uzbek Example," Kennan Institute for Advanced Russian Studies (Washington, D.C., 1979).

H. Gordon Skilling and Franklyn Griffiths, *Interest Groups in Soviet Politics* (Princeton, 1971).

Index

Afghanistan, 138
Agriculture, 14,115
Alcoholism, 91
Aliev, G. A., 19, 20
Alma Ata, 4, 8, 97, 215, 216
Andropov, Y., 14, 247
Arkhangelsk Medical Institute, 173
Armenia, 54-56, 58, 212
Ashkhabad, 7, 8, 96, 97
Australia, 113
Automobile (*See Transportation*)
Azerbaidzhan, 6, 19, 56, 58, 120, 147, 212, 213

Baku, 4, 7, 8, 97, 120, 159, 186, 214, 216
Baltic Republics, 66
Bangkok, 199
Barnaul, 4
Bauer, R., 144, 226
Bednyi, M., 90, 91
Belorussia, 31, 52, 54, 56, 58, 88, 101, 120, 211-13
Birthrate, 84, 85, 87-89, 92, 93, 98, 101, 104, 106, 247, 250
Bratsk, 21
Brezhnev, L., 12, 14, 15, 17, 89, 92, 98, 99, 106, 129
Bronfenbrenner, U., 170
Bureaucracy
  citizen demands on, 224-41
  citizen relations with, 222-26
  Communist Party, 240
  definition of, 224, 225
  evaluation of, 228-36

interaction with, 236-41
  militia (police) and, 233, 235, 240, 241
  policy, 224
Burnazian, A., 139

California, 171
Castro, F., 107
Caucasus, 6, 73, 93, 101, 102
Central Asia, 6, 26, 34, 66, 73, 79, 88, 89, 93, 96, 101, 102, 105, 211, 216, 227, 230, 235, 239-40
Cheliabinsk, 4, 8, 97, 215
Chicago, 217
Child care, 34-35, 72
Child support, 99, 101, 102, 106
Chile, 194
Chinn, J., 34, 106
Cincinnati, 217
Cities, 37, 84, 87, 90, 101, 115, 116, 135, 136, 182, 206, 207, 208, 211, 216, 245-47, 249, 250
City council, 18, 19, 245
City government (*See also Bureaucracy*)
  classification of, 21, 22
  financing of, 45-62, 245-50
    revenues, 46, 48-52, 54, 62
    expenditures, 46, 48, 50, 55-61
      factors associated with, 59-61
      fluctuations of, 58-59, 62
    limiting growth of, 116 (*See Internal passport*)
    size, 33
    tax policies, 50-52, 54, 62
    turnover tax, 49, 51-52

Commuting (*See Transportation*)
Constitution, 99, 131
Consumer, 5, 48, 49
  and bureaucrats (*See Bureaucracy*)
Consumer goods (*See also Retail trade*)
  consumption of, 202, 203
  hoarding, 205
  investment in, 203, 206, 207, 218
  price of, 203, 204
  quality of, 205, 218, 249, 250
  repair, 202, 205, 210, 211
  services, 190, 203
  shortage, 205, 250
Conviction rate, 120
Cook Islands, 194
Crime and criminals, 113, 114, 248
  rate of, 114, 117, 120, 121, 124
  statistics, 117
  urban, 117, 119, 122-124
  youth, 123
Criminologists, 122, 144

Danilov, A. T., 170
Demographic policy, 98-100
Deutscher, I., 229
Divorce (*See Family*)
Dnepropetrovsk, 4, 7, 8, 67, 97, 215
Doctors (*See Health care*)
Donetsk, 4, 7, 8, 67, 97
Dushanbe, 4, 7, 8, 27, 33, 94, 96, 97, 215

Education, 298
  administration of, 160-61, 165
  correspondence schools and, 166-68
  cost of, 162
  evening schools and, 166-68
  expenditure on, 56, 60, 62, 78
  general education schools
    curriculum of, 163-64, 166
    location of, 162-63
    sponsorship in, 165
    tracking in, 163-64, 166
  higher educational institutions, 159-60
  ministry of, 160
  policies, 157, 174-75
  problems of, 169-74, 170-72, 175

  second economy in, 168-69, 237, 238
  selection of students, 160-61, 237-39
  specialized secondary schools, 158-59
  special profile schools and, 165-66
  state committee for vocational-
    technical, 160
  teacher evaluation and, 171
  vocational-technical schools, 157-62
Employment (*See Labor force*)
Engels, F., 116
Enterprises (*See Ministries*)
Environmental protection, 107
Erevan, 4, 8, 27, 97, 215
Estonia, 26, 58, 68, 75, 119, 194, 212-13, 216, 230

Family, 34, 73, 84-85, 88, 92-94, 96, 98, 100-1, 105-7, 250
  abortions, 85, 93, 100, 146, 250
  constitutional rights, 99
  divorce, 73, 84, 91, 96, 97, 100, 103-105
  experts on, 85
  marriage, 99, 103-4
  rural, 87
Farmers markets, 206
Federal Republic of Germany, 226
Feshbach, M., 89
Finances (*See Cities*)
Food
  rationing, 13
  shortage, 14-15, 114
  supplies of, 6, 12-14, 95, 105-6, 150, 218, 245
France, 134, 194, 225
Frunze, 7, 8, 27, 96, 97, 215

Georgia, 9, 21, 52, 58, 68, 211-13, 216, 227, 230, 235
German Democratic Republic, 106
Goldman, M., 203
Gorky, 4, 8, 97, 189, 214
Great Britain, 225
Grossman, G., 146
Guatemala, 194

Hamburg, 199
Hanson, P., 203
Harrisburg, 217
Health care (*See also Family and Population*), 5, 68, 80, 116, 129, 148, 248
  budget of, 132, 149-50
  constitution and, 131
  doctors, 141
  equipment shortage, 144-45, 150
  falsification of, 138
  prepaid, 132
  second economy of, 140, 146-48
  stratification, 135-37
  system, 130, 133-34, 150-51
Hegedus, A., 221, 223
Helsinki, 135
Hospitals, 135, 137-38, 141-48, 150
Housing, 5, 36, 37, 92, 95, 105, 106, 116, 122, 123, 150, 208
  allocation of, 9, 10, 229-32, 236, 237
  conveniences, 9
  cooperative, 9, 12
  corruption in, 20, 232, 236
  cost of, 9
  dormitories, 117
  for workers, 5
  investment in, 12, 16
  living space, 7, 60, 62
  party and government role in, 16-18
  privately owned, 9
  shortage of, 5, 7, 9, 12, 14, 15, 68, 70, 183, 229, 230
Hungary, 103, 194

Infant mortality (*See Population*)
Inkeles, A., 226
Internal passport, 115, 116, 123
Iran, 194
Irkutsk, 4, 13, 137
Israel, 226
Italy, 202, 247
Ivory Coast, 194
Izhevsk, 4

Jacoby, S., 103
Japan, 113, 225

Jordan, 194

Kamchatka, 122
Kazakhstan, 56, 58, 89, 211-13
Kazan, 4, 8, 93, 94, 97
Kemerovo, 239
Khabarovsk, 4, 121, 145
Kharchev, 18
Kharkov, 4, 7, 8, 67, 97, 169, 186, 189, 214, 238, 239
Kholban, A.,
Khripkova, A., 172
Khrushchev, N., 12, 17, 129, 172, 173
Kiev, 4-8, 48, 67, 94, 97, 115, 116, 120, 140,159, 165, 186, 190, 214, 216
Kirghizia, 9, 54, 58, 212, 213
Kishinev, 4, 8, 27, 97, 137, 215, 237
Knaus, W., 130, 134, 136-38, 143, 145, 148
Kokand, 240
Komi, 122
Krasnoiarsk, 122, 239
Krivoi Rog, 4
Kuibyshev, 4, 8, 97, 145, 214

Labor force, 5, 6
  allocation of, 5, 36, 65, 70, 238, 239
  auxiliary, 71
  changes in, 66
  commuters, 78, 79, 185
  employment, 5, 65, 79
  exchanges, 71
  foreign, 78
  hoarding, 6, 70, 247
  part-time, 73-77, 80
  pensioners, 76, 77, 229, 230-32, 237
  productivity, 6, 7, 68 (*See also Shchekino*)
  shortage, 6, 65, 66, 68, 78, 98, 105, 161, 173
  students in, 77, 78
  supply, 7, 247
  training of (*See Education*)
  turnover of, 7, 65, 69, 70, 80
  women in, 34, 65, 71-73, 74-77
Latvia, 31, 52, 56, 68, 101, 119, 180,

194, 212, 213
Lenin, I., 84, 114, 136, 250
Leningrad, 3, 4, 5, 6, 8, 12, 18, 22, 33,
    66, 67, 73, 93, 97, 103, 114-16,
    123, 159, 166, 174, 184, 186-88,
    195, 214, 237, 238
Leningrad University, 166
Lithuania, 56, 58, 211-13
Los Angeles, 104, 199, 217
Lvov, 4

McAuley, A., 151
Magadan, 122
Markets, 211
Marriage (*See Family*)
Marx, K., 221
Maternity leave, 101
Medical care (*See Health care*)
Medicine, 143-45, 148, 149
Metro (*See Transportation*)
Michigan, 171
Migration, 35-39, 66, 67, 79, 87-89, 98,
    105, 114, 115, 117, 123, 247, 249
Milwaukee, 217
Ministries, 16, 17, 20, 22, 30, 47, 49
  enterprises of, 48, 49
    profit deduction tax, 52
    profits of, 49-52
    use of labor by (*See Labor allocation*)
Ministry of Communications, 206
Ministry of Defense, 206
Ministry of Health Protection, 95, 133,
    135, 150, 206
Ministry of Internal Affairs, 135, 206,
    208, 240
Ministry of Power and Electrification, 95
Ministry of Trade, 206, 208
Minsk, 7, 8, 27, 31, 33, 93, 96, 97, 159,
    186, 214, 216
Moldavia, 54, 56, 58, 76, 101, 167, 212,
    213, 216, 227, 237
Mortality rates, 89, 100, 104, 105, 149
  life expectancy, 91
  of infants, 89, 90, 132, 139, 149
Morton, H., 229, 236
Moscow, 3-8, 12, 13, 16-18, 22, 34, 66-
    68, 70, 73, 76, 87, 93, 94, 96, 97,
    103, 114, 115, 123, 136, 139, 142,

145, 148, 159, 164, 166, 171, 172,
    184, 186-88, 190, 195, 197, 198,
    214, 216-18, 230, 237, 238
Moslems, 88, 120

Nazimov, I., 173
New Economic Policy, 114
New York, 164, 180, 189, 199, 217
Novokuznetsk, 4
Novosibirsk, 4, 8, 21, 97, 186, 214

Odessa, 4, 7, 8, 67, 120, 171, 215
Ofer, G., 202, 203
Omsk, 4, 8, 97, 215, 239

Party and government, 16-18, 20, 89
Paustofsky, K., 89
Pedestrian, 192, 193
Pensioners, 6, 106, 250 (*See also
    Labor*)
Perm, 4, 8, 96, 97
Petrovskii, B., 139
Planning (*See Urban planning*)
Police, 122, 233, 235, 240, 241
Pollution, 90
Population, 6, 59, 62, 85, 92, 99, 105
  age of, 67, 68
  demographic forecast of, 6, 65-70, 73,
      79, 80, 173
  fertility, 84-87, 93, 107
  growth of, 31, 33, 38, 104, 203
  infertility, 85
  migration of (*See Migration*)
  nationality, 73
  politics and, 19
Production-training combines, 174
Prokof'ev, M., 170
Province (oblast), 46

Radiation, 90
Rent, 9, 245
Residence permit (*propiska*), 5, 29, 36,
    70, 87, 116, 250
Restaurants (*See Retail trade*)

Retail trade (*See also Consumer goods*)
202, 210, 212
distribution of, 202
growth of, 204
personnel, 202-3
planning, 207, 208, 218
private, 210
restaurants, 5, 210, 216
sales, 203, 204, 216
stores, 203, 208, 209-11
Retirement, 6
age of, 6
Riga, 73, 94, 96, 97, 103, 119, 120, 169, 180, 182, 183, 185, 189, 190, 193-95, 197, 215
Rochester, 180
Romania, 202
Rostov on-the-Don, 4
Rural life, 14, 35-36, 67
Russian Soviet Federated Socialist Republic (RSFSR), 31, 34, 52, 58, 66, 67, 71, 74, 93, 211-13, 225, 227, 230
Rustavi, 21
Rywkin, M., 230

Saratov, 4
Schools, 247 (*See also Education*)
Seattle, 217
Shchekino, 7, 70, 71
Shipping (*See Transportation*)
Siberia, 26, 36, 101, 102, 120, 121, 218, 239, 249
Skurski, R., 203
Smith, H., 171
Solovev, A., 173
Solzhenitsyn, A., 136
Stalin, J., 13, 16, 85, 100, 101, 105, 129, 135, 137, 197, 223, 245, 246, 250
State Committee for Civil Construction and Architecture, 207, 208
State Committee for Construction (*Gosstroi*), 17, 19, 183, 190
State Committee for Labor and Wages, 71
State Committee for Publishing, 206
State Planning Committee (*Gosplan*), 46, 183, 187, 207, 245
Suburbs, 5, 189, 193, 194, 247

Subways (*See Transportation*)
Sverdlovsk, 4, 7, 8, 67, 68, 96, 97, 189, 214
Sweden, 134

Tadzhikistan, 26, 31, 54, 56, 58, 101, 212, 213
Tallin, 8, 97, 119, 120, 215
Tashkent, 4, 8, 93, 94, 96, 97, 214
Taxation (*See Cities*)
Tbilisi, 4, 8, 97, 164, 186, 187, 215
Texas, 171
Tiumin, 122
Tobolsk, 120
Togliatti, 4, 79
Transportation
automobiles, 180, 194-97
bus, 188-91, 194
commuter, 185, 188, 193, 194
evaluation of, 199, 200
fares, 188
financing of, 190
goods of, 198, 199
metro (subway), 183, 185, 187, 191, 199
planning, 180, 185, 187, 190
street cars (trolley cars), 190
taxis, 191, 192
trolley bus, 188-91
Tula, 4
Turkmenistan, 58, 212, 213, 216
Tuvin, 122

Ufa, 4, 8, 97, 166
Ukraine, 9, 52, 58, 67, 68, 88, 212, 213, 216, 227, 239
United Kingdom, 202
United States, 3, 85, 90, 104, 132, 138, 150, 194, 202, 203, 217, 225, 226, 246, 247
Unwed mothers, 100
Uralsk, 173
Urban growth, 3, 66, 67, 245
history of, 26-29
sources of, 30-39
Urban planning, 15, 16, 47, 122, 245, 247

Urbanization, 3, 25, 45, 85, 87, 104,
    113, 115, 116, 244, 245, 247, 249
  levels of, 29
Uzbekistan, 9, 31, 52, 54, 58, 216, 230,
    240

Vilnius, 4, 8, 97, 159, 215
Vladivostok, 4, 121
Voinovich, V., 221
Volgodansk, 94, 95
Volgograd, 4
Volkov, A. 224
Voronezh, 4

Washington, D.C., 245

Whitney, C., 146
Wirszup, I., 164, 169
Women, 100, 101, 249

Yakutsk, 122
Yaroslavl, 4
Young Communist League (Komsomol),
    156

Zagorsk, 18
Zags (Civil Registration), 96, 103,
    104
Zaporozhe, 4
Zemtsov, L., 166
Zhdanov, 4